Rational and Irrational Beliefs

Rational and Irrational Beliefs

Research, Theory, and Clinical Practice

Edited by Daniel David,
Steven Jay Lynn, and Albert Ellis

OXFORD
UNIVERSITY PRESS

2010

OXFORD
UNIVERSITY PRESS

Oxford University Press, Inc., publishes works that further
Oxford University's objective of excellence
in research, scholarship, and education.

Oxford   New York
Auckland   Cape Town   Dar es Salaam   Hong Kong   Karachi
Kuala Lumpur   Madrid   Melbourne   Mexico City   Nairobi
New Delhi   Shanghai   Taipei   Toronto

With offices in
Argentina   Austria   Brazil   Chile   Czech Republic   France   Greece
Guatemala   Hungary   Italy   Japan   Poland   Portugal   Singapore
South Korea   Switzerland   Thailand   Turkey   Ukraine   Vietnam

Copyright © 2010, by Oxford University Press, Inc.

Published by Oxford University Press, Inc.
198 Madison Avenue, New York, New York 10016

www.oup.com

Library of Congress Cataloging-in-Publication Data

Rational and irrational beliefs : research, theory, and clinical practice / edited by Daniel David,
    Steven Jay Lynn, & Albert Ellis.
    p.   cm.
    Includes index.
    ISBN 978-0-19-518223-1
    1. Delusions.   2. Irrationalism (Philosophy)   3. Rationalism.   4. Health behavior.
    I. David, Daniel, Dr.   II. Lynn, Steven J.   III. Ellis, Albert, 1913–2007.
    RC553.D35R38 2009
    616.89—dc22

                                                                              2009003476

9   8   7   6   5   4   3   2   1

Printed in the United States of America
on acid-free paper

Preface

In the 1950s, influential researchers and theoreticians (e.g., Noam Chomsky, George Miller, Alan Newell, Herbert Simon) departed from the behaviorist tradition and broke the intellectual ground for the nascent field that Ulrich Neisser (1967) termed "cognitive psychology" in his book by the same name. During this fertile period, Albert Ellis parted ways with both psychodynamic and behavioral psychotherapists to delineate a cognitive approach to conceptualizing and treating psychological conditions. As early as 1955, Ellis applied the verb *catastrophize* (and later *awfulize*) to the way people think when they are anxious. After the publication of the article "Rational Psychotherapy" (Ellis, 1958) and the seminal book *Reason and Emotion in Psychotherapy* (Ellis, 1962, 1994), Ellis became a tireless advocate of a cognitive approach to psychotherapy. Although other professionals (e.g., Adler, Horney, Kelly) before him had stressed the importance of cognitions in the clinical field, they did not promote the cognitive paradigm as an entity in and of itself. It is fair to assert that Ellis's rational-emotive behavior therapy (REBT), which highlights the integral role of cognition in adaptive and maladaptive functioning, is the oldest form of cognitive-behavior therapy (CBT) and represents the prototype of contemporary cognitive-behavior therapies.

By identifying the manifold ways in which individuals react to similar situations, and by exploring how their attitudes, beliefs, and expectancies shape their reality and behavior, Ellis played a pivotal role in instigating the "cognitive revolution" in psychotherapy and psychology more broadly. Accordingly, it is not surprising that concepts derived from REBT have penetrated and/or been assimilated by cognitive psychology, psychotherapy, and many domains of mainstream psychology, including the psychology of stress, coping, and resilience. Indeed, contemporary cognitive-behavioral therapies, regardless of their stripe, share the following propositions, derived from or related to Ellis's REBT: *(1)* cognitions can be identified and measured, *(2)* cognitions play a central role in human psychological functioning and disturbance, and *(3)* irrational cognitions can be replaced with rational cognitions and thereby abet functional emotional, cognitive, and behavioral responses in keeping with personal goals and values.

Ellis's "ABC(DE)" model is the cornerstone of REBT and cognitive-behavioral therapies. In a nutshell, Ellis argued that individuals respond to an undesirable or unpleasant activating (internal or external) event (A) with a gamut of emotional, behavioral, and cognitive consequences (C). The diverse ways in which people respond to the same or similar events is largely the result of differences in their cognitions or belief systems (B). Rational beliefs can be characterized as efficient, flexible, and/or logical. Rational beliefs promote self-acceptance and adaptive coping with stressful events, reduce vulnerability to psychological distress, and play an instrumental role in achieving valued goals.

According to REBT, beliefs are infused with emotion. In fact, Ellis has argued that thoughts, feelings, and behaviors are intimately interconnected. Irrational beliefs (IBs) are related to unrealistic demands about the self (e.g., "I must be competent, adequate, and achieving in all respects to be worthwhile."), others ("I must become worried about other people's problems."), and the world or life conditions ("I must be worried about things I cannot control.") and are associated with a variety of dysfunctional feelings and behaviors. According to Ellis, vulnerability to psychological disturbance is a product of the frequency and strength of irrational beliefs, as compared to rational beliefs. Clients who engage in REBT are encouraged to actively dispute/restructure (D) their IBs and to assimilate more efficient (E) and rational beliefs in order to increase adaptive emotional, cognitive, and behavioral responses. It is notable that this general framework (at least the A-B-C part of Ellis's scheme) is at the heart of most, if not all, cognitive-behavior therapies.

Cognitive-behavioral therapies are the most popular contemporary therapeutic approaches (Garske & Anderson, 2004), and have steadily increased in acceptance and influence. Not surprisingly, thousands of books and scholarly publications have been devoted to cognitive psychology and CBT. Since its introduction to the psychological community, hundreds of papers have been published on the theory and practice of REBT. Some studies (e.g., Dryden, Ferguson, & Clark, 1989; McDermut, Haaga, & Bilek, 1997) have confirmed the main aspects of Ellis's original REBT theory (Ellis, 1962), whereas other studies (e.g., Bond & Dryden, 2000; Solomon, Haaga, Brody, & Friedman, 1998) have made critical contributions to the evolution of REBT theory and practice (for details, see Ellis, 1994; Solomon & Haaga, 1995). Furthermore, meta-analytic studies have supported the contention that REBT is an empirically supported form of CBT (e.g., Engels, Garnefski, & Diekstra, 1993).

Despite the centrality of rational and irrational beliefs to CBT and REBT, it is also legitimate to say that no available book, monograph, or resource provides a truly accessible, state of the science summary of research and clinical applications pertinent to rational and irrational beliefs. Our concern about this gap in the extant literature provided the impetus for this volume.

This book is designed to provide a forum for leading scholars, researchers, and practitioners to share their perspectives and empirical findings on the nature of irrational and rational beliefs, the role of beliefs as mediators of functional and dysfunctional emotions and behaviors, and clinical approaches to modifying irrational beliefs and enhancing adaptive coping in the face of stressful life events. Many of the chapters in this volume represent international collaborations, and bring together and integrate disparate findings, to offer a comprehensive and cohesive approach to understanding CBT/REBT and its central constructs of rational and irrational beliefs. The authors review a steadily accumulating empirical literature indicating that irrational beliefs are associated with a wide range of problems in living (e.g., drinking behaviors, suicidal contemplation, "life hassles"), and that exposure to rational self-statements can decrease anxiety and physiological arousal over time and can be a major tool in health promotion. The contributors identify areas that have been "underresearched," including the link between irrational beliefs and memory, emotions, behaviors, and psychophysiological responses.

The major focus of our book is on rational and irrational beliefs as conceptualized by proponents of REBT. However, the contents encompass other cognitive constructs that play an influential role in cognitive-behavior therapies including schemas, response expectancies, intermediate assumptions, automatic thoughts, and appraisal and coping. While important in their own right, these concepts are discussed in terms of their relation to rational and irrational beliefs and their role in cognitive-behavioral therapies and psychotherapy more generally. In addition to focusing on the ways irrational beliefs hamper adequate functioning, we highlight how rational beliefs contribute to positive coping and engender resilience in the face of stressful life events.

It bears emphasizing that our book is not be an "advocacy piece," slanted toward positive findings regarding REBT. In fact, where appropriate, the contributors directly challenge claims made by proponents of REBT and other cognitive therapies. Our intention was to produce a balanced, critical treatise that provides: *(a)* cogent summaries of what is known and what is not known about irrational beliefs, *(b)* suggestions for future research to address important unresolved questions and issues, and *(c)* up-to-date information for practitioners to guide their clincal practice.

Our book is organized in six parts. Part I (Foundations) introduces the reader to the fundamentals of understanding rational and irrational beliefs from a conceptual, historical, cultural, and evolutionary perspective. Chapter I (Ellis, David, and Lynn) traces the historical lineage of the concept of rational and irrational beliefs from the vantage point of REBT, but also discusses the role of rational and irrational beliefs in terms of an array of cognitive mechanisms and constructs. Chapter 2 (Still) approaches definitional issues surrounding irrationality from a logical and historical perspective, discussing the implications of different ways of construing irrationality. Chapter 3 (David and DiGiuseppe) and Chapter 4 (Wilson) contain provocative analyses of rational and irrational thinking from a sociocultural and evolutionary perspective, respectively.

Part II (Rational and Irrational Beliefs: Human Emotions and Behavioral Consequences) further explores the role of irrational and rational beliefs in human functioning. Chapter 5 (Szentagotai and Jones) examines the influence of these beliefs in human behavior, whereas Chapter 6 (David and Cramer) discusses the role of rational and irrational beliefs in human feelings, encompassing both subjective and psycho-physiological responses.

Part III (Clinical Applications) turns to clinical implications of understanding and modifying irrational beliefs and instating more rational ways of viewing the self and the world. The section begins with a foundational chapter (Chapter 7, Macavei and McMahon) on assessing irrational and rational beliefs, which provides many useful suggestions for measuring and evaluating beliefs in research and clinical contexts. The next two chapters (Chapter 8, Browne, Dowd, and Freeman; Chapter 9, Caserta, Dowd, David, and Ellis) review the literature on irrational and rational beliefs in the domains of psychopathology and primary prevention, respectively, whereas Chapter 10 (David, Freeman, and DiGiuseppe) explores the role of irrational beliefs in stressful and non-stressful situation in health promoting behaviors, cognitive-behavioral therapy, and psychotherapy in general. In Chapter 11, Mellinger examines the ways that mindfulness has been integrated into contemporary therapeutic approaches to the treatment of irrational thinking in emotional disorders and reviews approaches that stand in sharp contrast to REBT.

Part IV (Physical Health and Pain) extends consideration of rational and irrational beliefs to the arena of physical health and pain. Schnur, Montgomery, and David (Chapter 12) review the literature on irrational and rational beliefs and physical health, and propose a new model for testing the influence of irrational beliefs on health outcomes. Ehde and Jensen (Chapter 13) summarize what is now a compelling literature linking catastrophizing cognitions to the experience of pain, and provide an overview of theory, research, and practice of cognitive therapy for pain.

In the penultimate Part V (Judgment Errors and Popular Myths and Misconceptions), Ruscio (Chapter 14) underscores the ways that judgment errors can lead to suboptimal decisions, and describes ways to prevent this from happening. Next, Lilienfeld, Lynn, and Beyerstein (Chapter 15) illustrate how popular misconceptions of the mind and erroneous beliefs can interfere with effective treatment planning and execution. In the closing Part VI (A Look to the Future), David and Lynn (Chapter 16) summarize and critique extant knowledge regarding irrational beliefs, highlighting gaps in the clinical and research literature, nd propose an agenda for future research.

We hope that this volume will serve as an indispensable reference for practitioners of psychotherapy, regardless of their theoretical orientation or professional affiliation (e.g., psychologist, psychiatrist, social worker, counselor), and will be of value to instructors and their students in graduate psychotherapy courses. Academic psychologists with interests in cognitive sciences and the application of cognitive principles in treatment and in fostering resilience will find much of interest in the pages herein. Finally, we anticipate that curious laypersons will discover that this volume will enrich their understanding of themselves and their loved ones. We are honored to dedicate this book to the memory of Albert Ellis (see section "About Albert Ellis" that follows). He immersed himself in the writing and editing of this volume with his characteristic passion, involvement, and acumen. In the midst of his valiant battle with colon cancer, he made invaluable contributions to many chapters before his death, making them perhaps his final gifts to science and clinical practice. We fondly remember Albert Ellis as a vital, compassionate, and wise human being, and dedicate this book to his legacy of substantive and enduring contributions to psychological theory, research, and practice.

About Albert Ellis
(adapted with the permission of the Albert Ellis Institute)

Albert Ellis is widely recognized as a seminal figure in the field of cognitive-behavioral psychotherapy. His contributions to the psychological care, healing, and education of millions of people over the past six decades are virtually without precedent. Ellis devoted his life to working with people in individual and group therapy; educating the public by way of self-help books, popular articles, lectures, workshops, and radio and television presentations; training thousands of therapists to use his approach to helping others; and publishing a steady stream of scholarly books and articles. Dr. Ellis has been honored with the highest professional achievement and research awards of the leading psychological associations, and has been voted the most influential living psychologist by American and Canadian psychologists and counselors.

Ellis was born in Pittsburgh in 1913 and raised in New York City. He made the best of a difficult childhood by becoming, in his words, "a stubborn and pronounced problem-solver." A serious kidney disorder turned his attention from sports to books, and the strife in his family (his parents were divorced when he was 12) led him to work at understanding others.

In junior high school Ellis set his sights on becoming the Great American Novelist. He planned to study accounting in high school and college, make enough money to retire at 30, and write without the pressure of financial need. The Great Depression put an end to his vision, but he completed college in 1934 with a degree in business administration from the City University of New York. His first venture in the business world was a pants-matching business he started with his brother. They scoured the New York garment auctions for pants to match their customer's still-usable coats. In 1938, he became the personnel manager for a gift and novelty firm.

Ellis devoted most of his spare time to writing short stories, plays, novels, comic poetry, essays and nonfiction books. By the time he was 28, he had finished almost two dozen full-length manuscripts, but had not been able to get them published. He realized his future did not lie in writing fiction, and he turned exclusively to nonfiction, to promoting what he called the "sex-family revolution."

As he collected more and more materials for a treatise called "The Case for Sexual Liberty," many of his friends began regarding him as something of an expert on the subject. They often asked for advice, and Ellis discovered that he liked counseling as well as writing. In 1942 he returned to school, entering the clinical-psychology program at Columbia. He started a part-time private practice in family and sex counseling soon after he received his master's degree in 1943.

At the time Columbia awarded him a doctorate in 1947 Ellis had come to believe that psychoanalysis was the most effective form of therapy. He decided to undertake a training analysis, and "become an outstanding psychoanalyst in the next few years." The psychoanalytic institutes refused to take trainees without M.D.s, but he found an analyst with the Karen Horney group who agreed to work with him. Ellis completed a full analysis and began to practice classical psychoanalysis under his teacher's direction.

In the late 1940s he taught at Rutgers and New York University, and was the senior clinical psychologist at the Northern New Jersey Mental Hygiene

Clinic. He also became the chief psychologist at the New Jersey Diagnostic Center and then at the New Jersey Department of Institutions and Agencies.

But Ellis's faith in psychoanalysis was rapidly crumbling. He discovered that when he saw clients only once a week or even every other week, they progressed as well as when he saw them daily. He took a more active role, interjecting advice and direct interpretations as he did when he was counseling people with family or sex problems. His clients seemed to improve more quickly than when he used passive psychoanalytic procedures. And remembering that before he underwent analysis, he had worked through many of his own problems by reading and practicing the philosophies of Epictetus, Marcus Aurelius, Spinoza, and Bertrand Russell, he began to teach his clients the principles that had worked for him.

By 1955 Ellis had abandoned psychoanalysis entirely, and instead was concentrating on changing people's behavior by confronting them with their irrational beliefs and persuading them to adopt rational ones. This role was more to Ellis' taste, for he could be more honestly himself. "When I became rational-emotive," he said, "my own personality processes really began to vibrate."

He published his first book on REBT, *How to Live with a Neurotic*, in 1957. Two years later he organized the Institute for Rational Living, where he held workshops to teach his principles to other therapists. *The Art and Science of Love*, his first really successful book, appeared in 1960, and he has now published more than 70 books and 700 articles on REBT, sex, and marriage. Many of his books and articles have been translated and published in over 20 foreign languages. Until his death on July 24, 2007, Dr. Ellis served as President Emeritus of the Albert Ellis Institute in New York, which provides professional training programs and psychotherapy to individuals, families and groups, and continues to advance Albert Ellis's legacy.

Albert Ellis
Daniel David
Steven Jay Lynn

REFERENCES

Bond, F. W., & Dryden, W. (2000). How rational beliefs and irrational beliefs affect people's inferences: An experimental investigation. *Behavioural and Cognitive Psychotherapy, 28*, 33–43.

Dryden, W., Ferguson, J., & Clark, T. (1989). Beliefs and influences: A test of a rational-emotive hypothesis: I. Performance in an academic seminar. *Journal of Rational-Emotive & Cognitive-Behavior Therapy, 7*, 119–129.

Ellis, A. (1958). Rational psychotherapy. *Journal of General Psychology, 59*, 35–49.

Ellis, A. (1962). *Reason and emotion in psychotherapy*. New York: Stuart.

Ellis, A. (1994). *Reason and emotion in psychotherapy* (rev. ed.). Secaucus, NJ: Birscj Lane.

Engels, G. I., Garnefski, N., & Diekstra, F. W. (1993). Efficacy of rational-emotive therapy: A quantitative analysis. *Journal of Consulting and Clinical Psychology, 6*, 1083–1090.

Garske, J. P., & Anderson, T. (2004). Toward a science of psychotherapy research: Present status and evaluation. In S. O. Lilienfeld, S. J. Lynn, & J. M. Lohr (Eds.), *Science and pseudoscience in clinical psychology* (pp. 145–175). New York: Guilford.

McDermut, J. F., Haaga, A. A. F., & Bilek, L. A. (1997). Cognitive bias and irrational beliefs in major depression and dysphoria. *Cognitive Therapy and Research, 21*, 459–476.

Neisser, U. (1967). *Cognitive psychology*. Englewood Cliffs, NJ: Prentice-Hall.

Robins, R. W., Gosling, S. D., & Craik, K. H. (1999). An empirical analysis of trends in psychology. *American Psychologist, 54*, 117–128.

Solomon, A., Haaga, D. A. F., Brody, K., Kirk, K., & Friedman, D. G. (1998). Priming irrational beliefs in formerly depressed individuals. *Journal of Abnormal Psychology, 107*, 440–449.

Solomon, A., & Haaga, D. A. F. (1995). Rational emotive behaviour therapy research: What we know and what we need to know. *Journal of Rational-Emotive and Cognitive-Behaviour Therapy, 13*, 179–191.

Contents

Contributors, xvii

PART I: Foundations

1. Rational and Irrational Beliefs: A Historical and Conceptual Perspective, 3
   Albert Ellis, Daniel David, and Steven Jay Lynn

2. Rationality and Rational Psychotherapy: The Heart of REBT, 23
   Arthur Still

3. Social and Cultural Aspects of Rational and Irrational Beliefs: A Brief
   Reconceptualization, 49
   Daniel David and Raymond DiGiuseppe

4. Rational and Irrational Beliefs from an Evolutionary Perspective, 63
   David Sloan Wilson

PART II: Rational and Irrational Beliefs: Human Emotions
and Behavioral Consequences

5. The Behavioral Consequences of Irrational Beliefs, 75
   Aurora Szentagotai and Jason Jones

6. Rational and Irrational Beliefs in Human Feelings and
   Psychophysiology, 99
   Daniel David and Duncan Cramer

PART III: Clinical Applications

7. The Assessment of Rational and Irrational Beliefs, 115
    Bianca Macavei and James McMahon

8. Rational and Irrational Beliefs and Psychopathology, 149
    Christopher M. Browne, E. Thomas Dowd, and Arthur Freeman

9. Rational and Irrational Beliefs in Primary Prevention and
    Mental Health, 173
    Donald A. Caserta, E. Thomas Dowd, Daniel David, and Albert Ellis

10. Rational and Irrational Beliefs: Implications for Mechanisms of
    Change and Practice in Psychotherapy, 195
    Daniel David, Arthur Freeman, and Raymond DiGiuseppe

11. Mindfulness and Irrational Beliefs, 219
    David I. Mellinger

PART IV: Physical Health and Pain

12. Irrational and Rational Beliefs and Physical Health, 253
    Julie B. Schnur, Guy H. Montgomery, and Daniel David

13. Coping and Catastrophic Thinking: The Experience and Treatment of
    Chronic Pain, 265
    Dawn M. Ehde and Mark P. Jensen

**PART V: Judgment Errors and Popular Myths and
          Misconceptions**

14. Irrational Beliefs Stemming from Judgment Errors: Cognitive
    Limitations, Biases, and Experiential Learning, 291
    John Ruscio

15. The Five Great Myths of Popular Psychology:
    Implications for Psychotherapy, 313
    Scott O. Lilienfeld, Steven Jay Lynn, and Barry L. Beyerstein

PART VI: A Look to the Future

16. A Summary and a New Research Agenda for Rational-Emotive and Cognitive-Behavior Therapy, 339
Daniel David and Steven Jay Lynn

Index, 349

Contributors

Barry L. Beyerstein, Ph.D.[1]
Professor of Psychology
Simon Fraser University
Burnaby BC, Canada

Christopher M. Browne, Ph.D.
Staff Psychologist
Farmingdale State College
State University of New York
Private Practice
Commack, NY

Donald A. Caserta, M.A., MSSA,
   LISW-S
Clinical Social Worker
The Cleveland Clinic
Cleveland, OH

Duncan Cramer, Ph.D.
Professor, Social Sciences
   Department
Loughborough University
Leicestershire, UK

Daniel David, Ph.D.
Professor of Clinical Cognitive
   Sciences

Babeş-Bolyai University
Cluj-Napoca, Romania
Adjunct Professor
Mount Sinai School of Medicine
New York, NY

Raymond DiGiuseppe, Ph.D.
Chairperson and Professor
Department of Psychology
St. John's University
Jamaica, NY

E. Thomas Dowd, Ph.D, ABPP
Professor of Psychology
Kent State University
Kent, OH

Dawn M. Ehde, Ph.D.
Department of Rehabilitation
   Medicine
University of Washington School of
   Medicine
Seattle, WA

Albert Ellis, Ph.D.[2]
Albert Ellis Institute
New York, NY

---

[1] Deceased

[2] Deceased

Arthur Freeman, Ed.D., ABPP
Visiting Professor
Department of Psychology
Governors State University
University Park, IL

Mark P. Jensen, Ph.D.
Professor and Vice Chair for Research
Department of Rehabilitation
    Medicine
University of Washington School of
    Medicine
Seattle, WA

Jason Jones, Ph.D.
Consultant Clinical and Forensic
    Psychologist
Course Director, The Centre for
    REBT (UK Affiliate of the Albert
    Ellis Institute)
University of Birmingham
Birmingham, UK

Scott O. Lilienfeld, Ph.D.
Professor
Department of Psychology
Emory University
Atlanta, GA

Steven Jay Lynn, Ph.D., ABPP
Professor of Psychology
Director, Psychological Clinic
Binghamton University
Binghamton, NY

Bianca Macavei, M.A.
Department of Clinical Psychology
    and Psychotherapy
Babeş-Bolyai University
Cluj-Napoca, Romania

James McMahon, Psy.D., Ph.D.,
    Sc.D., Th.D.
University of Oradea
Oradea, Romania
Albert Ellis Institute
New York, NY

David I. Mellinger, M.S.W.
Anxiety Disorders Treatment
    Service Panorama City Service
Area
Kaiser Permanente Behavioral
    Health Care
Los Angeles, CA

Guy H. Montgomery, Ph.D.
Associate Professor
Department of Oncological
    Sciences
Director of the Integrative
    Behavioral Medicine
Mount Sinai School of Medicine
New York, NY

John Ruscio, Ph.D.
Psychology Department
The College of New Jersey
Ewing, NJ

Julie B. Schnur, Ph.D.
Assistant Professor
Department of Oncological
    Sciences
Integrative Behavioral Medicine
    Program
Mount Sinai School of Medicine
New York, NY

Arthur Still, Ph.D., FPBsS,
CPsychol Durham University
Durham, UK

Aurora Szentagotai, Ph.D.
Babeş-Bolyai University
Cluj-Napoca, Romania

David Sloan Wilson, Ph.D.
Distinguished Professor
Departments of Biology and
Anthropology
Binghamton University
Binghamton, NY

PART I

Foundations

I

Rational and Irrational Beliefs: A Historical and Conceptual Perspective

Albert Ellis, Daniel David, and Steven Jay Lynn

This introductory chapter will trace the historical evolution of the constructs of rational and irrational beliefs and provide an overview of the empirical support and practical implications of contemporary models that have been proposed to define and understand rational and irrational beliefs. We will define irrational and rational beliefs and approach them in terms of *(a)* computational, algorithmic/representational, and implementational models of cognition; *(b)* the similarities and differences between rational and irrational beliefs and cold cognitions (e.g., automatic thoughts, expectancies, schemas); and *(c)* denoting the place of rational and irrational beliefs in the broader skein of cognitive psychology and cognitive-behavior theory and therapy, as well as psychotherapy more generally. Our discussion will serve as a prelude to more in-depth discussion and elaboration of these topics in the chapters that follow.

Historical Development of the Constructs of Rational and Irrational Beliefs

In general terms, rational beliefs refer to beliefs that are logical, and/or have empirical support, and/or are pragmatic. As one can notice, a belief does not have to fit all three criteria to be rational. However, it is necessary that a belief meet at least one criterion, or a combination of criteria, to be considered rational (see also Chapter 4). Thus, the terms *rational* and *irrational* have a psychological rather than a philosophical and/or logical definition. Accordingly, rational beliefs are not necessarily related to a rational approach in epistemology and logic (e.g., Popper's critical rationalism), and criticisms of rationality stemming from other epistemological positions (e.g., Quine-Duhames thesis, postmodernism, and constructivism) and/or politics (e.g., feminist perspective) should not be regarded as direct critiques of rational and irrational beliefs constructs as used in psychology. Still, the discussion of the philosophical underpinnings of rational and irrational belief is important and it is approached in its basic components in Chapter 2. Other terms, used interchangeably for these beliefs, are: adaptive, healthy, positive, and functional. Irrational beliefs refer to beliefs that are illogical, and/or do not have empirical support, and/or are nonpragmatic.

Typically the terms *rational* and *irrational* are used to define the type of cognitions (i.e., evaluative/appraisal/hot cognitions) described by rational-emotive behavior therapy (REBT). In contrast, the terms *functional* and *dysfunctional* are often used to define the type of cognitions (mental representations like descriptions and inferences) described by cognitive therapy (e.g., automatic thoughts). Also, the terms *adaptive* and *maladaptive* are often used to describe the behaviors generated by various cognitions, whereas the terms *healthy* and *unhealthy* typically refer to the feelings and psychophysiological responses generated by various cognitions. The terms *positive* and *negative* are less commonly used because positive thinking is not necessarily rational (e.g., delusional positive thinking), and negative thinking is not necessarily irrational (e.g., realistic negative thinking). Accordingly, these terms are mostly used to described feelings, but again, positive feelings are not necessarily healthy or functional and negative feelings are not necessarily unhealthy or dysfunctional (see Chapter 4 in this volume for details).

According to the "*ABC*(DE)" model (see Ellis, 1994; David & Szentagotai, 2006a), often people experience undesirable activating events (A), about which they have rational and irrational beliefs/cognitions (B). These beliefs lead to emotional, behavioral, and cognitive consequences (C). Rational beliefs (RBs) lead to adaptive and healthy (i.e., functional) consequences, whereas irrational beliefs (IBs) lead to maladaptive and unhealthy (i.e., dysfunctional) consequences. Once generated, these consequences (C) can become activating events (A) themselves, producing secondary (meta)consequences (e.g., meta-emotions: depression about being depressed) through secondary (meta-cognitions) RBs and IBs. Clients who engage in REBT are encouraged to actively dispute (D) (i.e., restructure) their IBs and to assimilate more efficient (E) RBs, to facilitate healthy, functional, and adaptive emotional, cognitive, and behavioral responses.

The ABC(DE) model was been recently expanded by including the concept of unconscious information processing (David, 2003). More precisely, sometimes cognitions are not consciously accessible, insofar as they are represented in the implicit rather than the explicit memory system (David, 2003). In this case, their impact on individuals' responses can be controlled *(a)* by behavioral techniques (e.g., altering automatic associations), and *(b)* by a direct focus on primary responses generated by unconscious information processing (e.g., targeting arousal by relaxation) or on secondary processes produced by these primary responses (e.g., conscious beliefs and consequences). In this context, when we say that an emotion is postcognitive, we mean that its generation always involves computational/cognitive mechanisms (be it conscious and/or unconscious). Once the emotion is generated, it can prime other cognitions and can appear precognitive; however, as we have noted, the generation of the emotion priming these cognitions involves itself computational/cognitive mechanisms. Accordingly, emotions are postcognitive.

Indeed, a cognitive approach assumes that most complex human responses (e.g., feelings, behaviors) are cognitively penetrable (see for details David, Miclea, & Opre, 2004). Cognitive penetrability means two things: *(a)* that a response (e.g., emotions, behaviors) is the outcome of conscious or unconscious cognitive processing, and *(b)* that a change in cognition will induce a change in the expressed response. It bears note that the limits of cognitive penetrability define the boundaries of cognitive approach. That is, because some basic human responses are not cognitively penetrable (e.g., are genetically determined), they typically are not considered within the purview of the cognitive approach.

The general conception of humans having rational and irrational beliefs was originated by several ancient philosophers, although they didn't exactly use that terminology. Gautama Buddha spoke about the Four Noble Truths, which included rational beliefs, and destructive beliefs, which included irrational ones. The ancient Greek philosophers, including Aristotle, Plato, Socrates, Epicurus, and Zeno of Citium, and several ancient Roman philosophers including Cicero, Seneca, Epictetus, and Marcus Aurelius also held that beliefs significantly affect emotional problems. The general conception of rational and irrational beliefs is many centuries old and I (Albert Ellis; AE) probably would not have arrived at the more specific REBT conception had I not made a hobby of philosophy from my fifteenth year onward.

Let us define Rational Beliefs (RBs) and Irrational Beliefs (IBs) as I (AE) started to use them in rational-emotive behavior therapy (REBT) when I (AE) first began practicing it in January 1955, gave my first paper on it at the American Psychological Association annual convention in Chicago in August 1956, and published my (AE) first article on this topic "Rational Psychotherapy"

TABLE I.I. Desires That Finally Lead to Healthy Results

Wants and Desires	Thwarting of Desires and Wants	Healthy Results	Secondary Desires	Healthy Results
I want to perform well and win others' approval	Performing poorly and winning disapproval	Sorrow, regret, and/ or frustration	I don't like feeling sad, regretful, and frustrated	Sorrow and regret about feeling sad and frustrated
I need to perform well and win others' approval	Performing poorly and winning disapproval	Severe anxiety, depression, and/or rage	I don't like feeling anxious, depressed, or rageful	Sorrow and regret about feeling anxious and depressed

(Ellis, 1958) and my (AE) major book in REBT, *Reason and Emotion in Psychotherapy* in 1962. The REBT conception of RBs and IBs is rather complicated but includes several main hypotheses (see Table 1.1):

- Humans are constructivists and have a considerable degree of choice or free will. However, free will is constrained by the fact the individuals are also limited by strong innate or biological tendencies and by their community living and social learning to think, feel, and behave.
- People have many goals and purposes—especially the goal of continuing to live and be reasonably free from pain and to be happy.
- People's beliefs or cognitions are strong and influential in selecting their goals and values but they are rarely, if ever, pure. When they think, they also feel and behave. When they feel, they also think and behave. When they behave, they also think and feel. Thus, they *believe* they want to live and be happy, they *desire* to do so, and they *act* to implement their thoughts and desires. All three processes are interrelated and integrated.
- People's desires include, first, wishes and preferences—for example, "I want to perform well and be approved by significant others, *but* if I perform badly and am disapproved, I can still usually survive and have some happiness."
- People's desires also may include absolutistic shoulds, oughts, musts, and demands: "I absolutely *have* to perform well and win others' approval, *or else* it is awful (as bad as can be) and I have little worth as a *person!*"
- Human desires and preferences are usually healthy and productive but absolute musts and demands are often unhealthy and destructive.

- When people *wish* for something and don't achieve it, they usually have healthy feelings-thoughts-behaviors of sorrow, regret, and frustration—healthy because these feelings motivate them to get what they want, and avoid what they don't want *next* time.
- When peoples' desires escalate to arrogant demands, they often have unhealthy feelings-thoughts-behaviors of severe anxiety, rage, and depression.
- When people who wish that they perform well and be approved by others, perform badly and are not approved by others, they often make themselves sorry and regretful and also make themselves severely anxious, raging, and depressed. They frequently feel sorry about their sorrow, and we call this secondary feeling or meta-emotion.
- When people demand that they perform well and be approved by others, and they perform badly and are disapproved, they not only often are anxious, raging, and depressed, but also make themselves anxious about their anxiety, enraged about their raging, and depressed about their depression. They have primary symptoms of emotional disturbance but they also have secondary symptoms—disturbance *about* their disturbance.

The history of people being able to challenge and dispute their irrational beliefs, feelings, and behaviors goes back at least 2500 years, when Gautama Buddha began to preach enlightenment and traveled widely in India, China, and other Asian countries spreading his teachings. Guatama hypothesized that all humans are equipped with the ability to set goals and express desires when they encounter adversity or suffering. However, by fully experiencing their suffering and gaining awareness that much distress is self-induced by their turning their moderate wishes and preferences into self-centered, arrogant desires and cravings, they encounter needless confusion and pain. Instead, Guatama Buddha taught that people can encounter themselves and their turmoil, minimize cravings, empty their minds of desires, and even reach Nirvana, an ideal state of total desirelessness and peace. Buddha was hard-headed and practical, and not religious in the traditional sense, as were many of his followers later. Searching for enlightenment the Buddha advocated an action-oriented approach to life that encompassed the virtues of practicality, patience, fortitude, self-discipline, right morals, right livelihood, and mindfulness of the moment-to-moment flux of experience. Like Lao Tsu and his teachings that came to be known as Taoism, Buddhists respect all life and strive to be even-tempered and accepting of themselves and others.

Around 470 B.C. Socrates, Plato, Epicurus, and other Greeks began to also stress philosophic questioning of social and political standards and to advocate thinking for oneself and thinking about one's thinking. They followed social rules and customs, but also valued personal independence. Their teachings were then carried to Rome by the Stoics, particularly Zeno and Chrysippus in the third century B.C. Epictetus (55 to 135 A.D.), a Greek slave who was brought to Rome, popularized stoicism, as did his pupil Marcus Aurelius (121 to 180 A.D.). Epictetus is famous for his maxim "It is not the misfortunes that happen to you that upset you, but your view of them." This is one of the classiest early statements of the modern constructivist philosophy of human distress.

Early-nineteenth-century psychologists, such as Pierre Janet (1889) and Robert Thorndike (1919), stressed self-disturbance and believed that people created irrational beliefs, and could therefore challenge them and develop healthier rational beliefs. But their influence was eclipsed by Sigmund Freud and his psychoanalytic followers who displaced Janet and Thorndike, and promulgated the view that people's early childhood experiences were so powerful and deeply rooted in the unconscious that they could not be countered by reason alone. John B. Watson, the originator of behavior therapy, contended that direct encounters with what is feared or avoided (i.e., in vivo desensitization), rather than conscious reflection, could disabuse people of their irrational ways of thinking and behaving.

More contemporary psychoanalysts, especially Adler (1946), Horney (1950), and Fromm (1956) held that self-created idealized images that had the malign power to severely disturb people could be modified in the course of psychotherapy. However, they neglected to present viable pathways to achieve this end, and failed to elucidate methods for disputing maladaptive beliefs. Instead, they mainly used intellectual methods of countering irrational thoughts. Still other therapists, such as Rogers (1961) and Perls (1969), disputed their clients' dysfunctional beliefs, often indirectly yet purposefully via emotion-eliciting and behavioral stratagems, but not cognitively.

All this changed considerably in 1950, when Ellis (1956, 1957, 1958, 1962) began to practice rational-emotive behavior therapy (REBT), a pioneering form of cognitive-behavior therapy. In his first paper on REBT in 1958, Ellis argued that REBT was an eclectic approach that integrated cognitive, emotional, and behavioral techniques. REBT particularly emphasized the differences between creating rational beliefs (RBs) to produce healthy emotions, such as sorrow and regret when desires are thwarted, and creating irrational beliefs (IBs) that lead to unhealthy feelings such as anxiety, depression, and rage when people do not get what they "needed" or get what they "can't stand" (see Table 1.2).

TABLE 1.2. Demands That Finally Lead to Unhealthy Results

Demands and Needs	Thwarting of Demands and Needs	Unhealthy Results	Secondary Demands and Needs	Unhealthy Results
I need to perform well and win others' approval	Performing poorly and winning disapproval	Severe anxiety, depression, and/or rage	I absolutely must not be anxious, depressed, or enraged	Anxiety about anxiety, depression about depression, and/or rage about being enraged
I want to perform well and win others' approval	Performing poorly and winning disapproval	Sorrow, Regret, and/or Frustration	I absolutely must not be sorrowful, and frustrated	Anxiety about sorrow and frustration

At the inception of REBT, Ellis postulated three major ways in which clients and other people could challenge and dispute (i.e., restructure) their irrational beliefs (IBs):

1. Realistic and empirical disputing that challenges people's musts and imperatives: "Where is the evidence that I absolutely *must* be successful and approved by significant others?" Answer: "There in no evidence for this, it will only be inconvenient and not 'terrible' if I fail and experience disapproval."
2. Logical disputing of people's overgeneralized and illogical beliefs: "Because I didn't succeed at this important task, that makes me a stupid, hopeless person." Disputing: "How does one important failure make *me* a failure?" Answer: "It only makes me a person who failed this time. A *failure* would be someone who *always* and *only* fails. That is not I, nor anyone."
3. Pragmatic disputing. "Where will it get me if I think I absolutely must succeed at important tasks and am a hopeless failure when I don't?" Answer: "It will get me nowhere—it will only make me anxious and depressed, instead of healthily sorry and frustrated when I fail or get rejected."

To target a larger audience, over time these methods were complemented with other strategies such as:

- Metaphors and literature (e.g., reading poetry and stories as homework, etc.)
- Playing-type techniques for children
- Humor, irony, and self-irony

- Pastoral techniques for religious people
- Any other techniques and procedures from diverse therapies that are safe, can be cognitively conceptualized, and can be used to transform irrational beliefs into rational beliefs.

As such, REBT is not only an etiopathogenetic (causal) treatment, but also a prophylactic one, because it shows people that they have a strong tendency to upset themselves with absolutistic thinking, but are able to change such thinking to express preferences, rather than shoulds, musts, and oughts, and thereby "unupset" themselves. Consequently, REBT is one of the major self-help therapies and teaches people, by means of books, tapes, and other materials, how to help themselves with and without a therapist.

As the first form of cognitive-behavioral therapy (CBT), REBT overlaps with the cognitive-behavioral therapies (CBTs) of Aaron Beck (1976), Donald Meichenbaum (1994), David Barlow (1996), and other therapists. But, as Ellis has noted (Ellis, 2004, 2005), REBT not only shows clients how they think, feel, and behave irrationally, and how to become more preferential and less absolutistic, but it also actively and steadily keeps teaching them three main "rational" philosophies:

1. People can choose to have unconditional self-acceptance (USA) in spite of their failings at important tasks and their being rejected by significant people. Why? Because they—simply and strongly—can refuse to damn themselves for their doings. They still had better evaluate what they think, feel and do—but not *themselves* or their *totality* as *persons.*

2. People can choose to have unconditional other-acceptance (UOA) in spite of the frequent "bad" behavior of others. Just as they refuse to rate their *selves* for their effective and ineffective thoughts, feelings and acts, they can do the same for others. If they do so, they have compassion for others by accepting *them,* but not *their sins.* They often hate what people *do,* but not the *persons* who do what is hateful.

3. People can choose to have unconditional life-acceptance (ULA) in spite of the frequent unfortunate life conditions. They can accept their life when it is replete with adversities and still decide to be as happy as they can be in spite of these adversities. They can choose to focus on whatever is joyous and fortunate in the many things available in life, to change the changeable things, and observe and dislike the unchangeable things they cannot change, and have wisdom to know the difference. Life may never be as happy as they would like it to be, but they can still lead a reasonably good existence.

These are some of the main principles and practices of REBT and of some of the other CBTs. They are also largely the philosophies central to some forms of Buddhism, especially the Tibetan Buddhism of the 14th Dalai Lama and his followers, which emphasizes the importance of scientific research instead of the mysticism of some of the Zen Buddhist groups (Dalai Lama & Cutler, 1998).

Some CBT professionals such as Marsha Linehan (1992) and Steven Hayes and his collaborators, have integrated mindfulness into CBT methods. Hayes, Follette, and Linehan (2004) have also added nondisputing methods to CBT, and have made it more paradoxical, less confrontational, and less verbal. REBT holds that these indirect and nondisputing methods can be integrated with the REBT techniques (Ellis, 2005, see Chapter 11, this volume), but this proposal still remains to be tested. Continued research will determine whether major cognitive restructuring strategies from REBT and CBT will largely remain intact or will be integrated with other thinking, feeling, and behaving procedures.

The Nature of Irrational and Rational Beliefs

The nature of rational and irrational beliefs has been described and discussed in hundreds of papers and books. Albert Ellis (Ellis & Dryden, 1997) as well as Aaron Beck (1976) listed many dysfunctional beliefs that people often have that make them disturbed and ineffective, including overgeneralization, catastrophizing/awfulizing, personalizing, and jumping to conclusions. Ellis and Dryden (1997) hold that virtually all these irrational beliefs consciously or implicitly include one or more absolutistic musts. Thus, when people use awfulizing, personalize, and tell themselves "He frowned at me, and that means he doesn't like me and that means I'm no good," they imply *(1)* He *must not* frown at me! *(2)* His frowning proves that he doesn't like me, as he *must* like me, that I'm no good, as I *must not* be! *(3)* I *must* never be frowned upon and put down by anyone and *must* be perfectly approved all the time! REBT looks for people's automatic negative thoughts and shows them how to dispute them. But it also routinely looks for the absolutistic shoulds, oughts, and musts that lie behind them, finds these musts, shows them to patients, and teaches people how to dispute and change them into preferences. REBT shows people that they consciously and unconsciously choose to disturb themselves by escalating their *preferences* into *demands* and *cravings*, and that they can train themselves not to do so and thereby create healthy feelings and emotions.

Multilevel Analysis

All these ideas are interesting, but they need to be organized in a structured conceptual framework, such as the one offered by multilevel analysis (text based on David, 2003; David, Miclea, & Opre, 2004; David & Szentagotai, 2006). Following the theoretical foundations of cognitive psychology (e.g., Marr, 1982; Newell, 1990), it has become commonplace to analyze IBs/RBs on three different levels: computational, algorithmic-representational, and implementational (for details see David, 2003).

The *Computational Level Theory* describes the goal of a given computation and the logic of the strategy through which it is carried out. Basic questions that research at this level addresses are: "What is the goal of the computation?" "Is it appropriate?" "What is the input and what is the output?" "What knowledge do we need to transform the input into output?" "How is the general strategy carried out?," "What is the interaction between the goal and our knowledge. A basic question that research at this level addresses is: "What is the goal/function of computations based on IBs/RBs?"

There is a broad consensus in the REBT literature (e.g., Ellis, 1994) that IBs/RBs refer to evaluative or "hot" cognitions, and therefore serve an evaluative function. Abelson and Rosenberg (1958) use the terms "hot" and "cold" cognitions to make the distinction between appraising (hot) and knowing (cold). *Cold cognitions* (Lazarus & Smith, 1988) refer to the way people develop representations of relevant circumstances (i.e., activating events), whereas *hot cognitions* refer to the way people process and evaluate cold cognitions (David & McMahon, 2001; David, Schnur, & Belloiu, 2002). Cold cognitions are often analyzed in terms of surface cognitions that are easy to access consciously, and deep cognitions that are consciously accessible yet more difficult to access. *Surface cognitions*, often called automatic thoughts, refer to descriptions and inferences (e.g., expectancies, attributions), whereas *deep cognitions* refer to core beliefs (i.e., schemas) and other meaning-based representations (for details, see Eysenck & Keane, 2000). *Hot cognitions*, on the other hand, also called appraisals or evaluative cognitions, refer to how cold cognitions are processed in terms of their relevance for personal well-being (for details, see Ellis, 1994; Lazarus, 1991). Consequently, during a specific activating event, there seem to be four different possibilities for how cold and hot cognitions regarding the activating event are related: *(1)* distorted representation of the event/negatively appraised; *(2)* nondistorted representation/negatively appraised; *(3)* distorted representation/nonnegatively appraised; *(4)* nondistorted representation/nonnegatively appraised.

According to Lazarus (1991) and to the appraisal theory of emotions, although cold cognitions contribute to appraisal, only appraisal itself results directly in emotions. The effect of cold cognitions on emotions seems to be dependent on hot cognitions. Although past research suggested that cold cognitions are strongly related to emotions (e.g., Schachter & Singer, 1962; Weiner, 1985), it is now generally accepted that as long as cold cognitions remain unevaluated, they are insufficient to produce emotions (Lazarus, 1991; Lazarus & Smith, 1988; Smith, Haynes, Lazarus, & Pope, 1993). Different schools of CBT differ in the emphasis they place on various levels of cognition (for details, see David & Szentagotai, 2006; Wessler, 1982). Because the REBT theory (Ellis, 1962; 1994; Wessler, 1982) has always been focused on evaluative/hot cognitions as proximal causes of emotions (i.e., irrational beliefs), rather than on cold cognitions (e.g., descriptions, inferences), the theory is congruent with more recent developments in cognitive psychology. The way we represent—by cold cognitions—activating events in our mind depends on the interaction between activating events and our rational and irrational beliefs. Cold cognitions may generate various operant behaviors, and then cold cognitions and operant behaviors may be further appraised in a rational/irrational manner, producing feelings and psychophysiological responses.

Indeed, recent research (Szentagotai & Freeman, 2007) addressing the relations between hot (i.e., irrational beliefs) and cold cognitions (i.e., automatic thoughts), found support for the model. More precisely, in a study involving participants suffering from major depressive disorder, Szentagotai and Freeman (2007) determined that automatic thoughts generate depressed mood if they are associated with irrational beliefs, as described above. DiLorenzo, David, and Montgomery (2007) also confirmed the model in a study concerned with the connection between hot cognitions (i.e., irrational beliefs) and inferences (i.e., expectancies) in a sample of college students facing a difficult exam.

The *Algorithmic-Representational Level Theory* specifies representations in detail, as well as the algorithms defined by them. Although Ellis's original work (1962) proposes 11 irrational beliefs, more recent developments in CBT/REBT suggest that irrational beliefs fall into four categories of irrational (dysfunctional/maladaptive) cognitive processes: demandingness (DEM), awfulizing/catastrophizing (AWF), global evaluation/self-downing (GE/SD), and frustration intolerance (FI) (Campbell, 1988; DiGiuseppe, 1996). DEM refers to absolutistic requirements expressed in the form of "musts," "shoulds" and "oughts." Furthermore, DEM includes an evaluative component (how desirable is this?) and a reality component (what should I expect?). AWF refers to one's evaluating a situation as more than 100% bad, and the worst thing that could happen to him/her. FI refers to people's beliefs that they cannot endure, or envision being unable to endure a given situation, as well as their belief that they will have no happiness at all if what they demand should not exist, actually exists. GE/SD appears when individuals tend to be excessively critical of themselves (i.e., to make global negative evaluations of themselves), of others, and of life conditions. These four irrational cognitive processes cover various areas of content (e.g., performance, comfort, affiliation) and refer to ourselves, others, and life conditions. According to Ellis (1962; 1994), DEM is the core irrational belief, and all other irrational beliefs are derived from it. Indeed, recent data suggest the following information processing sequence: *(1)* DEM; *(2)* AWF and/or FI, and/or GE/SD, and *(3)* dysfunctional consequences (see DiLorenzo, David, & Montgomery, 2007). The line of research concerned with the algorithmic-representational level examines how IBs/RBs are represented in our cognitive system. At least two possibilities have emerged so far:

1. Irrational beliefs are evaluative (hot) cognitions that are organized as propositional representations (Ellis, 1994). A propositional representation is the smallest unit of knowledge that can stand as a separate assertion; that is, the smallest unit about which one can make the judgment of true or false (Anderson, 2000).
2. Irrational beliefs are evaluative cognitions that are organized as a specific type of schema ("evaluative schemas") (DiGiuseppe, 1996). A schema represents the structure of an object or event according to a slot format, where slots specify values that the object or event has on various attributes (Anderson, 2000). Thus, schemas are complex structures that represent the person's constructed concepts of reality and behavioral responses to that reality.

In the light of recent empirical data (see Szentagotai, Schnur, DiGiuseppe, Macavei, Kallay, & David, 2005) it seems that DEM and GE/SD are evaluative schemas, whereas AWF and FI are evaluative cognitions organized as propositional representations.

The *Implementational Level Theory* answers the question of how representations and algorithms are carried out from a physical point of view. For example, what happens in the human brain when IBs or RBs are activated? This fascinating field requires interdisciplinary research, partnering with the field of cognitive neuroscience. REBT research on this topic is still in a nascent phase. Studies that meld the study of belief and neuroscience are usually conducted within the framework of evolutionary psychology (Ruth, 1993), connectionist modeling (Ingram & Siegle, 2000), and modern brain-mapping techniques (e.g., MRI).

The Relationship between Rational and Irrational Beliefs

Early research conceptualized rational beliefs as low levels of irrational beliefs. However, recent data suggest that rational and irrational beliefs are not bipolar constructs (e.g., a low level of irrational beliefs does not necessarily signify high levels of rational beliefs), but are rather orthogonal to one another. As shown in Table 1.3 (see also, David & Szentagotai, 2006b), the relations between rational and irrational beliefs may be very complex (Bernard, 1998; David, 2003). Faced with a specific event (A), people can have simultaneously high irrational beliefs, low irrational beliefs, or no irrational beliefs. Similarly and simultaneously, they can have high rational beliefs, low rational beliefs, or no rational beliefs regarding the same event (A) (e.g., David, Schnur, & Belloiu, 2002). These potential interactions should be taken into account when designing research and conducting statistical procedures.

Rational and Irrational Beliefs in the Architecture of the Human Mind

REBT can be described in terms of a simple ABC(DE) format and hence taught to children and adults, and incorporated in materials that can be effectively used for self-help purposes. Thus, individual clients and self-help groups can be shown that:

1. When people have goals and encounter adversities (A) so that they don't get what they want or get what they don't want, they can *choose* to have healthy consequences (C) or unhealthy ones.
2. Their choice is largely at B, the level of their Belief—Feeling—Behavioral system (see the ABC model described above). At B they can decide and be determined to feel *healthily* sorry, regretful, or frustrated, or can decide to be *unhealthily* anxious, depressed, and raging.
3. Their decision at B can be strongly and actively (persistently) to healthily *prefer* that their adversities (A) be reduced, or to unhealthily *demand* that their adversities be reduced.
4. If people absolutistically and rigidly insist that adversities must not exist—"It is *awful* to be rejected. I can't *stand it*. Rejection makes me *totally unlovable!*"—they tend to severely upset themselves. If they only prefer success and approval but unconditionally accept failure and disapproval, they make themselves minimally or moderately upset.
5. When individuals feel (C) unhealthily anxious, depressed, and raging when faced with adversities (A), they can constructively realize that they have changed their *preferences* for success and approval into

TABLE 1.3. The Relations between Rational and Irrational Beliefs in a Stressful Situation (e.g., taking an important exam)

	High Level of Rational Beliefs	Low Level of Rational Beliefs	No Rational Beliefs
High Level of Irrational Beliefs	I must pass the exam (high IB) I very much want to pass the exam and make my mom happy (high RB)	I must pass the exam (high IB) It would be nice if I passed the exam and made my mom happy but this is not so important (low RB)	I must pass the exam (high IB) I don't care about making my mom happy by passing the exam (lack of RB)
Low Level of Irrational Beliefs	It would be nice if I passed the exam but this is not so important (low IB) I very much want to pass the exam and make my mom happy (high RB)	It would be nice if I passed the exam but this is not so important (low IB) It would be nice if I passed the exam and made my mom happy but this is not so important (low RB)	It would be nice if I passed the exam but this is not so important (low IB) I don't care about making my mom happy by passing the exam (lack of RB)
No Irrational Beliefs	I don't care about passing the exam (lack of IB) I very much want to pass the exam and make my mom happy (high RB)	I don't care about passing the exam (lack of IB) It would be nice if I passed the exam and made my mom happy but this is not so important (low RB)	I don't care about passing the exam (lack of IB) It would be nice if I passed the exam and made my mom happy but this is not so important (low RB)

arrogant, unrealistic, compulsive *demands*, and that they always have the therapeutic *choice* of returning to healthy preferences again.

6. People can be alert to their tendencies to think irrationally for the rest of their lives and whenever they identify these tendencies use a number of REBT thinking, feeling, and behaving methods to minimize them.

7. Thus, people can use the cognitive method of disputing (D) their irrational beliefs; rehearse coping statements; use the REBT self-help format; profit from psycho-educational methods of reading, listening to audio and audio-visual REBT-oriented cassettes; enroll in REBT-oriented lectures, courses, and workshops; do cost-benefit analysis of their harmful addictions; engage in REBT games and sports; and make use of other REBT cognitive techniques.

8. People can use several emotional evocative-experiential techniques that are described in the REBT literature that include forceful coping statements, shame attacking exercises, rational-emotive imagery, role-playing, and rational humorous stories and songs (for details see Ellis, 1962).

9. People can use several behavioral methods that are described in the REBT literature that include: modeling, in vivo desensitization, activity homework assignments, stimulus control, relaxation techniques, skill training, teaching friends and relatives how to use REBT, relapse prevention, and other action-oriented methods.

10. As many empirical studies have demonstrated, REBT is quite effective in individual and group therapy (Engels, Garnefski, & Diekstra, 1993). However, REBT also has been successfully used by many individuals in its self-help application, along with or without a therapist.
    It follows the tradition of Ralph Waldo Emerson (1803–1882), and Dale Carnegie (1888–1955), but is more comprehensive than they were, in that its self-help component offers a variety of cognitive, emotive, and behavioral methods for the individual to apply (Ellis, 1957, 1999/2007, 2001, 2003).

In summary, REBT and CBT hold that unfortunate adversities (A) in people's early and later lives often significantly contribute to their emotional problems and behavioral dysfunctions and have serious consequences (C). However, humans are innate constructivists and have strong tendencies to create and invent needless problems for themselves by the *views* or *philosophies* (B) they choose to take of frustrating events (A). Their beliefs (B) about the difficulties in their lives have cognitive, emotional, and behavioral implications, because they are frequently, strongly, and persistently held. When these beliefs are healthy, they consist of preferences and desires that adversities be ameliorated and REBT calls them rational or functional beliefs that lead to healthy feelings of sorrow and disappointment and to efforts to improve adverse circumstances.

When people's beliefs or philosophies are unhealthy and destructive, REBT calls them irrational or dysfunctional and actively disputes them (D) in multiple cognitive, emotional, and behavioral ways. Many empirically based research studies show that REBT (Smith, 1982; Engels, Garnefski, & Diekstra, 1993; Lyons & Woods, 1991; David, 2004) and other forms of CBT (Hollon & Beck, 1994) are effective. But these approaches are still evolving and can potentially be usefully added to or integrated with other methods. Indeed, REBT and CBT both emphasize science and faith founded on facts, in a manner not unlike the Tibetan Buddhism of the Dalai Lama. Along with Viktor Frankl (1963, 1967, 1975), REBT espouses "rational spirituality" that includes cultivating vital absorbing interest and purposiveness in life (Ellis & Harper, 1997). Some forms of CBT (like REBT) can integrate religious faith and/or techniques (e.g., meditation-like mindfulness) into treatment. How these integrations will be expressed in efficient and efficacious clinical protocols still needs to be researched (but see mindfulness cognitive therapy, which is an empirically supported treatment for severe depression according to National Institute for Health and Clinical Excellence, UK).

Conclusion

In general terms, rational beliefs refer to beliefs that are logical, and/or have empirical support, and/or are pragmatic; other terms, used interchangeably, for these beliefs are adaptive, healthy, and functional. Irrational beliefs refer to beliefs that are illogical, and/or do not have empirical support, and/or are nonpragmatic; other terms, used interchangeably for these beliefs are maladaptive, unhealthy, and dysfunctional. While the terms rational/functional and irrational/dysfunctional are typically used for beliefs, the terms adaptive and maladaptive are used for their behavioral consequences, and the terms healthy and unhealthy—for their emotional consequences. In rational-emotive and cognitive-behavioral therapy, however, they have received specific meanings. Irrational beliefs describe specific information processes, which are evaluative (hot cognitions), and involved in maladaptive and unhealthy behavioral and emotional consequences. These irrational cognitive processes are: (1) DEM, (2) AWF, (3) FI, (4) GE/SD. DEM seems to be the central irrational belief. Rational beliefs describe specific information processes, which are evaluative (hot cognitions), and involved in adaptive and healthy behavioral and emotional consequences. Near the end of his life, Ellis said that perhaps "dysfunctional" and "functional" beliefs would have been better terms, because of the negative philosophical and religious connotations of "rational" and "irrational" (Ellis, personal communication to David). This might have prevented unfair criticisms of REBT and contributed to a better integration of cognitive-behavioral therapies. However, there is also the significant advantage of the rational/ irrational concepts of individualizing these beliefs in the clinical field as a part of the rational-emotive and cognitive-behavioral approach of Ellis.

REFERENCES

Abelson, R., & Rosenberg, M. (1958). Symbolic psycho-logic: A model of attitudinal cognition. *Behavioral Science, 3*, 1–13.

Adler, A. (1946). *Understanding human nature* (W. B. Wolfe, Trans.). New York: Greenberg. (Original work published 1927).

Anderson, J. R. (2000). *Cognitive psychology and its implications* (5th ed.). New York: Worth Publishing.

Barlow, D. H. (1996). Health care policy, psychotherapy research, and the future of psychotherapy. *American Psychologist, 51*, 1050–1058.

Beck, A. T. (1976). *Cognitive therapy for emotional disorders.* New York: International University Press.

Bernard, M. E. (1998). Validation of the general attitude and beliefs scale. *Journal of Rational-Emotive and Cognitive-Behavior Therapy, 16*, 183–196.

Campbell, I. (1988). The psychology of homosexuality. In A. Ellis & M. E. Bernard (Eds.), *Clinical applications of rational-emotive therapy* (pp. 153–180). New York: Plenum.

Dalai Lama, H. H., & Cutler, H. (1998). *The art of happiness: A handbook for living.* New York: Riverhead Books.

David, D. (2003). Rational Emotive Behavior Therapy (REBT): The view of a cognitive psychologist. In W. Dryden (Ed.), *Theoretical developments in REBT.* London: Brunner/Routledge.

David, D. (2004). Special issue on the cognitive revolution in clinical psychology: Beyond the behavioral approach—Conclusions: Toward an evidence-based psychology and psychotherapy. *Journal of Clinical Psychology, 4*, 447–451.

David, D., & McMahon, J. (2001). Clinical strategies in cognitive behavioral therapy: A case analysis. *Romanian Journal of Cognitive and Behavioral Psychotherapy, 1*, 71–86.

David, D., Miclea, M., & Opre, A. (2004). The information processing approach to the human mind: Basic and beyond. *Journal of Clinical Psychology, 4*, 353–369.

David, D., Schnur, J., & Belloiu, A. (2002). Another search for the "hot" cognitions: Appraisal, irrational beliefs, attributions, and their relation to emotion. *Journal of Rational-Emotive and Cognitive-Behavior Therapy, 2*, 93–131.

David, D., & Szentagotai, A. (2006a). Cognition in cognitive-behavioral psychotherapies: Toward an integrative model. *Clinical Psychology Review, 26,* 284–298.

David, D., & Szentagotai, A. (2006b). The faster you move the longer you live: A test of rational emotive behavior therapy. In D. David (Ed.), *A critical review of the current trends in psychotherapy and clinical psychology.* New York: NovaScience.

DiGiuseppe, R. (1996). The nature of irrational and rational beliefs: Progress in rational emotive behavior theory. *Journal of Rational-Emotive & Cognitive-Behavior Therapy, 4,* 5–28.

DiLorenzo, T. A., David, D., & Montgomery, G. H. (2007). The interrelations between irrational cognitive processes and distress in stressful academic settings. *Personality and Individual Differences, 42,* 765–77.

Ellis, A. (1956). An operational reformulation of some basic principles of psychoanalysis. *Psychoanalytic Review, 43,* 163-180.

Ellis, A. (1957). *How to live with a neurotic: At home and at work.* New York: Crown. (Rev. ed., North Hollywood, CA: Wilshire Books, 1975).

Ellis, A. (1958). Rational psychotherapy. *Journal of General Psychology, 59,* 35–49.

Ellis, A. (1962). *Reason and emotion in psychotherapy.* New York: Lyle Stuart.

Ellis, A. (1994). *Reason and emotion in psychotherapy* (Rev. ed.). Secaucus, NJ: Birch Lane.

Ellis, A. (1999/2007). *How to make yourself happy, and remarkably less disturbable.* Atascadero, CA: Impact Publishers.

Ellis, A. (2001). *Feeling better, getting better, staying better: Profound self-help therapy for your emotions.* Atascadero, CA: Impact Publishers.

Ellis, A. (2003). *Ask Albert Ellis: Straight answers and sound advice from America's best-known psychologist.* Atascadero, CA: Impact Publishers.

Ellis, A. (2004). *Rational emotive behavior therapy: It works for me—it can work for you.* Amherst, NY: Prometheus Books.

Ellis, A. (2005). *The myth of self-esteem.* Amherst, NY: Prometheus Books.

Ellis, A., & Dryden, W. (1997). *The practice of rational emotive behavior therapy.* New York: Springer Publishing Co.

Ellis, A., & Harper, R. A. (1997). *A guide to rational living* (3rd rev. ed.). North Hollywood, CA: Melvin Powers/Wilshire Books.

Engels, G. I., Garnefski, N., & Diekstra, R. F. W. (1993). Efficacy of rational-emotive therapy: A quantitative analysis. *Journal of Consulting and Clinical Psychology, 61,* 1083–1091.

Eysenck, M., & Keane, M. (2000). *Cognitive Psychology: A student's handbook* (4th ed.). Hillsdale, NJ: Erlbaum.

Frankl, V. E. (1963). *Man's search for meaning: An introduction to logotherapy* (I. Lasch, Trans.). New York: Washington Square Press. (Earlier title, 1959: *From death-camp to existentialism.* Originally published in 1946 as *Ein Psycholog erlebt das Konzentrationslager.*)

Frankl, V. E. (1967). *Psychotherapy and existentialism: Selected papers on logotherapy.* New York: Simon and Schuster.

Frankl, V. E. (1975). *The unconscious god: Psychotherapy and theology.* New York: Simon and Schuster. (Originally published in 1948 as *Der unbewusste Gott.* Republished in 1997 as *Man's search for ultimate meaning.*)

Freud, S. (1926). *Hemmung, symptom, und angst* [Inhibition, symptom, and anxiety]. Vienna: Int. Psychoalytischer Verlag.

Fromm, E. (1956). *The art of loving*. New York: Harper & Row.

Hayes, S. C., Follette, V. M., & Linehan, M. M. (2004). *Mindfulness and acceptance: Expanding the cognitive-behavioral tradition*. New York: Guilford Press.

Hollon, S. D., & Beck, A. T. (1994). Cognitive and cognitive-behavioral therapies. In A. E. Bergin & S. L. Garfield (Eds.), *Handbook of psychotherapy and behavior change* (4th ed., pp. 428–466). New York: Wiley.

Horney, K. (1950). *Neurosis and human growth*. New York: W.W. Norton.

Ingram, R. E., & Siegle, G. J. (2000). Cognition and clinical science: From revolution to evolution. In K. Dobson (Ed.), *Handbook of cognitive therapy* (pp. 111–138). New York: Guilford.

Janet, P. (1889). *L'automatisme psychologique*. Paris: Félix Alcan. (New ed., Société Pierre Janet, 1973).

Lazarus, R. S. (1991). *Emotion and adaptation*. New York: Oxford University Press.

Lazarus, R. S., & Smith, C. A. (1988). Knowledge and appraisal in the cognition-emotion relationship. *Cognition and Emotion, 2*, 281–300.

Linehan, M. M. (1992). Behavioral treatment of borderline personality disorder. In D. Silver & M. Rosenbluth (Eds.), *The handbook on borderline disorders* (pp. 415–434). Madison, CT: International Universities Press.

Lyons, L. C., & Woods, P. J. (1991). The efficacy of rational-emotive therapy: A quantitative review of the outcome research. *Clinical Psychology Review, 11*, 357–369.

Marr, D. (1982). *Vision*. San Francisco: W.H. Freeman and Company.

Meichenbaum, D. (1994). *A clinical handbook/practical therapist manual*. Waterloo, Ontario, Canada: Institute Press.

Newell, A. (1990). *Unified theories of cognition*. Cambridge, MA: Harvard University Press.

Perls, F. (1969) *Ego, hunger, and aggression: The beginning of gestalt therapy*. New York: Random House. (Original work published 1947.)

Rogers, C. R. (1961). *On becoming a person*. Boston: Houghton Mifflin.

Ruth, W. J. (1993). Evolutionary psychology and rational emotive theory: Time to open the floodgates. *Journal of Rational Emotive and Cognitive Behavior Therapy, 11*, 235–248.

Schachter, S., & Singer, J. E. (1962). Cognitive, social, and physiological determinants of emotional state. *Psychologial Review, 69*, 379–399.

Smith, C. A., Haynes, K. N., Lazarus, R. S., & Pope, L. K. (1993). In search of the "hot" cognitions: Attributions, appraisals, and their relation to emotion. *Journal of Personality and Social Psychology, 65*, 916–929.

Smith, D. (1982). Trends in counselling and psychotherapy. *American Psychologists, 37*, 802–809.

Szentagotai, A., & Freeman, A. (2007). An analysis of the relationship between irrational beliefs and automatic thoughts in predicting distress. *Journal of Cognitive and Behavioral Psychotherapies, 7*, 1–9.

Szentagotai, A., Schnur, J., DiGiuseppe R., Macavei, B., Kallay, E., & David, D. (2005). The organization and the nature of irrational beliefs: Schemas or appraisal? *Journal of Cognitive and Behavioral Psychotherapies, 2*, 139–158.

Thorndike, R. L. (1919). *An introduction to the theory of mental and social measurements.* New York: Teachers College, Columbia University.

Watson, J. B. (1913). Psychology as the behaviorist views it. *Psychological Review, 20,* 158–177.

Weiner, B. (1985). *An attributional theory of motivation and emotion.* New York: Springer-Verlag.

Wessler, R. L. (1982). Varieties of cognitions in the cognitively-oriented psychotherapies. *Rational Living, 17,* 3–10.

2

Rationality and Rational Psychotherapy: The Heart of REBT

Arthur Still

In 1958 Albert Ellis published "Rational Psychotherapy," a brief paper marking the beginning of cognitive therapies (Ellis, 1958). As the therapy developed and he gained followers, he changed the name to "rational-emotive therapy," and then to rational-emotive behavior therapy (REBT). Meanwhile, Beck introduced his own version of cognitive therapy, cognitive-behavior therapy (CBT: Beck, 1963). There are differences between the Ellis and Beck approaches, and one of the most interesting lies in the bold use of the word *rational*, with all the ancient philosophical baggage it carries. The bland and relatively modern *cognitive, behavior,* and *therapy* carry no such baggage. The additions of *emotive* and *behavior* to "Rational Psychotherapy" served to soften the tough challenge of *rational*, but the word remains provocative in the field of psychotherapy, where feeling and empathy hold sway, and where the client's attempts to be rational about the difficulties that lead to therapy seem already to have failed miserably. This chapter looks at the logical and historical background to Ellis's use of *rational*, and why this use is so relevant in understanding the distinctive importance of REBT. It starts by exploring the different uses of the word that give rise to its different meanings; it then brings out two fundamental and apparently contrasting usages, referred to here as disciplinary and emancipatory rationality;

finally, it draws on the tension between these usages to display the full complexity of Ellis's use of the word *rational*, and to put some of the philosophical criticisms of Ellis and REBT into perspective.

Discursive Formations

To investigate a word like *rational* it can be helpful to recognize that its use always occurs within a context of a kind that Danziger (1997) called a "discursive formation." This is in part a verbal context: *rationality* and *rational* have close links with *reason, reflection, thought,* and *mental* (listed in rough order of proximity), so that a discursive formation is "a language that constitutes an integrated world of meanings in which each term articulates with other terms so as to form a coherent framework for representing a kind of knowledge that is regarded as true and a kind of practice regarded as legitimate" (Danziger, 1997, p. 13).

But a discursive formation is more than a semantic network, more for instance than a network of concepts or a meme. A meme is a historical unit for the evolution of words, according to Dawkins (1976), but it is too atomistic for the purposes of this chapter. It does not readily allow for the embedding in cultural and social practices (or "disciplinary mechanisms"; Foucault, 1980; Mitchell, 1991) of a word like *rationality*, and it is misleading at best to treat it in isolation from these factors. In the approach to rationality adopted here, the most significant unit is therefore the discursive formation, of which words and ideas are a part, rather than the individual words or ideas themselves. And in order to study discursive formations it is often necessary (as in the study of biological species) to pay at least some attention to their evolution.

Dryden and Still (1998) used this approach in order to separate two principal uses of the word *rationality*, whose differences are obscured by the common label. They were concerned to bring out the differences between its use in discourse about science, and in discourse within (rather than about) psychotherapy. In the first case, *rationality* has to do with the social and individual processes that serve to construct and maintain the objectivity of science, in the second it is about self-management. Failure to allow for these differences can lead to inappropriate criticisms of the usage in one discursive formation by importing the logical constraints proper to another. In this respect the development of modern cognitive psychotherapies, which attempt to ground themselves in science, and which therefore draw on both uses of the word *rationality*, offers an especially instructive field of study. This chapter builds on the earlier papers and draws on more recent work (Dryden and Still,

2007), which has tried to refine these distinctions and to put them more firmly within a historical context. We refer there to two aspects of rationality, rather than just uses of the word, though it is the uses that reveal the different aspects. Both aspects of rationality turn out to be essential to any discursive formation in which *rationality* forms a part, but they are weighted differently in the different discursive formations we discussed in Dryden and Still (1998).

Some Uses of Rational and Rationality

INSTRUMENTAL AND SCIENTIFIC RATIONALITY AND THE LOGIC OF JUSTIFICATION. In one use of *rationality* it is the guide that enables cognitive agents to "adopt beliefs on the basis of appropriate reasons" (Brown, 1995, p. 744). Related to this, it is an ideal for instrumental action: "To give a rational explanation of an action done by A is to show that on the basis of A's beliefs A did what he thought was most likely to realize his goals" (Newton-Smith, 1981, p. 271). Newton-Smith referred to this minimal rationality as minirat, which applies only to the action, and does not take into account the goals of the action. If you take pleasure in walking through the fields when there is a full moon, even when it is extremely cold, that in itself may be neither rational nor irrational, but it is rational (minirat) to look up the time of the full moon, and go out when the moon is up in order to enjoy yourself. If no belief is involved you may be criticized or mocked for your enjoyment, but it is not usually an issue of rationality.

But goals do become such an issue when there are beliefs that require justification. If you believe that there are fairies at the bottom of the garden, and that they appear at midnight in midwinter when the moon is full but are extremely shy, then if you wish to see them it would be rational (minirat) to conceal yourself and remain very quiet at the appropriate time, even though your belief (most people in Western cultures would probably agree) is not rational; it cannot be justified. If on the other hand a zoologist has good scientific reason to believe that a species of toad, long thought extinct, exists and comes out to mate in a dangerous and inhospitable (to us) swamp when the moon is full, it would be rational to mount a field trip to investigate this, not just because the action is appropriate to the goal (minirat), but also because the goal may well be rational. Whether or not the goal and the whole endeavor are rational will be a matter for debate within the discursive formation of zoology. It is up to the zoologist to justify it by appealing to current trends and long-term aims in this branch of the discipline, as well as current zoological knowledge. If the justification is successful, and survives peer criticism, then the zoologist's actions and beliefs will usually be regarded as rational (even though they may sound crazy when reported in the popular press) because zoology is a science, and science is generally accepted throughout most of the world as epitomizing a rational activity. This scientific rationality belongs to an amorphous and ill-defined discursive formation known as science, which contains within it a web of interlocking, specialized discursive formations, that make up the individual disciplines such as zoology and physics. Scientific rationality is what disciplines all aspire to, some of them (such as physics) with more certainty than others (such as scientifically based psychotherapy).

Notice that the physical details of the action may be similar in each of the above examples, but the ascriptions of rationality differs. In practice the battle-ground for earning this desirable label (or avoidance of the dismissive "irrational") is justification, or the giving of reasons. Traditional logic is the attempt to give this reasoning a formal basis. In the first case you may be asked why you are looking up the time of the full moon, but you are not required to justify your enjoyment. In the second you are also required (if you wish to be thought rational according to the standards of your time and place) to justify your goal, which follows from your belief in fairies. In the zoology case also you may be required to justify both action and goal; for instance to another zoologist (your career may depend on it), who questions the value of going to this particular swamp, or that toads of this species would only mate when the moon is full, or whether it is really possible that the species is not extinct. Participation in the discursive formation of zoology requires years of training, and penetrates every aspect of a zoologist's life *qua* zoologist; rationality applies to goals as well as actions, and all the practices that may require justification.

TECHNICAL RATIONALITY AND PSYCHOTHERAPY.   The practice of scientific medicine is generally of this form, with actions being justified by appealing to current good practice and to the body of knowledge that constitutes the science. The expert, the doctor, draws on her skills and knowledge in order to apply it to the patient. Still and Todd (1998) referred to this, following Schön (1983), as "technical rationality." Behind technical rationality is a body of knowledge based on both pure and applied research, and the global scientific institution, with its discursive formations molding together the practices and language of medical education, medical research, and medical writing, and linking these to other disciplines such as biochemistry, anatomy and physiology, and pharmacology. The practitioner has been initiated into the mysteries of this knowledge, and is thereby an expert in applying it to the case in hand. Any form of technical rationality is close to scientific rationality, but can be complicated here by a tension between the physician as expert and the more general demand placed on the physician as helper. In general practice she is still called on as helper when technical rationality fails, notably when the patient's illness turns out to be incurable and terminal. The discursive formation of technical rationality does not cover this, and when the patient is dying and beyond help, the physician may be at a loss, and as uncomfortable as many lay people are when confronted with the personal aspects of terminal illness. Or she may pause and reflect, and perhaps resort to a different discipline or subdiscipline, such as counseling or the new speciality of terminal care, or refer the patient on to experts in those disciplines. This pause and reflection is the exercise of another use or aspect of *rationality*, which is referred to later in this chapter as emancipatory rationality.

With partial success, practitioners of psychotherapy often strive for a structure of rationality that is similar to technical rationality, hoping that outcome studies and experimental psychology can provide a body of knowledge which is available to be drawn on by practitioners, who are thereby experts like physicians. And like physicians when technical rationality fails, they will then sometimes be obliged to draw on different resources, or to pass their clients on to experts. But an interesting difference from modern medicine in rational structure is the development of a number of distinct therapies, each often linked closely to the founder, as in REBT, CBT, IPT (interpersonal therapy; Klerman & Weissman, 1993) or ACT (acceptance and commitment therapy; Hayes, 2004). Thus if a therapist discovers something that works, instead of testing it and offering it as an addition to the body of psychotherapeutic knowledge he or she is apt to construct around it a distinct system of therapy, establishing itself as a distinct discursive formation, with its own language, research, therapeutic practices, and certificated training. This has been true of these and many other therapies, and a recent addition has been EMDR (eye movement desensitization and reprocessing). Francine Shapiro (1995) launched this and developed it as a going concern after discovering that she dealt with her worries as she walked on the beach by moving her eyes around. Instead of exploring this phenomenon and offering it to the world as knowledge, like a perceptual psychologist discovering a new visual or auditory phenomenon, she used it as the foundation of her own model of therapy.

As a result of this focus on models rather than knowledge, there is a different structure of rationality in these discursive formations. Justification in psychotherapy usually appeals to the model in question, rather than to a body of knowledge that all practitioners share as in medicine. Attempts have been made to do this in psychotherapy, as in Rogers's core conditions (Rogers,1961), or Egan's skilled helper (Egan, 1990), and these may be appealed to in justifying specific practices, but psychotherapy has not yet succeeded in providing anything like the kind of knowledge base available for medicine. Nevertheless, the logic of rationality is in some respects similar in both cases; psychotherapeutic practice is justified (rationally) by appeal to the principles of established models or published evidence, and even apparently irrational activities can be justified in this way. Thus the person who waits for fairies at midnight when the moon is full may turn out to be a client of an REBT therapist carrying out a shame-attacking exercise; a scientist perhaps, whose rigid demand that he always behave and talk in a logical manner is jeopardizing his marriage; the therapist finds that the demand is grounded in the irrational belief that it would be awful and unbearable and make him a worthless failure if people thought of him as irrational, and accordingly sets him this task, with instructions to dispute the irrational belief. This is justified and rational within REBT as a shame-attacking exercise, demonstrating to the client that being thought irrational does not make him a worthless failure. This justification and the deliberate shock effect make good sense (are rational) in REBT, but probably not within person-centered therapy, or even CBT. Here, as for scientific or technical rationality in general, the ascription of rationality follows successful justification.

RATIONALITY AND THE LOGIC OF JUSTIFICATION. Traditional and modern formal logic belong to the logic of justification, providing an abstract ideal to guide the discourse of instrumental rationality in scientific and other disciplines. Justifications are required not just to be based on agreed premises (whether empirical, as sometimes in science, or some other basis of agreement), but to proceed logically to warrant the beliefs or actions under question. At one time it was hoped that the rationality of scientific knowledge could be reduced to a logical structure, founded on a set of unquestionable observation statements. This was pushed to its limits in the Unity of Science movement 70 years ago, and since then foundationalism has been thoroughly undermined by philosophers and sociologists (Galison and Stump, 1996). Some of these have been critical of the pretensions of science, but others have been loyal allies like Karl Popper (1972) and Bartley (1988), who recognized that what survives as knowledge is never the ultimate truth, but has undergone and survived the critical scrutiny of other scientists, and always remains open to revision through further scrutiny. So a rational science depends on allowing and encouraging dissemination of research and informed criticism. It depends therefore on a social structure and practices rather than just on an internal logical structure. Bartley (1988) went so far as to dispense altogether with the logic of justification as an esssential part of the rationality of science, which relies he believes simply on a community with an informed and alert critical vigilance. Traditional logic remains important, of course, but no longer preeminent as a cornerstone of rationality.

RATIONALITY AS NORMATIVE. Audi's dictionary puts rationality's normative status strongly: "for any action, belief, or desire, if it is rational we ought to choose it" (Gert, 1995, p. 674). This may be too strong, since it is not obviously illogical to say "I agree that is the rational thing to do, but I don't feel it will work," or "I know it's irrational (i.e, I cannot give reasons for it), but I have a feeling it will turn out for the best." In many disciplines, and certainly psychotherapy, there is a recognition that hunches (the "feelings" in the above sentences) sometimes pay off—when this happens the justification and hence the rationality of the action may be bestowed retrospectively (though this can happen even if the hunch doesn't pay off) or it may remain a lucky guess. Nevertheless, the normative use of *rational* (the force of "ought" in Gert's definition) is stronger than what Ellis refers to as a conditional demand, like "if you want to pass the exam you must write more than a couple of sentences." Perhaps it reflects the pervasiveness of the discursive formations to which *rationality* belongs, just as the moral "oughts" and "shoulds" of so-called Western societies reflect not absolutes but a very broad discursive formation that defines this culture. This point is discussed further in Dryden and Still (1999).

RATIONALITY AS AN INSTRUMENT OF CULTURAL AND POLITICAL POWER BUT ALSO THE MEANS OF SUBVERTING THAT POWER. The claim has been put forth that rationality is *biased* because it is a class-based or male or Western or whatever notion (Nozick, 1993, p. xii). Being normative, rationality of thought and practices is apt to be defined and evaluated by the most powerful parts of a community, so has leant itself to the dissemination of power. Colonial expansion has for centuries been forcefully justified as rational, bringing education, health, and order to backward communities. Nowadays we are more likely to question this, recognizing that such appeals to reason may mask less creditable motives, or more simply serve to replicate the values of the colonizer. Tim Mitchell (1991) has traced this in great detail in the case of Britain and modern Egypt, bringing out how values are exported on the back of what Foucault (1980) referred to as disciplinary mechanisms. These replace the old practices, all in the name of good sense and rationality, but they carry with them the cultural values of the colonizing power. Feminist writers have pointed to a similar process across gender, with "reason" and "rationality" used in a way that maintains the power imbalance; there is a circular process in which "rationality" has been used to pick out intellectual skills that are supposed to belong especially to men, and this has been used to justify (in the name of reason!) the educational practices that ensure that women are given limited opportunity to acquire these skills (Griffiths & Whitford, 1988; Lloyd, 1993).

Yet it is part of rationality to be intent on noticing biases, including its own, and controlling and correcting these (Nozick, 1993, p. xii). Noticing biases is the task Tim Mitchell and feminist writers have set themselves, and they have exercised reason in doing so. So rationality is being used to criticize what had previously passed as rationality. This political dialectic is mirrored in the therapeutic processes considered here, and is especially well captured in REBT. Biased rationality derives from and maintains itself in the "shoulds" and "musts" and absolutist thinking that cause, according to REBT, unhealthy emotions. They are like the justifications of an outworn science or cultural practice (appealing to generalizations like "you must always wear a tie at work;" "biological species are fixed in time," so they cannot gradually evolve and separate; "homosexuality is a disease" so we must try to eradicate it; "women are less rational than men" so they should not be educated to a high level; and space and time are absolute). Such one-time "rational" generalizations are questioned by reason, just as Ellis used rationality to question the client's previously unquestioned reasons based on beliefs that he referred to as irrational.

RATIONALITY AS UNIQUELY HUMAN. Another aspect of rationality is that it is a uniquely human capacity, a natural power that distinguishes human beings from other animals ("Rationality refers to those intellectual capacities, usually involving the ability to use language, that distinguish persons from most other animals": Gert, 1995, p. 675). Aristotle made this a definition of being human—a rational animal with language. In the aspects of rationality considered so far human language seems an essential part. The knowledge of science and other disciplines are unthinkable without language and human communities held together through language. But there is another aspect of rationality, a power rather than a normative principle, that may not depend so thoroughly on language and may not be entirely confined to humans.

RATIONALITY AS REFLECTIVE PROBLEM-SOLVING. This power is the capacity for reflective problem-solving. It is the ability to step back when habits and old rules fail to achieve the goal, and to look at the situation afresh. This is pervasive in science when the well-established disciplinary mechanisms fail to come up with an answer, but this aspect of rationality can be brought out most clearly with everyday examples. Yesterday, having a wash, late for an appointment, and in a hurry to get out, I became irritated by the soap slipping off the shelf on the wash basin into the water. I put it back on and it slipped off again. A couple of impulses or thoughts went through my mind; complaining to (blaming) the person who had bought this new, smaller brand of soap, and slamming the soap angrily back; then I paused, reflected on the situation and put the soap in the soap container on the window sill above. This trivial sequence, lasting about a second, is rationality in action, and it is close to a form of trial and error behavior. Not the random trial and error described by Thorndike and many later psychologists, but the intelligent trial and error described by Campbell (1960) and Popper (1972), which involves trials guided by initial perception or hypotheses. The key difference lies in the reflective pause of the kind reported by Kohler (1957) in his study of "insight" in apes (one of the most famous in a long history of attempts to determine whether animals have rationality).

Or consider a driver who has been tailed closely for some time by another car eager to overtake; eventually the other driver overtakes perilously near a corner, and the driver is forced to brake, to allow this idiot in. The angry label "idiot" may prompt the first driver to do the same back, to tail very closely, "why should he be allowed to drive like this?" Sometimes this happens, but fortunately more often the driver pauses, reflects, sees his dangerous impulse from a wider perspective, and keeps a safe distance. The pause and reflection may be social rather than individual. Imagine a hobby gardener, who begins by trying to follow the rules laid down by the experts who write books or appear in radio and TV programs. After a time, she learns to reflect on her own experience, what has worked and what has not worked in her own garden, and to share this with others. A gardening miniculture develops, at odds with the offical line. An example of a similar process in medicine is described by Schou and Hewison (1999) in a grounded theory study of patients at a large cancer unit in Leeds. They found that patients became socialized into a subculture with other patients, and it was from this subculture that much of their practical knowledge of the disease came, as well as how to interpret the doctors' cryptic pronouncements, the significance of a change of treatment, and so on.

As a final example consider the thinking that led to Einstein's special theory of relativity, as described in Wertheimer's (1961) classic account. Faced with the discursive formation of nineteenth-century physics, with its absolute framework of space and time, Einstein struggled with the anomalies that arose from this when he reflected on problems of measurement and simultaneity, and the failure of Michelson and Morley to detect variations in the speed of light with the direction of the earth's movement. He resolved these anomalies in a simple and elegant way, by giving up the absolute framework of space and time, and retaining the speed of light as an invariant, giving up therefore the central assumption of the old discursive formation, and replacing it with a new one. Einstein's "pause," and perhaps the secret of his genius, was his refusal to be swept along by the apparent rationality of the absolutes he questioned, and this gave him time to work out a convincing alternative. The reflection, the puzzling over the anomalies, took years, but the mathematical alternative took only six weeks to work out.

In each of these cases, from the most trivial to the most profound, there is a stepping back from the smooth flow of old habits or the unquestioned assumptions of scientific rationality, into a different way of seeing things, and then a new way forward. A different kind of logic applies here. Not the formal logic of justification, but a logic similar to Dewey's logic of inquiry. Dewey's theories of thinking and inquiry were still influential at the time Ellis wrote "Rational Psychotherapy," and the possible direct or indirect influence on Albert Ellis are considered in Still and Dryden (1998). As described recently by Burke, the logic of inquiry consists of two aspects; a linear movement toward a resolution of a problem (sometimes, especially in science, toward a warranted judgement); and cyclical movement similar to trial and error:

> The agent observes the results of his/her/its actions, entertains possible courses of action and expected results based on those observations, experiments with more feasible alternatives to test their viability, observes the results of such experimentation, and around it goes—a process of exploring facts of the matter and narrowing the range of possible actions one can take, until, hopefully, a solution to the initial problem is settled on. (Burke, 1994, p. 160)

Insofar as this is a perceptual process, Burke argues that

> A notion of noncognitive rationality is suggested here, measured by the appropriateness of given habits in given instances. The rationality involved in determining which habits are triggered in a given instance and which are not is a function of the systematicity of the space of constraints and processes which make up the contents of various habits, matched against whatever actions and results are actually occurring in the present situation (Burke, 1994, p. 161).

The rationality in the examples above consisted in checking the immediate impulses (slamming the soap down, tailing the car in front, following the rules, accepting the word of the doctors without question, taking on board the assumptions of absolute space and time), pausing (for a fraction of a second, or for several years in the case of Einstein), and looking more closely at the situation, replacing the initial impulse, based on limited habits of looking and attending, with rational reflection on the situation as a whole, which enabled the participant to choose rationally. The exercise of this aspect of rationality is potentially emancipatory, since it involves the capacity to step back and loosen the grip of earlier habits, rules, or reasons. This does not entail that the other possibilities are not rational. They are not in the driving and soap examples, though in both cases they may be part of a belief system and reasons (justication) are forthcoming—most people would agree that they are not good reasons, which is why we see the actions as irrational. In the gardening example, on the other hand, following the known rules would be a good, rational justification for carrying on as before, even though pausing and reflecting may lead to better solutions of the problems that arise. Trusting the doctors without question could certainly be rationally justified, and following the assumptions of nineteenth-century physics appeared at the time the height of rationality.

We thus have a number of uses or aspects of *rationality*: "Minirat," which applies to actions rather than goals. Scientific and technical rationality, which applies to actions, goals, and beliefs, and is relative to its own discursive formation. A similar rationality is set up within other disciplines, such as history, literary criticism, and theology, where actions and beliefs are justified by appeal to the norms of the discipline. In general this is disciplinary rationality, or "discrat" for short; scientific rationality is an especially clearcut form of discrat. The root "disc" of *discrat* is taken to refer to the discursive formations of which discrat is a part, to the disciplinary mechanisms that hold together discrat in action, and also to any discourse to which the logic of justification applies. This chapter uses *discrat* to cover not just the academic disciplines in which the discursive formation is tightly organized but also loose disciplines such as the discourse of popular gardening, as well as irrational belief systems, like the soap and driving examples above, which are used as a source of justification. Thus the driver gripped by road rage *justifies* his behavior to himself with the thought, "he shouldn't have overtaken like that" and "he mustn't be allowed to get away with it." The "rat" of *discrat* refers not just to *rationality*, but to the semantic space to which the epithets *rationality* and *irrationality* apply.

The contrasting aspect of rationality is a process of reflective problem-solving, which serves to emancipate to some degree from the old rules and habits that are no longer satisfactory. So it is emancipatory rationality or "emanrat" for short (Dryden and Still, 2007). The separation of discrat and emanrat in what seem to be different meanings of rationality, may itself be historical in origin, rather than essential. Dryden and Still (2007) argue that what is essential, if anything, is the tension between the two aspects, and that to avoid the tension by separating into two meanings is misleading, even dangerous. But this is what has happened, and this chapter turns now to outline the historical context of this split. Not by tracing the history in a scholarly fashion, but by describing two historical figures who have been read as representing these two aspects of rationality, Plato and Epictetus, both of whom lurk in the rationalities of REBT.

As Danziger pointed out in elaborating on discursive formations, the classical notion of rationality was not the same as ours. Aristotle treated rationality not as instrumental intelligence, nor as reason within a discursive formation, nor as the capacity to break out of restrictive habits or patterns of thought, but as a kind of harmony between the rational order of the world, and human understanding of that order. This would be present in all human excellence, in theoretical knowledge as well as in practical skills (Danziger, 1997, p. 29). But out of that classical notion of rationality, different but still the ancestor of ours, a split seems to have developed between two aspects of rationality. On the one hand rationality as the capacity for knowledge and eventually science; on the other a capacity for problem-solving, including psychological problems. These are discrat and emanrat, represented here by Plato and Epictetus. The first is a psychological framework with reason like a ruler, aloof from appetites and emotions, yet striving to resolve the conflicts between them and achieve harmony. In the second, the faculties act harmoniously together as a system, but sometimes out of harmony with the world or in conflict with other systems within the mind.

Plato and Disciplinary Rationality

Semantically, rationality is closely linked to reason and thinking. These are psychological processes, and they are often contrasted with other psychological process, like emotion and desire. But why make divisions in the mind at all, separating thinking and reason from perception, from emotion, and from drives or appetites? Does this correspond to a psychological reality? It certainly seems to. For over 100 years textbooks of psychology and physiology have followed this classification, and it has been a system for distinguishing areas of research, as well as providing a framework for mapping psychological processes onto parts of the brain and nervous system. Who could doubt the validity of these divisions? Yet not every writer has taken it for granted, and its distant origin lies fairly clearly in Plato's tripartite division of the soul, or more accurately (since Plato's writings are not consistent in this matter) in the way Plato was read and used by later generations.

The three parts of Plato's division were reason, desire or appetite, and emotion. We can see they are distinct (Plato, or Socrates, as his spokesperson in the dialogue, argues) because they can be in opposition to each other, or one present without the other. Thus thirst is a desire that pulls the person toward drinking, but there is sometimes a prohibition "derived from reasoning," which pulls in the opposite direction. This is an opposition between the "rational principle of the soul" and the "irrational or appetitive" (Plato, 1970, p. 213). To show that emotion can be in opposition to desire, Plato told the story of Leontius, who had a strong desire to see some dead bodies at a place of execution, but also dread and abhorrence of them (emotion), and anger at himself for giving in to the desire. Finally, the example of children and animals shows us emotion without reason, so they too must be distinct.

This is a hierarchical view of the soul, with reason at the top, and it had an explicit political parallel. Reason is like a wise ruler necessary to bring order to the unruly energies of the hoi polloi, the appetites and the emotions. Throughout history it has been a two-way metaphor, with current political structures used to illuminate the mind, and vice versa. In Plato rationality is not just what distinguishes human beings in this world from animals, but provides a link with a transcendent higher world, of eternal essences or God. It is this aspect of Plato's rationality that was elaborated by the Neoplatonists, and then taken over by Christianity and eventually science and modern scientific psychology. Nowadays rationality provides a link not with God but with nature and with the truths that are forthcoming from the study of nature. The brain of Plato, we might say, is the brain of discrat.

EPICTETUS AND EMANCIPATORY RATIONALITY. The structure of Stoic psychology gave a different place to reason and rationality. Instead of a struggle between these and other forces in the mind, the main struggle in the psychology of Chrysippus, the most prolific and influential of the Hellenistic Stoics, was between right and wrong reason. Paraphrasing his views in a modern idiom, it appears that reason, emotion, and desire are not distinct, but always act together as a system, rather than in opposition to each other. Stoic human psychology followed Aristotle in defining the human being as a rational animal. Thus, although we experience strong impulses, directed toward or away from some object (explained as stemming directly from appetites or emotion in the Platonic system), they are always the *product* of reason in the case of adult humans; therefore they cannot be in conflict with reason.

Impulses are directed desires, a product of a sense impression and "assent." Assent is a product of reason, at least in adults, so that "Reason supervenes as the craftsman of impulse" (Chrysippus in Long & Sedley, 1987, p. 346; quoted in Long, 1986, p. 173). Obviously not all impulses are rational, and to be consistent, Chrysippus had to loosen the strong connection between reason and rationality that was present in Plato. In Chrysippus there can be a wavering between good and bad impulses, and hence between right and wrong reason (Inwood, 1985, p. 156). Thus

> At one moment (someone) may assent to the true Stoic proposition that pain is not a bad thing; but if this judgement is insecurely based it will not be strong enough to reject a contrary judgement, that pain is something very bad, which comes to mind and is accompanied by a bodily reaction as the dentist starts drilling his tooth. (Long, 1986, p. 177)

The conflict is between two impulses plus potential assent, each a system of reason, emotion, and sense impression. The example (and the thinking behind it) can readily be translated into REBT terms:

At one moment (someone) may assent to the true REBT proposition that pain (A) is unpleasant but not awful and absolutely unbearable; but if this belief (RB) is insecurely based it will not be strong enough to reject a contrary belief (IB), that pain is absolutely unbearable, which comes to mind and is accompanied by a bodily reaction (C) as the dentist starts drilling his tooth.

Still and Dryden (1999) conclude that

> just as in REBT an emotional or behavioral consequence is always (or nearly always) a product of belief (B), which may be rational or irrational; so in classical Stoicism choice is always controlled by reason, which may be right or wrong reason. When conflict occurs it is not between reason and emotion as in Plato, but between right and wrong reason, and the corresponding impulses, which contain within them what we call desire or appetite and emotion. (Still and Dryden, 1999, p. 152)

From the point of view of emanrat, the advantages of the Stoic structure of rationality over the Platonic are that it more readily enables reason to reflect on itself, and insists on the inseparability of reason, emotions, and appetite, as the rational problem-solver launches into the dynamic and interactive process of inquiry. Reason is more openly vulnerable and error prone in Stoic psychology than in Plato, and requires within itself a process of self-correction. But the self-reflection is not just turned inward; it is about achieving harmony between person and the world, and therefore the focus is on the interface between them. So the reflection is not primarily on the external world, discounting the interests of the observer, as in scientific rationality, but works together with emotion and appetite toward a mutual adjustment of world and person to bring them in harmony. The brain of the Stoics is the brain of emanrat.

A later Stoic, Epictetus, was a more practical philosopher than Chrysippus, and it is as a moral guide that his writings have remained influential over many centuries (Still & Dryden, 2003). As the teacher who appears in his *Dialogues* (Gill, 1995), he shows himself to be a close follower of Socrates' method, but not of the tripartite model that we have referred to as Platonic. The Stoic ideal was the sage, who lived in perfect harmony with nature, and a basic maxim from Epictetus captures this ideal: "There are things which are within our power, and there are things which are beyond our power." Whatever is not in our power to change cannot be bad or evil, and the sage therefore accepts it without conflict. If it can be changed it can be evil, and the Sage uses reason to find means to change it. In my trivial example of the soap, I started out of harmony; the soap kept slipping off and annoying me; by pausing, reflecting, and viewing the situation, I achieved harmony. At another extreme, Jim Stockdale described how he used Epictetus in order to survive imprisonment and torture in North Vietnam. It was not in anyone's power to withstand modern methods of torture, so he reflected on what was in his power for himself and for the men for whom, as the senior officer in the prison, he was responsible. Following another maxim from Epictetus ("Look not for any greater harm than this: destroying the trust-worthy, self-respecting well-behaved man within you," Stockdale, 1995, p. 8), he devised with the other prisoners a plan of resistance to retain self-respect under torture, by deciding among themselves what degrading demands they would refuse to obey. This was within their power, and they thus used rationality under the most extreme condition to plan their resistance. The choice was to submit and despair or submit and use reason to work out a plan of continued resistance.

Another reader of Epictetus was Albert Ellis, and Still and Dryden (2003) argued that he took much more from Epictetus than the familiar maxim made familiar by Beck as well. According to Ellis: "Men are disturbed not by things, but by the views which they take of them" (quoted in Still & Dryden, 2003, p. 43). Following Socrates closely, Epictetus used dialogue to help his listeners to see their psychological problems as within their power to solve, and Still and Dryden argued that it is partly this rational process (referred to here as emanrat rather than discrat), that influenced Ellis in creating rational psychotherapy.

Disciplinary and Emancipatory Rationality in Rational Psychotherapy

Rational Psychotherapy as Emanrat

In 1958, when Ellis published "Rational Psychotherapy," his approach contrasted in important ways from some of the popular therapies of the time. But there were

also similarities. Many forms of psychotherapy aim for emanrat, emancipating
from the restrictive and sometimes unarticulated assumptions that have been
acquired from parents, schools, peers, and the media, which are drummed in
usually in the name of reason. This is emancipation from a system of beliefs and
justifications, like any discursive formation; it therefore has the structure of
discrat. Psychoanalysis attempted to replace the discredited old discrat with
awareness and with an alternative that supposedly gave a completer picture.
Gestalt therapy undermined it by drawing attention to and changing the habits of
speech, movement, and perception that sustained it, like the disciplinary
mechanisms described by Michel Foucault and Tim Mitchell. Person-centered
therapy provided an ideal nonjudgemental audience, freeing the client from the
pressures maintaining the old discrat in his or her social milieu, and so enabling
the client's natural power of emanrat to emerge and open the way to a new,
mature discrat. But Ellis went directly to the heart of the struggle between the old
discrat and emanrat, to the "oughts" and "shoulds" whose coercive linguistic
function is to maintain discrat, in all its manifestations, and to counter the
reflective consideration of alternatives, from road rage to the unquestioned
assumptions of nineteenth-century physics. Like Epictetus he recognized that
psychological obstacles can be treated rationally (emanrat) like any others.

In time Ellis moved away from giving the words themselves causal
power, first by recognizing the necessity of the "hot cognitions" that come
with the words when they lead to unhealthy emotions (Ellis, 1994, p. 60),
and then the importance of Beck's unreflective, automatic thoughts in
maintaining irrational beliefs (Ellis, 1994, p. xv). Underlying these words
and thoughts are absolute demands, absolute in the sense that they are
assumed without question. Questioning or attacking such demands is a
key practice in emanrat, whether it is a driver who resists the temptation to
tail the driver who has cut in, or Einstein subverting the traditional assumptions of absolute time and space. But emanrat is not just negative or critical.
As Einstein recognized, it is not enough to undermine the old demands to
produce change. It is also necessary to have an alternative theory in place to
form the basis of a new discursive formation. Similarly Ellis found the need,
in his therapeutic emanrat, to replace the irrational beliefs with rational
beliefs, and to include effective new strategies, the E of the ABC(DE) model
(Ellis, 1994).

Rational Psychotherapy as Discrat

Thus the successful exercise of emanrat paves the way to a new discrat, and
REBT is potentially discrat in several senses; in each different sense a call

for justification is answered with an appeal to a different discursive formation. In this respect REBT is rational (discrat) in two ways that are shared with other psychotherapies. These are dealt with first, before considering what is distinctive about REBT vis-à-vis rationality.

The disciplinary mechanisms of psychotherapy itself make up a discursive formation, though as we have already seen this is not as impressive as in other technical rationalities. In this sense it is rational to adopt unconditional positive regard, because this has come to be adopted as a standard for psychotherapy. The therapist can justify her failure to condemn the client for his bad actions, not primarily because this is known to work, but because this attitude is regarded as essential to psychotherapy, as the removal of observational bias is to any experimental science. Another general sense in which REBT is rational (discrat) is in the use of outcome studies, and the explicit allegiance to a scientific outlook. The usual claim to scientific rationality amongpsychotherapies is participation in the discursive formation of experimental design and statistical testing, shared by a number of social, medical, and biological sciences. By 1958 several therapies had reported outcome studies. Ellis had not done so in 1958, but has always recommended them as necessary for a scientific therapy, though this has not been achieved as thoroughly as for CBT (Still, 2001).

The distinctive ways in which REBT is explicitly discrat are in the doctrine of "shoulds" and in teaching rationality to clients through the ABC(DE) model, including the distinction between two kinds of emotion and the rules for of disputing irrational beliefs. Ellis's emanrat, the rational process of stepping back, reflecting, and challenging the irrational discrat that remains coersive, and finding an alternative, itself became formulated as a discrat. It has its own disciplinary mechanisms and training, though the use of the traditional coercive language of "should" and "must" is studiously avoided by Ellis, unless qualified as conditional. Or unless cushioned with humor, as in "Cherchez le 'shoulds.'

The ABC(DE) model has been at the center of this discrat, especially in the training of therapists, and the socialization of clients into the requirements of therapy (Dryden, 1990) The process of therapy involves the emanrat of stepping back and articulating the perceptions (A), the thought processes and emotions or behavior (C) of the discursive system to be replaced, opening the way to a new discrat for the client. The goal is to change the unhealthy emotion into its healthy equivalent, anger into annoyance, anxiety into concern, and so on, or to develop alternative behavior. This is usually done by disputing (D) the irrational beliefs (IB), and replacing them with rational beliefs (RB). The change is aided and consolidated by developing effective new strategies

(E) for dealing with problems of living. The disputation makes some logical and philosophical assumptions in demonstrating the client's irrationalities. The client is assumed to make: *(a)* The logical mistake of deriving a modal statement from an empirical statement (Does "I must have this" follow logically from "I want this"?); *(b)* The empirical or scientific mistake of assuming a covering law that will enable this derivation ("What law of the universe states that I must have this because I want it?"); *(c)* The pragmatic mistake of assuming that the irrational belief ("I must have this") will help the client achieve his or her goals.

There are some anomalies in the ABC(DE) model from the point of view of Ellis's claims to rationality. First it seems inconsistent with another claim made by Ellis. The ABC(DE) model appears to separate perception, cognition, and emotion into logically distinct categories, but Ellis, from the first paper in 1958 onward, has been insistent that these are interdependent and cannot be separated in this way. By separating, the ABC(DE) model looks like an application of the Platonic model of the mind, though in theory Ellis's allegiance has been to a model that is similar to the Stoic. A defense could be that such separation is necessary for training and therapeutic purpose, though at a deeper level there is interdependence. Such compromise might weaken the claim to rationality, like a politician who claims to be morally upright, but is obliged on pragmatic grounds to indulge in practices that are morally questionable. That perhaps is how the world is; both politician and psychotherapist have to compromise their moral or theoretical purity in order to be effective. But *rationality* would then be in danger of becoming a technical term within the discursive formation of REBT, distinct from other uses of the word, which would dilute the bold claim to rationality as a distinctive feature, except as emanrat.

Second, although in this chapter I have given weight to Ellis's bold and explicit use of *emanrat* as justifying the "rationality" of rational psychotherapy and REBT, it is not clear that this is how Ellis himself has seen it. In Ellis (1958) and later much is made of details of the rational disputing itself. The possible problem is that the first two (a and b above) are questionable, or at best a matter of debate, according to the modern discursive formations from which they have been borrowed, philosophy and the philosophy of science. Their continued use could be justified on the grounds that they work, so they are rational in terms of the REBT discursive formation. But this would effectively reduce the first two to the third, the pragmatic dispute, which underlies the dynamic process of emanrat. These points are returned to below, in considering some of the criticisms that have been leveled at Ellis's use of *rationality*.

Criticisms of Ellis's Rationality

Bearing in mind this analytical description of the rationality or otherwise of Ellis's rational psychotherapy and its successors we turn to some of the less sympathetic critics of Ellis's concept, who claim that Ellis himself, the well-known champion of rationality, founder of the Institute for Rational Living, fails to live up to ordinary and philosophical standards of rationality.

Ellis Has Not One but Two Theories of Rationality

Evans (1984–1985) pointed out that Ellis uses "rationality" in more than one sense. This was noted above, but Evans puts it differently: "What is Ellis' theory of rationality? Unfortunately, it appears that Ellis has not one but two theories of rationality" (Evans, 1984–1985, p. 131). The first Evans refers to as the "'evolutionary' conception of rationality," since it appeals to something like a Darwinian conception of "survival value." He quotes Ellis: "By *irrationality* I mean any thought, emotion, or behavior that significantly interfere (sic) with the survival and happiness of the organism" (quoted in Evans, 1984–1985, p. 31).

The second theory is the "empirical" or scientific theory. Irrational beliefs lead to unhealthy emotions, and the therapist is "a scientific interpreter who teaches his clients—who in many ways resemble the students of other science teachers—how to follow the hypothetico-deductive method and to specifically apply it to their own value systems and emotional problems" (Ellis quoted in Evans, 1984–1985, p. 131). The problem is, according to Evans, that these theories or criteria of rationality may sometimes be incompatible: "It seems very possible that some beliefs which are warranted by the scientific method could actually make people unhappy, and even more plausible to claim that some beliefs which do lead to happiness and survival in the long run are not warranted by the scientific method" (Evans, 1984–1985, p. 131).

Evans appealed to Bertrand Russell's view "that it is only reasonable to accept beliefs which we have good reason to suppose to be true" (Evans, 1984–1985, p. 132), and contrasted this with Ellis, who "seems to posit as a standard for rational *belief* a view which seems only appropriate for *action*" (Evans, 1984–1985, p. 133; author's italics). This appeal to Russell is instructive, in view of the argument of this chapter that Dewey's pragmatist logic abstracts from emanrat rather than discrat, and that Ellis's initial claim to be a rational psychotherapy is most safely justified as an exercise in emanrat. Throughout their long careers, Russell and Dewey were at loggerheads about logic. Russell refused to accept what we refer to as emanrat as the basis of a logic, and Burke's book, quoted above, is subtitled *A Reply to Russell.*

The distinctions made by Evans correspond to those between disciplinary and emancipatory rationality, though I do not see them as incompatible, but necessary parts of scientific rationality or of living rationally. By allying himself with Russell, Evans gives priority to rationality applied to beliefs and truth, rather than to actions; it is largely restricted to discrat.

In his reply to Evans, Ellis explicitly chose a pragmatic criterion as the essence of rationality, close to emanrat rather than discrat:

> Absolutistic, dogmatic, extreme thinking is irrational because it *often* (not *always*) leads to poor emotional and behavioral results—and thereby *tends* to sabotage happiness and survival. It is also unscientific by the usual rules of the scientific method because it sets up as "true" and "factual" many propositions that are overgeneralized and unfalsifiable . . . . Therefore, RET holds, many unscientific propositions are significantly *correlated* with "irrational" (antisurvival and antihappiness) views. Possibly the two are so closely related that they are almost identical. But this is not what RET now claims. (Ellis, 1984–1985, p. 137; author's italics)

Ellis resolves the dilemma here by denying that something that is normally called rational (a scientific statement or belief justified by impeccably correct reasons) is in itself rational (as is entailed by discrat), and asserting the empirical proposition that such scientific statements are *correlated* with rationality ("the Goals of survival and happiness," Ellis, 1984–1985, p. 136): "So I would now say that beliefs that are scientifically warranted are *usually* rational in the sense that they *normally* lead to human survival and happiness— or at least do so more often than do unscientific, absolutistic beliefs" (Ellis, 1984–1985, p. 137).

This pragmatic view could hardly be more different from Russell's view of rationality, quoted by Evans. Russell asserted the disciplinary aspect of rationality as its essence, Ellis an aspect closer to the emancipatory. It is not the same, since emanrat is a dynamic process, and Ellis here is defining rationality of a belief in terms of its consequences; but they are similar since the process of emanrat always involves a close attunement to the consequences of every action.

The view of this chapter is that both Russell and Ellis are partly wrong, firstly in assuming that *rationality* has a true definition or essence, secondly in denying the other aspect of rationality. The word's usage embraces both meanings, since rationally following a rule (discrat), entails the possibility of rationally not following it, the outcome of emanrat (this is discussed in more detail in

Dryden and Still, 2007). Ellis's great achievement is not as a logician, but in discovering how the demands of any discrat in the life of an individual are not and cannot be absolutes, how failing to recognize this can cause great suffering, and by carrying through the practical consequences of this.

Is It Rational to Rate Human Beings?

Erwin (1997) challenges Ellis's view that "The idea that certain people are bad, wicked, or villainous and that they should be severely punished and blamed for their villainy" (Erwin, 1997, p. 106) is irrational. Why, he asked, must the belief that this is true "about the most notorious tyrants and serial killers of the twentieth century" be irrational? "Is it impossible that my belief [that this is true] be supported by good reasons?" (Erwin, 1997, p. 106). Ellis would probably not deny this, but would argue that this is a matter of how you define human beings (Ellis, 1962, pp. 155–156). So the belief that human beings are nonratable is arrived at through a decision that belongs to emancipatory rationality rather than disciplinary; though once the decision is made it could become the basis of a new discursive formation with its own discrat. Ellis chose a discursive formation within which it is not rational to rate human beings (like Buddhism, some forms of Christianity, Rogerian psychotherapy, and to some extent the liberal views that prevailed when Ellis was first writing), rather than one within which it is (such as Calvinism and neoconservatism).

Ellis Fails to Lay Down Decision Procedures for Ascribing Rationality

According to O'Donohue and Vass (1996), Ellis has failed to give the client a "systematic method for the decision procedure that takes criteria of rationality and beliefs and renders reliable judgments about the rationality of these beliefs," and "no heuristics or other hints on how this might be done are offered" (O'Donohue and Vass, 1996, p. 308). This is a demand for the rules of discrat rather than the rational problem-solving approach of emanrat. In practice REBT clients do not usually have difficulty in applying the word "rational" (perhaps because of the compromises referred to above), and there are certainly heuristics, such as "Cherchez le 'shoulds.'" But the main criticism by O'Donohue and Vass is more general. Ellis's use of *rationality* fails to match up to Bartley's belief that "How can we be rational?" reduces to how can we "arrange our lives and institutions to expose our positions, actions, opinions, beliefs, aims, conjectures, decisions, standards, frameworks, ways of life, policies, traditional practices, etc., to optimum examination, in order to counteract and eliminate as much error as possible" (Bartley, 1988, p. 213; quoted in O'Donahue and Vass, 1996).

Taken literally this could lead to a nightmare society in which official scrutiny of every detail of our lives is justified in the name of rationality. As a political and social policy *optimum* and *error* are too vulnerable, like rationality itself (or at least discrat) to official control, and thus to the dissemination of power through disciplinary mechanisms. But perhaps to make sense of Bartley's definition we do not need such loaded words as *optimum* and *error*, but to accept that what is meant is a healthy balance between discrat and emanrat. But according to the argument of this chapter, restoring this balance in individual lives is what Ellis's therapy is about.

Wessler: Ellis as Pesudoscientist

Wessler (1992, 1996) wrote as a once prominent follower of Ellis and REBT who had come to believe that Ellis's philosophical account of the therapy is inconsistent with his practice. Thus in theory Ellis is a constructivist, by which Wessler means one who "maintains that humans construct a private reality and that objective reality is unknowable if it exists at all" (Wessler, 1992, p. 620). But in practice Ellis has been quite dogmatic in his beliefs about REBT, as in the "musturbation axiom" ("that absolute musts have a pivotal role in any form of psychological disturbance," Wessler, 1996, p. 48) and the parallel process model of emotions ("that there are qualitative differences between certain similar emotions, and that each is mediated by a different type of belief," Wessler, 1996, p. 48). Since these are dogmatically held, and not scientifically supported, Wessler accused Ellis of being a pseudoscientist, a label which, if it sticks, banishes him from sharing in the desirable rationality offered by true science. In arguing his case Wessler appealed to Popper's notion of falsifiability before it had been shaped by the debates with Thomas Kuhn during the 1960s and 1970s, and brought more closely into line with how science is actually practiced. Popper himself recommended that a good conjecture or hypothesis be held onto fairly dogmatically and improved in the face of falsified predictions, until it eventually becomes untenable. Lakatos (1970) referred to the empirical "hard core" of a science, which is unquestioned and protected from falsification during normal scientific activity, though the latter may involve hypothesis testing and attempts at falsification as described in Popper's earlier work. Thus in classical physics it took much more than a falsification of a prediction by Michelson and Morley to dislodge the very dogmatically held belief in the absolute framework of space and time.

However, as described earlier, the structure of rationality (discrat) is different in psychotherapy. It is not the same as scientific or technical rationality, because the source of justification is usually not a body of knowledge, but a therapeutic model. Models are organized around a set of ideas and procedures, often reported by a clearly identified founder as described above. These define the model. Over time the model will be expanded and refined, but the original ideas and procedures must still be recognizable and as such must necessarily still remain sacrosanct, otherwise it will no longer be the same model. IPT must continue to give priority to interpersonal issues, ACT must continue to involve acceptance and commitment, and REBT must continue to focus on musturbation. If these are the equivalent of the hard core in science, they are even more dogmatically held; even an Einstein could not shift them fundamentally without destroying the model. So Wessler's criticism of Ellis may be valid, but only because it is partly true for all psychotherapies with this structure of rationality.

Conclusion

This chapter has not attempted to criticize or defend Ellis's REBT, but to describe his use of the word *rational*, and to place it within a wider historical and philosophical context. If Ellis's rationality turns out to be complex and imprecise, this is not necessarily a criticism; precision is not a good in itself, and a certain degree of ambiguity may turn out to be fruitful, as the phenomena to which the word refers are unraveled together with the meaning of the word itself. Ellis's main contribution is, it is argued, the successful insistence that many psychological difficulties can be treated rationally like any other problems or obstacles in living, rather than as medical, moral, or personality issues. This involves setting up a dialogue in which client and therapist cooperate in reflecting on the problem and its possible solutions. To clarify this and the magnitude of Ellis's achievement, it was necessary to separate two aspects of rationality. First, disciplinary rationality (discrat), which is prominent in the discursive formations of science, medicine, and other disciplines where knowledge is paramount as the source of justification of beliefs and practices. It is also important in everyday life in following rules and routines, which are justified in relation to a belief system, whether or not the belief system would be regarded as rational by another person or another culture. Second, emancipatory rationality (emanrat), which is a process of pausing and reflecting on the problem situation faced, sometimes due to a failure of discrat, and aiming toward a workable solution through intelligent trial and error. This is also important in science, when discrat is not working or inapplicable. When emanrat takes over from discrat, the coercive "shoulds" and "musts" ("you should do this," "you must do it that way") are suspended while the problem-solver searches for a novel approach to try out, or searches for an alternative within the discursive formations available.

With confidence and vigor (encouraged it is suggested by his reading of Epictetus), Ellis and his clients applied emanrat directly to psychological difficulties, targeting the coercive language of discrat ("shoulds" and "musts"), which holds the old system together and is therefore the trigger point for change. In addition he described an alternative discrat to replace the irrational belief systems (the discredited old discrats). This is the ABC(DE) model, including the principles of disputing and the parallel process theory of emotions. For many commentators, this model seems to be what makes REBT rational, discrat rather than emanrat. To some extent this is understandable, since Ellis draws on the rhetoric of discrat in his ABC(DE) model, but it is clear that, when pressed, he leans toward emancipatory rationality (emanrat) in his definition of rationality, and the direct application of this to psychological problems is his greatest achievement.

REFERENCES

Bartley, W. W. (1988). Theories of rationality. In G. Radnitzky & W. W. Bartley (Eds.), *Evolutionary epistemology, rationality, and the sociology of knowledge*. La Salle, IL: Open Court.

Beck, A. T. (1963). Thinking and depression. *Archives of General Psychiatry, 9*, 324–333.

Brown, H. I. (1995). Rationality. In T. Honderich (Ed.), *The Oxford companion to philosophy*. Oxford: Oxford University Press.

Burke, T. (1994). *Dewey's new logic: A reply to Russell*. Chicago & London: University of Chicago Press.

Campbell, D. T. (1960). Blind variation and selective retention in creative thought as in other knowledge processes. *Psychological Review, 67*, 380–400.

Danziger, K. (1997). *Naming the mind*. London: Sage.

Dawkins, R. (1976) *The selfish gene*. Oxford: Oxford University Press.

Dewey, J. (1938). *Logic: The theory of inquiry*. New York: Henry Holt.

Dryden, W. (1990). *Rational-emotive counselling in action*. London: Sage.

Dryden, W., & Still, A. W. (1998). REBT and rationality: Philosophical approaches. *Journal of Rational-Emotive & Cognitive-Behavior Therapy, 16*, 77–99.

Dryden, W., & Still, A. W. (1999). When did a psychologist last discuss 'chagrin'? America's continuing moral project. *History of the Human Sciences, 12*, 93–110

Dryden, W., & Still, A. W. (2007). Rationality and the shoulds. *Journal for the Theory of Social Behaviour, 2007, 37*, 1–23.

Egan, G. (1990). *The skilled helper: A systematic approach to effective helping* (4th ed.). Pacific Grove, CA: Brooks/Cole.

Ellis, A. (1958). Rational psychotherapy. *Journal of General Psychology, 59,* 35–49.

Ellis, A. (1962). *Reason and emotion in psychotherapy.* Secaucus, NJ: Citadel.

Ellis, A. (1984–1985). Yes, how reasonable is rational-emotive therapy? *Review of Existential Psychology and Psychiatry, 10,* 135–139.

Ellis, A. (1994). *Reason and emotion in psychotherapy* (2nd ed.). New York: Carol Publishing.

Erwin, E. (1997). *Philosophy and psychotherapy.* London: Sage.

Evans, C. S. (1984–1985). Albert Ellis' conception of rationality: How reasonable is rational-emotive therapy? *Review of Existential Psychology and Psychiatry, 10,* 129–134.

Foucault, M. (1980). Two lectures. In C. Gordon (Ed.), *Power/Knowledge: Selected interviews and other writings 1972–1977.* Brighton: Harvester Press.

Galison, P., & Stump, D. J. (Eds.). (1996). *The disunity of science: Boundaries, contexts, and power.* Stanford, CA: Stanford University Press.

Gert, B. (1995) Rationality. In R. Audi (Ed.). *The Cambridge dictionary of philosophy* (pp. 674–675). Cambridge, UK: Cambridge University Press.

Gilbert, P. (Ed.). (2005). *Compassion: Conceptualisations, research, and use in psychotherapy.* London: Routledge.

Gill, C. (Ed.). (1995). *The discourses of Epictetus.* London: J.M. Dent.

Griffiths, M., & Whitford, M. (1988). *Feminist perspective in philosophy.* Basingstoke, UK: Macmillan Press.

Hayes, S. C. (2004). Acceptance and commitment therapy, relational frame theory, and the third wave of behavioral and cognitive therapies. *Behavior Therapy, 35,* 639–665.

Inwood, B. (1985). *Ethics and human action in early Stoicism.* Oxford: Oxford University Press.

Klerman, G. L., & Weissman, M. M. (1993). *New applications of interpersonal psychotherapy.* Washington, DC: American Psychiatric Press.

Kohler, W. (1957). *The mentality of apes.* Harmondsworth, Middlesex, UK: Penguin Books.

Lakatos, I. (1970). Falsification and the methodology of scientific research programmes. In I. Lakatos & A. Musgrave (Eds.). *Criticism and the growth of knowledge.* (pp. 91–195). Cambridge, UK: Cambridge University Press.

Lloyd, G. (1984). *The man of reason: 'Male' and 'female' in western philosophy.* London: Routledge.

Long, A. A. (1986). *Hellenistic philosophy* (2nd ed.). London: Duckworth.

Long, A. A., & Sedley, D. N. (1987). *The hellenistic philosophers* (Vol. 1). Cambridge, UK: Cambridge University Press.

Mahoney, M. J., & Gabriel T. J. (1987). Psychotherapy and cognitive sciences: An evolving alliance. *Journal of Cognitive Psychotherapy, 1,* 39–59.

Mitchell, T. (1991). *Colonising Egypt.* Berkeley and Los Angeles: University of California Press.

Newton-Smith, W. H. (1981). *The rationality of science.* London: Routledge & Kegan Paul.

Nozick, R. (1993). *The nature of rationality.* Princeton, NJ: Princeton University Press.

O'Donohue, W., & Vass, J. S (1996). What is an irrational belief? Rational-emotive therapy and accounts of rationality. In W. O'Donohue & R. F. Kitchener (Eds.), *The Philosophy of Psychology.* London: Sage.

Plato (1970). *The Dialogues of Plato* (Vol. 4, Benjamin Jowett, Trans.). London: Sphere Books.

Popper, K. R. (1972). *Objective knowledge: An evolutionary approach.* Oxford: Oxford University Press.

Rogers, C. R. (1961). *On becoming a person.* Boston: Houghton Mifflin.

Schou, K. C., & Hewison, J. (1999). *Experiencing cancer.* Milton Keynes, UK: Open University Press.

Schön, D. A. (1983). *The reflective practitioner: How professionals think in action.* London: Temple Smith.

Segal, Z., Williams, J. M. G., & Teasdale, J. (2002). *Mindfulness-based cognitive therapy for depression.* London: Guilford.

Shapiro, F. (1995). *Eye movement desensitization and reprocessing: Basic principles, protocols, and procedures.* New York: Guilford Press.

Still, A. W. (2001). Marginalisation is not unbearable: Is it even desirable? *Journal of Rational-Emotive & Cognitive-Behavior Therapy, 19,* 55–66.

Still, A. W., & Dryden, W. (1998). The intellectual origins of rational psychotherapy. *History of the Human Sciences, 11,* 63–86.

Still, A. W., & Dryden, W. (1999). The place of rationality in Stoicism and REBT. *Journal of Rational-Emotive & Cognitive-Behavior Therapy, 21,* 37–55.

Still, A. W., & Dryden, W. (2003). Ellis and Epictetus: Dialogue vs. method in psychotherapy. *Journal of Rational-Emotive & Cognitive-Behavior Therapy, 21,* 37–55.

Still, A. W., & Dryden, W. (2004). The social psychology of "pseudoscience": A brief history. *Journal of the Theory of Social Behaviour, 34,* 265–290.

Still, A. W., & Todd, C. J. (1998). When technical rationality fails: Thinking about terminally ill patients. *Journal of Health Psychology, 3,* 137–148.

Stockdale, J. B. (1995). Testing Epictetus's doctrine in a laboratory of human behaviour. *Bulletin of the Institute of Classical Studies, 40,* 1–13.

Wertheimer, M. (1961). *Productive thinking.* London: Tavistock Publications.

Wessler, R. L. (1992). Constructivism and rational-emotive therapy: A critique. *Psychotherapy, 29,* 620–625.

Wessler, R. L. (1996). Idiosyncratic definitions and unsupported hypotheses: Rational emotive behavior therapy as pseudoscience. *Journal of Rational-Emotive & Cognitive-Behavior Therapy.*

Note: This is a revised draft of the article published in the *Journal of Cognitive and Behavioral Psychotherapies* (with permission).

3

Social and Cultural Aspects of Rational and Irrational Beliefs: A Brief Reconceptualization

Daniel David and Raymond DiGiuseppe

Behavioral predispositions shape culture and are shaped through it.

—(McGuire & Troisi, 1998)

Humans have motives and needs that drive their behaviors. Valence is associated with the properties of our physical and social environments that satisfy diverse needs. More specifically, valence is a basic component of our emotional life that derives from judging whether something is helpful or harmful in terms of satisfying important needs (Barrett, 2005). When valences are shared by a group of people, they form the crux of values and norms. For example, food and the activities associated with eating are related to a variety of values and norms because they satisfy one of our fundamental needs (e.g., hunger). Culture can be thought of as the sum of these values and norms, and civilization can be conceptualized as culture in action. In other words, culture is a construct referring to beliefs, representations, behavioral patterns, and artifacts that are transmitted socially across many generations within a group, resulting in patterns of within-group similarities and between-group differences (Buss, 2001; Cosmides & Tooby, 1992).

To understand the impact of the social and cultural factors on rational and irrational beliefs, it is necessary to understand the complex relation between biology and culture in terms of modern evolutionary psychology. This chapter aims to reconceptualize the way we typically think about the role that culture and environment play in shaping rational and irrational beliefs.

Controversies regarding the relative contribution of nature and nurture during development have been among the most important in psychology, as well as the narrower domain of conceptualizing the construct of rational and irrational beliefs. Our contention (see also Cosmides & Tooby, 1992, 2006) is that the assumption that nature and nurture are separate "entities," more or less interacting, is flawed. However, this dichotomy is so deeply represented in scientific thinking and professional practice that many lay people and even professionals have difficulty considering alternative ways to think about the nature-nurture issue (see also Cosmides & Tooby, 2006). Indeed, confusing individuals with populations has led many professionals to approach the nature-nurture question in the following way: Is biology (i.e., genes) or the environment (e.g., culture) more important in determining rational and irrational beliefs?

From a scientific point of view this is a meaningless question (see also Cosmides & Tooby, 1992, 2006). It is widely accepted that all phenotypic characteristics (i.e., visible characteristics) of an organism, including rational and irrational beliefs, are the joint product of genes and environment: genes allow the environment to influence the development of phenotypes. To ask which is more important is similar to asking, what is more important in determining the area of a physical location—the length or the width of its sides? (Cosmides & Tooby, 2006). If one of these components is "zero," then the phenotype is "zero." In the discussion that follows, we will discuss rational and irrational beliefs within this interactive framework proposed by Cosmides and Tooby (2006).

Rational and Irrational Beliefs in the Standard Social Science Model

According to the standard social science model (see also Cosmides & Tooby, 1992, 2006), the specific contents of the human mind (e.g., attitudes, knowledge, and beliefs) consist mainly of information derived from "outside"—that is, our environment and the social-cultural world. Moreover, the architecture of the human mind consists of a number of general purpose mechanisms related to the ability to learn, for example, that are often content-independent, although they themselves can have a biological basis (Cosmides & Tooby, 2006). The same general mechanisms are involved in learning diverse information contents such as beliefs (e.g., rational and irrational), language, and so forth.

Thus, according to this paradigm, rational and irrational beliefs derive from our social-cultural environment. More precisely, the environment injects rational and/or irrational meanings into our understanding of us and the world, and the architecture of our brain has no distinctive structures to influence these meanings. The human mind thus consists mainly of representations of social/cultural information (e.g., rational and irrational beliefs), representations produced by general purpose mechanisms, which are often content-independent. Accordingly, an individual exposed to an environment rich in irrational beliefs will likely develop irrational beliefs, whereas an individual exposed to an environment rich in rational beliefs will mainly develop rational beliefs. In summary, according to this model, we become rational and irrational mainly depending on our education and learning history and the social/cultural environment we live in.

This model possesses both face and common-sense validity. Most people would acknowledge that their beliefs, including rational (e.g., I would prefer to succeed but I do not absolutely have to) and irrational (e.g., I must succeed, and it is awful if I don't) ones, are acquired by the same mechanisms associated with learning other cognitive contents (e.g., The earth is round), during the course of living. Although scant research addresses the learning of rational or irrational beliefs, some data suggest that children reared in environments rich in irrational beliefs (e.g., their parents display a high level of irrational beliefs or related psychopathology) also tend to display high level of irrational beliefs (see Barlow & Coren, 2004).

However, in science, things are not always what they seem. A description of a difference between two groups (populations) is not the same as an explanation for that difference (Buss, 2001). For example (see Buss, 2001), Bulgarians and Estonians value physical attractiveness in a mate more than do Scandinavian Finns. Saying that cultural differences explain this specific behavior in specific individuals is nothing more than a tautology that does not explain, but merely describes a salient difference across populations.

Theoretical and empirical research has determined that the difference in question can be better explained from an evolutionary point of view (Buss, 2001). Because pathogens can compromise physical appearance, valuing beauty in mating is a way of avoiding pathogens and choosing a healthy mating partner. An abundance of environmental pathogens can thus contribute to an emphasis or focus on physical attractiveness in a given population

(Gangestad & Buss, 1993). If this hypothesis is correct, one (see also Buss, 2001) would expect a correlation between cultural variation in the prevalence of pathogens and average cultural importance placed on physical attractiveness in a potential mate. Indeed, Gangestad and Buss (1993) found a high correlation between environmental pathogens and concern about physical attractiveness (r = .71). Thus cultural variations in the prevalence of pathogens account for 50% of the cultural variations in factors involved in mate choice (e.g., physical attractiveness). Therefore, the evolutionary re-conceptualization of various psychological differences that appear to be culturally determined must be taken into account. A similar evolutionary perspective can also be applied to the rational and irrational beliefs constructs.

Rational and Irrational Beliefs in the Evolutionary Framework

Adopting an evolutionary framework, Ellis (1976) has long proposed that rational and irrational beliefs have a strong biological basis, which can be manifested in various ways, which we will describe in the discussion that follows (after Buss et al., 1998).

Rational and Irrational Beliefs as Adaptations

From an evolutionary/biological perspective, rational and irrational beliefs develop by natural selection. That is, both rationality and irrationality would now have, or once have had, some adaptive value for our ancestors. At first blush, the adaptive value of rationality seems much more obvious than the adaptive value of irrationality, but this topic deserves closer analysis. Buss et al. (1998) have outlined characteristics of psychological attributes prone to shaping by evolutionary influences:

- Evolutionary designed features are complexly specialized for solving adaptive problems in the past environment of a species. An adaptive problem has two main characteristics. First, it appears frequently during the evolutionary history of a species. Second, solving the problem positively affects the reproduction of individual organisms.
- These features are unlikely to appear due to chance.
- These features are not better explained as a by-product of mechanisms designed to solve other adaptive problems. Gould refers to features that evolved in this latter way as spandrels. (Gould, 2002)

Based on this analysis, some authors have proposed that irrational beliefs evolved by design (Pelusi, 2003; Ruth, 1992, 1993). For example, demandingness (e.g., placing excessive demands on oneself and others) resulting in frustration, intolerance, and anger might have been adaptive for our ancestors at the time humans evolved in our environment of evolutionary adaptiveness (EEA, the statistical composite of the kind of environments our ancestors faced during the past 1,000,000 years, Pelusi, 2003). If our status and/or mating access were challenged by a rival, demanding that the challenge must not occur, and taking forceful and sometimes drastic actions to ensure this eventuality, may have been useful in solving an adaptive problem. Indeed, data suggest that most homicides are committed by men toward men, in relation to rivalry over status and females (Pelusi, 2003).

In our current environment, such extreme measures may not be adaptive, and may instead generate emotional and social problems, according to the mismatch theory (i.e., mismatch between the function of irrationality in the EEA and our current environment). Based on these potentially adaptive functions of demandingness in our evolutionary history, corroborated by the fact that the current prevalence of irrationality is very high, and that irrationality is unlikely to appear due to chance (Ellis, 1994), conceptualizing irrationality as the byproduct of evolutionary design should be seriously considered.

Rational and Irrational Beliefs as By-products

Another possibility is that rational and irrational beliefs are merely artifacts of the evolution of a larger brain, and conferred little or no adaptive advantage on problem-solving. However, this possibility does not mean that rational or irrational beliefs do not today have salient consequences on emotions and behaviors, be they with evolutionary or nonevolutionary effects.

Rational and Irrational Beliefs as Noise

Genetic "noise" can be produced by mutations that neither contribute to nor detract from the functional design of an organism (Buss et al., 1998). In this regard, irrational beliefs are outcomes of random mutation. Again, this possibility does not mean that rational or irrational beliefs do not today have salient consequences on emotions and behaviors, be them with evolutionary or nonevolutionary effects.

Rational and Irrational Beliefs as Exaptations

Rational and irrational beliefs may have served an adaptive function in the past; however, in the present they have a new function correlating with fitness (survival and reproduction) (see for details Buss et al., 1998). That is, the role of the adaptation has shifted from the original role it played in the past.

Rational and Irrational Beliefs as Spandrels

In this paradigm, rational and irrational beliefs are considered by-products of a large brain. However, in the present they have acquired new functions, correlating with fitness (see Buss et al., 1998; Gould, 2002).

Whereas the argument for the biological basis of irrationality has been previously analyzed and discussed (see Ellis, 1976, and the below analysis), less is known regarding the biological basis of rationality. Moreover, the second part of the evolutionary hypothesis, namely that irrationality may have evolved for adaptive reasons, in various forms discussed above, seems less certain. We remain unsure if irrationality was ever adaptive,—whether it evolved because irrationality provided our ancestral humans with better genetic fit, or whether irrationality is a spandrel. Although irrationality seems to be a ubiquitous human trait, whether it ever served an adaptive function is open for debate and research.

Ellis (see for details, 1976, 1979, 1994) and Dryden, David, and Ellis, (in press) have argued that the following points constitute evidence in favor of his hypothesis concerning a biological basis of human irrationality.

1. Irrationality is independent of intellectual ability and intelligence. All human beings show evidence of irrational thinking and beliefs.
2. Irrationality is culturally ubiquitous. Disturbance-creating irrationalities that are present in our society are also present in all social and cultural groups that have been studied historically and anthropologically. Psychotherapists from every country and culture that have been studied report the presence of irrationality as described herein.
3. Irrationality occurs despite teaching rational thinking. Many of the irrational behaviors we exhibit in are in opposition to what our parents, peers, and the mass-media teach us to do.
4. Irrationality is a recurring phenomenon. People often adopt new irrational thinking patterns and beliefs after relinquishing old ones.
5. Irrationality occurs despite individual efforts to challenge it. People who vigorously oppose various kinds of irrational behaviors often fall prey to

these very same irrationalities. Atheists and agnostics exhibit zealous and absolutistic philosophies, and highly religious individuals act immorally.

6. Irrationality occurs despite knowledge or insight of its existence. Insight into the irrationality of thoughts and behaviors helps only partially to change them.

7. Irrationality resists change. People often return to irrational habits and behavioral patterns even after they have worked hard to change and overcome them.

8. Humans are predisposed to learn irrationality. People are often more prone to acquire self-defeating than self-enhancing behaviors and beliefs.

9. Irrationality is present even in individuals we might expect to be more rational. Psychotherapists, who by virtue of their knowledge and skills, might be expected to be good role models of rationality, often act irrationally in their personal and professional lives (see Chapter 15 in this book for details).

These postulates may leave the impression that REBT paints a negative image of humans (Dryden et al., in press). However, REBT theory stresses the existence of a second basic biological tendency. Humans have a corresponding ability to think rationally about their thinking, and the ability to exercise their power to choose to work toward changing their irrational thinking into rational thinking. Thus, people are by no means powerless over their natural tendency toward irrational thinking; they can transcend (although maybe not completely) irrationality by deciding to actively and continuously work toward modifying their thinking by employing cognitive, emotive, and behavioral challenging methods. Nevertheless, little research has investigated the biological basis of rationality and the constraints associated with instating rational beliefs. For example, it is possible—taking into account its hypothesized evolutionary past—that while irrationality (i.e., irrational beliefs) has both prefrontal and subcortical (e.g., amygdala) implementation, rational beliefs have mainly a prefrontal implementation. This could explain the difficulty of changing irrationality—as it is coded in old, evolutionary subcortical structures—as it suggests that rather than replacing irrational beliefs with rational beliefs we only learn to control the output of irrational beliefs by strengthening the rational beliefs. Future studies should investigate this hypothesis in evolutionary and implementational (e.g., fMRI) paradigms. In the final analysis, then, the REBT image of humans is complex and optimistic (Dryden et al., in press; Ellis, 1994).

Rational and Irrational Beliefs in the Context of Culture and
Evolution (based on the framework of Cosmides & Tooby, 2006)

As we noted previously, modern psychological approaches (Buss, 2001;
Cosmides & Tooby, 2006) reject the nature versus nurture dichotomy (e.g.,
innate versus acquired, biological versus cultural influences). The effect of the
environment on an organism (e.g., human mind) depends on the evolved
cognitive architecture. What we really need to understand and explain is the
nature and the number of these evolved mechanisms, not necessarily the
relative influence of biology and culture (Cosmides & Tooby, 2006). Indeed,
the developmental mechanisms of many organisms were designed by natural
selection to produce different phenotypes in different environments. However,
this does not imply that any aspect of the environment can affect the organism
(e.g., playing music to a child does not affect the color of his or her eyes).

People often tend to think about genes in terms of "Aristotelian essences"
that inevitably lead to certain behaviors, regardless of the environment in which
they are expressed (Cosmides & Tooby, 2006). Rather, genes are simply
regulatory factors that mediate the impact of the environment on the development of the organism. All aspects of the phenotype can be influenced by
environmental manipulation, the extent of such influence depending on the
creativity or invasiveness of the change in the environment. For example (see
also Cosmides & Tooby, 2006), if the human embryo is exposed to powerful
radiation, it will never develop into a normal fetus.

A thorough analysis also reveals the existence of numerous myths and/or
debates concerning this issue of biology versus culture relevant to various
phenotypic aspects of our organism, in the case at hand the development of
rational and irrational beliefs. We briefly outline them (based on Cosmides and
Tooby, 1992, 2006).

About the Presence at Birth

A common error people make is related to their belief that in order for a
phenotypic aspect (e.g., irrationality) to be considered part of our evolved
architecture, it must be present from birth. This conception confounds the
initial state of an organism with its evolved architecture. For example (after
Cosmides & Tooby, 2006), young boys typically do not have a beard—it usually
grows during adolescence; however, this does not mean that they learn to have a
beard. This misconception frequently leads to misguided arguments and
heated debates. People believe that if they can show that there is information
in the culture that mirrors the way people think (e.g., rationally and/or

irrationally), that such information is the cause of their thinking style. For example (adapted after Cosmides & Tooby, 2006), if parents see that men characters portrayed in books are more demanding than women characters, they assume that this explains why their boy is more demanding than their girl. However, what is cause versus the effect? Does the fact that men characters are more demanding in the books (i.e., culture/environment) "teach" boys to be more demanding, or does it merely "reflect" the way boys normally develop? In the absence of research on the causal determinants of demandingness, there is, of course, no way of knowing. An aspect of our evolved architecture can mature at any point in the life cycle, a fact that applies to the cognitive programs of our brain, including rational and irrational beliefs, just as much as it does to other aspects of our phenotype (e.g., beards) (Cosmides & Tooby, 2006).

About the Innate versus Learned Debate

As we have noted, scientists will gain little from dichotomizing the role of biological versus cultural factors (and their interaction) in understanding the origin and expression of beliefs in terms of learning versus innateness or learning versus instinct. It is clear that the brain must have a certain kind of innate structure for us to be able to learn anything. Because learning can only occur in the presence of a mechanism causing it, it logically follows that the mechanisms that create the potential for learning must themselves be unlearned. Therefore, certain learning mechanisms must be components of our evolved architecture that have developed in the same way regardless of the environmental variations that humans have faced during their evolution.

The interesting question (see Cosmides & Tooby, 2006) is what are these unlearned programs? Are they specialized for learning particular kind of things (e.g., learning either language or beliefs), or are they designed to solve more general problems (e.g. learning both language and beliefs)? Based on the modern evolutionary psychology paradigm (Cosmides & Tooby, 2006) learning programs, including those for learning rational and irrational beliefs, could be specialized evolved mechanisms.

About More Nature Brings More Nurture

It is assumed that the richer the architecture of these specific evolved mechanisms, the more an organism will be capable of learning (Cosmides & Tooby, 2006). For example, children can learn Romanian while the family pets cannot because the cognitive architecture of humans contains mechanisms that are not present in that of pets (e.g., cats). Similarly, humans learn spoken language quite easily, and humans living in isolation have created thousands of different languages. However, written language is far more difficult to learn than spoken language, and humans learn both writing and reading with significantly greater difficulty than speaking. This appears to be the case because, while we seem to have evolved mechanisms for efficiently learning spoken language (i.e., see Chomsky's learning acquisition device; Chomsky, 1965), comparable mechanisms have not evolved for written language.

Thus, learning is not a unitary phenomenon: the mechanisms that cause the acquisition of grammar, for example, are different from those causing the acquisition of rational and irrational beliefs (see Chomsky, 1965). A common conception among scientists and philosophers (both before and after Darwin) has been that our mind is like a blank page that is free of any information until the hand of experience writes on it. The accumulation and convergence of data in the field of cognitive sciences and evolutionary psychology and biology show that this view of the human mind is wrong (Cosmides & Tooby, 2006). Evolutionary psychology provides an alternative paradigm that is beginning to replace this simplistic view. Pinker (2002), for example, has shown that many aspects of human behavior are ubiquitous and the result of evolution. According to this perspective, all normal human minds develop a standard collection of reasoning and regulatory circuits that are functionally specialized and, frequently, domain-specific. These evolved circuits, including those for learning rational and irrational beliefs, shape the way we organize and interpret our experiences, determine the constants of our mental life, and provide universal frames of meaning that allow us to understand the actions and intentions of others (see also Cosmides & Tooby, 2006). Beneath the level of surface differences, all humans share certain assumptions about the world and human actions due to these human universal evolved mechanisms (Buss, 2001; Cosmides & Tooby, 2006).

Conclusion

We believe that at least three main ideas should be derived from this chapter. First, a description of the differences between two groups or categories such as rational and irrational beliefs, does not explain the differences (Buss, 2001). Stating that culture explains or determines these differences contributes little to knowledge (i.e., cognitive profit); the question still remains why do these differences exist? Second, specific mechanisms that mediate the ability to learn, for example, are inherent to human nature (e.g., evolution-based), and go a long way to account for cultural differences. Third, culture is not an independent causal agent, divorced from individuals. Thus, it is important to not ignore the role of evolution in creating, maintaining, transmitting, and changing culture.

Regarding the application of these conclusions to rational and irrational beliefs, we can say the following:

- Humans seem to have a biological predisposition towards rational and irrational beliefs. However, investigators have devoted less attention to studying the predisposition toward rationality as compared to the predisposition toward irrationality. Predisposition, however, is not equivalent to genetic determinism (e.g., specific genes or a combination of genes fully determine rational and/or irrational cognitions). Rather, predisposition implies that given a certain environment, based on our genes, we will assimilate more rational and/or irrational beliefs. Innate tendencies to develop irrational beliefs may thus explain the difficulty of changing them during psychotherapy (e.g., they are more difficult to change than automatic thoughts). Ellis (1994) acknowledged that the recognition of the biological basis of irrationality motivated him to work harder with his clients.
- If a predisposition to irrationality is biologically based in the brain, it is likely to result in irrational beliefs and, consequently, in the recurrence of the disturbed emotions these beliefs cause. Thus, relapse of emotional disturbance is to be expected, and clients need to learn how to manage relapse and how to respond to it without feeling hopeless.
- Disturbed and nondisturbed groups both endorse irrational beliefs. Accordingly, some other aspects of irrationality, besides its mere presence and interaction with a specific activating event, will be needed to distinguish disturbed from nondisturbed groups. We suggest that it may be the ratio of irrational to rational beliefs. If irrational beliefs dominate, rational beliefs will be unable to overshadow the disturbing or debilitating effects of irrational thinking.
- Irrational beliefs are likely to always be present; that is, rational beliefs may not replace or eliminate irrational beliefs entirely. Learning to discriminate rational and irrational beliefs and instituting rational thinking beliefs can be thought of as a coping strategy to counter irrational thought patterns. Although activating events such as failure or loss may inevitably first trigger irrational beliefs, we can learn to subsequently activate more rational modes of thinking. As we become more facile with the practice of countering or replacing irrational with rational thoughts, the period during which irrational beliefs are activated shortens, and may eventually reach the point that they are no

longer consciously recognized, even though their activation does not disappear altogether. This model was first proposed by the philosopher Spinoza (Damasio, 2003), and aptly describes the human condition (Gilbert 1991).

- The biological predisposition to rational or irrational thinking is not well understood, but it may be related to the concept of evolutionary design, mainly in the case of irrationality; future studies should investigate the concept of rational beliefs through this evolutionary lens.
- Rational and irrational beliefs specific to our social and cultural environment will be assimilated and filtered by evolved biological predispositions.
- People will develop irrational beliefs and thereby create psychological disturbance even if they are raised in an ideal culture, in which rational thinking is modeled. This process is analogous to the unfolding of innate language programs. Children raised without adults to model a specific language develop speech and create their own language, with minimum exposure to linguistic stimuli (Pinker, 1994). In much the same way, we can create our own irrationality.

Well-represented in individual human consciousness, rational and irrational beliefs are expressed in the broader culture, which, in turn, maintains and transmits irrational beliefs in a recursive cycle. Thus, our cognitive predispositions shape our culture, and the expression of such predispositions is at least partly shaped via cultural influences (McGuire & Troisi, 1998).

REFERENCES

Barlow J., & Coren, E. (2004). *Cochrane database syst rev.* 1: CD002020.

Barrett, L. F. (2005). Valence is a basic building block of emotional life. *Journal of Research in Personality, 40,* 35–55.

Buss, D. M. (2001). Human nature and culture: An evolutionary, psychological perspective. *Journal of Personality, 69,* 955–978.

Buss, D. M., Haselton, M. G., Bleske, A. L., & Wakefield, J. C. (1998). *American Psychologist, 53,* 533–548.

Chomsky, Noam (1965). *Aspects of the theory of syntax.* Cambridge, MA: MIT Press.

Cosmides, L., & Tooby, J. (1992). Cognitive adaptations for social exchange. In J. Barkow, L. Cosmides, & J. Tooby (Eds.), *The adapted mind.* New York: Oxford University Press.

Cosmides, L., & Tooby, J. (2006). *Evolutionary psychology: A primer.* http://www.psych.ucsb.edu/research/cep/primer.html.

Damasio, A. R (2003). *Looking for Spinoza: Joy, sorrow, and the feeling brain.* Orlando, FL: Harcourt.

Dryden, W., David, D., & Ellis, A. (in press). Rational emotive behavior therapy, In
    K. S. Dobson (Ed.), *Handbook of cognitive-behavioral therapies.* New York: Guilford.
Ellis, A. (1976). The biological basis of human irrationality. *Journal of Individual
    Psychology, 32,* 145–168.
Ellis, A. (1979). The theory of rational-emotive therapy. In A. Ellis & J. M. Whiteley
    (Eds.), *Theoretical and empirical foundations of rational-emotive therapy.* Monterey,
    CA: Brooks/Cole.
Ellis, A. (1994). *Reason and emotion in psychotherapy* (Rev. ed.). New York: Carol
    Publishing Group.
Gangestad, S. W., & Buss, D. M. (1993). Pathogen prevalence and human mate
    preferences. *Ethology and Sociobiology, 14,* 89–96.
Gilbert, D. T. (1991). How mental systems believe. *American Psychologist, 46,* 107–119.
Gould, S. J. (2002). *The structure of evolutionary theory.* Cambridge, MA: Belknap Press of
    Harvard University Press.
McGuire, M., & Troisi, A. (1998). *Darwinian psychiatry.* New York: Oxford University
    Press.
Pelusi, N. M. (2003). Evolutionary psychology and rational emotive therapy. In
    W. Dryden (Ed.), *Rational emotive behaviour therapy: Theoretical developments.* New
    York: Brunner-Routledge.
Pinker, S. (1994). *The language instinct.* New York: W. Morrow and Co.
Pinker, S. (2002). *The blank slate: The modern denial of human nature.* New York: Viking.
Ruth, W. (1992). Irrational thinking in humans: An evolutionary proposal for Ellis'
    genetic postulate. *Journal of Rational-Emotive & Cognitive-Behavior Therapy, 10,* 1,
    spring.
Ruth, W. (1993). Evolutionary psychology and rational-emotive therapy: Time to open
    the floodgates. *Journal of Rational-Emotive and Cognitive-Behavior Therapy, 11,* 4,
    winter.

4

Rational and Irrational Beliefs from an Evolutionary Perspective

David Sloan Wilson

The term *rationality* has at least two major meanings in everyday language. First, it refers to beliefs that are logically consistent and supported by empirical evidence. This is the kind of rationality associated with scientific and intellectual thought. Second, it refers to beliefs that enable people to achieve their goals. A corporation is said to behave rationally, for example, when it adopts a strategy that maximizes its profits. These two meanings can be called "factual rationality" and "practical rationality" respectively.

Both of these meanings are combined when CBT/REBT defines irrational beliefs as being nonlogical, nonempirically based (invoking factual rationality), and nonhelpful (invoking practical rationality). The purpose of this essay is to show that the two meanings cannot be combined in such a simple manner. A complex relationship exists between factual and practical rationality that can result in all four outcomes. A belief can be logically consistent and well supported by evidence, but spectacularly nonhelpful. Conversely, a belief can defy all the canons of logic and evidence but nevertheless function as an essential survival tool.

This essay examines the relationship between factual and practical rationality from an evolutionary perspective. A number of foundational conclusions can be drawn that are highly relevant to a modern application such as CBT/REBT.

Deception Begins with Perception

All organisms—even bacteria—are behaviorally flexible. An organism that is instructed by its genes to "do X" in all situations would never survive. Instead, organisms are instructed to "do X" in situation 1, "do Y" in situation 2, and so on. This kind of flexibility inherently requires environmental input. An organism can't "do X" in situation 1 unless it senses that 1 is the relevant situation. All forms of perception and information processing in organisms can be regarded as a transformation of environmental information into behavioral output. This general statement enabled John Almann (1999, p. 3) to begin his panoramic survey of brain evolution with a discussion of the brainlike mechanisms of bacteria:

> Some of the most basic features of brains can be found in bacteria because even the simplest motile organisms must solve the problem of locating resources and avoiding toxins in a variable environment. Strictly speaking, these unicellular organisms do not have nervous systems, but nevertheless they exhibit remarkably complex behavior: They sense their environment through a large number of receptors and store this elaborate sensory input in the form of brief memory traces. Moreover, they integrate the inputs from these multiple memory sensory channels to produce adaptive movements. The revolution in our understanding of genetic mechanisms has made it possible to determine how these brainlike processes work at a molecular level in bacteria.

From this perspective, it is obvious that the perception and processing of information must be highly selective to function adaptively. There is a nearly infinite variety of environmental stimuli that might be perceived, which can be processed in nearly infinite number of ways. Only a very small fraction of these possibilities lead to adaptive behavioral outcomes. Thus, organisms perceive only the stimuli that matter for their survival and reproduction and process them in just the right ways. Migratory birds are genetically programmed to stare at the night sky as nestlings. That information is processed by their brains and enables them to navigate by the stars as adults. If the nestlings are raised indoors, they lose their ability to migrate because they did not receive the appropriate environmental input at the appropriate stage of their life cycle. Bird species that don't migrate, such as the black-capped chickadee, are genetically programmed to remember the locations of thousands of food items that they store during the fall and revisit during the winter. Every species is elaborately programmed in this way, giving them abilities that are often truly superhuman, as in the two examples just described (e.g., Gaulin and McBurney, 2001, ch. 7).

Environmental stimuli that don't matter for survival and reproduction become invisible. Humans can see only a narrow slice of the light spectrum, hear only a narrow slice of the sound spectrum, can't sense electrical and magnetic fields at all, and so on. In addition, that which is perceived is often highly rendered. Our brains transform a continuous spectrum of light waves into discrete colors, for example (Shepard, 1992).

All of these adaptive mental processes are distortions of what is actually out there in the world, independent of any particular organism. The fact that there *is* a world out there can be established objectively by the tools of science. We know that there are magnetic and electrical fields, for example, but we had to go beyond the perceptual and information processing abilities that evolution provided us. In that sense, accurately perceiving objective reality is *unnatural*.

We lack a good vocabulary for thinking about adaptive distortions of reality. The word *deception* comes close, but in everyday usage it usually implies adaptively distorting reality for personal gain at the expense of others. The kind of deception that we are discussing is much more general. If we could somehow strip the word of its narrow and pejorative connotations, we could say that deception truly begins with perception.

The Evolution of Symbolic Belief Systems

Beliefs are a special form of mentality. Migratory birds and winter residents such as the chickadee might have sophisticated mental adaptations, but they do not necessarily have beliefs. Philosophers and psychologists have not reached a consensus on exactly what qualifies as a belief, but in this essay I will follow the reasoning of Terrence Deacon (1998) in his highly stimulating book *The Symbolic Species.*

Suppose that I train a rat to associate cheese with the word "cheese" by pairing the two in classic Pavlovian style. There is now a mental association, but it will be broken if I start to say the word without actually providing cheese. In contrast, I could say the word "cheese" to you a million times without providing cheese, and you would still associate the word with the object. That, according to Deacon, is the difference between simple associative learning and symbolic thought. With associative learning, the mental pairing is firmly linked to an environmental pairing. With symbolic thought, the mental associations become liberated from environmental associations, taking on a life of their own.

According to Deacon, our species is unique in its capacity for symbolic thought. This is not because symbolic thought is especially difficult. In fact, an intriguing part of Deacon's thesis is that other animals can be taught to think symbolically, more like us than their own kind. The rudiments of symbolic thought don't require a bigger or different brain than our ape ancestors possessed; they simply weren't *useful* for survival and reproduction. The key event in human evolution was an environmental context that made rudimentary symbolic thought adaptive.

Once it evolved, the ability to create a nearly infinite variety of mental representations gave our ancestors a new kind of behavioral flexibility, enabling them to spread over the planet, occupying hundreds of ecological niches. It is awesome to contemplate that a single biological species can acquire the adaptations to survive in environments as different as the frozen artic, the arid desert, the humid rain forest, and remote islands thousands of miles from the mainland. Then, with the advent of agriculture, population density expanded by many orders of magnitude, leading to modern life as we know it. None of this would be possible without the cultural evolution of symbolic belief systems, guided by a genetically evolved psychological architecture unique to our species.

An analogy with the mammalian immune system is instructive. It is a mind-bogglingly complex set of genetic adaptations for fighting disease organisms, but its centerpiece is a process of random antibody formation and selective retention of those that successfully bind to antigens. In other words, the slow-paced process of genetic evolution built a fast-paced process of antibody evolution. That is how we should think about the rapid formation and selective retention of symbolic belief systems. It is a faced-paced evolutionary process in its own right, made possible by a psychological architecture that evolved by genetic evolution.

Factual and Practical Rationality

The fast-paced process of cultural evolution differs from the slow-paced process of genetic evolution in numerous details (Richerson and Boyd, 2005), but it is equally subject to adaptive distortions of factual reality. Before Darwin, philosophers could comfortably assume that God endowed humans with the ability to see the world as it really is. After Darwin, they tended to assume that the word *evolution* could simply be substituted for *God*—that it is always adaptive to see the world as it really is. From a modern evolutionary perspective, this assumption is extraordinarily naïve. *Sometimes* it is adaptive to see the world as it really is, such as knowing the precise location of a deer so that it can be hit with a spear, but other situations favor adaptive distortions of reality. For example, regarding your enemy as an inhuman monster is more motivating than regarding him as much like yourself. An authentic evolutionary epistemology predicts that factual rationality will be the servant of practical rationality, showing up when useful and quietly excusing itself otherwise (Wilson, 1990, 1995, 2002, 2007).

An example from the anthropological literature will bring these abstract ideas to life. Micronesian Islanders are master navigators, spending days out of sight of land as they travel between islands in their outrigger canoes. Unlike migratory birds, their ability to navigate is not genetically innate but based on a system of cultural beliefs, some of which appear crazy from the standpoint of factual rationalism. For example, they believe that the islands move while their boat stands still. They also believe in the existence of certain islands that do not, in fact, exist. Cognitive psychologist Edwin Hutchins has shown that these beliefs are highly adaptive, despite the fact that they are manifestly false. It is computationally more efficient for them to think of themselves as a single fixed point in a constellation of islands that move, rather than to think of themselves as a moving point in a constellation of fixed islands. And if there is not an actual island for them to imagine passing to keep track of their movement, they invent one (Hutchins & Hinton, 1984; Hutchins, 1995).

Once we begin to think of cultural beliefs as a transformation of environmental information into behavioral output, it makes perfect sense for them to depart from factual rationality, just like our genetically evolved perceptual systems such as vision and hearing. The example of the Micronesian Islanders is beautiful because it is so concrete. The superiority of the false beliefs can be demonstrated in computational terms and we can easily imagine the factual rationalist, stubbornly insisting that the islands don't move and certain islands don't exist, disappearing over the horizon in his canoe, never to return.

Religions and Stealth Religions

We needn't travel to exotic lands to discover adaptive distortions of reality. They are all around us, especially in the form of religion.

Why is religion so puzzling to the scientific imagination? *Because it appears so factually irrational.* How can people believe so fervently in agents and events for which there is no objective proof whatsoever? It should be obvious by now that this stance toward religion, so common that it doesn't attract notice, is naïve and wrongheaded from an evolutionary perspective. Why should *factual rationality* be the gold standard for evaluating religious belief or any other belief? From an evolutionary perspective, there is only one gold standard—*what do the beliefs cause the believers to do?* Once we adopt the appropriate gold standard, much of the mystery and paradox surrounding religion melts away (Wilson, 2002, 2005, 2008). Most enduring religious systems are impressively designed to define groups, coordinate the activities of their members, to foster cooperation and suppress free-riding, exploitation, and factionalism in all their forms. Often (but by no means always) the purpose of solidarity within a religious group is to compete with other groups, a lamentable fact that is nevertheless to be expected from an evolutionary perspective. It should surprise no one, at least in retrospect, that religious beliefs obtain much of their power in motivating adaptive behaviors by departing from factual rationality. An example from Jainism is eloquently described by James Laidlaw (1995, p. 7) in a book whose title says it all: *Riches and Renunciation: Religion, Economy, and Society among the Jains.*

> How then, is it possible to live by impossible ideals? The advantage for addressing this question to Jainism is that the problem is so very graphic there. The demands of Jain asceticism have a pretty good claim to be the most uncompromising of any enduring historical tradition: the most aggressively impractical set of injunctions that any large number of diverse families and communities has ever tried to live by. They have done so, albeit in a turbulent history of change, schism, and occasionally recriminatory "reform," for well over two millennia. This directs our attention to the fact that yawning gaps between hope and reality are not necessarily dysfunctions of social organization, or deviations from religious systems. The fact that lay Jains make up what is—in thoroughly worldly material terms—one of the most conspicuously successful communities in India, only makes more striking and visible a question that must also arise in the case of the renouncers themselves.

As for religions, so also for many other cultural belief systems, which do not invoke supernatural agents but massively depart from factual realism in other respects in their drive to motivate an adaptive suite of behaviors. Patriotic histories of nations are as irrational, factually incorrect, and purpose-driven as any religion. Intellectual movements and scientific theories are not immune. Respectable doctors and scientists during the nineteenth century believed that intellectual development interfered with ovarian development in women. Scientific theories do not approximate factual reality when they are proposed, but only after they have been winnowed by empirical evidence, such as women graduating from college with functioning ovaries.

I have coined the term *stealth religion* to describe a cultural belief system that doesn't qualify as religious in the narrow sense of invoking supernatural agents, but which nevertheless departs from factual reality in its drive to motivate a suite of adaptive behaviors (Wilson, 2007). I also provide a detailed example of a stealth religion in the form of Ayn Rand and her philosophy of objectivism. Ironically, Rand was an atheist who claimed that her philosophy was based entirely on rationalism, but her movement can be shown to be just as distorted and purpose-driven as any fundamentalist religion. It is humbling to contemplate that the problems often associated with religions also exist for stealth religions, perhaps even more so, because stealth religions do a better job of masquerading as factual reality.

Factual Rationalism's Niche

It might seem that the dominance of practical over factual rationalism makes a mockery of the hallowed status of factual rationalism among scientists and intellectuals. On the contrary, I think that factional rationalism deserves its hallowed status—as an adaptive strategy that can succeed under appropriate environmental conditions.

One of the most important lessons to learn about evolution is that adaptations do not always correspond to what is true, good or useful in an absolute sense. To pick an example relevant to therapy, John Bowlby (1969), who pioneered the study of child development from an evolutionary perspective, identified three attachment styles in children. The secure style is clearly superior to the two insecure styles (avoidant and ambivalent) in terms of child development and adult functioning. Nevertheless, the two insecure styles can still be interpreted as adaptations to suboptimal childhood environments (Chisholm 1999). If a parent is unable or unwilling to invest in a child's development, it can be more adaptive to cling to the parent (ambivalent) or seek resources elsewhere (avoidant) than to employ the so-called secure attachment style. The fact that making the best of a bad situation has lifelong repercussions, which perhaps can be ameliorated by therapy, does not prevent the two **insecure** strategies from being interpretable as adaptive in the evolutionary sense of the word.

To pick a second example at the societal level, Norris and Inglehart (2004) show that worldwide trends in religiosity and secularization can be explained in terms *existential security,* which they define as "the feeling that survival is secure enough that it can be taken for granted." Geographical regions that are high in existential security, such as Western Europe, become secular and favor modes of thought associated with factual rationality. Regions that are low in existential security, such as the Middle East, adopt modes of thought associated with religious fundamentalism. Using international data from the World Values Survey, Norris and Inglehart show that the world as a whole is becoming more religious—less factually rational, if you will—for the simple reason that it is becoming less secure.

This result is alarming but also points to an optimistic solution. Factual rationalism can be a highly adaptive strategy in cultural evolution, but only under appropriate environmental conditions. The modes of thought associated with rationalism are time and labor intensive. At the individual level, they require an enormous amount of information processing, starting from childhood. At the societal level, they require an elaborate infrastructure associated with education and science. These activities can flourish under conditions of high existential security, but they cannot survive otherwise. It is unreasonable to expect people to invest their personal and collective resources on such activities when they feel, often for the best of reasons, that their very lives are at stake. For rationalism to succeed, we need to initiate a positive feedback cycle in which rational strategies increase existential security, which in turn favors the cultural evolution of factually rational strategies over their factually irrational alternatives.

Conclusion

As an evolutionist who is not trained specifically in CBT/REBT, my main contribution to this volume is to summarize what evolutionary theory has to say about the nature of rational and irrational beliefs. Those who are trained in CBT/REBT are best qualified to relate my comments to their own area of expertise. I will conclude this essay by offering a few suggestions of my own.

- *Rationality cannot be defined, at the outset, as both factually and practically rational.* The relationship between factual and practical rationality is too complex for them to be combined in such a simple manner. Even if the goal of CBT/REBT is to promote beliefs that are both factually and practically **rational**, they need to be defined separately and their complex relationship needs to be understood in detail to achieve the goal.

- *Factual rationalism contributes to practical rationalism only under certain conditions.* The primary goal of any form of therapy is to help people function better in their everyday lives—to make them more practically rational. CBT/REBT attempts to achieve this goal by getting people to think about their problems in a factually rational way. Understanding the complex relationship between practical and factual rationality can help to predict when the particular therapeutic strategy employed by CBT/REBT is likely to succeed or fail, to devise novel strategies for "expanding factual rationalism's niche," and even to judiciously incorporate strategies that involve departures from factual rationality.
- *Paying attention to the details of human evolutionary psychology.* In this essay I have concentrated on fundamental trade-offs between practical and factual rationality and basic evolutionary principles that apply to all species. A second essay could be written on the relevance of specific psychological mechanisms that evolved in our particular species, which make us especially prone to certain kinds of irrational beliefs. The field of human evolutionary psychology is still in its infancy and some of its bold initial claims are being moderated. In particular, Tooby and Cosmides (1992) developed a massive modularity thesis that portrayed the human mind as a collection of hundreds of special-purpose adaptations that evolved in Pleistocene environments and are often expressed maladaptively in modern environments. The massive modularity thesis marginalizes the importance of open-ended and domain-general learning mechanisms associated with behaviorism, which Tooby and Cosmides pejoratively called the standard social science model (SSSM). Fortunately, this polarized view is yielding to a more balanced view that recognizes the importance of both special-purpose adaptations and domain-general learning abilities that adapt individuals and societies to the present environments (Buller, 2005). All branches of psychology are in the process of becoming integrated from an evolutionary perspective and there is every reason for a therapeutic method such as CBT/REBT to be firmly anchored in the emerging synthesis.

REFERENCES

Almann, J. M. (1999). *Evolving brains.* New York: Scientific American Library.

Bowlby, J. (1969). *Attachment and Loss: Vol. 1. Attachment.* New York, Basic Books.

Buller, D. J. (2005). *Adapting minds: Evolutionary psychology and the persistent quest for human nature.* Cambridge, MA: MIT Press.

Chisholm, J. S. (1999). *Death, hope, and sex.* Cambridge, UK: Cambridge University Press.

Deacon, T. W. (1998). *The symbolic species.* New York: Norton.

Gaulin, S. J. C., and McBurney, D. H. (2001). *Psychology: An evolutionary approach.* Upper Saddle River, NJ: Prentice Hall.

Hutchins, E. (1995). *Cognition in the wild.* Cambridge, MA: MIT Press.

Hutchins, E., and Hinton, G. E. (1984). Why the islands move. *Perception, 13,* 629–632.

Laidlaw, J. (1995). *Riches and renunciation: Religion, economy, and society among the Jains.* Oxford: Oxford University Press.

Norris, P., and Inglehart, R. (2004). *Sacred and secular: Religion and politics worldwide.* Cambridge, UK: Cambridge Univeristy Press.

Richerson, P. J., and Boyd, R. (2005). *Not by genes alone: How culture transformed human evolution.* Chicago: University of Chicago Press.

Shepard, R. N. (1992). The perceptual organization of colors: An adaptation to regularities of the terrestrial world? In J. H. Barkow, L. Cosmides, & J. Tooby (Eds.), *The adapted mind: Evolutionary psychology and the generation of culture* (pp. 495–532). Oxford: Oxford University Press.

Tooby, J., & Cosmides, L. (1992). The psychological foundations of culture. In J. H. Barkow, L. Cosmides, & J. Tooby (Eds.), *The adapted mind: Evolutionary psychology and the generation of culture* (pp. 19–136). Oxford: Oxford University Press.

Wilson, D. S. (1990). Species of thought: A comment on evolutionary epistomology. *Biology and philosophy, 5,* 37–62.

Wilson, D. S. (1995). Language as a community of interacting belief systems: A case study involving conduct toward self and others. *Biology and Philosophy, 10,* 77–97.

Wilson, D. S. (2002). *Darwin's cathedral: Evolution, religion, and the nature of society.* Chicago: University of Chicago Press.

Wilson, D. S. (2005). Testing major evolutionary hypotheses about religion with a random sample. *Human Nature, 16,* 382–409.

Wilson, D. S. (2007). *Evolution for everyone: How Darwin's theory can change the way we think about our lives.* New York: Delacorte.

Wilson, D. S. (2008). Evolution and religion: The transformation of the obvious. In J. Bulbulia, R. Sosis, E. Harris, R. Genet, C. Genet, & K. Wyman, (Eds.), *The evolution of religion: Studies, theories, critiques* (p. 11–18). Santa Margarita, CA: Collins Foundaton Press.

PART II

Rational and Irrational Beliefs: Human Emotions and Behavioral Consequences

5

The Behavioral Consequences of Irrational Beliefs

Aurora Szentagotai and Jason Jones

Human behavior flows from three main sources: desire, emotion, and knowledge.

—Plato

According to the rational-emotive behavior theory (REBT) of mental health and disturbance, emotional problems and self-defeating behaviors are learned maladaptive responses resulting from faulty thinking\g patterns. For many years, Ellis (e.g. 1962, 1994) has cogently argued that diverse manifestations of psycho-pathology are the outcome of holding *irrational* beliefs. When assessing people's psychological problems, REBT therapists and theorists rely on the ABC model, a framework that has strong commonalities with other cognitive-behavior approaches. The main components of this model are:

Activating events (A), which refers to events that the person is potentially able to discern and attend to (Dryden, 2002). Activating events can be: *(1)* objective situations; *(2)* present thoughts, feelings, and behaviors related to objective situations; and *(3)* past or future thoughts and memories that are in some way related to the present situation (David, 2006a). Internal events, such as the experience of pain, can also comprise situations that provoke distress (Dryden, 2002). The dimension of the A that is important in REBT, because it differs from other forms of cognitive-behavior therapy (CBT), is that inferences (cognitions

75

that exist along a true-false continuum) are included as activating events. Indeed, Dryden (2003) has renamed A as adversity, representing the inference that can be drawn about the activating event.

Activating events trigger the person's Beliefs (B), which, according to REBT, are fully and explicitly evaluative. An important distinction is made between rational beliefs (RB) that are flexible, consistent with reality, logical, and constructive to the person, and irrational beliefs (IB) that are rigid, inconsistent with reality, illogical, and largely detrimental to the person (Dryden, 2003). One element key to the experience of beliefs, be they rational or irrational, is the degree of conviction with which they are held at the moment of a particular emotional episode.

When people experience emotions, beliefs do not present as self-talk or internal dialogue, nor are people usually consciously aware of their beliefs, but a careful examination of any unhealthy emotional experience will typically disclose a number of irrational beliefs. In many ways, therefore, we consider beliefs to be fused with their emotional and behavioral consequences. Beliefs can be determined by their directional source (self, other, or world/life/conditions), and their evaluative content (demands vs. preferences, awfulizing vs. anti-awfulizing, low frustration tolerance vs. high frustration tolerance, and conditional acceptance vs. unconditional acceptance) (see below).

One of the central tenets of REBT is that beliefs mediate the view people have about events and come between the actual event and the Consequences (C) that the person experiences, which can be emotional, cognitive-behavioral, and physiological in nature. Whereas rational beliefs lead to functional consequences, irrational beliefs lead to dysfunctional ones (e.g., Ellis & Harper, 1961; David, 2006a).

Although the ABC model used within REBT appears to offer a sequential view of emotional experience and the associated action tendencies, it is important to note that people usually do not experience emotion as a sequential process. Typically, people report "feeling" at all levels of the ABC model, thus representing the importance of each aspect of the model. Although first described in 1955, the ABC model still accommodates recent advances in cognitive theory, such as automatic or nonconscious processing (e.g. Power & Dalgleish, 1997). The purpose of imposing a simple framework on complex experiences is to facilitate therapeutic change.

With this brief overview in mind, we now turn to our main point of interest in this chapter: the relation between rational/irrational thinking and behavior. REBT theory specifically states that beliefs, rational and/or irrational, engender emotional experiences that have specific action tendencies. Generally, it is considered that irrational beliefs function to generate emotions that in turn facilitate tendencies to engage in avoidant or escape behaviors, whereas rational beliefs generate emotions that facilitate approach behaviors (Ellis, 1994; Dryden, 2002). In hypothesizing about the relation between beliefs and their consequent emotions and action tendencies, Dryden (2002) delineates a gamut of behaviors/action tendencies associated with endorsing irrational beliefs, including withdrawing from reinforcement, physically or verbally attacking others, isolating oneself from others, avoiding feared situations, self-harming, shutting down communication, seeking constant reassurance, disclaiming responsibility, ignoring attempts from others to restore social equilibrium, and engaging in superstitious behavior. Unfortunately, to date, there is little empirical research that has been devoted to identifying the action tendencies associated with emotional experiences (see David, Szentagotai, Kallay, & Macavei, 2005).

The rationale for this oversight is not apparent from reviewing the literature. However, we offer three reasons for the paucity of research on action tendencies of emotions. First, developments in cognitive-behavioral theory generally have focused on syndromes, usually associated with existing nosological systems. Depression, for example, has been studied more as a syndrome or cluster of identifiable characteristics, rather than purely an emotional experience that is a disordered variant of sadness. Hence, there has been less emphasis on understanding the beliefs associated with specific action tendencies than there has been on the beliefs associated with categorically specified syndromes. Unfortunately, the REBT position, which addresses emotions explicitly, irrespective of syndromal definitions, has been largely overlooked in research. Second, although Ellis emphasized the role of behavior in his seminal works, behavior was not formally folded into general REBT until the mid-1980s, reflected in the modification of *rational-emotive therapy* to *rational-emotive behavior therapy*. Third, there are substantive methodological difficulties in determining the specific relation between beliefs and behaviors. Most, if not all, cognitive theories recognize that beliefs lead to emotional experiences, and, consequently, to specific action tendencies that accompany emotions. From a research perspective, this implies that teasing apart any specific relationship between beliefs and behavior explicitly is likely to be artifactual, as it would prove extremely difficult to remove the effects of associated emotions.

Before we proceed with our analysis, some other points need to be made. In this chapter, our focus will be on *overt operant behavior*. Overt behaviors are responses that can be observed and measured, directly or with certain instruments, independent of the subjectivity of the person producing them. Operant behaviors are learned [motor] behaviors, which are under our voluntary control, and have a direct impact on our physical or social environment (Spiegler &

Guevremont, 1993; David 2006b). Examples of overt operant behaviors include being physically aggressive toward someone (e.g., hitting) for not treating us with the respect we demand, or avoiding something that we are anxious about because we have told ourselves that we must not experience it because to do so would be truly awful.

We acknowledge that behavior does not occur in a vacuum, and is usually the response to a set of emotional experiences generated by rational and/or irrational beliefs. However, to illuminate our account as clearly as possible we have chosen to focus on each of the four main irrational beliefs proposed by the rational-emotive behavior theory independently, rather than discussing all aspects of the theory as a whole. We hope this approach will make our review comprehensive and coherent within this constraint, considering the diversity of theoretical and empirical aspects that could otherwise prove difficult to present coherently. Accordingly, our analysis will focus on research findings that assess and discuss the four irrational beliefs and their consequences separately, rather than on research evaluating the behavioral outcomes of global irrationality/ rationality or on assessment methods that do not make the distinction among the four types of irrational beliefs described by the theory.

Although in his earlier works Ellis describes 11 types of irrational beliefs (Ellis, 1962), later developments suggest that they fall into 4 main categories: (1) demandingness (DEM), (2) awfulizing (AWF), (3) low frustration tolerance (LFT), and (4) global evaluation/self or other-downing (SD). These four types of irrational beliefs cover various content areas (e.g. performance, comfort, affilia-tion) and can refer to ourselves, others, or life in general (Ellis & Harper, 1961; David et al., 2005). The alternative rational beliefs are: (1) preferences, (2) anti-awfulizing, (3) high frustration tolerance, and (4) unconditional self/other acceptance. REBT also specifies the relationships among these beliefs (Ellis, 1994), namely that both rational and irrational beliefs consist of a primary and secondary belief. Whereas the former expresses the demanding or preferential nature of the belief, the latter conveys a personally meaningful context or theme (Dryden, 2002; MacInnes, 2004). An example would be: *I must get the highest grades in my class* (primary belief—DEM), *and I cannot stand it if I don't* (secondary belief—LFT).

The Behavioral Consequences of Demandingness

In Ellis's words, demands are "commands on the universe to be the way you want it to be" (DiGiuseppe, 1996). As rigid assertions of desires, demands are beliefs characterized by a dogmatic insistence that a certain condition must or must not exist. Such absolutistic requirements are commonly expressed in the form of "must," "ought," absolute "shoulds," "have to," and so forth. Demands concern oneself, others, and life conditions. The rational alternatives of demands are full preferences, which are flexible assertions of what the person wants, coupled with the acceptance of the fact that we cannot insist absolutely that we get what we want; hence, the demanding element is negated.

Demandingness is viewed as the core (or root) irrational belief from which the other irrational beliefs stem (Ellis (1962, 1994). However, this assumption is clinically derived, and has not yet received sufficient and definitive empirical support (David et al., 2005; DiGiuseppe, 1996). In response to the lack of empirical investigation into the primacy of demandingness, Ellis (e.g., 2003a) often offers what is fundamental common sense: How can a derivative exist (such as awfulizing, LFT, or self-downing) in the absence of a demand? It is unlikely that these derivatives (e.g., awfulizing) would stem from a full preference. For example, if people strongly prefer to be approved of by others but recognize that they cannot insist on or guarantee approval, then being disapproved of cannot be evaluated as a truly awful experience.

What has been established, however, is the role of demandingness in generating a range of unhealthy negative (dysfunctional) emotions (David, Schnur, & Belloiu, 2002; David et al, 2005). A review of the literature on the correlates of demandingness also shows it to be related to several types of behavioral maladaptive consequences (see Table 5.1) in both adults and children. According to Ellis (2003a; 1997), there are three main types of demands that create problems for people: (1) demands that they should perform well, (2) demands that others must treat them nicely, and (3) demands that living conditions must be free of hassles and that life should be fair. We will use this distinction in extracting the behavioral consequences of demandingness.

Demands on the behavior of the self (e.g. "I must achieve," "I must be competent," "I must act perfectly") have been associated with self-defeating behaviors such as comfort eating, medication use, the tendency to engage in routine or repetitive behaviors (Harrington, 2005), and reduced attempts to inhibit aggression (e.g. Bernard, 1998). Also, behavioral demands are predictive of interpersonal behavioral difficulties such as relational problems, and social avoidance and isolation (Watson, Sherbak, & Morris, 1998). In a study designed to examine the action tendencies of anxiety, Nicastro, Luskin, Raps, and Benisovich (1999) explored the behavioral consequences (amount of time speaking in front of an audience) of demandingness in potentially anxiety provoking social situations. According to the REBT theory, social anxiety may be produced by demands to achieve some personal standard in order to be appreciated by others. The investigators' results revealed that participants who

TABLE 5.1. Behavioral Consequences of Irrational Beliefs

Irrational belief	Dysfunctional behavior	Study
Demandingness		
Self-related demands for achievement and competence	• Comfort eating • Medication use • Increased anger expression • Social avoidance and isolation • Decreased performance in social context • Internalized and externalized behavioral disorders in children	Harrington (2005) Bernard (1998) Watson, Sherbak, and Morris, (1998) Nicastro, Luskin, Raps, and Benisovich (1999) Silverman and DiGiuseppe (2001)
Demands for comfort and fairness/ entitlement	• Self-harming • Behavioral avoidance • Comfort eating • Overspending • Procrastination • Reduced anger control • Increased anger expression • Relational problems	Harrington (2005); Harrington (2003); Bridges and Roig (1997) Bernard (1998) Addis and Bernard (2002)
Demands for control	• Hostile-dominant interpersonal style	Goldberg (1990)
Other related demands	• Marital problems • Aggressive anger expression	Möller and De Beer (1998); Möller and Van der Merwe (1997) Jones and Trower (2004)
Awfulizing		
	• Submissive interpersonal style • Social isolation • Increased anger suppression • Increased anger expression • Externalized behavioral disorders in children	Goldberg (1990) Watson, Sherbak, and Morris, (1998) Martin and Dahlen (2004) Silverman and DiGiuseppe (2001)
Low frustration tolerance		
	• Decreased anger control • Increased anger expression	Watson, Sherbak, and Morris (1998) Möller and Van der Merwe (1997)_ Martin and Dahlen (2004) Jones and Trower (2004)

- Increased anger suppression
- Social isolation
- Marital problems

• Behavioral avoidance	Harrington (2005)
• Comfort eating	
• Routine behavior	
• Procrastination	
• Overspending	
• Medicationuse	
• Self-harm	

Global-evaluation/
  self-downing

• Defensiveness to negative feedback	Chamberlain and Haaga (2001)
	Martin andDahlen (2004)
• Increased anger suppression	Jones and Trower (2004)
	Addis and Bernard (2002); Möller and
• Aggressive anger expression	Van der Merwe (1997); Möller, Rabe
	and Nortje (2001); Möller and De Beer
• Marital problems	(1998)
• Internalized and externalized behavioral disorders in children	Silverman and DiGiuseppe (2001)

endorsed high levels of demandingness spent significantly less time talking about themselves in front of others than individuals who endorsed low levels of demands in social situations.

A significant amount of research has documented the link between a demand of self-oriented perfectionism and maladaptive behaviors such as disordered eating (e.g., Pearsons & Gleaves, 2006; Sherry, Hewit, Besser, McGee, & Flett, 2004), alcohol abuse (e.g., Hewit & Flett, 1991), problems in interpersonal interactions (e.g., Haring, Hewit, & Flett, 2003), suicide (e.g., Blatt, 1995), diminished task performance (Frost & Marten, 1990), and reduced willingness to discuss and share personal results on various tasks with others (Frost, Turcotte, Heimberg, & Mattia, 1995).

Harrington (2005) conducted a study with nonpsychotic psychiatric patients to study demands for personal comfort (e.g., beliefs that life should be free of hassles and inconvenience) and entitlement/fairness (e.g., beliefs that life should be fair, and that one should enjoy immediate gratification), and their relation to maladaptive behaviors. Harrington (2005) determined that individuals holding comfort and/or entitlement beliefs were prone to self-defeating behaviors, including self-harming, behavioral avoidance, comfort eating, the use of medication, overspending, and procrastination. Procrastination has been previously linked to irrationality in general and demandingness in particular in both clinical and nonclinical populations (e.g. Beswick, Rothblum, & Mann, 1988; Bridges & Roig, 1997). Demands for comfort, fairness, and approval are also related to the expression and control of anger. As these demands increase, anger control diminishes, while relationship problems (Addis & Bernard, 2002) and behavioral expression of anger-aggression increases (Bernard, 1998).

Demands for absolute control have been linked theoretically to the tendency to exhibit rigid and domineering behaviors. Although empirical data are scarce, there is some evidence that demands for control are related to a hostile-dominant interpersonal style (Goldberg, 1990).

Finally, we will briefly examine other-related demandingness (e.g., absolutistic beliefs regarding how others should behave or treat the person), which predicts relational/marital problems. REBT distinguishes between *couple dissatisfaction*, which consists of *moderately* intense negative emotions and rational beliefs, in one or both partners, and *couple disturbance*, which consists of *highly* intense negative emotions and irrational beliefs experienced by one or both partners (Addis & Bernard, 2002). According to REBT, relationship disturbances stem from unrealistic expectations characterized by irrational demands for approval and performance, which partners tend to express in terms of each other and the marital relationship itself (Ellis, 2003b).

Clinical observations suggest that failing to meet these irrational demands (by self or by the partner) leads to awfulizing, underestimating the ability to cope with problems (low frustration tolerance), and to blaming the self or the other person (Ellis, 1991). In a series of studies examining these hypotheses, Möller and colleagues (Möller & De Beer, 1998; Möller & Van der Merwe 1997) found that other-directed demands (but not self-directed demands) played a significant role of in predicting poor marital adjustment and marital conflict.

Ellis (1977) also argues that other-related demands fuel the dysfunctional behavioral reactions of individuals with anger related problems. Jones and Trower (2004) garnered support for this hypothesis in a study that examined evaluative beliefs in a clinical sample of individuals with anger disorders, most of whom reported expressing violence during their anger episodes.

Although most of the studies in this area have been conducted on adults, there is also evidence of demandingness-related behavioral problems in children. Silverman and DiGiuseppe (2001) assessed the relationship between irrational beliefs and emotional and behavioral problems in schoolchildren (aged 9–13). They reviewed both internalizing and externalizing problems, a broad grouping of behavior problems in the literature regarding child psychopathology that distinguishes between overcontrolled, depressive, and fearful behavior on the one hand, and undercontrolled, aggressive, antisocial behavior on the other (Achenbach & Edelbrock, 1983). Their results (based on teachers' ratings of children's problems) showed a significant association between demandingness and internalizing disorders. Moreover, children displaying both internalized and externalized behavior problems endorsed significantly higher levels of demandingness than children without overt behavior problems (Silverman & DiGiuseppe, 2001).

Based on the data reviewed, we can draw the empirically supported conclusion that demandingness is related to a variety of behavioral problems ranging from addictive behavior and eating disorders to aggression and disturbed social relationships, in both adults and children. Thus, the REBT hypothesis that demandingness is at the heart of psychological disturbance has a broad and solid foundation.

The Behavioral Consequences of Awfulizing/Catastrophizing

Awfulizing beliefs refer to the extreme dichotomous evaluation of a negative event as worse than it absolutely should be. Awfulizing beliefs exaggerate the consequences of past, present, or future events, conceptualizing people or events as terrible, horrible, or the worst thing that could happen (MacInnes, 2004). A person who holds an awfulizing belief is unable to allow for the fact that there are worse possible present or future outcomes (Dryden, 2003). According to the REBT theory, awfulizing derives from demandingness: when people do not get what they believe they are entitled to, they conclude that "it is awful" (Dryden, 2002; but see DiGiuseppe, 1996 for a discussion regarding the relationship between demandingness and the other irrational beliefs). Anti-awfulizing beliefs are the rational counterparts of awfulizing. They refer to the evaluation that when people's full preferences are not met, they conclude that the circumstances may be "bad" but not awful. This approach allows for the fact that worse outcomes are possible (Dryden, 2002), and relies on a continuum of badness, rather than a dichotomous judgment of either awful or not bad at all.

Whereas the relationship between awfulizing and dysfunctional emotions has received extensive attention in the REBT literature (e.g., David et al., 2002), significantly less research has focused on the impact of awfulizing on overt behavior (Table 6.1). The rational-emotive behavior theory of emotions has traditionally tied awfulizing to the experience of anxiety (David, 2003), although clinical anecdotes suggest that awfulizing can pervade most if not all emotional problems, including unhealthy anger, depression, shame, guilt, and hurt (Dryden, 2002).

Ellis distinguishes between two major forms of anxiety: *ego and discomfort anxiety* (Ellis, 2003c, 2003d), both of which have to do with awfulizing. Discomfort anxiety results when people feel that: *(1)* their comfort is threatened, *(2)* they must get what they want, and that *(3)* *it is awful or catastrophic* when they do not get what they demand. In contrast, ego anxiety appears when people feel that: *(1)* their self or personal worth is threatened, *(2)* they must perform well and/or be approved by others, and that *(3)* *it is awful or catastrophic* when they fail to perform well and/or are not approved by others. In Ellis's opinion, these two constructs help explain several phenomena related to emotional disturbance (Ellis, 2003c), including a range of self-defeating behaviors (e.g., avoidance). However, Ellis's assumptions are based primarily on clinical observations, rather than empirical data.

The domain of social interactions is one area in which awfulizing may have an impact on behavior. Goldberg (1990), for example, found that awfulizing is significantly correlated with a submissive interpersonal style, whereas Watson, Sherbak, and Morris (1998) documented a significant relationship between awfulizing and social isolation. Considering the involvement of awfulizing in anxiety, it is possible that when people adopt a submissive, other-directed relational style and they avoid social contact, it is a way of reducing or eliminating the unpleasant emotional consequences (e.g., anxiety) of negative interpersonal encounters (Goldberg, 1990).

Awfulizing also influences the experience and control of anger (e.g., Hazaleus & Deffenbacher, 1985; Zwemer & Deffenbacher, 1984). High levels of awfulizing are related to both unhealthy anger suppression and to aggressive anger expression (Martin & Dahlen, 2004). Finally, in the case of children, awfulizing significantly correlates with externalized behavioral disorders (Silverman & DiGiuseppe, 2001). Although empirical evidence on the behavioral effects of awfulizing is scarce, compared to research on demandingness, several studies have begun to establish the relation between awfulizing and maladaptive behaviors, providing preliminary confirmation of theoretical assumptions and clinical observations of REBT. However, because the research base is largely correlational in nature, researchers have yet to determine the causative role of awfulizing in dysfunctional behaviors.

The Behavioral Consequences of Low Frustration Tolerance

Low frustration tolerance beliefs assert the fact that one cannot tolerate or bear an event or set of circumstances, thereby making a situation appear to be intolerable. As in the case of awfulizing, many REBT theorists hold that low frustration tolerance stem from demands—when people do not get what they believe they must get, they conclude that the situation is intolerable and they cannot stand it (Dryden, 2002). On the other hand, high frustration tolerance beliefs assert that events may be difficult to tolerate, but they are not intolerable.

According to REBT, low frustration tolerance discourages people from contending with unpleasant circumstances, and short-circuits their ability to confront obstacles to goal-attainment. Alternatively, high frustration tolerance promotes active efforts to confront or eliminate obstacles to happiness and achievement (Dryden, 2002).

Not uncommonly, anger is conceptualized in terms of frustration tolerance. Power and Dalgleish (1997) summarized the clinical and cognitive psychology literature and concluded that anger is aroused most typically following the perception that one's goal has been intentionally blocked by another, which may then be further evaluated as being unbearable (Ellis, 1977). Several studies highlight the role of low frustration tolerance in the experience and expression of anger. Martin and Dahlen's (2004) study of college students determined that low frustration tolerance is related to trait anger—the aggressive expression of anger—and inversely related to the tendency to control the outward expression of anger.

Interestingly, low frustration tolerance is also related to anger suppression, which can also yield maladaptive effects. According to Spielberger (1999), the tendency to inhibit anger becomes increasingly problematic as trait anger increases. Indeed, low frustration tolerance is related to state anger following provocation. Jones and Trower (2004) also found evidence of low frustration tolerance beliefs in participants with anger disorder who were asked to describe a typical, recent, or vivid example of their experience of anger (18% of the sample).

An overview of the literature with an eye to behavioral consequences (Table 5.1), also points to the impact of low frustration tolerance belief in the social domain. The endorsement of this belief is associated with self-reports of poor social adjustment in general (e.g., social isolation, normlessness; Watson et al., 1998), as well as with poor marital adjustment. As already mentioned, in discussing the nature of disturbed marital interactions, Ellis points out that they arise from unrealistic expectations resulting from irrational demands that partners tend to have not only about each other, but also about the marital relationship itself (Ellis, 2003b; Möller & Van der Merwe, 1997). Failing to meet these irrational demands leads, among other things, to underestimating the ability to cope with the marital problems, or the dogmatic insistence that the problems are too grave to bear (low frustration tolerance). When one of the partners reacts badly to the normal frustrations or abnormal demands of the other one, these frustrations and demands are accentuated (Ellis, 2003b).

The other partner, in turn, can also react poorly to the marital difficulties. This pattern increases low frustration tolerance and outbursts of temper by both partners (e.g., anger). Indeed, there are data confirming the relationship between high levels of LFT (in both husbands and wives) and low dyadic adjustment (e.g., low cohesion, low affectional expression). Researchers have failed to document such a relationship in high dyadic adjustment couples (Möller & Van der Merwe, 1997). Thus, in marital affiliations, it appears that LFT beliefs are related to unhealthy behavioral patterns that can in turn further exaggerate conflict, withdrawal, or submission.

Moving from the interpersonal to the individual level, theorists have suggested that low frustration tolerance exacerbates certain types of disorders and conditions, particularly self-control problems (e.g., procrastination; see Ellis & Knauss, 1977). In the attempt to explain self-control problems (e.g., binge eating, self-harm), behavioral theorists have emphasized that self-control involves the ability to tolerate costs such as gratification delay, effort expenditure, and punishment (Eisenberger, 1992). Harrington (2005) also includes the ability to tolerate emotional discomfort/distress among these costs. A low ability to tolerate such costs would result in a range of self-control problems. Although empirical data are still sparse, some evidence (Harrington, 2005) links low frustration tolerance beliefs to a variety of maladaptive coping mechanisms such as behavioral avoidance, procrastination, comfort eating, overspending, the use of medication, and self-harm (the latter is also associated with chronic anger).

Another self-defeating behavior, addiction, is also hypothesized to be associated with LFT beliefs (Bishop, 2001; Ellis, 2001). REBT formulates most addiction-related problems as stemming from the following sequence: *(a)* people believe or infer (at A) that they cannot cope with the discomfort caused by the absence of a substance (e.g., food, alcohol, nicotine, or illicit substances); *(b)* they demand that they should not have to tolerate such discomfort because it is unbearable, and *(c)* at C they seek relief by using the substance. Unfortunately, few empirical studies have investigated this conceptual scheme.

Silverman and DiGiuseppe's study (2001), one of the few to investigate the association between irrational beliefs and behavioral problems in children, found no correlations between the LFT subscale scores of the Child and Adolescent Scale of Irrationality (CASI) and externalized or internalized behavioral problems.

To conclude our discussion on low frustration tolerance, we believe that the empirical data synthesized above support some of the important assumptions of REBT regarding the involvement of LFT in human disturbance (e.g., dysfunctional behaviors). In fact, research conducted by DiGiuseppe and colleagues (DiGiuseppe, 1996); DiGiuseppe, Leaf, Exner, & Robin, 1988suggests that of the four irrational beliefs, LFT, along with self-downing, which we discuss in the next section, correlate most strongly with emotional disturbance.

The Behavioral Consequences of Global Evaluation/Self-Downing

People exhibit a natural tendency to make global evaluations (i.e., overgeneralize) about themselves, others, and the world. This tendency is probably a result of the cognitive system's innate ability to generalize rapidly from specific occurrences to facilitate learning or ensure safety, for example. More specifically, people tend to draw global, stable, and more or less definitive conclusions based on low-frequency behaviors or events. From a logical point of view, this process can yield erroneous inferences, so no firm and general conclusions can be drawn based on inductive reasoning (David, 2006b; Ellis, 1997). Or as Aristotle put it, "The whole is more than the sum of its parts" (from *Metaphysica*, tr. 1963).

Self-downing refers to making global negative evaluations about oneself (e.g., *The fact that I failed the exam proves that I am a failure*). The person evaluates a specific trait, behavior, or action according to a standard of desirability or worth and then applies the evaluation to his or her entire being (MacInnes, 2004). When such negative overgeneralizations are applied to others or the world, it is called other-downing and world-downing, respectively.

The rational correspondent of self-, other-, and world-downing is unconditional self-, other-, and world-acceptance. With regards to unconditional self-acceptance (which we will focus on in this chapter), a person understands that although people do bad or stupid things, they cannot be globally rated as bad or stupid, and that people's fallibility and foibles (including the self) must be accepted. REBT teaches that people are valuable in themselves, even though their behaviors may not always be laudable; however, unconditional self-acceptance does not mean that individuals do not strive to change or improve their behavior when it is called for (e.g., maladaptive behaviors).

Ellis and other REBT theorists (Dryden, 2002, 2003; Ellis, 1987) suggest that self-downing also results from demandingness. When people do not get what they believe they must get, and they attribute this failure to themselves, they will tend to engage in global self-condemnation, rather than disapprove of a specific behavior. To date, researchers have failed to secure support for this contention. Factor analytic studies have found that self-downing beliefs and demands, awfulizing, and LFT load onto different factors (DiGiuseppe et al.,

1988; DiGiuseppe & Leaf, 1990), contrary to REBT theory. That is, acceptance beliefs are somehow independent of other irrational beliefs. One possibility is that conditional acceptance beliefs are especially easy to access. In our clinical practice we often find that clients who depress themselves are quick to identify that they are worthless or a failure, but less able to readily establish what demand they are failing to achieve. It may therefore be that previous studies have not employed methods with sufficient sophistication to examine how diverse irrational beliefs interrelate.

Before we turn to the relationship between self-downing and self-defeating behavior, let us mention again that self-downing is one of the irrational beliefs that exhibits the highest correlations with emotional disturbance and negative affect (DiGiuseppe, 1996; DiGiuseppe et al., 1988; Kassinove, 1986). Perhaps unsurprisingly, unconditional self-acceptance is positively correlated with happiness and life satisfaction, and negatively correlated with dysfunctional emotions such as depression and anxiety (Chamberlain & Haaga, 2001a). In fact, the hypothesis that unconditional self-acceptance is associated with emotional well-being has been one of the core assumptions of REBT for decades (Ellis, 1997; Chamberlain & Haaga, 2001a).

Our response to negative feedback can be considered a strong indicator of the presence or absence of unconditional self-acceptance, whether we behave competently or not, and whether we are accepted and approved by others. People who are not self-accepting tend to be easily threatened by criticism, as it generates evaluations of worthlessness (Ellis & Dryden, 1997), whereas self-acceptors, who rate their behavior and not themselves, are more likely to be nondefensive about negative feedback when their performance on a specific task is poor, and also more likely to use criticism as an opportunity to improve their performance (Ellis & Dryden, 1997). Chamberlain and Haaga (2001b) found that subjects who unconditionally accepted themselves were: *(1)* less prone to denigrate people who provided negative evaluations (e.g., depict the person that criticized them as unkind, unintelligent, or imperceptive); *(2)* more objective in evaluating their own performance on the task; and *(3)* significantly less defensive in receiving negative feedback.

Self-downing has also been associated with aggressive reactions. Beck (1999) postulates that people with anger problems tend to infer that others perceive them in keeping with how they truly see themselves. For example, if people hold a core belief such as "I am no good," they will infer that others also see them as "no good." Anger thus represents an attempt to refute this projection.

Empirical data shows that self-downing is related to both unhealthy anger suppression (Martin & Dahlen, 2004) and to violent anger expression. Jones and Trower (2004) found that the activation of self-downing beliefs was central in the experience of anger in a sample of clinically angry individuals (i.e., physically and verbally aggressive). The Jones and Trower (2004) study did not consider the role of hurt in relation to anger. It is quite natural for the wounded to attack, as if fighting for survival. In REBT, clients with anger problems also frequently present with hurt-related problems, and defend with anger against anticipated hurt when they perceive a looming threat or attack. Although REBT therapists have been aware of this relationship for many years, little empirical support has been established for the hypothesized link between hurt and anger.

Researchers who have investigated the relations between marital adjustment and core irrational beliefs have consistently found that self-downing is associated with relational/marital problems (e.g. Addis & Bernard, 2002; Möller & Van der Merve, 1997; Möller, Rabe, & Nortje, 2001). To take one example, in one of their studies on marital conflict, Möller and De Beer (1998) presented couples with several marital scenes with conflict present or absent, and found self-downing to be one of the core beliefs associated with conflict. Self-downing is also related to children's emotional and behavioral problems, and is associated with both internalized (i.e., controlled, depressive, fearful behavior) and externalized (i.e., aggressive, antisocial behavior) symptoms, as reported by both teachers and children (Silverman & DiGiuseppe, 2001).

Among the ideas that REBT (and Albert Ellis in particular) has promoted over the past decades is the importance of unconditional self-acceptance and the detrimental effects of self-downing for psychological health and well-being. As we have indicated, this claim is supported by research focusing on functional/dysfunctional emotions, and by studies exploring adaptive/maladaptive behavior (Table 6.1).

Other Behavioral Consequences of Irrational Beliefs

Our analysis has focused on research that examines the behavioral impact of the four irrational beliefs rather than on research evaluating (a) the behavioral outcomes of global irrationality/rationality or (b) studies using assessment methods that do not distinguish among the four types of irrational beliefs. However, several studies are also worth mentioning that have garnered evidence for detrimental effects of irrational beliefs on behavior beyond the irrational beliefs categorized by recent REBT theory.

One line of research has focused on behavioral performance on different motor tasks. These studies (Bonadies & Baas, 1984; Kombos, Fournet, & Estes, 1989; Schill, Monroe, Evans, & Ramanaiah, 1978) indicate that irrational beliefs are associated with underachievement in various perceptual-motor tasks (e.g., trail making, mirror tracing). However, other authors have found only partial or no support for this hypothesis (Rosin & Nelson, 1983). A similar detrimental impact of irrational thinking on performance has been observed in some intellectual performance tasks, especially verbal tasks (Prola, 1984, 1985). Interestingly, highly intelligent people seem to learn rational beliefs more easily than people with lower intelligence (Wilde, 1996a, 1996b).

Another line of research has found evidence for an association between irrational beliefs and procrastination (Beswick, Rothblum, & Mann, 1988; Bridges & Roig, 1997), with very few disconfirming results (e.g., Ferrari & Emmons, 1994). Finally, a relationship has been discerned between irrational beliefs and behavioral measures of social skills (Monti, Zwick, & Warzak, 1986). As we have seen, some of these results (e.g., procrastination, social skills) have been reconfirmed in studies using more specific measures of irrational beliefs.

In summary, the available evidence provides strong evidence in support of the role of irrational beliefs in a variety of self-defeating behaviors. Research has yet to examine their role specifically in regard to the potential link between emotional experience and consequent action tendencies. The problem of procrastination offers a straightforward research paradigm for future investigation. REBT holds that procrastination may be either driven by anxiety (i.e., anxious about performance and therefore procrastination) or anger (i.e., angry about having to perform and therefore procrastination). The direct comparison of the same behavior driven by two separate emotional pathways would suggest that manifestations of irrational beliefs may be tied to specific and diverse feelings.

The Maintenance of Maladaptive Behavior

Ellis (1987) argues that disturbed emotions and behaviors are very difficult to overcome, even by those who understand (e.g., as a result of therapy) how they actually disturb themselves, and what they should do to change their circumstances. Once people become disturbed, their problems tend to self-reinforce and grow stronger. Irrational beliefs lead to dysfunctional emotions, which, in turn, perpetuate and aggravate irrational thinking. Similarly, irrational beliefs lead to dysfunctional or maladaptive behaviors, which, in turn, reinforce and exacerbate irrational beliefs (Ellis, 1987). Thus, "vicious circles," often acknowledged in cognitive models of emotional disorders (e.g., anxiety, depression), play a role in perpetuating maladaptive cognitive-behavioral-emotional patterns.

Let us consider the example of an elevator phobia. REBT theory argues that phobic behavior (e.g., avoidance) is both cognitively and behaviorally reinforced (Ellis, 1962). Every time phobic individuals avoid entering an elevator, they rehearse and strengthen the belief that something awful that they cannot tolerate will happen if they do (e.g., the elevator would malfunction and they would be trapped). Moreover, as behavioral models of phobia have pointed out, every time they avoid the elevator, they also avoid experiencing anxiety, which negatively reinforces further avoidance.

It is also possible for self-defeating behaviors to be maintained because of secondary gains. The angry husband who strikes his wife might succeed in influencing her future behavior that provokes his anger, and thus feel vindicated in the moment. However, his wife's anger at his outburst may exacerbate relationship problems in the longer term. Accordingly, short-term gains serve to maintain otherwise self-defeating behaviors.

Ellis (1987) argues that this destructive process is similar to "almost any neurotic thought and action," and that if people do not get help, they progressively deepen their disturbance, and end up in a state of hopelessness in which they relinquish efforts to change or improve their circumstances. Dispirited individuals are less likely to seek professional help, and even when they do seek therapy, they do not invest, or invest insufficiently in learning and practicing new, more adaptive ways of thinking and acting. It is worth mentioning that in a study assessing the relationship between rationality/irrationality and marital adjustment, Addis and Bernard (2002) determined that rationality was one of the predictors of whether or not married individuals, confronted with various problems, were receiving marital counseling.

Behavioral Intervention Techniques in Rational-Emotive Behavior Therapy

REBT is often perceived as mainly focused on cognition (i.e., rational/irrational thinking) and on using cognitive techniques (e.g., Socratic questioning and disputation) to help people give up their irrational beliefs and reach a deep, philosophical change in their orientation to life (Ellis, 1999). Cognition also probably receives most attention in REBT textbooks and manuals. Whereas a focus on cognition is a vital part of REBT (Ellis, 1987), it is also true that a sole focus on cognition neglects the highly behavioral nature of REBT. The following quotations illustrate the accent REBT places on behavior change:

> "Rational emotive therapy is one of the relatively few techniques which include large amounts of actions, work and "homework" assignments of so called nonverbal nature." (Ellis, 1962, p. 334)
>
> "REBT insists on homework assignments, desensitizing and deconditioning actions both within and without the therapeutic sessions, and on other forms of active work on the part of the patient." (Ellis, 1962, p. 188)
>
> "Humans rarely change and keep believing a profound self-defeating belief unless they often act against it." (Ellis, 1975, p. 20)
>
> "REBT has always held that human disturbance stems from a combination of cognitive, emotional, behavioral, and biological "causes," thus: effective therapy needs to be heavily integrated and multimodal." (Ellis, 1997, p. 336)

A review of the literature regarding the practice of REBT reveals that among the behavioral techniques frequently employed by its practitioners are in vivo desensitization or exposure, behavioral risk-taking experiments, shame-attacking exercises, and reinforcement management techniques. These interventions are used both during the sessions as well as outside the therapeutic meetings, as behavioral homework assignments (Dryden, 2002; Ellis, 1999) designed to modify clients' irrational thinking patterns as well as their maladaptive operant behaviors (David, 2006b).

Conclusion

Rational-emotive behavior therapy is very specific about the fact that irrational beliefs lead not only to dysfunctional emotional consequences, but also to self-defeating behaviors that are integral to understanding the overall picture of human psychological health and disturbance. However, a review of the literature shows that, to date, behavioral patterns have received less empirical attention compared to the emotional consequences of irrational thinking.

In this chapter we have reviewed studies assessing the irrational beliefs–dysfunctional/maladaptive behavior relationship, and focused mainly on research that evaluates the four types of beliefs separately, rather than global irrationality. However, despite an obvious degree of specificity in the behavioral consequences of individual irrational beliefs, there is also an overlap in their effects (e.g., the aggressive expression of anger is related to high levels of low frustration tolerance, self-downing, and demandingness). We believe this is not surprising considering the hypothesized mutual interdependence among diverse irrational beliefs (i.e., awfulizing, low frustration tolerance, and self-downing are all derivatives of demandingness; Ellis, 1962, 1994).

Despite the significant advancements in the arenas of basic and applied research in REBT (David et al., 2005), many questions still remain to be asked and answered. Hopefully, our review will stimulate inquiry to clarify the relation between irrational beliefs and behavior that will lead to more effective ways of treating dysfunctional behavior.

REFERENCES

Achenbach, T. M., & Edelbrock, C. S. (1983). *Manual for the child behavior checklist and the revised child behavior profile.* Burlington, VT: University Associates in Psychiatry.

Addis, J., & Bernard, M. E. (2002). Marital adjustment and irrational beliefs. *Journal of Rational-Emotive & Cognitive-Behavior Therapy, 2(1),* 3–13.

Beck, A. T. (1999). *Prisoners of hate: The cognitive basis of anger, hostility, and violence.* New York: Guilford Press.

Bernard, M. E. (1998). Validation of the general attitude and belief scale. *Journal of Rational-Emotive & Cognitive-Behavior Therapy, 16(3),* 183–196.

Besser, A., Flett, G. L., & Hewit, P. L. (2004). Perfectionism, cognition, and affect in response to performance failure versus success. *Journal of Rational-Emotive & Cognitive-Behavior Therapy, 22(4),* 301–328.

Beswick, G., Rothblum, E., & Mann, L. (1988). Psychological antecedents of student procrastination. *Australian Psychologist, 23,* 207–217.

Bishop, F. M. (2001). *Managing addictions: Cognitive, emotive, and behavioral techniques.* New Jersey: Aronson.

Blatt, S. J. (1995). The destructiveness of perfectionism. *American Psychologist, 50(12),* 1003–1020.

Bridges, R., & Roig, M. (1997). Academic procrastination and irrational thinking: A re-examination with context controlled. *Personality and Individual Differences, 22,* 941–944.

Bonadies, G. A., & Bass, B. A. (1984). Effects of self-verbalizations upon emotional arousal and performance: A test of rational-emotive theory. *Perceptual and Motor Skills, 59(3),* 939–948.

Chamberlain, J. M., & Haaga, D. A. (2001a). Unconditional self-acceptance and psychological health. *Journal of Rational-Emotive & Cognitive-Behavior Therapy, 19(3),* 163–176.

Chamberlain, J. M., & Haaga, D. A. (2001b). Unconditional self-acceptance and response to negative feedback. *Journal of Rational-Emotive & Cognitive-Behavior Therapy, 19(3),* 177–189.

David, A., Ghinea, C., Macavei, B., & Kallay, E. (2005). A search for "hot cognitions" in clinical and non-clinical contexts: Appraisal, attributions, core irrational themes, and their relations to emotion. *Journal of Cognitive and Behavioral Psychotherapies, 5(1),* 1–43.

David, D. (2006a). *Psihologie clinică și psihoterapie: Fundamente* [Clinical psychology and psychotherapy: Fundamentals]. Iași: Polirom.

David, D. (2006b). *Tratat de psihoterapie cognitiv-comportamentală* [Treaty of cognitive-behavioral psychotherapy]. Iaşi: Polirom.

David, D. (2003). Rational emotive behavior therapy (REBT): The view of a cognitive psychologist. In W. Dryden (Ed.), *Rational Emotive Behaviour Therapy: Theoretical developments* (pp. 130–159). New York: Brunner Routledge.

David, D., Szentagotai, A., Kallay, E., & Macavei, B. (2005). A synopsis of rational-emotive behavior therapy (REBT): Fundamental and applied research. *Journal of Rational-Emotive & Cognitive-Behavior Therapy, 23(3)*, 175–221.

David, D., Schnur, J., & Belloiu, A. (2002). Another search for "hot" cognitions: Appraisal, irrational beliefs, attributions, and their relation to emotion. *Journal of Rational-Emotive & Cognitive Behavior Therapy, 20(2)*, 93–131.

DiGiuseppe, R. (1996). The nature of irrational and rational beliefs: Progress in rational emotive behavior theory. *Journal of Rational-Emotive & Cognitive-Behavior Therapy, 14(1)*, 5–28.

DiGiuseppe, R., & Leaf, R. C. (1990). The endorsement of irrational beliefs in a clinical population. *Journal of Rational-Emotive & Cognitive-Behavior Therapy, 26(2)*, 235–247.

DiGiuseppe, R., Leaf, R., Exner, T., & Robin, M. W. (1988). *The development of a measure of irrational/rational thinking.* Paper presented at the meeting of the World Congress of Behavior Therapy, Edinburgh, Scotland.

Dryden, W. (2002). *Fundamentals of rational emotive behaviour therapy.* London: Whurr Publishers Ltd.

Dryden, W. (2003). "The cream cake made me eat it": An introduction to the ABC theory of REBT. In W. Dryden (Ed.), *Rational emotive behaviour therapy: Theoretical developments* (pp 1–21). New York: Brunner Routledge.

Eisenberger, R. (1992). Learned industriousness. *Psychological Review, 99*, 248–267.

Ellis, A. (1962). *Reason and emotion in psychotherapy.* New York: Stuart.

Ellis, A. (1975). The rational-emotive approach to sex therapy. *Counseling Psychologist, 5(1)*, 14–22.

Ellis, A. (1977). *Anger: How to live with and without it.* Secaucus, NJ: Citadel Press.

Ellis, A. (1987). The impossibility of achieving consistently good mental health. *American Psychologist, 42(4)*, 364–375.

Ellis, A. (1991). The revised ABC's of rational emotive therapy. *Journal of Rational-Emotive & Cognitive-Behavior Therapy, 9(3)*, 139–172.

Ellis, A. (1994). *Reason and emotion in psychotherapy* (2nd ed.). Secaucus, NJ: Birscj Lane.

Ellis, A. (1997). Extending the goals of behavior therapy and cognitive behavior therapy. *Behavior Therapy, 28(3)*, 333–339.

Ellis, A. (1999). Why rational-emotive therapy to rational emotive behavior therapy. *Psychotherapy, 36*, 154–159.

Ellis, A. (2001). *Overcoming destructive beliefs, feelings, and behaviors: New directions for rational emotive behavior therapy.* New York: Prometheus Books.

Ellis, A. (2003a). Differentiating preferential from exaggerated and musturbatory beliefs in rational emotive behavior therapy. In W. Dryden (Ed.), *Rational emotive behaviour therapy: Theoretical developments* (pp. 22–34). New York: Brunner Routledge.

Ellis, A. (2003b). The nature of disturbed marital interaction. *Journal of Rational-Emotive & Cognitive-Behavior Therapy, 21(3/4)*, 147–153.

Ellis, A. (2003c). Discomfort anxiety: A new cognitive-behavioral construct (Part I). *Journal of Rational-Emotive & Cognitive-Behavior Therapy, 21(3/4)*, 183–191.

Ellis, A. (2003d). Discomfort anxiety: A new cognitive-behavioral construct (Part II). *Journal of Rational-Emotive & Cognitive-Behavior Therapy, 21 (3/4)*, 193–202.

Ellis, A., & Dryden, W. (1997). *The practice of rational emotive behavior therapy* (2nd ed). New York: Springer.

Ellis, A., & Knaus, W. J. (1977). *Overcoming procrastination*. New York: Institute for Rational Living.

Ellis, A., & Harper, R. A. (1961). *A guide to rational living*. Englewood Cliffs, NJ: Prentice Hall.

Ferrari, J., & Emmons, R. (1994). Procrastination as revenge: Do people report using delays as a strategy for vengeance? *Personality and Individual Differences, 17(4)*, 539–544.

Frost, R. O., & Marten, P. A. (1990). Perfectionism and evaluative threat. *Cognitive Therapy and Research, 14(6)*, 559–572.

Frost, R. O., Turcotte, T., Heimberg, R. G., & Mattia, J. I. (1995). Reactions to mistakes among students high and low in perfectionistic concern over mistakes. *Cognitive Therapy and Research, 19(2)*, 195–205.

Goldberg, G. M. (1990). Irrational beliefs and three interpersonal styles. *Psychological Reports, 66(3)*, 963–969.

Haring, M., Hewit, P. L., & Flett, G. L. (2003). Perfectionism, coping, and quality of intimate relationships. *Journal of Marriage and Family, 65(1)*, 143–158.

Harrington, N. (2005). Dimensions of frustration intolerance and their relationship to self-control problems. *Journal of Rational-Emotive & Cognitive-Behavior Therapy, 5(1)*, 1–20.

Hazaleus, S. L., & Deffenbacher, J. L. (1985). Irrational beliefs and anger arousal. *Journal of College Student Personnel, 26(1)*, 47–52.

Hewit, P. L., & Flett, G. L. (1991). Perfectionism in the self and social context: Conceptualization, assessment, and association with psychopathology. *Journal of Personality and Social Psychology, 60(3)*, 456–470.

Hogg, J. A., & Deffenbacher, J. L. (1986). Irrational beliefs, depression, and anger among college students. *Journal of College Student Personnel, 27(4)*, 349–353.

Hutchinson, G. T., Patock-Peckham, J. A., Cheong, J., & Nagoshi, C. T. (1998). Irrational beliefs and behavioral misregulation in the role of alcohol abuse among college students. *Journal of Rational-Emotive & Cognitive-Behavior Therapy, 16(1)*, 61–74.

Jones, J., & Trower, P. (2004). Irrational and evaluative beliefs in individuals with anger disorder. *Journal of Rational-Emotive & Cognitive-Behavior Therapy, 22(3)*, 153–169.

Kassinove, H. (1986). Self-reported affect and core irrational thinking: A preliminary analysis. *Journal of Rational-Emotive & Cognitive-Behavior Therapy, 4(2)*, 119–130.

Kombos, N. A., Fournet, G. P., & Estes, R. E. (1989). Effects of irrationality on a trail making performance task. *Perceptual and Motor Skills, 68(2)*, 591–598.

MacInnes, D. (2004). The theories underpinning rational emotive behaviour therapy. *International Journal of Nursing Studies, 41(6)*, 685–695.

Martin, R. C., & Dahlen, E. R. (2004). Irrational beliefs and the experience and expression of anger. *Journal of Rational-Emotive & Cognitive-Behavior Therapy, 22(1)*, 3–20.

Möller, A. T., & De Beer, Z. C. (1998). Irrational beliefs and marital conflict. *Psychological Reports, 82(1)*, 155–160.

Möller, A. T., Rabe, H. M., & Nortje, C. (2001). Dysfunctional beliefs and marital conflict in distressed and non-distressed married individuals. *Journal of Rational-Emotive & Cognitive-Behavior Therapy, 19(4)*, 259–270.

Möller, A. T., & Van der Merwe, J. D. (1997). Irrational beliefs, interpersonal perception, and marital adjustment. *Journal of Rational-Emotive & Cognitive-Behavior Therapy, 15(4)*, 269–279.

Monti, R., Zwick, W., & Warzak, W. (1986). Social skills and irrational beliefs: A preliminary report. *Journal of Behavior Therapy and Experimental Psychiatry, 17(1)*, 11–14.

Nicastro, R., Luskin, F., Raps, C., & Benisovich, S. (1999). The relationship of imperatives and self-efficacy to indices of social anxiety. *Journal of Rational-Emotive & Cognitive-Behavior Therapy, 17(4)*, 249–263.

Pearson, C. A., & Gleaves, D. H. (2006). The multiple dimensions of perfectionism and their relation with eating disorder features. *Personality and Individual Differences, 41(2)*, 225–235.

Power, M., & Dalgleish, T. (1997). *Cognition and emotion: From order to disorder*. East Sussex, UK: Hove, Psychology Press.

Prola, M. (1984). Irrational beliefs and reading comprehension. *Perceptual and Motor Skills, 59*, 777–778.

Prola, M. (1985). Irrational beliefs and intellectual performance. *Psychological Reports, 57*, 431–434.

Rosin, L., & Nelson, W. M. (1983). The effects of rational and irrational self-verbalizations on performance efficiency and levels of anxiety. *Journal of Clinical Psychology, 39(2)*, 208–213.

Schill, J., Monroe, S., Evans, R., & Ramanaiah, N. (1978). The effects of self-verbalization on performance: A test of the rational-emotive position. *Psychotherapy: Theory, Research, and Practice, 15(1)*, 2–7.

Sherry, S. B., Hewit, P. L., Besser, A., McGee, B. J., & Flett, G. L. (2003). Self-oriented and socially prescribed perfectionism in the Eating Disorder Inventory perfectionism subscale. *International Journal of Eating Disorders, 35(1)*, 69–79.

Silverman, S., & DiGiuseppe, R. (2001). Cognitive-behavioral constructs and children's behavioral and emotional problems. *Journal of Rational-Emotive & Cognitive-Behavior Therapy, 19(2)*, 119–134.

Spiegler, M. D., & Guevremont, D. C. (1993). *Contemporary Behavior Therapy*. Pacific Grove: Brooks/Cole Publishing Company.

Spielberger, C. D. (1999). *State-Trait Anger Expression Inventory-2: Professional manual*. Odessa, FL: Psychological Assessment Resources, Inc.

Watson, P. J., Sherbak, J., & Morris, R. J. (1998). Irrational beliefs, individualism–collectivism, and adjustment. *Journal of Personality and Individual Differences, 24(2)*, 173–179.

Wilde, J. (1996a). The efficacy of short-term rational-emotive education with fourth-grade students. *Elementary School Guidance and Counselling, 31(2)*, 131–138.

Wilde, J. (1996b). The relationship between rational thinking and intelligence in children. *Journal of Rational-Emotive & Cognitive-Behavior Therapy, 14(3)*, 187–192.

Zwemer, W. A., & Deffenbacher, J. L. (1984). Irrational beliefs, anger, and anxiety. *Journal of Counselling Psychology, 31(3)*, 391–393.

6

Rational and Irrational Beliefs in Human Feelings and Psychophysiology

Daniel David and Duncan Cramer

People can be analyzed with respect to at least four interrelated levels: *(1)* biological structure (i.e., anatomy and physiology), *(2)* behavioral output, *(3)* cognitive processes, and *(4)* subjective experience. Whereas physicians/biologists focus on the biological level, psychologists typically focus on the other three levels: *(1)* behaviors (e.g., observable and measurable operant reactions of the organism), *(2)* cognitions (e.g., information processing), and *(3)* subjective experience (e.g., feelings and emotions). Of course psychologists also study physiological reactions (e.g., unconditioned and conditioned responses) that are often defined as behaviors, and discussed in connection with either behaviors or feelings. In this chapter we will consider such physiological reactions in the course of our discussion of feelings.

Theories of Feelings: Fundamentals

Early theories of feelings focused mainly on the role of physiological factors such as arousal (Cannon, 1927; Ekman, 1992). Although early theories offered important insights into the mechanisms (e.g., physiological) involved in generating emotions, they did not cover the gamut of these mechanisms. More recent theories, however, have included cognition as a major component of affect (Schachter & Singer, 1962; Smith & Lazarus, 1993). Indeed, the relation between emotion and cognition is one of the central themes of modern psychological science. Because rational and irrational beliefs are a particular type of cognition, research relating rational and irrational beliefs to feelings can be considered part of *the cognitive approach to emotions.*

Several lines of research can be identified that fall within the cognitive approach. The first line of research (e.g., Schachter & Singer, 1962) explores the role of representational cognitions (e.g., how we represent the environment in our mind)—namely cold cognitions such as schemata, attributions, and automatic thoughts—in human feelings. The second line of research (e.g., Smith & Lazarus, 1993) explores the role of appraisal in human feelings. Cognitions associated with appraisal are not representational, but evaluate the personal significance of transactions in the environment and/or representational cognitions, as we will explain below. The third line of research (e.g., LeDoux, 2000) focuses on the role of unconscious information processing on human feelings.

David and his colleagues (see for details David, 2003) have proposed that it is possible to integrate these diverse research streams in terms of the distinction between "hot" and "cold" cognitions. Abelson and Rosenberg (1958) use the terms *hot* and *cold cognitions* to distinguish between appraising (hot) and knowing (cold). *Cold cognitions* refer to the way people develop representations (be they conscious and/or unconscious) of relevant circumstances (i.e., activating events), whereas hot cognitions refer to the way people process and evaluate (consciously and/or unconsciously) cold cognitions in terms of their relevance to personal well-being (for details, see David & McMahon, 2001; David, Schnur, & Belloiu, 2002; Ellis, 1994; Lazarus, 1991).

Consequently, during a specific activating event, there seem to be four different possibilities for how cold and hot cognitions regarding the activating event can be related (see for details David, 2003): *(1)* distorted representation of the event/negatively appraised, *(2)* nondistorted representation/negatively appraised, *(3)* distorted representation/nonnegatively appraised, and *(4)* nondistorted representation/nonnegatively appraised. Although past research has suggested that cold cognitions are strongly related to emotions (e.g., Schachter & Singer, 1962; Weiner, 1985), it is now generally accepted that as long as cold cognitions remain unevaluated, they are insufficient to produce emotions (Lazarus, 1991; Lazarus & Smith, 1988; Smith, Haynes, Lazarus, & Pope, 1993). Thus, according to Lazarus (1991) and to the appraisal theory of emotions, although cold cognitions contribute to appraisal, only appraisal itself results directly in emotions. Accordingly, the effect of cold cognitions (conceptualized as distal causes) on emotions seems to be influenced by hot cognitions (conceptualized as proximal causes). More precisely, the way we represent—by cold cognitions—activating events in our mind depends on the interaction between activating events and our rational and irrational beliefs. Cold cognitions may generate various operant behaviors, and then both cold cognitions and operant behaviors may be further appraised in a rational/ irrational manner, generating feelings and psychophysiological responses.

Ellis's cognitive theory of emotion (i.e., REBT theory of feelings) that centers on the role of rational and irrational beliefs in human feelings, falls within the appraisal paradigm in attempting to integrate cold cognitions with the cognitive unconscious. The REBT efforts at such integration will be elaborated in the following section.

REBT Theory of Feelings: Fundamentals (based on David, 2003; David et al., 2002)

According to REBT, people experience undesirable events (A) about which they have rational or irrational beliefs. Irrational beliefs are defined as evaluative beliefs that are not empirically supported, nonpragmatic, and/or illogical. Rational beliefs, on the other hand, are empirically supported, pragmatic, and/or logical. Rational beliefs promote functional (healthy/appropriate/ adaptive/rational) feelings, whereas irrational beliefs promote dysfunctional (unhealthy/inappropriate/maladaptive/irrational) feelings. We use the terms *functional/healthy* and *dysfunctional/unhealthy* feelings, to differentiate between cognitions (rational and irrational), behaviors (adaptive vs. maladaptive), and some physiological responses (healthy vs. unhealthy).

Ellis originally suggested basing the distinction between functional and dysfunctional feelings on their intensity (Ellis & Harper, 1961). Dysfunctional negative feelings (e.g., anger, depressed mood, anxiety, guilt) are more intense and related to irrational beliefs, whereas functional negative feelings (e.g., annoyance, sadness, concern, remorse) are generally less intense and related to rational beliefs. This perspective is consistent with the idea that emotional distress (negative affect) is a unitary construct, a hypothesis we refer to as the *unitary model of distress* (e.g., David, Montgomery, Macavei, & Bovbjerg, 2005). According to this model, distress levels range along a continuum from low to high, regardless of whether researchers measure specific negative affect (e.g., anxious, concerned) or general affect (e.g., distressed), obtained by summing the scores of specific negative affect items.

Specific labels describing different negative affects (e.g., anxious and concerned) are considered (see for details David et al., 2005): *(1)* to be synonyms for the same emotional experience (e.g., anxious and concerned are two different labels for the same emotional experience); *(2)* to refer to the same underlying construct (e.g., dysphoria), with labels (e.g., anxious vs. concerned) representing differences in intensity (e.g., moving from concerned to anxious); or *(3)* to be qualitatively different negative feelings, which can be functional or dysfunctional depending on their intensity (e.g., high anxiety and concern are dysfunctional whereas low anxiety and concern are functional).

In a revised version of the theory (Ellis & Harper, 1975), Ellis suggested that the distinction between functional and dysfunctional feelings is mainly qualitative. According to this perspective, the *binary model of distress*, functional negative feelings (e.g., concern) and dysfunctional negative feelings (e.g., anxiety) are qualitatively different. The functionality or dysfunctionality of feelings depends on their subjective experience (e.g., concern vs. anxious), associated cognitions (e.g., rational vs. irrational), and consequences (e.g., adaptive vs. maladaptive behaviors and/or healthy vs. unhealthy physiological responses). Defined in this way, dysfunctional negative feelings correspond to clinical problems, whereas functional negative feelings reflect normal reactions people might have during stressful events.

There are fundamental differences in the implications of these two cognitive theories. From a clinical point of view, trying to reduce all negative feelings as a whole might be inappropriate (according to the binary model). Is it adaptive to feel calm and relaxed during a stressful event? Indeed, reacting in a neutral or unemotional manner in the face of a stressor can reduce motivational resources necessary to confront or cope with the stressor (Anderson, 1994; Yerkes & Dodson, 1908). Should we then try to reduce negative feelings only to a point that preserves their motivational valences? We are not aware of such an approach in either research or clinical practice. For example, facing a difficult exam is seen by many as a stressful situation. However, experiencing a functional negative feeling (e.g., concern) can enhance performance in this context by stimulating learning. Being very calm or too anxious however, is typically associated with lower motivation to work hard to succeed at a difficult task (see also David et al., 2005).

From a methodological point of view, many professionals quantify distress (negative feelings) as a whole. For example, the Beck Depression Inventory (BDI) (Beck, Steer, & Brown, 1996) and the State-Trait Anxiety Inventory (STAI) (Spielberger, 1983; Spielberger, Gorusch, & Lushene, 1970) combine *depressed mood* and *sadness* scores (BDI) and *anxiety* and *concern* scores (STAI) to reveal the global level of *depressed mood* (BDI) and *anxiety* (STAI). However, this procedure is seriously flawed, if the binary model of distress is correct. We will analyze the current state of the science regarding these two cognitive theories of emotions, based on the REBT constructs of rational and irrational beliefs.

The Unitary Model of Distress—The Quantitative Theory

Cramer and various collaborators have initiated a rigorous research program to investigate the role of rational and irrational beliefs in human feelings. Their first set of studies used a correlational design, investigating the relations between irrational beliefs and functional and dysfunctional negative feelings, either under nonstressful circumstances or during imagined stressful situations. Cramer (1985) found that irrational beliefs were positively correlated with both functional and dysfunctional negative feelings. In a second set of experimental studies, Cramer and colleagues (e.g., Cramer, 2004, 2005; Cramer & Buckland, 1996; Cramer & Fong, 1991; Cramer & Kupshik, 1993) used rehearsal of irrational beliefs in imagined stressful situations to determine their impact on functional and dysfunctional negative feelings. Once again, they found that irrational beliefs are related to both functional and dysfunctional negative feelings.

Based on these findings, Cramer argued that the unitary model of distress is more strongly supported, in line with Ellis's original hypothesis (Ellis & Harper, 1961), and reinforced by Wessler (1996), who dismissed the binary model of distress based on logic and available empirical data. On logical grounds, Wessler noted that according to the binary model, one can feel both sad and depressed at the same time, and even mild feelings of anger and anxiety would be seen as dysfunctional feelings in REBT. Weber claimed that this conclusion was difficult to understand clinically. Wessler (1996) also pointed out that no major theory of emotions takes the binary model of distress seriously, and suggested that REBT should renounce it as well. On empirical grounds, Wessler (1996) pointed to data inconsistent with the binary model of distress. For example, he pointed out that Kassinove, Eckhardt, and Endes (1993) found that people are able to identify variations in emotional intensity, but not variations in emotional quality, a serious challenge, in his view, to the binary model of distress.

Binary Model of Distress—The Qualitative Theory

However, the unitary model has not gone unchallenged. From a theoretical point of view, a positive correlation between irrational beliefs and both functional and dysfunctional negative feelings is not an invalidation of the binary model of distress. Because dysfunctional feelings involve functional feelings (e.g., if one is depressed he/she is also sad), a correlation between irrational beliefs and both sadness and depressed mood is not unexpected. According to REBT theory, rational beliefs should be positively associated with functional negative feelings (e.g., sadness), whereas irrational beliefs may or may not be associated with functional negative feelings (see David et al., 2002, for details). Also, according to the appraisal theory (Lazarus, 1991), the coexistence of negative and positive feelings and/or of various negative feelings (be they functional or dysfunctional) makes perfect sense (see also David et al., 2002). That is, considering that multiple goals may be present during specific activating events, a diversity of feelings also makes sense. For example, not passing an exam may be related to anxiety, depressed mood, and anger. The goal of "proving your value by passing the exam" may be associated with anger and depressed mood, if you did not pass the exam. However, the goal of "passing the exam in order to avoid being criticized by your father" may be associated with anxiety, but not necessarily depression, in the case of failure.

From a methodological point of view, most previous studies have used imagined rather than real stressful events, a major shortcoming, as Ellis (1994) has always underscored the idea that irrational beliefs may be activated during real stressful events but not imagined situations. Recently, David and his collaborators have initiated a line of research to investigate the binary model, with an updated methodology. They first elaborated a nuanced binary model (see David, 2003; David et al., 2002; David et al., 2005), relating rational and irrational beliefs to specific feelings, following the appraisal framework of Smith and Lazarus (1993) (see Table 5.1, based on David, 2003; David et al., 2002).

Second, they attempted to validate this model (see Table 6.1) by using multiple paradigms for investigating the emotion-cognition relation. Using the appraisal paradigm, David et al. (2002) found that high levels of irrational beliefs generate dysfunctional feelings (e.g., depressed mood, anxiety), whereas low levels of irrational beliefs (interpreted as rational beliefs) generate functional feelings (e.g., sadness, concern), according to the model presented in Table 6.1. This study was criticized for its reliance on undergraduate psychology students, who might have been aware of the theory under investigation; indeed, correlations between irrational beliefs and dysfunctional feelings were quite high. Consequently, David, David, Ghinea, Macavei, and Kallay (2005) replicated these results (correlations were significant but smaller than in the first study) in a sample that was not "contaminated" by psychological knowledge (physics undergraduates), and extended the findings to a clinical sample (i.e., psychotherapy patients), thus providing support for the robustness and generalizability of the data.

TABLE 6.1. Relations between Rational and Irrational Beliefs and Human Feelings

Appraisal Theory (Smith et al., 1993)			REBT Theory in the Terms of Appraisal Theory; A hypothesized model		
Emotion	Core relational theme	Appraisal components	Emotion: Dysfunctional and Functional	Core relational theme	Important appraisal components
Anger	Other-blame	Motivationally relevant; Motivationally incongruent; Other accountability (e.g., the others, life conditions)	Anger	Other-blame	Motivationally relevant; Motivationally incongruent with DEM; Other-accountability (i.e., the others, life conditions)
			Annoyance		Motivationally relevant; Motivationally incongruent with preferences; Other-accountability (i.e., the others, life conditions)
Guilt	Self-blame	Motivationally relevant; Motivationally incongruent; Self-accountability (e.g., myself)	Guilt	Self-blame	Motivationally relevant; Motivationally incongruent with DEM; Self-accountability (i.e., myself)
			Remorse		Motivationally relevant; Motivationally incongruent with preferences; Self-accountability (i.e., myself)
Fear-Anxiety	Danger-threat	Motivationally relevant; Motivationally incongruent; Low or uncertain emotion-focused potential	Fear-Anxiety	Danger-threat	Motivationally relevant; Motivationally incongruent with DEM; Low or uncertain emotion-focused potential (i.e., AWF, LFT)
			Concern		Motivationally relevant; Motivationally incongruent with preferences; High emotion-focused potential (i.e., non-AWF; non-LFT)
Sadness	Irrevocable loss; Helplessness about harm or loss	Motivationally relevant; Motivationally incongruent; Low problem focused potential; Negative future expectations	Depression	Irrevocable loss; Helplessness about harm or loss	Motivationally relevant; Motivationally incongruent with DEM; Low problem-focused coping potential (i.e., SD); Negative future expectations
			Sadness		Motivationally relevant; Motivationally incongruent with preferences; Low problem-focused coping potential (i.e., non-SD)

David, Schnur, and Birk (2004) evaluated the robustness of the binary model by investigating it in another cognitive paradigm, the bifactorial model of emotions. According to the bifactorial model, emotional experience is the result of the cognitive interpretation of physiological arousal (see Schachter & Singer, 1962). The researchers found that arousal levels did not differentiate between functional and dysfunctional feelings, as would be expected on the basis of the unitary model. Finally, this research group investigated the binary model using a third paradigm called the factorial paradigm. Ellis and DiGiuseppe (1993) argued that a principal component analysis was necessary to rigorously test the binary model of distress. If the binary model of distress best fits the data, two principal components should emerge. The first principal component should demonstrate that high levels of irrational beliefs are associated with both functional and dysfunctional feelings, whereas the second principal component should demonstrate that high levels of rational beliefs are positively associated with functional negative feelings and negatively associated with dysfunctional negative feelings. David et al., (2005) confirmed this pattern in clinical samples (Romania and United States), offering further support for the binary model of distress.

Other research also supports the binary model, beyond the data secured by the David research group. For example, Zisook et al. (1994) found that depression, but not grief (sadness), is associated with suppression of the immune system. Spörrle and Försterling (2007) found that commonsense (naïve) theories of emotions are consistent with Ellis's ABC(DE) model (see Chapter 1, More specifically, whereas rational beliefs are associated with functional feelings and adaptive behaviors, irrational beliefs are associated with dysfunctional feelings and maladaptive behaviors. Harris, Davies, and Dryden (2006) experimentally demonstrated that whereas rational beliefs are associated with concern, irrational beliefs are associated with anxiety.

However, there are several limitations to this line of research related to the binary model of distress. The most important limitation refers to the fact that researchers operationalized rational beliefs as low scores on irrational beliefs (see Chapter 7, this volume for a discussion of this issue). Moreover,as noted earlier, some studies used mostly imagined and rehearsed activating events and beliefs rather than real ones (see Ellis, 1994).

Physiological Reactions and Rational and Irrational Beliefs

As we mentioned in the introduction, the relationship between rationality of beliefs and emotionality has been mainly studied in relation to verbal reports of feelings. At present, there are few empirical studies specifically focused on physiological responses.

According to REBT, rational beliefs should be accompanied by biological indicators of health, whereas irrational beliefs should be accompanied by unhealthy biological indicators of maladaptive or disease-related physiological responding. Indeed, Papageorgiou et al. (2006) found that irrational beliefs were positively associated with C-reactive protein, interleukin-6, tumor necrosis factor-alpha, and white blood cells; these results remained significant after controlling for age, sex, years of school, body mass index, physical activity status, depression level, and food items. The results suggest that irrational beliefs are associated with indicators of increased inflammation, among apparently healthy people. Therefore, future studies should focus on the psychophysiological concomitants of beliefs, using a variety of measures of rational and irrational beliefs, and biological indicators of health and disease. To understand the role of rational and irrational beliefs on physical health see Chapter 12 of this volume.

Conclusion

Empirical research regarding the unitary and the binary model of distress has resorted to imagined, verbally rehearsed, or recalled stressful events. To date, only one study has investigated Ellis's cognitive theory of emotions using real stressful events. Thus, although the conclusions tend to support the binary model of distress, the binary and unitary models continue to vie for definitive empirical support.

We suggest that research relating rational and irrational beliefs to human feelings should: (a) investigate the role of unconscious information processing (e.g., implicit memories); (b) correlate rational and irrational beliefs with other cognitive constructs relevant to feelings (e.g., response expectancies); and (c) be connected to influential contemporary conceptualizations of affect, namely the bipolar framework (assuming that positive and negative feelings are bipolar; Russell & Carroll, 1999) and the independence framework (assuming that positive and negative feelings are independent; Watson & Tellegen, 1999).

Recently, theorists have enriched the ABC(DE) model by including the concept of unconscious information processing (David, 2003). Sometimes beliefs are not consciously accessible, but are nevertheless represented in the implicit rather than the explicit memory system (David, 2003; Tobias et al., 1992). We will describe four ways in which the ABC(DE) model and the cognitive unconscious construct are linked (for details, see David, 2003). First, unconscious information processing is subserved by subcortical processes. These subcortical processes preserve the cognitive (computational) component of emotions and connect the theory of emotions to the concept of the cognitive unconscious, widely investigated in current cognitive psychology (David, 2000; LeDoux, 2000). Second, subcortical and automatic processes can be countered by activating higher (conscious) order modes of thinking (Beck & Clark, 1997; Ellis, 1994), and their effects can be controlled by conscious strategies. Third, REBT does not assume that verbal mediation is the only modality of emotional control. Some very successful exposure methods work specifically on unconscious information processing involved in emotion formation (Ellis, 1962, 1994). Fourth, an emotion generated by subcortical mechanisms may become a stimulus, which in turn may be consciously appraised, generating a secondary emotional problem (Ellis, 1962, 1994). For example, anxiety generated by unconscious information processing (e.g., implicit expectancies involved in classical conditioning) can be further appraised by irrational beliefs (e.g., "being anxious makes me a weak person"), and a meta-emotion (secondary emotion) can be generated (i.e., depressed mood).

Rational and irrational beliefs are only one of the cognitive mechanisms involved in emotions. Therefore, it is essential to incorporate the impact of other cognitive mechanisms on feelings in a more general model. For example, Montgomery et al. (2007) found that the impact of irrational beliefs (both general and exam-related irrational beliefs) on distress (exam-related distress) is partially mediated by response expectancies about exam-related distress (Kirsch, 1999), However, the construct of response expectancy (i.e., expectancies for nonvolitional responses such as anxiety) has not yet been included in the REBT model. Thus, future studies should include rational and irrational beliefs in a more comprehensive cognitive model of emotions (see Chapter 10, this volume for such an attempt).

We have suggested several ways in which REBT theory could be integrated into the broader arena of affect research (David et al., 2005). Dysfunctional negative feelings generated by irrational beliefs during stressful situations seem to correspond to: *(a)* negative affect/high arousal (e.g., rage), *(b)* negative affect/low arousal (e.g., depressed mood) in a bipolar framework of research (Russell & Carroll, 1999), or *(c)* high negative affect (e.g., rage) and low positive affect (e.g., depressed) in the independence framework (Watson & Tellegen, 1999). Functional negative feelings generated by rational beliefs in stressful situations may correspond to negative affect/medium arousal in the bipolar framework of affect (Russell & Carroll, 1999) or unpleasantness in the independence framework of affect (Watson & Tellegen, 1999). These distinctions can help guide future studies of the relation between the REBT theory of emotion and more general models of affect and information processing.

Finally, another important research topic concerns the distinction between functional and dysfunctional positive feelings, and how they relate to rational and irrational beliefs. Ellis proposed a model (Ellis, 1994; Ellis & Harper, 1961) in which he claimed that rational beliefs are related to functional positive feelings, whereas irrational beliefs are related to dysfunctional positive feelings. However, the model lacks specificity and empirical support.

We are aware of only one empirical study that evaluates and is consistent with Ellis's claims (Tiba & Szentagotai, 2005). More specifically, the authors determined that rational (flexible) beliefs are related to positive functional feelings (e.g., healthy happiness resulting from passing an exam that students think they would very much like to pass), whereas irrational beliefs are related to positive dysfunctional feelings (e.g., unhealthy happiness resulting from passing an exam that students think they must absolutely pass). The functionality and/or dysfunctionality of positive feelings were measured in terms of subjective experiences and behavioral tendencies (for details see Tiba & Szentagotai, 2005). It is, however, premature to draw conclusions based on this study alone. Future research should examine this topic because the theoretical (e.g., see the positive psychology movement focusing on enhancing positive affect and traits; Seligman & Csikszentmihalyi, 2000) and practical (e.g., what feelings to enhance in therapy) implications are important. Indeed, as we have stressed here, not all negative feelings are dysfunctional, and probably not all positive feelings are functional. Thus, a good therapist will focus on enhancing functional feelings, be they positive and/or negative.

REFERENCES

Abelson, R. P., & Rosenberg, M. J. (1958). Symbolic psycho-logic: A model of attitudinal cognition. *Behavioral Science, 3*, 1–13.

Anderson, K. J. (1994). Impulsivity, caffeine, and task difficulty: A within-subjects test of the Yerkes-Dodson law. *Personality and Individual Differences, 6*, 813–829.

Beck, A. T., & Clark, D. A. (1997). An information processing model of anxiety: Automatic and strategic processes. *Behavior Research and Therapy, 35*, 49–58.

Beck, A. T., Steer, R. A., & Brown, G. K. (1996). *Manual for Beck Depression Inventory II (BDI-II)*. San Antonio, TX: Psychology Corporation.

Beck, A. T., Ward, C. H., Mendelson, M., Mock, J., & Erbaugh, J. (1961). An inventory for measuring depression. *Archives of General Psychiatry 4*, 561–571.

Cannon, W. B. (1927). The James-Lange theory of emotions: A critical examination and an alternative theory. *American Journal of Psychology, 39*, 106–124.

Cramer, D. (1985). Irrational beliefs and strength versus inappropriateness of feelings. *British Journal of Cognitive Psychotherapy, 3,* 81–92.

Cramer, D. (2004). Effect of the destructive disagreement belief on relationship satisfaction with a romantic partner or closest friend. *Psychology and Psychotherapy, 77,* 121–133.

Cramer, D. (2005). Effect of four aspects of rational statements on expected satisfaction with a close relationship. *British Journal of Guidance & Counselling, 33,* 227–238.

Cramer, D., & Buckland, N. (1996). Effect of rational and irrational statements and demand characteristics on task anxiety. *The Journal of Psychology, 129,* 269–275.

Cramer, D., & Fong, J. (1991). Effect of rational and irrational beliefs on intensity and "inappropriateness" of feelings: A test of rational-emotive theory. *Cognitive Therapy and Research, 4,* 319–329.

Cramer, D., & Kupshik, G. (1993). Effect of rational and irrational statements on intensity and "inappropriateness" of emotional distress and irrational beliefs in psychotherapy patients. *British Journal of Clinical Psychology, 32,* 319–325.

David, D. (2000). Implicit memory: Remarks after a deccenium of disputes. *Erdely Pszichologiai Szemle, 2,* 49–64.

David, D. (2003). Rational emotive behavior therapy; The view of a cognitive psychologist. In W. Dryden (Ed.), *Theoretical developments in REBT.* London: Brunner/Routledge.

David, D., David, A., Ghinea, C., Macavei, B., & Kallay, E. (2005). A search for "hot" cognitions in a clinical and non-clinical context: Appraisal, attributions, core relational themes, irrational beliefs, and their relations to emotion. *Journal of Cognitive and Behavioral Psychotherapies, 5,* 1–42.

David, D., & McMahon, J. (2001). Clinical strategies in cognitive behavioral therapy: A case analysis. *Romanian Journal of Cognitive and Behavioral Psychotherapy, 1,* 71–86.

David, D., Schnur, J., & Belloiu, A. (2002). Another search for the "hot" cognition: Appraisal irrational beliefs, attribution, and their relation to emotion. *Journal of Rational-Emotive and Cognitive-Behavior Therapy, 20,* 93–131.

David, D., Schnur, J., & Birk, J. (2004). Functional and dysfunctional emotions in Ellis' cognitive theory: An empirical analysis. *Cognition and Emotion, 18,* 869–880.

David, D., Montgomery, G. H., Macavei, B., & Bovbjerg, D. (2005). An empirical investigation of Albert Ellis' binary model of distress. *Journal of Clinical Psychology, 61,* 499–516.

Ekman, P. (1992). An argument for basic emotions. *Cognition and Emotion, 6,* 169–200.

Ellis, A. (1962). *Reason and emotion in psychotherapy.* New York: Lyle Stuart.

Ellis, A. (1994). *Reason and emotion in psychotherapy* (Rev. ed.). Secaucus, NJ: Birch Lane.

Ellis, A., & DiGiuseppe, R. (1993). Are inappropriate or dysfunctional feelings in rational-emotive therapy qualitative or quantitative? *Cognitive Therapy and Research, 17,* 471–477.

Ellis, A., & Harper, R. A. (1961). *A guide to rational living.* Englewood Cliffs, NJ: Prentice-Hall.

Ellis, A. & Harper, R. A. (1975). *A new guide to rational living.* North Hollywood, CA: Wilshire Book Company.

Harris, S., Davies, M. F., & Dryden, W. (2006). An experimental test of a core REBT hypothesis: Evidence that irrational beliefs lead to physiological as well as psychological arousal. *Journal of Rational-Emotive & Cognitive-Behavior Therapy, 24*, 101–111.

Kassinove, H., Eckhardt, C. I., & Endes, R. (1993). Assessing the intensity of "appropriate" and "inappropriate" emotions in rational-emotive therapy. *Journal of Cognitive Psychotherapy: An International Quarterly, 7*, 227–238.

Kirsch, I. (Ed.). (1999). *How expectancies shape experience.* Washington, DC: American Psychological Association.

Lazarus, R. S. (1991). *Emotion and adaptation.* New York: Oxford University Press.

Lazarus, R. S., & Smith, C. A. (1988). Knowledge and appraisal in the cognition-emotion relationship. *Cognition and Emotion, 2*, 281–300.

LeDoux J. E. (2000). Emotion circuits in the brain. *Annual Review of Neuroscience, 23*, 155–184.

Montgomery, G. H., David, D., DiLorenzo, T. A., & Schnur, J. B. (2007). Response expectancies and irrational beliefs predict exam-related distress. *Journal of Rational-Emotive & Cognitive Behavior Therapy, 25*, 17–34.

Opriş, D., & Macavei, B. (2005). The distinction between functional and dysfunctional negative emotions: An empirical analysis. *Journal of Cognitive and Bahavioral Psychotherapies, 5*, 181–195.

Papageorgiou, C., Panagiotakos, D. B., Pitsavos, C., Tsetsekou, E., Kontoangelos, K., Stefanadis, C., & Soldatos, C. (2006). Association between plasma inflammatory markers and irrational beliefs: The ATTICA epidemiological study. *Progress in Neuro-Psychopharmacology and Biological Psychiatry, 30*, 1496–1503.

Russell, J. A., & Carroll, J. M. (1999). On the bipolarity of positive and negative affect. *Psychological Bulletin, 1*, 30–30.

Schachter, S., & Singer, J. E. (1962). Cognitive, social, and physiological determinants of emotional state. *Psychological Review, 69*, 379–399.

Seligman, M. E. P., & Csikszentmihalyi, M. (2000). Positive psychology. *American Psychologist, 55*, 5–15.

Smith, C. A., & Lazarus, R. (1993). Appraisal components, core relational theme, and the emotions. *Cognition and Emotion, 7*, 233–269.

Smith, C. A., Haynes, K. N., Lazarus, R. S., & Pope, L. K. (1993). In search of the "hot" cognitions: Attributions, appraisals, and their relation to emotion. *Journal of Personality and Social Psychology, 65*, 916–929.

Spielberger, C. D. (1983). *State-trait anxiety inventory (Form Y).* Palo Alto, CA: Consulting Psychologists Press.

Spielberger, C. D., Gorusch, R. L., & Lushene, R. E. (1970). *Manual for the state-trait anxiety inventory.* Palo Alto, CA: Consulting Psychologists Press.

Spörrle, M., & Försterling, F. (2007). Which thoughts can kill a boxer? Naïve theories about cognitive and emotional antecedents of suicide. *Psychology and Psychotherapy, 80*, 497–512.

Tiba, A., & Szentagotai, A. (2005). Positive emotions and irrational beliefs: Dysfunctional positive emotions in healthy individuals. *Journal of Cognitive and Behavioral Psychotherapies, 1*, 53–72.

Tobias, B. A., Kihlstrom, J. F., & Schacter, D. L. (1992). Emotion and implicit memory. In S.-A. Christianson (Ed.), *Handbook of emotion and memory* (pp. 67–92). Hillsdale, NJ: Erlbaum.

Watson, D., & Tellegen, A. (1999). Issues in the dimensional structure of affect: Effects of descriptors, measurement error, and response formats: Comment on Russell and Carroll (1999). *Psychological Bulletin, 125,* 601–610.

Weiner, B. (1985). An attributional theory of achievement motivation and emotion. *Psychological Review, 92,* 548–573.

Wessler, R. L. (1996). Idiosyncratic definitions and unsupported hypotheses: Rational-emotive behavior therapy as pseudoscience. *Journal of Rational-Emotive & Cognitive-Behavior Therapy, 14,* 41–61.

Yerkes, R. M., & Dodson, J. D. (1908). The relation of strength of stimulus to rapidity of habit-formation. *Journal of Comparative Neurology and Psychology, 18,* 459–482.

Zisook, S., Shuchter, S. R., Irwin, M., Darko, D. F., Sledge, P., & Resovsky, K. (1994). Bereavement, depression, and immune function. *Psychiatry Research, 52,* 1–10.

PART III

Clinical Applications

7

The Assessment of Rational and Irrational Beliefs

Bianca Macavei and James McMahon

Everything should be made as simple as possible, but not simpler.

—Albert Einstein

The B in the ABC: Comments on Rational and Irrational Beliefs

The central tenet of the REBT theory, originally developed by Albert Ellis in the 1950s, is that irrational and rational beliefs are associated with dysfunctional and functional emotions. As far back as the 1980s, the scientific community identified important issues regarding the assessment of irrational beliefs (IBs) (Smith, 1982). First, there was confusion regarding the *structure of IBs*: some practitioners believed they were more like transient thoughts, whereas others claimed that irrational beliefs were enduring cognitive structures (Smith, 1982). Second, it was not clear whether irrational beliefs had a specific (e.g., "My husband MUST love me") or a more general (e.g., "Wifes MUST be loved by their husbands") content (Smith, 1982).

Psychological instruments designed to assess irrational beliefs also received severe criticism because they were based exclusively on self-reports, and because the items reflected a mixture of cognitive, emotional, and behavioral elements, which led to low discriminant validity (Smith, 1982). The *theory* behind the first efforts to assess irrational beliefs was also problematic, insofar as many instruments were based on Albert Ellis's early theory that described ten or eleven specific irrational beliefs, instead of the more encompassing four IBs outlined in later revisions of the theory (David, Szentagotai, Kallay, & Macavei, 2005).

Another problem was related to the *exclusive focus on IBs*. That is, disputing irrational beliefs is generally not considered sufficient to reduce emotional distress, absent changes in more adaptive thinking (i.e., rational beliefs or RBs). Moreover, researchers have shown that IBs and RBs are not polar opposites: more rational beliefs do not necessarily signify fewer irrational beliefs (DiGiuseppe, Robin, Leaf, & Gormon, 1989; Bernard, 1998). Accordingly, it is necessary to measure both irrational and rational beliefs, either with different instruments, or with different items in the same instrument (i.e., separate scores for IBs and RBs). Additionally, cognitive psychologists have increasingly emphasized the need to disambiguate cognitive *processes* from the *content* of thoughts (David et al., 2005). Taking these considerations into account, the new generation of IBs/RBs assessment instruments share the following characteristics: *(1)* they contain noncontaminated items (i.e., items that assess only cognition), *(2)* they include separate scores for IBs and RBs, and *(3)* they possess the ability to separate the process from the content of thought (Lindner, Kirkby, Wertheim, & Birch, 1999).

In this chapter, we will discuss a variety of conceptual and methodological issues regarding the assessment of rational and irrational beliefs. We will review two major ways of identifying and assessing IBs/RBs: *(1)* psychological instruments and *(2)* therapy oriented assessment, and discuss state of the science developments in assessment including approaches based on virtual reality.

Finding the B: Ways of Identifying Rational and Irrational Beliefs

The assessment of IBs/RBs can have a significant impact on both clinical practice and research. IBs and RBs are often assessed with *psychological instruments* (i.e., tests and questionnaires) that are rigorous, well standardized, and cost- and time-effective, and evaluate an array of cognitive mechanisms of emotional distress and maladaptive behavior.

Therapists can also identify specific beliefs on a more informal, client-centered basis, and share their knowledge in an educative manner with patients in the early stages of cognitive-behavior therapy (CBT). This method, albeit nonstandardized, permits a thorough and personalized assessment of cognitions (Ellis & Dryden, 1997) based on an idiographic rather than a nomothetic approach, and may avoid defensiveness, anxiety, and discomfort associated with more formal standardized testing.

Identifying maladaptive cognitions associated with dysfunctional emotions and behaviors is fundamental to relieving symptoms. Accordingly, when therapists periodically assess IBs/RBs, they have an opportunity to: *(a)* develop a common language for gauging the progress of therapy on an ongoing basis, and *(b)* strengthen the therapeutic alliance via collaboration. Relatedly, assessment also provides a way to investigate the efficacy and effectiveness of interventions in general, and specific strategies in particular (e.g., how restructuring IBs affects dysfunctional emotions and behaviors). In research, the accurate assessment of evaluative beliefs is vital for validating the REBT model and theory of change (e.g., how cognition relates to behavior and emotion).

Psychological Instruments

By 1981, more than fifteen different scales designed to assess irrational beliefs had been reported in the literature (Sutton-Simon, 1981). Since that time, test developers have created more sophisticated and reliable scales that benefited from understanding the limitations of previous scales. The most commonly used early instruments were the Irrational Beliefs Test—IBT (Jones, 1968), and the Rational Behavior Inventory—RBI (Shorkey & Whiteman, 1977) (McDermut, Haaga, & Bilek, 1997). Similar to another measure of irrationality—the Idea Inventory II (Kassinove, Crisci, & Tiegerman, 1977), the IBT and RBI were based on the list of 11 irrational beliefs described by Ellis in 1962. The structure of IBs-assessment instruments was initially simple and straightforward, with each of the 11 IBs assessed by a single item, but their complexity or breadth gradually increased (i.e., more items to assess the same IB). Although conceptually outdated, as they were based on Ellis's early theory (Dryden & Ellis, 1988; Ellis, 1984) and lacking in discriminant validity (Zurawski & Smith, 1987), these measures were used into the 1990s (Bridges & Sanderman, 2002). Later, Malouff and Schutte (1986) attempted to respond to criticisms concerning early IBs measures, and developed the Irrational Belief Scale—IBS. Whereas the theoretical basis of the instrument was the same as earlier ones, the IBS separated cognition-related from affect-related items. Discriminant validity was thus increased, and the likelihood of having two measures of the same variable was reduced (Smith, 1989).

Paralleling the development of scales for adults, test developers created instruments specifically designed to measure IBs/RBs in children and adolescents. The Children's Survey of Rational Beliefs—Forms B and C (Knaus, 1974) focused on rationality only, and was designed for children aged 7 to 10 (form B, 18 items), and 10 to 13 (form C, 38 items). These instruments also mixed cognition, affect, and behavior, providing a global score of rationality. In response to changes in the REBT theory, Bernard and Laws (1988) developed the Child and Adolescent Scale of Irrationality, which was later updated and improved by Bernard and Cronan, (1999). This new measure addressed the four types of irrational beliefs described in the updated REBT theory. The test separated cognitive processes from the content of thoughts, covering a variety of different contents (e.g., comfort, achievement, control, and autonomy), a feature specific to second-generation instruments measuring IBs and RBs.

At present, the most valid, up-to-date, and widely used self-report instruments for measuring irrational and rational beliefs in adults are:

- The Attitude and Belief Scale 2/ General Attitude and Belief Scale (ABS 2/GABS—Burgess, 1986; DiGiuseppe, Leaf, Exner, & Robin, 1988);
- The Shortened General Attitude and Belief Scale (SGABS—Lindner, Kirkby, Wertheim, & Birch, 1999);
- The Survey of Personal Beliefs (SPB—Kassinove, 1986);
- The Common Beliefs Survey-III (CBS-III—Bassai, 1976; Bassai, 1977; Tosi, Forman, Rudy, & Murphy, 1986);
- The Irrational Beliefs Inventory (IBI—Koopmans, Sanderman, Timmerman, & Emmelkamp, 1994);
- The Evaluative Beliefs Scale (EBS—Chadwick, Trower, & Dagnan, 1999).

COMMENTS ON THE ATTITUDE AND BELIEF SCALE 2/GENERAL ATTITUDE AND BELIEF SCALE (ABS 2/GABS). An important distinction in the assessment of IBs/RBs is between the *process* and the *content* of a particular belief (David, 2003). Regardless of the specific content they encompass, irrational processes or modes of thinking such as demandingness, awfulizing, low frustration tolerance, and global evaluation lead to dysfunctional consequences. These processes can reflect specific contents or beliefs (e.g., "My family must respect me"), or very general contents or beliefs (e.g., "Everybody must respect me"). Additionally, DiGiuseppe et al. (1989) point out three main domains that irrational beliefs cover: affiliation, achievement, and comfort. Rationally and irrationally phrased items can be created to refer to different contents associated with irrational/rational processes. Developing instruments that target specific irrational/rational processes about particular contents is important for the accurate assessment of evaluative beliefs.

In 1986, Burgess developed the General Attitude and Belief Scale (GABS) as a measure of irrationality. The scale consisted of ninety-six items assessing cognition (i.e., irrational beliefs). Although it did not separate the process from the content of thought, it had good discriminant validity, differentiating depressed, agoraphobic, and anxious clients (DiGiuseppe & Leaf, 1990; DiGiuseppe et al., 1988; Shaw, 1989). DiGiuseppe et al. (1988) improved the instrument by *(1)* reducing it to 76 items (4 items for practice that are not scored and 72 scored items), and *(2)* structuring items so that the process and the content would be separated. The resulting instrument was named the Attitudes and Belief Scale 2 (ABS 2). The ABS 2 is a 72-item scale that measures IBs/RBs in adults. It can be described in terms of a 4x3x2 matrix, with three items in each of the twenty-four cells. The first factor is named Cognitive Process, and it has four levels representing demandingness (DEM), global evaluation or self-downing (SD), low frustration tolerance (LFT), and awfulizing (AWF). The second factor is represented by Content/Context information and has three levels referring to beliefs about affiliation, achievement, and comfort. The third factor has two levels and refers to the way items are worded—rationally or irrationally. The scale allows for the discrete and valid evaluation of the four beliefs central to REBT: demandingness, self-downing, low frustration tolerance, and awfulizing. The measure possesses high internal consistency and discriminant validity (e.g., DiGiuseppe et al., 1989, for American population; Macavei, 2002, for Romanian population).

David (2007a) developed a shortened, 8-item version of the ABS 2 (ABSs) in Romanian. Each of the 8 items reflects an irrational or rational belief (demandingness-DEM; global evaluation-GE; low frustration tolerance-LFT; awfulizing-AWF; preference-PREF; nonglobal evaluation-nonGE; frustration tolerance-FT; and badness-BAD). The eight items are combined into two scales—rationality and irrationality. The scale has good psychometric properties (David, 2007a—Romanian population).

Bernard (1990) further refined The General Attitude and Belief Scale (GABS), and reduced the measure to 55 items. The scale has one rationality subscale and six irrationality subscales (need for achievement, need for approval, need for comfort, demand for fairness, self-downing, and other-downing).

COMMENTS ON THE SHORTENED GENERAL ATTITUDE AND BELIEF SCALE (SGABS). Although the 55-item GABS had good psychometric properties, a further reduction in length was considered necessary (Lindner et al., 1999). Following thorough investigation, the GABS was reduced to a 26-item scale (the Shortened General Attitude and Belief Scale—SGABS—Lindner et al., 1999) that measures all 7 dimensions covered by the 55-item GABS. The SGABS has a few major advantages: besides the brief time required for completion (i.e., about four minutes), it is comprehensive enough to measure all major categories of irrational beliefs. Also, the significantly higher association between SGABS scores and IBs scores than between SGABS scores and Beck Depression Inventory scores indicates lack of contamination (Lindner et al., 1999). The fact that one measure of absolutistic cognition (IBs) correlates more with another measure of irrationality (SGABS) than with a measure of depressive symptoms (a mixture of cognitions, emotions, behaviors) argues for the power (i.e., discriminant validity) of the instrument.

COMMENTS ON THE SURVEY OF PERSONAL BELIEFS (SPB). The SPB is a 50-item self-report questionnaire designed to measure irrational processes in adults. It has five subscales, reflecting the updated REBT theory (Steel, Möller, Cardenas, & Smith, 2006): awfulizing, self-directed shoulds, other-directed shoulds, low frustration tolerance, and negative self-rating. Emphasizing demandingness as the primary absolutistic process, the SPB also identifies the type of demands in terms of being oriented toward the self or others. The questionnaire exhibits good internal consistency and adequate test-retest reliability (Demaria, Kassinove, & Dill, 1989).

The SPB has been extensively used in clinical studies designed to investigate the relationship between IBs and different emotional consequences, such as anger (Azoulay, 2000; Ziegler & Smith, 2004), anxiety, and depression (Chang & Bridewell, 1998; Chang & DiZurilla, 1996), negative affect (Muran, Kassinove, Ross, & Muran, 1989), as well as many other cognitive and behavioral variables such as perfectionism (Di-Biase, 1999) (for an extensive list, see Steel et al., 2006). The SPB remains, along with the GABS/ABS 2, one of the best validated irrational beliefs measures available.

COMMENTS ON THE COMMON BELIEFS SURVEY-III (CBS-III). The CBS-III is a 54-item self-report inventory of general irrational attitudes, based on REBT theory (Ellis & Harper, 1975). It focuses on higher-order, general categories of beliefs (Thorpe, Walter, Kingery, & Nay, 2001). Nine existing surveys have been combined and refined into one final scale, with a six-factor structure (Ciarrochi, 2004). Bassai (1977) identified the factor structure of the measure, which was replicated by Tosi, Forman, Rudy, and Murphy (1986) in a study involving 264 medical patients.

The CBS-III contains the following six scales, four of which measure low acceptance and the tendency to make global evaluations:

- the *perfectionism* scale (i.e., high expectations of events and people);
- the *self-downing* scale (i.e., the inability to accept fallibility and the conviction that self-worth is negatively affected by errors and inability to achieve one's goals);

- the *need for approval* scale (i.e., the inability to accept oneself if not approved by others);
- the *blame proneness* scale (i.e., negative global evaluation of other people when they make mistakes);
- the *importance of the past* scale (i.e., the belief that one's emotions and behaviors are determined by past events); and
- the *control of emotions* scale (i.e., the belief that one's emotions are determined by external events) (Ciarrochi, 2004).

The six factors of the CBS-III also combine into two higher-order scales:

- the *evaluation* scale consisting of Blame Proneness, Self-Downing, and Perfectionism; and the *locus of control* scale—consisting of Importance of the Past, Importance of Approval, and Control of Emotions.

Although some irrational processes (e.g., awfulizing and low frustration tolerance), central to the REBT theory, are less extensively covered by the fifty-four items of the survey, the CBS-III investigates a fundamental element of the ABC model that has been ignored by other instruments—the strength of the A-C connection. The belief that one's emotions are caused by external events rather than by one's thoughts is one of the major, but frequently overlooked, cognitive errors. This misconception is a primary target of REBT.

Among all forms of CBT, REBT is the one that most fervently advocates self-acceptance; developing unconditional acceptance entails a profound change and is the focal point of intervention (McMahon, 2008). With four of its six scales focused on "low acceptance," the CBS-III targets the core element of REBT. The CBS-III has good internal reliability and correlates with other measures of dysfunctional thinking; it also discriminates between respondents in both clinical and nonclinical settings (Thorpe, Parker, & Barnes, 1992; Thorpe et al., 2001).

Thorpe and Frey (1996) developed a 19-item short form of the CBS-III that has good internal consistency, convergent validity, and discriminant validity. Of the 19 items in the short version of the CBS-III, 16 are part of the Self-Downing, Perfectionism, and Importance of the Past scales (Thorpe & Frey, 1996). The scales significantly correlate with the Situational Self-Statement and Affective State Inventory (i.e., a measure of unhelpful self-statements), proving their convergent validity (Thorpe et al., 2001).

COMMENTS ON THE IRRATIONAL BELIEFS INVENTORY (IBI). The IBI is a 50-item self-report measure of IBs, originally developed in Dutch by Koopmans, Sanderman, Timmerman, and Emmelkamp (1994). It is based on a 137-item pool derived from the Irrational Beliefs Test—IBT (Jones, 1968) and the Rational Behavior Inventory—RBI (Shorkey & Whiteman, 1977) (Bridges & Sanderman, 2002).

Following factor analysis, a five-factor structure of the IBI emerged:

- *Worrying* (I = 12) about future accidents and misfortune;
- *Rigidity* (I = 14) regarding self and others' values and norms;
- *Need for Approval* (I = 7) of others and fear of failure and rejection;
- *Problem Avoidance* (I = 10) and difficulty in confronting problems, and being dependent on others in decision making; and
- *Emotional Irresponsibility* (I = 7) reflecting the belief that emotions are caused by external factors.

A total score can be computed by summing all 50 items. Higher scores reflect higher irrationality (Bridges & Sanderman, 2002).

As a response to the major criticisms of the IBT and RBI, the IBI was meant to be a noncontaminated instrument for assessing evaluative cognitions (i.e., irrational beliefs), independent of emotions and behaviors (Bridges & Sanderman, 2002). Similar to the CBS-III, the IBI includes items designed to investigate the strength of the A-C connection.

Although originally developed in Dutch (Koopmans et al., 1994), the IBI was later translated into English, and used to investigate the association of irrational beliefs with paranormal beliefs (Roig, Bridges, Renner, & Jackson, 1998), procrastination (Bridges & Roig, 1997), and obsessive-compulsive symptoms (Kirby et al., 2000). The relationship between irrational beliefs and self-efficacy was also investigated using an Estonian version of the IBI (Rimm & Jerusalem, 1999). The Dutch version of the IBI was used in numerous studies as an instrument to investigate the correspondence of irrational beliefs with depression (Emanuels-Zuurveen, & Emmelkamp, 1997), dental phobia (de Jongh, Muris, Schoenmakers, & ter Horst, 1995), obsessive-compulsive disorder (van Oppen et al., 1995), and social phobia (Mersch, Jansen, & Arntz, 1995).

All these versions of the IBI have been shown to have good internal consistency and validity (Koopmans et al., 1994; Bridges & Sanderman, 2002; Rimm & Jerusalem, 1999). A major shortcoming of this instrument is the lack of explicit reference to unconditional self-acceptance, central to the REBT theory.

COMMENTS ON THE EVALUATIVE BELIEFS SCALE (EBS). The EBS (Chadwick, Trower, & Dagnan, 1999) is an 18-item, easy-to-complete (i.e., it takes around five minutes) self-report measure, assessing negative global evaluative beliefs.

In response to the criticisms of some of the first generation IBs measures, the EBS is one of the few instruments dealing exclusively with negative personal evaluations (Zurawski & Smith, 1987; Robb & Warren, 1990). It measures three types of negative personal evaluations that comprise three subscales:

- *Other-self* (i.e., how the person believes others evaluate him/her);
- *Self-self* (i.e., how the person evaluates himself/herself); and
- *Self-other* (i.e., how the person evaluates others).

Unlike other evaluative beliefs assessment instruments, the EBS focuses specifically on one irrational process, global evaluation of self and others, emphasizing and detailing the direction (i.e., self-other) of global evaluation, which is a core element of the REBT theory. Studies have shown that, in accordance with the REBT theory, depressed individuals mostly endorse negative evaluative beliefs in the form of self-self and other-self, whereas people experiencing paranoid disorders mostly hold beliefs of other-self and self-other type (Chadwick & Trower, 1997). The EBS possesses good internal reliability and predictive validity for symptoms of anxiety and depression (Chadwick et al., 1999).

All IBs/RBs assessment instruments described above are self-report measures. Whereas they have good psychometric properties, some questions remain regarding the availability of these beliefs and their sensitivity to coping/defense mechanisms (David et al., 2005). A particularly relevant aspect to consider in the assessment of IBs/RBs is the compatibility between the way beliefs are *organized* and the type of *method* employed to identify them. More than a decade ago, DiGiuseppe (1996) argued that more studies were needed to help clarify how IBs/RBs were represented in the cognitive system. The idea that different types of IBs are represented in a different format (David, 2003) has received some empirical support. Szentagotai et al. (2005) have shown that whereas DEM and GE seem to be core evaluative schemas (i.e., encompassing both factual and evaluative components), LFT and AWF are better conceptualized in terms of appraisal.

This specification brings about a further distinction between structurally and/or functionally conscious or unconscious contents and processes. Some cognitive contents and processes are structurally unconscious, represented in our memory in a format that cannot be readily accessed (Schacter & Tulving, 1994). In such cases, priming methodologies and other implicit tasks can be used to help access them. Other processes and contents, while structurally conscious, are functionally unconscious due to automatization (e.g., cognitive schemas), and can sometimes can be made conscious, if properly primed (Solomon, Haaga, Brody, Kirk, & Friedman, 1998). IBs seem to be structurally conscious cognitions, functioning consciously or unconsciously, although more research is needed to explore the possibility that demandingness is also structurally unconscious (David, 2007, personal communication). The first steps in this direction were represented by the development of the Articulated Thoughts in Simulated Situations (ATSS—Davidson, Robins, & Johnson, 1983) and implicit tasks and priming methodologies (David et al., 2005).

The Psychotherapy Oriented Assessment

Some professionals claim that the early use of extensive assessment procedures (e.g., filling out a test battery before the psychotherapeutic intervention) could be iatrogenic to certain clients (Ellis & Dryden, 1997). More specifically, Ellis and Dryden (1997) argued that some clients could develop additional symptoms during the time-consuming evaluation procedure, perhaps due to the large number of questions they must answer. When central cognitive mechanisms such as IBs/RBs are assessed, the procedure may involve remembering personal difficulties and negative emotions that could prime IBs in some clients (Solomon et al., 1998). In addition, some clients might mistake prolonged diagnosis and general case conceptualization for treatment, and believe that "therapy" can offer little to contribute to their rehabilitation (Ellis & Dryden, 1997).

An alternative strategy would be to assess cognitive factors (i.e., irrational and rational beliefs) and inappropriate feelings and dysfunctional behaviors over several therapy sessions. This way, clinical assessment is combined with education for CBT; clients learn about the importance of case conceptualization, homework and collaboration, disputing self-defeating cognitions, and working toward changing maladaptive behaviors (Ellis & Dryden, 1997). An advantage of psychometric assessment, however, is that it can provide a baseline against which the client can observe progress (or lack of progress) in psychotherapy.

The Assessment Process

The *assessment process* includes several important aspects. First, client and therapist work together to identify the client's dysfunctional feelings and behaviors and to separate them from functional ones, thereby identifying and clarifying the "C" in the ABC model. In CBT it is essential to separate functional emotions (e.g., sadness, concern, remorse, annoyance), from dysfunctional emotions (e.g., depression, anxiety, guilt, or anger). Likewise, addictions, compulsions, procrastination, and other maladaptive behaviors are distinguished from idiosyncratic but nonharmful ones (e.g. socializing excessively, overworking). Usually, the A (activating event) and the C (cognition) are assessed before the B (behavior). It is important to reveal and evaluate both

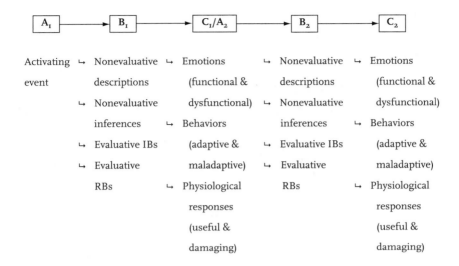

FIGURE 7.1. The ABC Components

primary and secondary emotions (e.g. anxiety about anxiety, depression about depression). When the client begins by describing an A, the therapist will inquire about the C, and vice versa. A specific activating event, which occurs prior to the maladaptive consequence is then targeted and briefly described, focusing on the part that triggers the B. Next, the B is evaluated and discussed in detail, focusing on evaluative beliefs (IBs /RBs).

*IB—irrational beliefs / RB—rational beliefs / C1—primary consequences / C2—secondary consequences / B1—primary beliefs (beliefs about the activating event) / B2—secondary beliefs (beliefs about own reactions to the activating event).

Techniques/Procedures for Identifying Irrational/Rational Beliefs

Some of the most commonly used methods for identifying specific IBs/RBs are detailed below.

SOCRATIC QUESTIONING/ OPEN-ENDED QUESTIONING/INDUCTIVE QUESTIONING/ GUIDED DISCOVERY. According to Padesky (1993), Socratic questioning

> involves asking the client questions which: (a) the client has the knowledge to answer, (b) draw the client's attention to information that is relevant to the issue being discussed but may be outside the client's current focus,

(c) generally move from the concrete to the more abstract so that (d) the client can, in the end, apply the new information to either reevaluate a previous conclusion or construct a new idea. (p. 4)

The main assumption is that clients are capable of answering questions posed to them, and that therapeutic strategies serve to reorganize existing cognitions to promote an effective response.

This evocative procedure is described in the literature under many different names, including: "Socratic questioning" (DiGiuseppe, 1991), "Socratic method" (DiGiuseppe, 1991), "Socratic disputation" (Bishop & Fish, 1999), "Socratic education" (Pateman, 1999), "Socratic interrogation" (Meyer, 1980), "Socratic rhetoric" (Frusha, 2002), "Paradoxical inquiry" (Burns & Auerbach, 1992), "Open-ended questioning" (DiGiuseppe, 1991; Neenan & Dryden, 2000), and "Guided discovery" (Beck, Wright, Newman, & Liese, 1993). Moorey (1996) equated "Socratic questioning" to an "inductive process of guided discovery" (p. 268). Although there is some discrepancy regarding terminology, definition, components, and purpose of Socratic questioning (Carey & Mullan, 2004), it can be seen as a fundamentally important psychotherapeutic procedure, which offers the client a strategy for introspective exploration and self-discovery.

Young and Beck (1980, p. 10) point out some of the functions of guided discovery/Socratic questioning.

1. To encourage the patient to initiate the decision-making process by pointing out alternative approaches.
2. To assist the patient in making a decision by weighing the pros and cons of alternatives that have already been generated, thus narrowing the range of desirable possibilities.
3. To prompt the patient to consider the consequences of continuing to engage in dysfunctional behaviors.
4. To examine the potential advantages of behaving in more adaptive ways.
5. To discover the meaning for the patient of a particular event or set of circumstances.
6. To help the patient define criteria that apply to maladaptive self-appraisals.
7. To show the patient how he or she is selectively focusing on only negative information in drawing conclusions.

Basically, the therapist asks the client questions about his/her thoughts. Open-ended questions can be phrased in several ways; some of them are described in the literature. For example, Dryden and DiGiuseppe (1990) suggest that therapists question clients about what they are telling themselves ("What were you telling yourself about A to make yourself disturbed at C?" in the ABC framework of REBT). Others (Walen, DiGiuseppe, & Wessler, 1980) offer alternative possibilities, such as "What was going through your mind?" "Were you aware of any thoughts in your head?" "What was on your mind then?" or "Are you [now] aware of what you were thinking at that moment?" Additional ways to inquire about the client's thoughts include framing questions such as: "Was there any particular thing you were thinking of when you felt disturbed?" "Is there a particular thought that makes you sad/worried?" or "What are you thinking of, when you experience negative emotions?"

Whereas using open-ended questions to determine the cognitive mechanisms of psychological disturbance offers the advantage of allowing clients to identify their own thoughts, the process frequently results in identifying automatic thoughts instead of evaluative cognitions. In such cases, the proper use of inferential chaining (e.g., moving from descriptions and inferences to their evaluations) can help clients experience a moment of insight, when they encounter their dysfunctional and irrational thinking.

Some authors recommend the Socratic dialogue be used mainly during the exploration and assessment phase of the therapeutic process (Dattilio, 2000; Beck et al., 1993), whereas others suggest it should be employed mostly when therapists prepare clients to function independently (DiGiuseppe, 1991).

THEORY-DRIVEN QUESTIONING. Questions during therapy can also be derived directly from CBT/REBT theory (Dryden & DiGiuseppe, 1990). These lines of questioning prompt clients to be more specific in formulating their answers and focus on "hot" cognitions rather then on automatic thoughts. For example, Dryden and DiGiuseppe (1990) suggest that in order to help client identify their absolutistic demands therapists should ask, "What *demand* were you making about other people's criticism to make yourself disturbed at point C?" Other possible ways of phrasing such questions could be:

- "What did you think he/she *should* have done in that situation to make yourself angry at him/her?" or "How did you think you *should* have reacted at that point to make yourself guilty about not doing so?" or "How did you expect that life *should be* to make yourself miserable when it was not?" (to focus on absolutistic demands);
- "What *kind of person* did you think would lie like you did?" Or "How do you describe *a person* that acts unjustly like you did?" or "What did you *call yourself* for making such a mistake?" (to focus on negative global evaluation);

- "Was his lack of interest in you very *hard to stand?*" Or "Was losing your job *unbearable* for you?" or "Did you have difficulty *putting up with* your child's behavior?" (to focus on low frustration tolerance);
- "Did you expect the criticism from your boss to be *awful* for you?" or "Did you think it was *terrible* to fail that exam?" or "Did you think it would be *horrible* to be rejected like that? (to focus on awfulizing).

Although efficient in many instances, posing these questions risks "putting words into the client's mouth." Therapists can reduce this risk by carefully evaluating dysfunctional emotions prior to assessing thoughts. Accordingly, questions can anticipate possible cognitive mechanisms associated with previously identified dysfunctional Cs.

IMAGERY. Assessing IBs/RBs on a retrospective basis involves recalling an activating event (A) associated with dysfunctional/maladaptive consequences (C), and determining the cognitive mechanisms that generate or are habitually associated with those consequences (B). When the client encounters difficulties answering the therapist's questions regarding the A, B, or C, imagery and/or guided imagery can be used to facilitate patient reports (Young & Beck, 1980; David, 2006).

Imagery is used in CBT interventions for different purposes: *(1)* to expose clients to phobic stimuli (behavior therapy—Wolpe, 1973); *(2)* as part of stress management training (SIT—Meichenbaum, 1985; Selye, 1974); and *(3)* as a way to access and restructure clients' automatic thoughts and core beliefs (cognitive therapy and rational-emotive behavior therapy—Dryden & DiGiuseppe, 1990; Edwards, 1990). Guided imagery can range from very specific (e.g., therapist-created scenarios the client is instructed to imagine) to a flexible script that the therapist and client construct together (Arbuthnott et al., 2001). The technique can be used alone or in combination with other methods such as hypnosis, relaxation training, and listening to music. The content of the images can be either realistic (i.e., things that are likely to happen in the client's real life, such as seeing a cat on the street) or fantastic/metaphoric (i.e., scenarios that are highly unlikely to happen in real life, such as being visited by a ghost at night) (Arbuthnott et al., 2001).

Whereas some therapeutic interventions require the use of realistic images (e.g., exposure to phobic stimuli), in other cases clients seem to benefit more from the inclusion of metaphorical scenes (e.g., imagining irrational beliefs as balls to be thrown away). Arbuthnott et al. (2001) and Courtois (2001) maintain that, whenever possible, therapists should use metaphorical images, in order to help clients bring to conscious awareness and express desires, thoughts, emotions, and emotionally laden behaviors. In this way, the risk of mistaking imagined experiences for perceived life situations, and thus creating false memories, is drastically reduced (Arbuthnott et al., 2001). For example, one could use unusual settings or fictional characters to reproduce activating events that trigger the client's IBs/RBs. Another possible benefit of using metaphoric images to identify irrational beliefs can be the highlight on the B-C connection. Because people often believe that life events (A) directly cause or contribute to their psychological disturbance (C) (Ellis & Dryden, 1997), it could be helpful to emphasize that any activating event that resembles the salient event can prime and interact with cognitive vulnerability factors. Therefore, the proximal cause of dysfunctional emotions and maladaptive behaviors resides at point "B" in the ABC model, and not at point "A."

ROLE PLAYING. When clients' psychological disturbances are mainly activated in social contexts, it is often possible to identify dysfunctional thinking during role-playing. According to Norton and Hope (2001), "Role-played scenarios involve the simulation of an interaction between the client and another individual or a group in the clinical setting" (p. 59). Situational analogue assessment methods, in contrast to naturalistic observational assessment, have been used mostly to evaluate social functioning, particularly social skill deficits and social anxiety in both adults and children (Norton & Hope, 2001; Levenson Jr. & Herman, 1991). Goal setting and evaluation play an important role in both social skill deficits and social anxiety. Whereas social skills combine the ability to perceive social cues, integrate them with personal goals, then produce and enact responses that will help attain those goals (Norton & Hope, 2001), social anxiety entails the fear of negative evaluations, and low self-confidence when confronted with social situations that people tend to avoid (American Psychiatric Association, 1994).

Standardized role-play scenarios were developed in order to compare the performance of individuals in clinical and nonclinical populations, on a normative basis. For example, the Social Skill Behavioral Assessment System was developed to measure skill and anxiety in opposite-sex interactions in nonclinical populations (Caballo & Buela, 1988), The Ideographic Role-Play measures global assertion in nonclinical populations (Kern, 1991), whereas the Disability and Assertiveness Role-Play Test (Glueckauf & Quittner, 1992) assesses general assertion skills in physically disabled adults. The modified version of the Behavioral Assertiveness Test-Revised (Bellack, Hersen, & Turner, 1979) is a global measure of assertion for adult psychiatric inpatients and outpatients.

As a means of assessing dysfunctional thinking in individuals, role-playing can be employed to recreate social situations that potentially trigger clients' maladaptive beliefs. In such instances, clients play themselves, while therapists play the role of the other participant in the dialogue (Young & Beck, 1980). Although this kind of role sharing is frequently used (Hope & Heimberg, 1993), in order to promote external validity, multiple role-plays with different individuals is a better option (Norton & Hope, 2001). Involvement in the enacted scenario is often necessary to trigger dysfunctional thinking and promote satisfactory results (Young & Beck, 1980).

OBSERVING THE PATIENT'S REACTIONS IN THE SESSION (MOOD SHIFT DURING THE SESSION). During the session, when clients experience changes in their moods, it can accurately reflect the activation of dysfunctional thinking. Therefore, instead of dismissing these emotions and helping clients feel better by distracting their attention from troubling thoughts, therapist can deliberately focus on them (Young & Beck, 1980). Mood shifts can be indicated by sudden changes in behavior (e.g., becoming aggressive, crying, lowering the head and wringing the hands) and in physiological responses (e.g., hyperventilating and blushing).

When clients display visible reactions, inquiries about the thoughts coupled with their responses (Beck, 1995) can pave the groundwork for an effective and accurate in vivo assessment of dysfunctional cognitions. This approach underscores the point for clients that dysfunctional feelings are not caused by situations alone, and is entirely consistent with a cognitive conceptualization of psychological distress.

DAILY RECORDS OF DYSFUNCTIONAL THOUGHTS AND DIARIES. When clients acknowledge the presence of particular thoughts associated with negative and dysfunctional emotions and behaviors but cannot recall them accurately during the session, one solution is to start monitoring thoughts as they occur. The client is instructed to keep a diary or to complete a self-monitoring form at the time of or shortly after the activating event takes place. It is a method similar to an "in vivo" exposure to activating events while monitoring cognitive, emotive, physiological, and behavioral reactions. In CBT, the self-monitoring of dysfunctional thoughts is often prescribed as homework, thus involving the client as a collaborator in the therapeutic process. Client and therapist then review the beliefs that were identified between sessions and discuss them as well as their impact on emotions and behaviors. Only beliefs that appear on the monitoring form are discussed, avoiding suggesting beliefs to clients and fostering self-efficacy in clients' ability to identify irrational thinking (Young & Beck, 1980). The self-monitoring form in Table 7.1 is based on the REBT self-help form (Sichel & Ellis, apud Ellis & Dryden, 1997) and the CBT synthetic form (David, 2006).

TECHNIQUES AND METHODS PRIMARILY USED WITH CHILDREN AND ADOLESCENTS. With children and adolescent clients, identifying dysfunctional thoughts sometimes requires more work and less reliance on verbal methods. Most of the time, young clients can only identify surface cognitions (e.g., specific automatic thoughts) and secondary irrational processes such as awfulizing, self-downing, and low frustration tolerance (Ann Vernon, personal communication).

Thought records are also used with young clients, although their form and content are typically adjusted to the developmental level of the child or adolescent (Kendall, 1990; Seligman, Reivich, Jaycox, & Gillham, 1995). Thought bubbles, animal, and plant drawings can all be used to represent cognitions, and it is encouraging that even very young children understand that a thought bubble is a way to represent cognitive content (Wellman, Hollander, & Schult, 1996). Bernard and Joyce (1984) created a child-friendly thought record, called the *Thought Flower Garden*. In this garden, flower blossoms represent feelings, stems stand for thoughts, and the soil is the activating event. This exercise clearly represents the relation between thoughts and emotions in an easy-to-remember format. Padesky (1986) shows that recording thoughts in a thought bubble floating over a cartoon-like face can be used to depict emotion, as expressed in the face, as well as cognition, which is recorded in the bubble. Additional space can be provided in the picture for drawing or writing the activating event and the intensity of the emotion

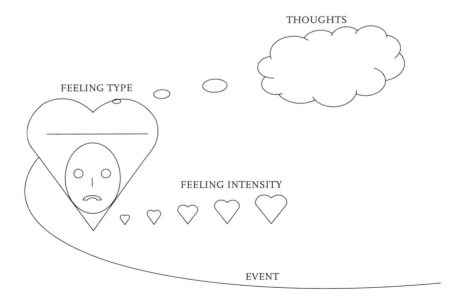

FIGURE 7.2. Example of a Thought Bubble with Rating Scale for the Intensity of Emotions

Board games are another useful method of identifying cognitions in children and adolescents. They are relatively complex exercises or strategies, involving emotions, cognitions, and ways to come up with rational self-statements. Berg (1990a, 1990b, 1990c) developed a series of such games, highly appreciated by children.

Rational stories that foster identification with animals that represent rational and irrational attitudes and behaviors can also be an effective means of assessing thoughts in children (Waters, 1980). The "Rational Stories for Children" (Waters, 1980) and "The Story of Retman" (David, 2007b; available at www.psychotherapy.ro) are examples of creative methods for helping children challenge and change their self-defeating beliefs.

Sentence completion tasks are appropriate mostly for adolescents, and allow for considerable creativity, flexibility, and complexity (Friedberg & McClure, 2002). This type of exercise requires that clients fill in the blanks of an incomplete sentence (Friedberg, Fidaleo, & Mason, 1992). The complexity of the exercise can range from easier forms that require teenagers to say what they think when a particular event occurs and a given emotion is experienced, to more complex variations, when only the basic elements of the ABC model are provided (i.e., "When X happens, I feel Y, and I think Z") and the entire content needs to be filled in.

The Next Generation of Assessment Methods and Technologies

The assessment of evaluative beliefs was, and still is, dominated by methods such as clinical interviewing, self-report questionnaires, and more recent indirect measures like the ATSS. However, a new wave of assessment tools is emerging, making use of the latest technological developments (Trull, 2007).

The hesitant integration of these new methods into mainstream psychological assessment is mainly due to the following reasons, most of them outdated themselves:

- the alleged costs of modern equipment;
- the supposed lack of technological sophistication of some clients and therapists; and
- the lack of information about the possibilities and the advantages of importing new technologies into more traditional practices (Trull, 2007).

The high costs of equipment and the lack of savvy of some users are no longer realistic arguments given the prevalence of simple to operate, inexpensive miniature electronic devices that accompany people even when they walk down the street or sleep (Trull, 2007). However, there is a real lack of studies to ground the elaboration and testing of ways to incorporate the advanced equipment into more traditional, yet effective intervention strategies (Trull, 2007).

The major advantages of employing novel technologies for cognitive assessment procedures include:

1. an increase in reliability and the efficient use of time and other resources;
2. a decrease in memory bias and reconstruction of events and personal reactions to these events;
3. the elimination of transcripts of entries, which can contribute to the creation of precise and unbiased summaries; and
4. the stimulation of client memory to reveal sensitive information (Trull, 2007).

Another possible benefit could be the optimization of the therapeutic alliance, mostly with younger clients who tend to associate electronic equipment with leisure activities and computerized games. The most relevant limitation of equipment-mediated assessment at present is the insufficient capability to monitor body language. However, studies investigating this issue reveal that coding the client's body language does not result in a significant increase in clinical judgment validity (Garb, 2007).

The most promising ways of making use of technological advancements in clinical assessment are listed below.

- Virtual reality assessment—Virtual reality is an advanced type of computer-human interface, which allows users to immerse themselves into a simulated complex environment resembling the real world, and to interact with elements of this virtual environment in ways similar to those found in real life interaction (Schultheis & Rizzo, 2001). The main feature of all virtual environments is the 3D interaction space, which helps generate a feeling of present, past, and potentially future problematic life situations—thus better approximating in vivo reactions (Riva, 2003). General irrational processes are sometimes hard to trigger because of their high levels of automatization and interference with coping and defense mechanisms (David et al., 2005). However, exposure to activating events in controlled environments not only activates evaluative processes, but also protects the client's right to safety and dignity. Virtual reality assessment techniques are currently used by psychologists in the Department of Clinical Psychology and Psychotherapy at Babeş -Bolyai University (www.clinicalpsychology.ro) in the assessment of ADHD, based on a technology developed by Rizzo,

Bowerly, Buckwalter, Schultheis, Matheis, Shahabi, Neumann, Kim, and Sharifzadeh (2002).

- Electronic diary assessment—Electronic diaries (EDs) are records obtained by means of mobile electronic devices. These devices are used to record data relevant for personal and interpersonal problems and deficits that are later addressed in counseling or therapy. Although EDs do not completely eliminate retrospective biases, they drastically reduce memory distortions of relevant data (Piasecki, Hufford, Solhan, & Trull, 2007). In the process of assessing evaluative beliefs, electronic diaries are the updated version of self-monitoring forms used in real-life situations. The major advantage expected is in terms of time saving, because electronic data capture eliminates the need for data entry (Piasecki et al., 2007).

- Computer-assisted interviewing and rating scales—Computer-assisted psychological instruments are the most widely used modern clinical assessment methods. They consist of structured interviews and other scales that can be safely self-administered. Although most evaluative beliefs questionnaires are designed for a paper and pencil format, many of them could also be administered in an electronic format. New IBs/RBs computer-assisted assessment instruments could also be developed, particularly given the insufficient number of IBs measures used in research (Kendall et al., 1995).

- Computer-based adaptive testing—Forbey and Ben-Porath (2007) launched the idea of computer-based adapted versions of questionnaires. Unlike more traditional computerized versions of questionnaires that basically parallel paper and pencil forms, computer-based adaptive tests terminate when an algorithm determines that answers to additional questions will not result in a change in the respondent's scores. Consequently, there can be a drastic reduction in the length of extensive questionnaires (e.g., personality inventories). The thorough assessment of general evaluative beliefs involves using different scales for each process, and separating rationally from irrationally worded items. Therefore, most contemporary IBs/RBs assessment instruments have fifty or more items, which has led to the subsequent development of numerous shortened versions. A main criticism of shortened versions is that there are too few items to reliably measure each dimension. Computer-based adaptive tests could very well be a future solution to this problem.

- Neuroimaging—Neuroimaging generally refers to the employment of electronic devices for visualizing specific neural areas of the brain and central nervous system, including brain activity. Currently, the high costs of such complex devices, the requirement of technological expertise, and technical limitations make neuroimaging a less accessible method. However, considering the fast technological advancement recorded over the last years, neuroimaging does hold promise for the future of identifying the biological correlates of both emotional symptoms and underlying irrational/rational processes (Trull, 2007).

- Ambulatory biosensors—Ambulatory biosensors (AB) are devices that record physiological and motor activity in real-life situations (Trull, 2007). There are three main domains of assessment relevant to clinical conditions that can benefit from the use of AB: *(1)* cardiovascular measurement, *(2)* motor activity and movement, and *(3)* cortisol levels as neurotransmitters inferred through blood draws (Haynes & Yoshioka, 2007). Changes in heart rate and blood pressure, hyperactivity, sleep problems, and fluctuations in inferred cortisol levels are all physiological correlates of emotions and therefore relevant indicators of the presence of IBs/RBs. The challenge of the future would be to pinpoint physiological fluctuations that specifically match or complement rational or irrational processes, providing the therapist with clear landmarks for the presence of clinically relevant targets (i.e., irrational beliefs and other cognitive distortions).

Conclusion

The assessment of irrational and rational beliefs has a major impact on both practice and research. In practice, the accurate identification of irrational processes and contents associated with psychopathology plays a fundamental role in ensuring the focus and efficacy of the psychological intervention, and influences client adherence to the psychotherapeutic process. In research, distinguishing different types of content, as well as processes and cognitions grounds not only the development of efficient intervention techniques, but also empirically based theories and models of change.

Based on current knowledge regarding the nature, organization, and functioning of IBs/RBs, the assessment process and development of test instruments should focus on:

- distinguishing cognition from its behavioral and emotional consequences to avoid contamination of measures;

- distinguishing RBs from IBs to reflect more recent theoretical developments and point out that RBs and IBs are not necessarily bipolar, opposite constructs;
- distinguishing the process from the content of thought;
- distinguishing different types of irrational processes (e.g., demandingness, low frustration tolerance, awfulizing, global evaluation);
- distinguishing different types of thought contents (e.g., need for achievement/performance, comfort, affiliation, approval, and fairness);
- distinguishing specific and contextual from general IBs/RBs;
- distinguishing conscious processing from unconscious processing;
- adjusting assessment instruments to the nature of IBs and RBs (i.e., enduring vs. transient, conscious vs. unconscious); and
- adjusting the instruments to fit the user (e.g., children or adults).

There are two major ways of identifying and assessing IBs/RBs: *(1)* psychological instruments and *(2)* therapy oriented assessment. Psychological instruments (i.e., tests and questionnaires) share the advantage of rigor, standardization, efficacy, and time-effectiveness, offering a broad perspective on the cognitive mechanisms of emotional distress. Therapy oriented assessment is a client-centered assessment, allowing the identification of cognitive contents and mechanisms along with education for CBT during a few initial sessions.

This chapter has reviewed the main psychological self-report measures and therapy-oriented assessment methods that are currently used for the identification and evaluation of IBs/RBs. Future work in the area should consider adjusting assessment tools to the nature and organization of IBs and RBs, by the development of indirect measures and implicit assessment tests.

A new wave is emerging in the field of clinical assessment, making use of the latest technological developments via electronic devices that assist psychological assessment. More research is needed to integrate these promising new directions into everyday practice and research.

The clinical assessment of IBs/RBs is an ongoing process, which informs the clinician throughout the treatment of the client's progress and of cognitive vulnerabilities that still need to be tackled. It is therefore of great importance to implement a valid strategy of evaluating and reevaluating underlying cognitive mechanisms in a manner that is relevant to the clinician and stimulating for the client. To this end, the effort to find new, more accurate and client-friendly assessment methods is an encouraging and ongoing development.

TABLE 7.1. CBT Self-Monitoring Form

The ABC(DE) Framework	CBT Self-Monitoring Form
A—Activating event/s (that happened just before you felt emotionally disturbed or acted in a self-defeating manner)	Describe the particular aspect/s of the situation that you are mostly disturbed about: _____ _____ _____ _____ _____ Major maladaptive / self-defeating behaviors (check all that apply): • Procrastination • Compulsions • Addictions • Aggression • Social isolation • Other (Specify): _____ Unhealthy physiological responses: _____ _____ _____
C—Consequences Disturbing, self-defeating or unhealthy: • emotions • behaviors • physiological responses that you produced by thinking irrationally and want to change. Major dysfunctional/ unhealthy negative emotions (check all that apply):	• Fear/anxiety • Depression • Anger • Shame • Guilt • Morbid jealousy • Other (Specify): _____

TABLE 7.1. (Continued)

The ABC(DE) Framework	CBT Self-Monitoring Form	
B—Irrational Beliefs (IBs) IBs that you tell yourself to cause your disturbing emotions, behaviors, physiological responses.	• I demand it happens:	• I cannot stand this:
	_____	_____
	_____	_____
	_____	_____
		_____
	• It is awful, the worst thing possible:	• I am a person without value or use:
	_____	_____
	_____	_____
	_____	_____
	_____	
D—Disputing / Restructuring Irrational Beliefs	For each IB previously checked ask yourself the following questions and offer answers.	Your answers:
	• Is my belief helping me achieve my goals; am I pleased with the consequences of upholding this belief?	_____
	• Is my belief consistent with reality; things always happen the way I want them to?	_____
	• Is it logical to expect all my wishes and desires to come true?	_____
		_____
		_____
		_____

E—Effective new beliefs (Rational beliefs)

Rational beliefs that will uphold my goals and replace old irrational beliefs.

- I would prefer, but I do not demand it happens:

- It is bad but not awful, not the worst thing possible:

- It is difficult to stand, but I can do it even if I do not like it:

- Nonglobal evaluation of self and others if mistakes are made:

TABLE 7.1. (Continued)

The ABC(DE) Framework	CBT Self-Monitoring Form	
F—Feelings and/or Behaviors (functional emotions and adaptive behaviors resulting from disputing your irrational beliefs and arriving at your rational beliefs). Major functional/healthy negative emotions:	• Concern • Sadness • Annoyance • Regret • Remorse • Nonmorbid jealousy • Other (Specify):	Major adaptive / self-enhancing behaviors: • Good time management • Nonimpulsive/Controlled behavior • Healthy eating and drinking habits • Assertive communication • Other (Specify): Healthy physiological responses:

REFERENCES

American Psychiatric Association. (1994). *Diagnostic and statistical manual of mental disorders* (4th ed.). Washington, DC: American Psychiatric Association.

Arbuthnott, K. D., Arbuthnott, D. W., & Rossiter, L. (2001). Guided imagery and memory: Implications for psychotherapists. *Journal of Counseling Psychology, 48,* 123–132.

Azoulay, D. (2000). Cognitive distortions in the experience and expression of anger. *Dissertation Abstracts International, 60*(8-B), 4200.

Bassai, J. L. (1976). Self-rating scales of rationality: An update. *Rational Living, 11,* 28–30.

Bassai, J. L. (1977). *The Common Beliefs Survey: A factored measure of irrational beliefs.* Paper presented at the 2nd National Conference on Rational Psychotherapy, Chicago.

Beck, A. T., Wright, F. D., Newman, C. F., & Liese, B. S. (1993). *Cognitive therapy of substance abuse.* New York: Guilford Press.

Beck, J. S. (1995). *Cognitive therapy: Basics and beyond.* New York: Guilford Press.

Bellack, A. S., Hersen, M., & Turner, S. M. (1979) The relationship of role-playing and knowledge of appropriate behavior to assertion in the natural environment. *Journal of Consulting and Clinical Psychology, 47,* 670–678.

Berg, B. (1990a). *The anxiety management game.* Dayton, OH: Cognitive Counseling Resources.

Berg, B. (1990b). *The depression management game.* Dayton, OH: Cognitive Counseling Resources.

Berg, B. (1990c). *The self-control game.* Dayton, OH: Cognitive Counseling Resources.

Bernard, M. E. (1990). *Validation of General Attitude and Belief Scale.* Presented at the World Congress of Mental Health Counselling, Keystone, Colorado.

Bernard, M. E. (1998). Validation of General Attitude and Belief Scale. *Journal of Rational-Emotive and Cognitive-Behavior Therapy, 16,* 183–196.

Bernard, M. E., & Cronan, F. (1999). The Child and Adolescent Scale of Irrationality: Validation data and mental health correlates. *Journal of Cognitive Psychotherapy: An International Quarterly, 13,* 121–132.

Bernard, M. E., & Joyce, M. R. (1984). *Rational-emotive therapy with children and adolescents.* New York: Wiley.

Bernard, M. E., & Laws, W. (1988). *Childhood irrationality and mental health.* Paper presented at the 24th International Congress of Psychology, Sydney, Australia.

Bishop, W., & Fish, J. M. (1999). Questions as interventions: Perceptions of Socratic, solution-focused, and diagnostic questioning styles. *Journal of Rational-Emotive & Cognitive-Behavior Therapy, 17,* 115–140.

Bridges, K. R., & Roig, M. (1997). Academic procrastination and irrational thinking: A re-examination with context controlled. *Personality and Individual Differences, 22,* 941–944.

Bridges, K. R., & Sanderman, R. (2002). The Irrational Beliefs Inventory: Cross cultural comparisons between American and Dutch samples. *Journal of Rational-Emotive & Cognitive-Behavior Therapy, 20,* 65–71.

Burgess, P. (1986). *Belief systems and emotional disturbance: Evaluation of the rational emotive model.* Unpublished doctoral dissertation, University of Melbourne, Parkville, Melbourne, Australia.

Burns, D. D., & Auerbach, A. H. (1992). Does homework compliance enhance recovery from depression? *Psychiatric Annals, 22,* 464–469.

Caballo, V. E., & Buela, G. (1988). Molar/molecular assessment in an analogue situation: Relationship among several measures and validation of a behavioral assessment instrument. *Perceptual and Motor Skills, 67,* 591–602.

Carey, T. A., & Mullan, R. J. (2004). What is Socratic questioning? *Psychotherapy: Theory, Research, Practice, Training, 41,* 217–226.

Chadwick, P., & Trower, P. (1997). To defend or not to defend: A comparison of paranoia and depression. *Journal of Cognitive Psychotherapy: An International Quarterly, 11,* 63–71.

Chadwick, P., Trower, P., & Dagnan, D. (1999). Measuring negative person evaluations: The Evaluative Beliefs Scale. *Cognitive Therapy and Research, 23,* 549–559.

Chang, E. C., & Bridewell, W. B. (1998). Irrational beliefs, optimism, pessimism, and psychological distress: A preliminary examination of differential effects in a college population. *Journal of Clinical Psychology, 54,* 137–142.

Chang, E. C., & DiZurilla, T. J. (1996). Irrational beliefs as predictors of anxiety and depression in a college population. *Personality and Individual Differences, 20,* 215–219.

Ciarrochi, J. (2004). Relationships between dysfunctional beliefs and positive and negative indices of well-being: A critical evaluation of the Common Beliefs Survey-III. *Journal of Rational-Emotive & Cognitive-Behavior Therapy, 22,* 171–188.

Courtois, C. A. (2001). Commentary on "Guided Imagery and Memory": Additional considerations. *Journal of Counseling Psychology, 48,* 133–135.

Dattilio, F. M. (2000). Cognitive-behavioral strategies. In J. Carlson & L. Sperry (Eds.), *Brief therapy with individuals and couples* (pp. 33–70). Phoenix, AZ: Zeig, Tucker, & Thiesen.

David, D. (2003). Rational emotive behavior therapy (REBT): The view of a cognitive psychologist. In W. Dryden (Ed.), *Rational emotive behaviour therapy: Theoretical developments.* New York: Brunner-Routledge.

David, D. (2006). *Tratat de psihoterapii cognitive si comportamentale* [The cognitive and behavioral therapies]. Iasi: Polirom.

David, D. (2007a). Scala de atitudini si convingeri, Forma scurta [The shortened version of the Attitudes and Belief Scale 2]. In D. David (Ed.), *Sistem de evaluare clinica* [Clinical assessment system]. Cluj-Napoca: RTS.

David, D. (2007b). The story of Retman. Retrieved from www.psychotherapy.ro.

David, D., Szentagotai, A., Kallay, E., & Macavei, B. (2005). A synopsis of rational-emotive behavior therapy (REBT): Fundamental and applied research. *Journal of Rational-Emotive & Cognitive-Behavior Therapy, 23,* 175–221.

Davidson, G. C., Robins, C., & Johnson, M. K. (1983). Articulated thoughts during simulated situations: A paradigm for studying cognition in emotion and behavior. *Cognitive Therapy and Research, 7,* 17–40.

de Jongh, A., Muris, P., Schoenmakers, N., & ter Horst, G. (1995). Negative cognitions of dental phobics: Reliability and validity of the Dental Cognitions Questionnaire. *Behaviour Research and Therapy, 33*, 507–515.

Demaria, T. P., Kassinove, H., & Dill, C. A. (1989). Psychometric properties of the Survey of Personal Beliefs: A rational-emotive measure of irrational thinking. *Journal of Personality Assessment, 53*, 329–341.

Di-Biase, M. (1999). Perfectionism in relation to irrational beliefs and neuroticism in community college students. *Dissertation Abstracts International, 59*(11-A), 4053.

DiGiuseppe, R. (1991). Comprehensive cognitive disputing in RET. In M. Bernard (Ed.), *Using rational emotive therapy effectively* (pp. 173–195). New York: Plenum.

DiGiuseppe, R. (1996). The nature of irrational and rational beliefs: Progress in rational emotive behavior theory. *Journal of Rational-Emotive & Cognitive-Behavior Therapy, 14*, 5–28.

DiGiuseppe, R., & Leaf, R. C. (1990). The endorsement of irrational beliefs in a general clinical population. *Journal of Rational-Emotive and Cognitive-Behavior Therapy, 8*, 235–247.

DiGiuseppe, R., Leaf, R., Exner, T., & Robin, M. V. (1988). *The development of a measure of rational/irrational thinking.* Paper presented at the World Congress of Behavior Therapy, Edinburgh, Scotland.

DiGiuseppe, R., Robin, M. W., Leaf, R., & Gormon, B. (1989). *A discriminative validation and factor analysis of a measure of rational/irrational beliefs.* Paper presented at the World Congress of Cognitive Therapy, Oxford, UK.

Dryden, W., & DiGiuseppe, R. (1990). *A primer on rational-emotive therapy.* Champaign, IL: Research Press.

Dryden, W., & Ellis, A. (1988). Rational-emotive therapy. In K. S. Dobson (Ed.), *Handbook of cognitive-behavioral therapies.* New York: Guilford.

Edwards, D. (1990). Cognitive therapy and the restructuring of early memories through guided imagery. *Journal of Cognitive Psychotherapy: An International Quarterly, 4*, 33–50.

Ellis, A. (1962). *Reason and emotion in psychotherapy.* New York: Lyle Stuart.

Ellis, A. (1984). The essence of RET-1984. *Journal of Rational-Emotive Therapy, 2*, 19–25.

Ellis, A., & Dryden, W. (1997). *The practice of rational emotive behavior therapy.* New York: Springer Publishing Company, Inc.

Ellis, A., & Harper, R. A. (1975). *A new guide to rational living.* New York: Prentice-Hall.

Emanuels-Zuurveen, L., & Emmelkamp, P. M. G. (1997). Spouse-aided therapy with depressed patients. *Behavior Modification, 21*, 62–77.

Forbey, J. D., & Ben-Porath, Y. S. (2007). Computerized adaptive personality testing: A review and illustration with the MMPI-2 computerized adaptive version. *Psychological Assessment, 19*, 14–24.

Friedberg, R. D., & McClure, J. M. (2002). *Clinical practice of cognitive therapy with children and adolescents: The nuts and bolts.* New York: Guilford.

Friedberg, R. D., Fidaleo, B. A., & Mason, C. A. (1992). *Switching channels: A cognitive-behavioral work journal for adolescents.* Sarasota, FL: Psychological Assessment Resources.

Frusha, C. E. (2002). Rhetoric of change: A Socratic rhetorical inquiry into family therapy dialogue. *Dissertation Abstracts International: Section B-The Sciences & Engineering, 63*(5-B), 2297.

Garb, H. N. (2007). Computer-administered interviews and rating scales. *Psychological Assessment, 19,* 4–13.

Glueckauf, R. L., & Quittner, A. L. (1992). Assertiveness training for disabled adults in wheelchairs: Self-report, role-play, and activity pattern outcomes. *Journal of Consulting and Clinical Psychology, 60,* 419–425.

Haynes, S. N., & Yoshioka, D. T. (2007). Clinical assessment applications of ambulatory biosensors. *Psychological Assessment, 19,* 44–57.

Hope, D. A., & Heimberg, R. G. (1993). Social phobia and social anxiety. In D. H. Barlow (Ed.), *Clinical handbook of psychological disorders: A step-by-step treatment manual* (2nd ed., pp. 99–136). New York: Guilford.

Jones, J., & Trower, P. (2004). Irrational and evaluative beliefs in individuals with anger disorders. *Journal of Rational-Emotive & Cognitive-Behavior Therapy, 22,* 153–169.

Jones, R. (1968). A factored measure of Ellis' irrational belief system with personality maladjustment correlates. *Dissertation Abstracts International, 29*(II-B), 4379–4380.

Kassinove, H. (1986). Self reported affect and core irrational thinking: A preliminary analysis. *Journal of Rational-Emotive Therapy, 4,* 119–130.

Kassinove, H., Crisci, R., & Tiegerman, S. (1977). Developmental trends in rational thinking: Implications for rational-emotive school mental health programs. *Journal of Community Psychology, 5,* 266–274.

Kendall, P. C. (1990). *The coping cat workbook.* Philadelphia, PA: Temple University.

Kendall, P. C., Haaga, D. A. F., Ellis, A., Bernard, M., DiGiuseppe, R., & Kassinove, H. (1995). Rational-emotive therapy in the 1990s and beyond: Current status, recent revisions, and research questions. *Clinical Psychology Review, 15,* 169–185.

Kern, J.M. (1991). An evaluation of a novel role-play methodology: The standardized idiographic approach. *Behavior Therapy 22(1),* 13–29.

Kirby, K. C., Berrios, G. E., Daniels, B. A., Menzies, R. G., Clark, A., & Romano, A. (2000). Process-outcome analysis in computer-aided treatment of obsessive-compulsive disorder. *Comprehensive Psychiatry, 41,* 259–265.

Knaus, W. (1974). *Rational-emotive education: A manual for elementary school teachers.* New York: Institute for Rational-Emotive Psychotherapy.

Koopmans, P. C, Sanderman, R., Timmerman, I., & Emmelkamp, P. M. G. (1994). The Irrational Beliefs Inventory (IBI): Development and psychometric evaluation. *European Journal of Psychological Assessment, 10,* 15–27.

Levenson, Jr., R. L., & Herman, J. (1991). The use of role playing as a technique in the psychotherapy of children. *Psychotherapy, 28,* 660–666.

Lindner, H., Kirkby, R., Wertheim, E., & Birch, P. (1999). A brief assessment of irrational thinking: The Shortened General Attitude and Belief Scale. *Cognitive Therapy and Research, 23,* 651–663.

Macavei, B. (2002). A Romanian adaptation of the Attitudes and Belief Scale 2. *Romanian Journal of Cognitive and Behavioral Psychotherapies, 2,* 105–122.

Malouff, J. M., & Schutte, N. S. (1986). Development and validation of a measure of irrational beliefs. *Journal of Consulting and Clinical Psychology, 54,* 860–862.

McDermut, J. F., Haaga, D. A. F., & Bilek, L. A. (1997). Cognitive bias and irrational beliefs in major depression and dysphoria. *Cognitive Therapy Research, 21,* 459–476.

McMahon, J. (2008). A glimpse in the philosophical psychology and the pragmatics of REBT: A suggestion by Wessler. *Journal of Cognitive and Behavioral Psychotherapies, 8,* 95–116.

Meichenbaum, D. (1985). *Stress inoculation training.* New York: Pergamon Press.

Mersch, P. P. A., Jansen, M. A., & Arntz, A. (1995). Social phobia and personality disorder: Severity of complaint and treatment effectiveness. *Journal of Personality Disorders, 9,* 143–159.

Meyer, M. (1980). Dialectic and questioning: Socrates and Plato. *American Philosophical Quarterly, 17,* 281–289.

Moorey, S. (1996). Cognitive therapy. In W. Dryden (Ed.), *Handbook of individual therapy* (pp. 254–281). London: Sage.

Muran, J. C., Kassinove, H., Ross, S., & Muran, E. (1989). Irrational thinking and negative emotionality in college students and applicants for mental health services. *Journal of Clinical Psychology, 45,* 188–193.

Neenan, M., & Dryden, W. (2000). *Essential cognitive therapy.* London: Whurr.

Norton, P. J., & Hope, D. A. (2001). Analogue observational methods in the assessment of social functioning in adults. *Psychological Assessment, 13,* 59–72.

Padesky, C. A. (1986, September). *Cognitive therapy approaches for treating depression and anxiety in children.* Paper presented at the 2nd International Conference on Cognitive Psychotherapy, Umea, Sweden.

Padesky, C. A. (1993, September 24). *Socratic questioning: Changing minds or guided discovery?* Keynote address to European Congress of Behavioural and Cognitive Therapies, London.

Pateman, T. (1999). Psychoanalysis and Socratic education. In S. Appel (Ed.), *Psychoanalysis and pedagogy* (pp. 45–51). Westpoint, CA: Bergin & Garvey.

Piasecki, T. M., Hufford, M. R., Solhan, M., & Trull, T. J. (2007). Assessing clients in their natural environments with electronic diaries: Rationale, benefits, limitations, and barriers. *Psychological Assessment, 19,* 25–43.

Rimm, H., & Jerusalem, M. (1999). Adaptation and validation of an Estonian version of the general Self-Efficacy Scale (ESES). *Anxiety, Stress, and Coping, 12,* 329–345.

Riva, G. (2003). Virtual environments in clinical psychology. *Psychotherapy: Theory, Research, Practice, Training, 40,* 68–76.

Rizzo, A., Bowerly, T., Buckwalter, J., Schultheis, M., Matheis, R., Shahabi, C., Neumann, U., Kim, L., & Sharifzadeh, M. (2002, September 17–19). Virtual environments for the assessment of attention and memory processes: The virtual classroom and office. In *Proceedings of the International Conference on Disability, Virtual Reality, and Associated Technology* (pp. 3–12). Vesaprem, Hungary.

Robb, H. B., & Warren, R. (1990). Irrational beliefs tests: New insights, new directions. *Journal of Cognitive Psychotherapy, 4,* 303–311.

Roig, M., Bridges, K. R., Renner, C. H., & Jackson, C. R. (1998). Belief in the paranormal and its association with irrational thinking controlled for context effects. *Personality and Individual Differences, 24,* 229–236.

Schacter, D.L., & Tulving, E. (Eds.) (1994). *Memory systems.* Cambridge, MA: The MIT Press.

Schultheis, M. T., & Rizzo, A. A. (2001). The application of virtual reality technology in rehabilitation. *Rehabilitation Psychology, 46,* 296–311.

Seligman, M. E. P., Reivich, K., Jaycox, L., & Gillham, J. (1995). *The optimistic child.* Boston: Houghton Mifflin.

Selye, H. (1974). *Stress without distress.* Philadelphia: Lippincott.

Shaw, E. (1989). *The assessment of rationality/irrationality: The psychometric properties of the Attitudes and Belief Scale in a student population.* Unpublished master's thesis, University of Melbourne, Australia.

Shorkey, C. T., & Whiteman, V. L. (1977). Development of the rational behaviour inventory: Initial validity and reliability. *Educational and Psychological Measurement, 37,* 527–534.

Smith, T. W. (1982). Irrational beliefs in the cause and treatment of emotional distress: A critical review of the rational-emotive model. *Clinical Psychology Review, 2,* 505–522.

Smith, T. W. (1989). Assessment in rational-emotive therapy: Empirical access to the ABCD model. In M. E. Bernard & R. DiGiuseppe (Eds.), *Inside rational-emotive therapy: A critical appraisal of the theory and therapy of Albert Ellis* (pp. 135–153). San Diego, CA: Academic Press.

Solomon, A., Haaga, D. A. F., Brody, C., Kirk, L., & Friedman, D. G. (1998). Priming irrational beliefs in recovered-depressed people. *Journal of Abnormal Psychology, 107,* 440–449.

Steel, H. R., Möller, A. T., Cardenas, G., & Smith, P. N. (2006). The Survey of Personal Beliefs: Comparison of South African, Mexican, and American samples. *Journal of Rational-Emotive & Cognitive-Behavior Therapy, 24,* 125–142.

Sutton-Simon, K. (1981). Assessing belief systems: Concepts and strategies. In P. C. Kendall and S. D. Hollon (Eds.), *Assessment strategies for cognitive-behavioral interventions.* New York: Academic Press.

Szentagotai, A., Schnur, J., DiGiuseppe, R., Macavei, B., Kallay, E., & David, D. (2005). The organization and the nature of irrational beliefs: Schemas or appraisal? *Journal of Cognitive and Behavior Psychotherapies, 5,* 139–158.

Thorpe, G. L., & Frey, R. B. (1996). A short form of the Common Beliefs Survey III. *Journal of Rational-Emotive & Cognitive-Behavior Therapy, 14,* 193–198.

Thorpe, G. L., Parker, J. D., & Barnes, G. S. (1992). The Common Beliefs Survey III and its subscales: Discriminant validity in clinical and nonclinical subjects. *Journal of Rational-Emotive & Cognitive Behavior Therapy, 10,* 95–104.

Thorpe, G. L., Walter, M. I., Kingery, L. R., & Nay, W. T. (2001). The Common Beliefs Survey-III and the Situational Self-Statement and Affective State Inventory: Test-retest reliability, internal consistency, and further psychometric considerations. *Journal of Rational-Emotive & Cognitive Behavior Therapy, 19,* 89–103.

Tosi, D. J., Forman, M. A., Rudy, D. R., & Murphy, M. A. (1986). Factor analysis of the Common Beliefs Survey III: A replication study. *Journal of Consulting & Clinical Psychology, 54,* 404–405.

Trull, T. J. (2007). Expanding the aperture of psychological assessment: Introduction to the special section on innovative clinical assessment technologies and methods. *Psychological Assessment, 19,* 1–3.

van Oppen, P., de Haan, E., van Balkom, A. J. L. M., Spinhoven, P., Hoogduin, K., & van Dyck, R. (1995). Cognitive therapy and exposure *in vivo* in the treatment of obsessive compulsive disorder. *Behaviour Research and Therapy, 33,* 379–390.

Walen, S. R., DiGiuseppe, R., & Wessler, R. L. (1980). *A practitioner's guide to rational-emotive therapy.* New York: Oxford University Press.

Waters, V. (1980). *Rational stories for children.* New York: Institute for Rational-Emotive Therapy.

Wellman, H. M., Hollander, M., & Schult, C. A. (1996). Young children's understanding of thought bubbles and of thought. *Child Development, 67,* 768–788.

Wolpe, J. (1973). *The practice of behavior therapy* (2nd ed.). New York: Pergamon Press. Retrieved from www.padesky.com/clinicalcorner/pdf/socquest.pdf.

Young, J. E., & Beck, A. T. (1980). *Cognitive therapy scale manual.* Retrieved from http://www.academyofct.org/upload/documents/CTRS_Manual.pdf.

Ziegler, D. J., & Smith, P. N. (2004). Anger and the ABC model underlying rational-emotive behavior therapy. *Psychological Reports, 94,* 1009–1014.

Zurawski, R. M., & Smith, T. W. (1987). Assessing irrational beliefs and emotional distress: Evidence and implications of limited discriminant validity. *Journal of Counseling Psychology, 34,* 224–227.

8

Rational and Irrational Beliefs and Psychopathology

Christopher M. Browne, E. Thomas Dowd, and Arthur Freeman

The rational-emotive behavior therapy (REBT) theory of emotional disturbance (Ellis, 1962) is a cognitively based model that posits that emotional disturbances (e.g., depression, anxiety, anger, guilt, etc.) result from irrational beliefs (IBs). IBs are evaluative thoughts that are illogical, anti-empirical, and dogmatic. Ellis and Dryden (1997) have identified several core irrational beliefs including demandingness (the belief that things absolutely *must* or *should* be a certain way), awfulizing and catastrophizing (when things go wrong it is *awful* and *terrible*), low frustration tolerance (the belief that when things do not go one's way it is *unbearable*), and global ratings of self and others (judging peoples' *total worth*, including one's own, based on behavior). Conversely, rational beliefs (RBs) are those best characterized as preferences and desires. According to Ellis (1962), these more moderate thoughts are much less likely to result in emotional disturbance.

The REBT theory is conceptualized in terms of the ABC model, in which (A) represents an activating event, (B) is the belief (RB or IB) related to the event, and (C) is the emotional or behavioral consequence of the belief (e.g., depression, anger, anxiety, alcohol and drug use, social withdrawal, etc.). According to to Ellis, it is not events (As) that cause individuals to become upset. Rather, beliefs/thoughts (Bs) mediate the effect events have on emotional and behavioral outcomes (Cs). To the extent that these consequences are negative, attainment of both short- and long-term goals is hindered. Furthermore, Ellis (1994) has made a distinction between the types of emotions that result from IBs and those that result from RBs. Emotions such as depression, anxiety, guilt, and anger are the consequences of irrational thinking. These emotions are dysfunctional; they differ in content from their more functional counterparts of sadness, concern, remorse, and annoyance; and as noted above, represent obstacles to goal attainment (David, Ghinea, Macavei, & Kallay, 2005).

Although for didactic purposes Ellis's ABC model is often presented separately, it should be noted that the model is an interactive one. Events, beliefs, and consequences interact and influence one another. For example, in response to getting reprimanded by her boss (A), Emily says to herself, "she absolutely *cannot* treat me that way! She has *no right* to do that!" (B), which results in a negative emotional experience (C) such as anger. This negative consequence is then likely to be accompanied by, or lead to, behaviors such as yelling back at her boss, treating others poorly, or hastily resigning from her job. As can be seen, these behaviors are maladaptive and reduce the likelihood that Emily will realize her goals. Further, according to Ellis (1997), individuals are predisposed to think irrationally. Put simply, people upset themselves by reacting negatively to their negative reactions. In the above example Emily's maladaptive emotional reaction is likely to upset her, particularly if this reaction results in a regrettable consequence such as losing her job or alienating her boss and coworkers.

Ellis (1997) proposes that IBs result from both biological (innate patterns of thinking and behaving) and social factors (family and peer relationships, schools, churches, and other social institutions, and the media). Evidence for the influence of social factors has been considerable. Recently, however, Leahy (2004) argued that negative thinking has possessed significant evolutionary advantage over the millennia for the human species and therefore is deeply ingrained in thinking patterns. The goal of REBT is to replace IBs with more moderate and functional beliefs (RBs) that represent preferences, tolerance, and acceptance rather than demandingness, intolerance, and global ratings of human worth (David et al., 2005). This is done through identifying IB's (i.e., demands, shoulds, musts, global ratings), actively disputing these beliefs through the use of logic and an examination of the consequences of continuing to hold on to IBs, and working to replace them with rational alternatives (i.e., preferences).

REBT theory also postulates that IBs and RBs mediate the relationship between environmental events and emotional distress, known as the REBT diathesis-stress model (David, Szentagotai, Kallay, & Macavei, in press). IBs are hypothesized to act as "cognitive vulnerability" factors in stressful situations, while RBs are hypothesized to act as "protective factors."

Evidence of REBT's efficacy is reflected in both clinical settings and in empirical research. REBT is one of the most widely used forms of therapy seen in clinical practice (Ellis & Dryden, 1997). Additionally, reviews of REBT efficacy using meta-analytic methods (e.g., Engels, Garnefski, & Diekstra, 1993; Lyons & Woods, 1991) have drawn favorable conclusions regarding its efficacy. The focus of this chapter will be on reviewing research on the association between IBs and general psychiatric symptoms including depression, anxiety, assertiveness problems, and Type A coronary-prone behavior.

Irrational Beliefs and General Emotional Disturbance

It follows from Ellis's model of psychopathology then, that endorsement of IBs should be related to increased levels of emotional disturbance and, conversely, reductions in IBs should be associated with clinical improvement. In both clinical and nonclinical samples, research has indeed supported this relationship. Endorsement of IBs has been positively associated with overall psychopathology (Lipsky, Kassinove, & Miller, 1980; Muran, Kassinove, Ross, & Muran, 1989; Newmark, Frerking, Cook, & Newmark, 1973; Smith, 1983), depression (McDermut, Haaga, & Bilek, 1997; Solomon, Arnow, Gotlib, & Wind, 2003; Solomon, Haaga, Brody, Kirk, & Friedman, 1998), anxiety (Deffenbacher, Zwemer, Whisman, Hill, & Sloan, 1986; Himle, Thyer, & Papsdorf, 1982; Lorcher, 2003), nonassertive behavior (Alden & Safran, 1978; Lange & Jakubowski, 1976), and Type A coronary-prone behavior (Smith & Brehm, 1981; Woods, 1987).

In what was at the time the first published study to evaluate the efficacy of REBT with a range of clinical problems, Lipsky et al. (1980) used a sample of community outpatient clients who presented with many of the classic neurotic symptoms such as anxiety, depression, guilt, and marital and family problems to assess REBT's effectiveness. Upon presenting for treatment, clients were randomly assigned to one of five groups: RET (at the time of the study REBT was called rational emotive therapy), RET and rational role reversal, RET and rational imagery, alternative treatment (relaxation and supportive counseling), and a no contact control group. Measures of irrational ideation, emotional adjustment, depression, anxiety, and neuroticism were administered at pre- and post-test (a measure of intelligence was also given to control for I.Q.). Results were consistent, and supported the comparative efficacy of the three RET treatments. Participants receiving RET and rational role reversal, and RET plus rational-emotive imagery evidenced significantly fewer symptoms of self-reported depression, anxiety, and neuroticism as compared to participants in the two control groups (Lipsky et al., 1980). Interestingly, participants in the RET plus rational role reversal group improved significantly more than participants in the RET only group, although participants in the RET only group evidenced significant reductions in symptoms of depression, anxiety, and neuroticism, as compared to participants in either control group. A possible explanation for this finding is that in order to be effective at rational role reversal, in which the patient conducts REBT with the therapist, one must demonstrate a thorough understanding of the principles of REBT (H. Kassinove, personal communication, November 13, 2005).

As noted above, the goal of REBT is to promote more rational thinking. Implicit in REBT is the assumption that reductions in irrational thinking mediate the positive effects of REBT. Whereas the Lipsky et al. (1980) study offers support for the assertion that thinking more rationally can improve psychological functioning, it cannot answer the question of whether or not this improvement is attributable to increases in rational thinking. Smith (1983) sought to evaluate REBT's hypothesized mechanism of action. Analyzing the data in the Lipsky et al. (1980) study, Smith (1983) used pre- to posttest difference scores to measure changes in IBs as a function of treatment group. Using multiple regression analysis, Smith (1983) found significant correlations between difference scores in the IB measure and measures of depression, anxiety, and neuroticism, thus supporting the hypothesized association between decreases in IBs and concurrent decreases in emotional disturbance. However, correlations between measures of anxiety, depression, and neuroticism were significant for both control groups as well.

In attempting to explain these findings, Smith (1983) hypothesized that the positive associations between measures of irrational beliefs and neurotic symptoms in both the treatment and control groups could represent true changes in thinking or, conversely, could be an artifact of the instrument used to assess irrational beliefs (the IDEA Inventory; Kassinove, Crisci, & Tiegerman, 1977). This methodological issue is addressed further below.

Muran et al. (1989) examined further the fundamental premise of REBT that irrational thinking results in emotional disturbance. These researchers hypothesized that individuals self-referring for psychological treatment would evidence significantly higher levels of irrational thinking compared to a sample of college students, and that there would be a positive association between IBs and depression, anxiety, anger, guilt, and general emotional distress. With respect to the first hypothesis, the only difference between the clinical and nonclinical group was that the nonclinical group evidenced significantly higher tolerance for frustration as compared to the clinical group. There were no other significant differences between the two groups on any of the other IB's (i.e., awfulizing, self- and other-directed shoulds, and ratings of self-worth).

Because anxiety and depression are among the most common clinical problems for which treatment is sought (Muran et al., 1989), the authors further examined the relationship between IBs and these specific disturbances. Results showed that there were no new differences between groups on ratings of anxiety; the nonclinical group again showed a higher tolerance for frustration than the clinical group. When depression was examined however, higher levels of irrational thinking emerged in the clinical group. This group evidenced significantly higher levels of self-directed shoulds, lower frustration tolerance, and higher total irrationality than the nonclinical group.

With respect to the hypothesis that a relationship between irrational thinking and specific indices of emotional disturbance would be found, results showed that for both groups total irrationality was significantly related to trait anger and guilt; awfulizing, self-directed shoulds, and low frustration tolerance were associated with guilt; and low frustration tolerance was significantly related to trait anger. Taken together, results of the above studies provide support for the REBT prediction that higher levels of IBs are associated with various forms of emotional disturbance.

Irrational Beliefs and Depression

Ellis has addressed the role of IBs in depression. Specifically, Ellis (1987) has cited Demandingness as the central IB in depressive disorders. According to Ellis, individuals who hold demands rather than preferences (e.g., "my friends *must always* treat me with respect"), are at higher risk for depression. If, on the other hand, the same individual merely said to herself, "It would be *nice* if my friends always treated me with respect, but I'll live if they don't," then it is likely that negative events will result in the functional emotions of disappointment and sadness rather than depression.

Research on the association between depression and IBs has generally found a positive relationship (e.g., Nelson, 1977; Prud'homme & Barron, 1992; Smith, 1989), although the findings in several studies (Hirschfeld et al., 1989; Rosenbaum, Lewinsohn, & Gotlib, 1996) have been equivocal. Using Jones's (1968) Irrational Beliefs Test (IBT), Nelson (1977) found that unrealistically high self-expectations, low frustration tolerance, anxious over-concern, and helplessness were significantly correlated with self-reported depression in college students as measured by the Beck Depression Inventory

(BDI; Beck, Rush, Shaw, & Emery, 1979). Similarly, Prud'homme and Barron (1992) used the IBT (IBT; Jones, 1968) and the Rational Behavior Inventory (RBI; Shorkey & Whiteman, 1977) to examine the pattern of IBs associated with clinical depression in three groups of participants: depressed patients, psychiatric patients, and a normal control group (a measure of anxiety was also included because of its common association with depression). Results were similar to Nelson's (1977) findings. Discriminant analysis was used to elucidate the cluster of irrational beliefs underlying depression. Results showed that demand for approval, frustration reactivity (analogous to low frustration tolerance), anxious overconcern, and helplessness significantly discriminated among the groups.

While the above findings are informative with respect to the types of distorted cognitions that may underlie depression, the results have been questioned on methodological grounds. Specifically, the studies discussed above used measures of IBs that have been shown to have questionable discriminant validity. The RBI and the IBT have been shown to be associated with measures of overall negative affect in addition to IBs, thus calling into question exactly what construct is being measured. Additionally, a common measure of depression used in these studies is the BDI. Some researchers suggest that high BDI scores should be regarded as indicative of dysphoria, not clinical depression (McDermut et al., 1997). If this is indeed the case, then drawing inferences regarding the relationship between IBs and depression based on studies using the BDI as the sole measure of depression may be misleading.

With these issues in mind, McDermut et al. (1997) and Solomon et al. (1998, 2003) in a series of studies, sought to improve on past investigations by using multiple measures of IBs (Solomon et al., 1998, 2003) and a measure of IBs (the Belief Scale, BS; Malouff & Schutte, 1986) that has shown good discriminant validity (McDermut et al., 1997). Also, the additional step of controlling for negative affect was taken by administering the Positive and Negative Affect Schedule—Trait Version (PANAS; Watson, Clark, & Tellegen, 1988).

McDermut et al. (1997) examined both attributions of events and IBs in three groups of community residents and college students: individuals diagnosed with major depression, a group with dysphoria, and a nondepressed group. One of the questions examined was the extent to which depression was related to endorsement of IBs. Additionally, exploratory analysis was conducted to examine differences in the endorsement of IBs between both the depressed and the dysphoric group, and the nondepressed and dysphoric group.

With respect to overall IBs (as measured by the BS total score) results showed that the depressed group had a significantly higher score than the nondepressed group. Additional partial correlation analysis showed that the BS was not significantly associated with overall negative affect, and that after controlling for negative affect, depression level remained a significant predictor of BS scores. This shows more conclusively that the effect was not attributable to a spurious association between the BS and general negative emotionality.

Finally, McDermut et al. (1997) examined the specific types of IBs among the three groups. The depressed group endorsed the following IBs significantly more than the nondepressed group: "To be a worthwhile person I must be thoroughly competent in everything I do," "Life should be easier than it is," "Many events from my past so strongly influence me that it is impossible to change," "I must keep achieving in order to be satisfied with myself," "Things should turn out better than they usually do," and "I cannot help how I feel when everything is going wrong." As can be seen, themes of perfection, low frustration tolerance, and helplessness characterized these thoughts.

By using a measure of IBs that has demonstrated good discriminant validity, controlling for overall negative affect, and employing a dysphoric comparison group in addition to a nondepressed group, the McDermut et al. (1997) study makes important methodological improvements over past research. These improvements notwithstanding, several issues still remain. Researchers (e.g., Bernard, 1981) have questioned whether self-report measures are sensitive enough to detect individuals' thoughts. It has been proposed that IBs operate at a preconscious level (Bernard, 1981). If this is indeed the case, then access to these thoughts may be possible only through indirect methods, such as asking individuals to articulate their thoughts and then analyzing these thoughts for irrational content.

An additional psychometric criticism of traditional measures of IBs is that their content is too general. Having individuals choose from a preselected list of thoughts may not accurately represent the types of specific, idiosyncratic thoughts held by individuals with emotional disturbances. In addition, McDermut et al. (1997) used a group of currently depressed individuals which makes inferring causality between depression and irrational thinking difficult. One cannot determine if irrational thinking leads to depression, as the REBT model would predict, or if being depressed leads to irrational thinking, which runs counter to the REBT model.

Two studies by Solomon et al. (1998, 2003) sought to address these issues. In the first study (Solomon et al., 1998), they used the BS and the articulated thoughts in simulated situations paradigm (ATSS; Davison, Robins, & Johnson, 1983) to assess IBs in recovered-depressed (RD) and never-depressed participants (ND). This design allows for an evaluation of the extent to which endorsement of IBs is a risk factor for depression or a correlate of depression (i.e., IBs change as depression level changes). If IBs are a risk factor, then it follows that the RD group should evidence higher levels of irrational thinking. Conversely, if IBs are a correlate, then they should not differ significantly between the two groups because both groups were currently not depressed.

In the ATSS paradigm, participants are presented with an audiotape of a situation and are asked to articulate their thoughts in reaction to the scenario. Incidentally, in a study investigating the construct validity of the ATSS procedure (Davison, Feldman, & Osborn, 1984), it was shown that participants in the stressful situation evidenced higher levels of IBs as compared to those in the neutral situation, and participants higher on measures of IBs were more anxious than participants who scored lower on measures of IBs (in the ATSS paradigm, situations can be tailored to the specific construct being examined, for example, social criticism, anger, or anxiety).

Solomon et al. (1998) sought to extend research by Rosenbaum et al. (1996), who used the RD-ND design and found no differences in IBs as measured by a self-report questionnaire. Solomon et al. (1998) point out however, that if IBs represent a cognitive vulnerability for depression (i.e., a latent variable), then these researchers may not have been able to uncover differences in IBs because both groups were, at the time of the study, not depressed. If this is indeed that case, then IBs may be accessible in nondepressed individuals only through priming. To address this issue, these researchers examined whether or not IBs can be primed and, if so, what type of prime would be effective in eliciting these beliefs: a negative mood state, negative events, or specific events that represent obstacles to goal attainment and include themes identified by participants as personal vulnerabilities (the fundamental-goals hypothesis).

Solomon et al. (1998) found the hypothesis that the RD group would have higher levels of IBs relative to the ND group was not supported. Baseline BS levels of IBs were not significantly different. Regarding the question of which prime, if any, would be effective in accessing latent IBs, the results provide some support for the negative mood prime hypothesis. In the RD group, negative mood was more strongly correlated with IBs. With respect to the negative event prime, there were no significant differences in IBs between groups. Finally, while the trend was consistent with the fundamental-goals hypothesis, differences between groups did not reach statistical significance. Taken together, these results suggest that IBs fluctuate with depression level, a conclusion that is not consistent with the REBT model of depression.

As noted above, Ellis has identified demandingness as the core IB most closely associated with depression. Accordingly, most widely used measures of IBs, such as the BS, include items assessing demandingness. These items tend to be general and absolute however, and the extent to which they represent the specific types of demanding thoughts held by depressed individuals is questionable (Solomon et al., 2003).

As a way to more accurately capture the types of specific, idiosyncratic beliefs thought to be most representative of REBT clients, Solomon et al. (2003) developed a more individualized measure, the Specific Demands on Self scale (SDS; Solomon, 1998), which contains items addressing demandingness "in regards to one's self-nominated worst personal shortcomings" (Solomon et al., 2003). The scale contains 15 self-evaluative domains that include physical abilities, physical appearance, emotions, achievement, and personality. For each of the 15 domains participants indicate whether there is anything about the domain that they would prefer to change. They hypothesized that the mixed findings in studies of IBs and depression may be due to the lack of sensitivity of traditional measures of IBs that use preselected items. To this end, they tested this hypothesis by comparing responses on the BS (preselected, closed-ended measure) to SDS (open-ended) responses. The RD-ND design was again used so that the question of whether IBs are risk factors or correlates could more clearly be evaluated. The authors hypothesized that group differences in IBs would only be associated with the SDS.

Results showed that neither group differed significantly on BS scores. As hypothesized however, there was a significant difference between groups on the SDS. The RD group identified significantly greater self-demands than the ND group. In terms of Cohen's (1988) criteria for effect size, the difference between groups was large. Furthermore, simultaneous regression analysis using group membership as the criterion indicated that the SDS was associated with unique variance, while the BS was not. Finally, results showed that 70% of the RD group evidenced at least one strongly held demand as compared to only 20% of the ND group, and that the RD group was nine times more likely than the ND group to endorse a strong demand.

These findings are important with respect to investigations of IBs and depression. They suggest that using a more specific, individualized measure of IBs, rather than a closed-ended, preselected measure, may be required to uncover IBs in individuals at risk for depression.

Irrational Beliefs and Anxiety

This section will review the research on the relationship between IBs and anxiety in both clinical and nonclinical samples, and will include studies of specific types of anxiety including general anxiety and worry, test anxiety, social anxiety, and speech anxiety.

As with other forms of emotional disturbance, Ellis (1994) proposes that holding thoughts related to themes of perfectionism ("I *must always* do a *perfect* job"), demandingness ("Things *have to* go as planned"), self-directed shoulds ("I *should* be able to get everything I need done in time for the party") and awfulizing/catastrophizing ("It's just *awful* that I have to do this presentation on Monday. My weekend is *ruined!*") result in anxiety. Furthermore, Ellis (1997) believes that anxious individuals have a propensity to get anxious *about their anxiety*. Once they feel themselves becoming anxious, they are likely to say to themselves, "I *must not* become anxious." This anxiety about anxiety serves only to exacerbate the problem. Ellis encourages anxious clients to accept their anxiety as something unpleasant but manageable, as opposed to something to be feared and avoided. Continuing to view anxiety in these maladaptive terms prevents people from attaining their goals and from living a more fulfilling, rewarding life, according to Ellis (1997).

Following from this conceptualization, REBT for anxiety focuses on working with clients to reduce their absolutist IBs and replace them with preferential RBs. Like studies of depression and IBs, research on the relationship between IBs and anxiety has found a positive association between irrational thinking and measures of anxiety (e.g., Deffenbacher et al., 1986; Gormally, Sipps, Raphael, Edwin, & Varvil-Weld, 1981; Himle et al., 1982; Lorcher, 2003; Thyer, Papsdorf, & Kilgore, 1983). In a preliminary investigation of the concurrent validity of the RBI (Whiteman & Shorkey, 1978), Himle et al. (1982) found that higher RBI scores (i.e., higher levels of rational thinking) were negatively correlated with measures of state, trait, and test anxiety in both clinical (test anxious) and nonclinical (college students) samples.

Thyer et al. (1983) extended this research by using a measure of psychiatric symptoms (the Symptom Checklist-90; SCL-90, DeRogatis & Cleary, 1977), in addition to the RBI to examine the association between IBs and clinical symptoms, including general anxiety, phobic anxiety, and obsessive-compulsive disorder. Results showed that correlations between the total RBI score and general anxiety, phobic anxiety, and obsessive-compulsiveness were significantly negatively correlated, indicating that higher levels of irrational thinking (i.e., lower RBI total scores) were associated with higher levels of self-reported anxiety symptoms (i.e., higher SCL-90 scores).

Deffenbacher et al. (1986) examined IBs and measures of trait anxiety, test anxiety, speech anxiety, social avoidance, and fear of evaluation and criticism in two samples of undergraduates. Results showed that all measures of anxiety were significantly and moderately correlated with IBs associated with need for

approval, catastrophizing, anxious overconcern, problem avoidance, helplessness, and perfectionism, and significantly, but minimally associated with
blame-proneness, emotional irresponsibility, dependency, and perfect solutions. Stepwise regression was then conducted to examine which specific IBs
were most predictive of high levels of anxiety. Results showed that anxious
overconcern, perfection, helplessness, and catastrophizing best predicted high
scores on trait anxiety measures; problem avoidance, anxious overconcern, and
helplessness predicted high speech anxiety scores; anxious overconcern, helplessness, and demand for approval predicted high levels of test anxiety; demand
for approval, perfectionism, and anxious overconcern best predicted high fear
of evaluation and criticism scores; and helplessness, perfectionism, and dependency (negatively weighted) best predicted high social avoidance scores.
Deffenbacher et al. (1986) discussed these findings in the context of treatment,
arguing that targeting specific IBs associated with the above forms of anxiety
would likely be therapeutically beneficial.

Recently, Lorcher (2003) investigated the relationship between worry and
endorsement of irrational beliefs. Worry is a central component of anxiety
(*DSM-IV*, American Psychiatric Association, 1994) and is defined as excessive
preoccupation with real or imagined negative consequences. It has been
hypothesized that the principal cognitive component of worry is irrational
thinking. Specifically, beliefs centering on themes of helplessness, danger,
and perfectionism have been proposed as characteristic of individuals who
worry excessively (Kelly & Miller, 1999).

Lorcher (2003) evaluated this hypothesis using a large sample of college
students. Participants completed the Worry Domains Questionnaire (WDQ;
Tallis, Davey, & Bond, 1994), a self-report measure that assesses frequency of
worry across the areas of relationships, lack of confidence, the future, work, and
financial problems, and the Irrational Beliefs Inventory (IBI; Alden & Safran,
1978), a measure of the extent to which individuals endorse 11 IBs
(e.g., "I believe that most human unhappiness is caused by external factors:
that people have little ability to control their own sorrows and disturbances,"
"I believe there is one right solution to any given problem. If I do not find this
solution I feel I have failed"). As expected, scores on the WDQ and the IBI were
significantly associated.

Stepwise multiple regression was then conducted to identify the specific IB items most closely associated with worry. Results showed that the
following IBI items contributed unique variance to scores on the WDQ,
"It is very important for me to be loved or approved of by almost
everyone I meet," "I believe that once something strongly affects my life
it will always affect my behavior," and "I become more upset than I would

when things are not the way I want them to be." These items accounted for 10%, 8%, and 3% of variance respectively. Results support the general assertion that IBs are associated with excessive worry, and are partially supportive of Kelly and Miller's (1999) hypothesis that worry is primarily the result of the IBs of helplessness ("My past history is an important determinant of my present behavior. I believe that once something strongly affects my life it will always affect my behavior"), and perfectionism ("I become more upset than I should when things are not the way I want them to be"). The third cognitive component of Kelly and Miller's (1999) model, the belief that everything is potentially dangerous, did not emerge as a significant predictor of elevated WDQ scores.

Finally, the efficacy of REBT plus relaxation in the treatment of test anxiety was evaluated by Dendato and Diener (1986). These researchers compared relaxation and REBT (R/REBT), study-skills training (SST), relaxation and REBT plus SST (R/REBT + SST), and a no-treatment control group (NT) to evaluate transient anxiety (STAI-State Form; Spielberger, Gorsuch, & Lushene, 1970) and academic performance (high school GPA and ACT scores). Results showed that R/REBT was effective in reducing anxiety (as measured by significant pre- to post-treatment differences in STAI-State Form scores), but did not significantly improve academic performance. R/REBT + SST was effective both in reducing anxiety and in improving academic performance as compared to NT, and more effective on both dependent variables than either treatment component alone. The studies reviewed above provide evidence that IBs are indeed associated with multiple types of anxiety including both transient anxiety (state) and trait anxiety, general worry, specific phobias, test, speech, and social anxiety (including fear of evaluation and criticism), and obsessive-compulsive symptoms.

Irrational Beliefs and Assertiveness Deficits

According to Lange and Jakubowski (1976), the content of IBs held by individuals with assertiveness deficits is related to themes of universal love and approval ("I must be loved by everyone I care about"), Awfulizing ("It would be just awful if I hurt his feelings"), and total competence ("I need to be good at everything I do"). Furthermore, by adhering to such unrealistic expectations of themselves and others, the nonassertive individual sets up a situation where failure (both personally and interpersonally) is almost certain. The result is frustration, inhibition, and negative and ineffective personal interactions (Lange & Jakubowski, 1976).

Alden and Safran (1978) examined the relationship between IBs and assertiveness through the use of both standardized measures and role-playing. Using two groups of "very unassertive" (Alden & Safran, 1978) university students and staff, one group who endorsed Ellis's IBs and another group who did not, these researchers sought to address two questions. First, what if any, is the effect of strong endorsement of IBs on the performance of assertive behavior and the experience of anxiety in situations where assertiveness is appropriate? It was hypothesized that nonassertive individuals who held strong IBs would experience more anxiety and would perform worse than nonassertive participants who did not endorse IBs as strongly. Additionally, it was predicted that the same group would engage in assertive behavior less often and would experience more anxiety when put in a situation in which assertiveness was appropriate.

Second, what is the relationship between IBs and nonassertiveness? That is, are IBs more closely related to *not knowing* how to be assertive (i.e., IBs may lead to distorted and biased social information processing, which may in turn hinder one's ability to accurately identify situations where assertiveness may be appropriate), or as evidence would suggest (Schwartz & Gottman, 1976), do IBs adversely affect the *performance* of assertive behaviors? This second question was handled in an exploratory vein. As such, no prediction was made regarding either explanation.

Both groups of participants completed a measure of IBs (the IB total score was used to identify a high and low endorsement group) and two measures of assertiveness, the Gambrill-Ritchey Assertion Inventory (AI; Gambrill & Ritchey, 1975) and the Assertion Information Form (AIF; Alden & Safran, 1978), an open-ended measure intended to assess participants' awareness of appropriate assertive responses. The AIF includes eight situations where assertive behavior may be appropriate and requires participants to rate how an assertive individual would respond. Subsequent to obtaining participants' ratings of the eight situations, all participants role-played these situations. Independent judges then rated participants' level of assertiveness and anxiety.

Results showed that the three IBs most frequently endorsed by the entire sample were related to themes of total competence, absolute approval, and what can be labeled as overconcern for the welfare of others ("I become more upset than I should about other people's problems and disturbances"). These findings are consistent with the IBs identified by Lange and Jakubowski (1976) as those most closely associated with nonassertiveness.

Scores on the AI for the two groups (high and low endorsement of IBs) showed that the high endorsement group engaged in assertive behavior significantly less frequently and experienced significantly higher levels of anxiety than the low endorsement group. Ratings of the assertiveness role-play are in agreement with AI scores: the high endorsement group was rated as signifi- cantly less assertive. While there was a trend for higher anxiety ratings for the high endorsement group, the difference in anxiety ratings did not reach statis- tical significance. The high endorsement group did, however, rate themselves as significantly more anxious than the low endorsement group. Finally, dis- criminant analysis was conducted to identify the specific types of IBs that most clearly differentiated high and low endorsement groups. Results of this analysis showed that IBs related to themes of total competence and overconcern for the welfare of others best discriminated among the two groups (Alden & Safran, 1978).

The second research question was whether or not the relationship between IBs and nonassertiveness was due to a lack of knowledge about how to engage in assertive behavior or to IBs interfering with appropriate assertive responses. Findings did not support the lack of knowledge hypothesis. The high endorse- ment group was not significantly different from the low endorsement group on knowledge of appropriate assertive responses. Despite apparently having the knowledge of appropriate assertive responses, the high endorsement group was not able to apply this knowledge. Although this group knew the types of assertive responses that would be appropriate for the situation, they did not perform these responses when given the opportunity in the role-play situation (Alden & Safran, 1978).

Taken together, these results support previous findings by Lange and Jakubowski (1976) and support Alden and Safran's (1978) primary predictions that those non-assertive individuals who endorsed Ellis's IBs to a greater extent would be less assertive and would experience greater levels of anxiety during a role-play situation than those nonassertive individuals who endorsed fewer IBs, and that the high endorsement group would rate themselves as significantly less assertive in actual situations and as experiencing more anxiety in these situations. Finally, results are consistent with the hypothesis that it is not lack of knowledge that hinders assertive responding. Rather, it appears that an over- concern for the feelings of others and a desire to be approved of by others serves to inhibit assertiveness, even in situations where the individual believes an assertive response is appropriate. These findings have implications for cogni- tively based assertiveness treatment. Practitioners would be wise to assess the content of IBs for themes of overconcern for others and absolute approval. Results of this study suggest that targeting these specific IBs in the context of REBT for assertiveness deficits would be indicated.

Woods (1987) also examined the relationship between IBs and assertive- ness in the context of a stress management workshop for industrial workers (he also included anxiety, depression, somatization, anger, and Type A coronary-prone behavior, which will be addressed below). Using a pretest-posttest design, Woods examined changes in these variables as a function of weekly REBT workshops for 49 employees. He hypothesized that changes in the variables of interest would occur following group training in REBT.

Workshop sessions were conducted for 1.5 hours each week for four weeks. Pretest measures of the variables of interest were administered about two weeks before the workshops began. In addition to workshops, participants were instructed to read several booklets describing the REBT model and a book titled, *The Assertiveness Option* (Jakubowski & Lange, 1978). Workshops were conducted in groups of eight to 14 employees, and consisted of lectures and active discussions about the role of IBs in emotional disturbances. The central REBT techniques of identifying and disputing IBs were used and a specific emphasis was placed on replacing IBs with RBs. Follow-up measures were completed between three and four months after the workshops ended.

For assertiveness, comparisons of pretest and posttest scores shows that almost half of the employees (46.9%) were classified as assertive based on scores on the AI (Gambrill & Ritchey, 1975) at pretest, as compared to nearly 70% at follow-up. Additionally, changes in ratings of discomfort and assertive response probability evidenced statistically significant decreases and increases respectively, from pretest to follow-up. Woods (1987) also examined changes in IBs from pretest to follow-up. Results show statistically significant reductions on seven of the 10 IBs assessed. The IBs that showed the largest decreases were in demand for approval, high self-expectations, anxious overconcern, and frustration reactivity.

Irrational Beliefs and Type A Coronary-Prone Behavior

The Type A coronary-prone behavior pattern (Friedman & Rosenman, 1974) describes individuals who are highly motivated to achieve, competitive across many situations, feel near-constant time pressure, and are high in hostility and anger. This pattern of behaviors, particularly hostility and anger (Siegman, Anderson, Herbst, Boyle, & Wilkinson, 1992) has been implicated as a risk factor for coronary disease.

Smith and Brehm (1981) examined the relationship between cognitions (IBs and self-statements) and Type A behavior. Following from the REBT model, these researchers hypothesized that specific IBs and self-statements related to themes of perfection, achievement, and mastery and control over events would emerge as mediators of Type A behaviors.

One hundred forty-nine college students completed measures of Type A behavior, IBs, and self-consciousness. Results for the total sample showed that the belief that one should avoid problems rather than face them (i.e., problem-avoidance) was strongly negatively correlated with high scores on the Type A behavior measures; indicating that participants high in measures of Type A strongly prefer to address problems directly rather than avoid them. Significant correlations were also found for Type A behaviors and the belief that blame should be assigned when others make mistakes or fail to live up to expectations (blame-proneness), anxious overconcern (concern about the potential of negative events occurring in the future), and social anxiety (negatively correlated).

To examine potential gender differences, males and females were analyzed separately. Results showed that males and females did indeed differ with respect to the types of beliefs that were associated with Type A behavior. Significant correlations were found for high Type A males and high achievement ("One should be thoroughly competent and achieving in all possible respects if one is to consider oneself worthwhile"), perfectionism ("There is a perfect solution to all problems and it is catastrophic if this perfect solution is not found"), and, as in the total sample, problem-avoidance and low social anxiety. For females, frustration reactivity ("It is catastrophic when things are not the way one would like them to be"), anxious overconcern ("If dangerous or frightening events could take place, one should think about the possibility of their occurrence"), and self-consciousness were all significantly associated with ratings of Type A behavior. As expected, problem-avoidance was also significantly negatively correlated with Type A behavior ratings for females (Smith & Brehm, 1981).

Results suggest that individuals scoring high in Type A behavior display an active rather than passive coping style (i.e., prefer to address problems rather than avoid them). Males endorsed achievement and perfectionism to a greater extent than females, who evidenced a pattern suggestive of a desire to control environmental demands. REBT treatment focusing on modifying IBs associated with these themes of perfectionism, control, and the belief that one has to continually achieve to be worthwhile would likely be beneficial in reducing Type A behaviors.

Results of the Woods (1987) study (see above) also suggest that REBT can be effective in reducing Type A behaviors. Comparing pre-REBT scores on the Jenkins Activity Survey (JAS; Jenkins, Zyzanski, & Rosenman, 1979) with scores at follow-up, it was shown that nearly 35% of employees scored above the 70th percentile, while just over 14% scored below the 30th percentile before the REBT workshop. This pattern was essentially reversed at follow-up.

Following REBT training, just over 14% were above the 70th percentile whereas over 32% were below the 30th percentile.

Results from the Woods (1987) and the Smith and Brehm (1981) studies suggest that REBT is effective in reducing the types of beliefs associated with the Type A behavior pattern. While this is encouraging, particularly considering the potential risk the Type A pattern confers with respect to CHD, whether or not these cognitive changes lead to long-term behavioral change is still unclear. Future studies should evaluate the extent to which these changes in thinking also lead to concomitant changes in maladaptive behaviors, such as overt anger, aggression, and hostility.

Conclusion

The REBT model proposes that irrational beliefs result in emotional disturbances, including depression, anxiety, anger, and guilt. Modifying IBs and substituting more adaptive rational beliefs (RBs) is the goal of REBT. It is thought that thinking more rationally better enables individuals to reach their goals and to live happier, more rewarding lives. Rather than experiencing emotional disturbances, individuals who adopt a rational cognitive set are likely to experience the more moderate, less dysfunctional emotions of sadness, concern, annoyance, and remorse (David et al., 2005).

The foregoing review examined the research on the association between IBs and emotional disturbances, including general psychiatric symptoms, depression, various forms of anxiety, assertiveness deficits, and Type A coronary prone behavior. The overall pattern of findings suggests that increased levels of IBs are associated with emotional disturbances. Now that this relationship appears to be established, several directions for future REBT research are proposed. First, measurement of IBs should continue to move in the direction of more ecologically valid, individualized methods. Merely presenting individuals with a preselected set of IBs and asking them to rate the extent to which they agree with these items may not accurately capture the specific, idiosyncratic nature of individuals' thought patterns. The end result may then be an inability to find differences between groups in the endorsement of IBs. The articulated thoughts in simulated situation paradigm (ATSS; Davison et al., 1983) and the Specific Demands on Self-scale (SDS; Solomon, 1998) appear promising as more sensitive, ecologically valid measures of IBs.

Second, research should continue to examine the nature of the relationship between IBs and dysfunctional emotions to attempt to answer the question of whether IBs are risk factors or correlates of emotional disturbances. To date, attempts to address this issue (Solomon et al., 1998) suggest that IBs fluctuate with level of depression (i.e., are correlates of depression), which runs counter to the REBT prediction that IBs represent risk factors for emotional disturbance. More causal-relationship studies, rather than correlational, should be conducted to answer this question. It should be noted, however, that this is a problem with the entire cognitive therapy literature. It is not clear if cognitive change causes behavioral and attitudinal change or if it results from and is reflective of that change.

Third, as addressed by David et al. (2005), researchers have tended to infer that rational thinking represents low scores on measures of irrationality, assuming that rational thinking is simply the absence of irrational thinking. Factor analysis suggests that this assumption may not be warranted (Bernard, 1998). Future REBT research, then, should measure IBs and RBs independently. Considering that the goal of REBT is more rational thinking, not just less irrational thinking, this issue should not be overlooked. Fourth, it may be helpful to determine the exact nature of certain types of irrational beliefs. Both the clinical and research literature have treated them as unitary constructs. However, David, Schnur, et al. (2005) found that demandingness and global evaluation/self downing appear to be evaluative schemas and that awfulizing/catastrophizing and frustration intolerance can be better conceptualized as evaluative cognitions that are not organized as schemas. In addition, they found that demandingness seems to be associated with each of the other three irrational beliefs, as a sort of core or meta-IB, although the direction of causality is unclear.

Fifth, the diathesis-stress model of REBT should be further investigated empirically. The results of studies investigating the REBT diathesis-stress model to date do not provide unequivocal evidence for it (David, Szentagotai, Kallay, & Macavei, in press). They tentatively suggest that the REBT diathesis-stress model can predict some outcomes (e.g., hostility) but not others (e.g., trait anxiety). However, they also suggest that when implemented and tested correctly (e.g., in prospective designs and real stressful events), hypotheses generated by the REBT diathesis-stress model tend to be empirically supported. This topic would benefit from further research.

Clinical Examples

A few short clinical examples may illustrate these concepts. Consider the case of Melissa, who has an IB schema, "I must be perfect" (i.e., demandingness) that might generate a number of thoughts and behaviors in all areas of her functioning. Melissa may become a perfectionist in order to increase the probability that other people will like her and think that she is better or smarter than others. In her relationships as well as in her work environment, Melissa may also expect the people around her to offer her praise and shower her with compliments. All goes well for Melissa when she is viewed and treated as being the perfect employee, friend, and wife. However, in situations that defeat her expectations, she becomes more vulnerable. For example, one day at work Melissa accidentally misplaced her report for a meeting at work, and was told by her boss that she had to work on developing her organizational skills. Given Melissa's attempts at being perfect at all times, and her boss's response to her as being unprepared for the meeting, Melissa may be far more reactive to this particular situation. She may react quickly to this comment, place greater weight on her thoughts, and find her schema of "I must be perfect" far more compelling than when she had a higher threshold and was not under any stress. Melissa's schema of "I must be perfect" is exacerbated once again and continues the vicious cycle of her thoughts and behaviors of being perfect.

Consider also the case of John. John, an individual with borderline personality disorder is tempted to maintain his cycle of acting helplessly in interpersonal relationships. He consistently continues to seek out the attention that he desires and craves. Although John desperately wants to be loved and cared for, his beliefs center on his deeply held IB schema that he is a vulnerable, weak, and worthless person (i.e., self-downing). His maladaptive schema continues to serve as a template for understanding and governing his world.

Third, consider the case of Mary. Mary is a 28-year-old woman who is currently experiencing symptoms of depression due to her recent break-up with her boyfriend of four years. Mary's depiction of her break-up and being single again is directly related to her feelings of helplessness and worthlessness. In her sessions, Mary reports that as a teenager and adolescent she felt constantly rejected by men due to her stocky weight and disheveled appearance. She would wait on the sidelines to be approached by a man who might find her to be attractive. In situations where people laughed and joked about her being overweight, she withdrew and isolated herself from others. Over the years, Mary has developed IB schemas that represent herself as being inadequate (i.e., self-downing), others as being overly critical (i.e., other-downing), and the world as being unjust and unfair (i.e., world-downing). When Mary was involved in satisfying and meaningful relationships with men, her maladaptive schema remained dormant. However, now faced with an unexpected break-up, Mary is in a depressive state where she ruminates on her previously dormant schema.

REBT continues to be one of the most widespread psychotherapies used in clinical practice. Continued refinement of its constructs and assumptions will likely only serve to enhance its utility and acceptability as both a system of psychotherapy and a philosophical framework that can be used to improve functioning across a wide range of domains and assist individuals in attaining their goals.

REFERENCES

Alden, L., & Safran, J. (1978). Irrational beliefs and nonassertive behavior. *Cognitive Therapy and Research, 2,* 357–364.

American Psychiatric Association (1994). *Diagnostic and statistical manual of mental disorders* (4th ed.). Washington, DC: American Psychiatric Association.

Beck, A. T., Rush, A. J., Shaw, B. F., & Emery, G. (1979). *Cognitive therapy of depression.* New York: Guilford Press.

Bernard, M. E. (1981). Private thought in rational emotive psychotherapy. *Cognitive Therapy and Research, 5,* 125–142.

Bernard, M. E. (1998). Validation of the General Attitude and Beliefs Scale. *Journal of Rational-Emotive and Cognitive-Behavior Therapy, 16,* 183–196.

Cohen, J. (1988). *Statistical power analysis for the behavioral sciences* (2nd ed.). Hillside, NJ: Erlbaum.

David, A., Ghinea, C., Macavei, B., & Kallay, E. (2005). A search for "hot" cognitions in a clinical and a non-clinical context: Appraisal, attributions, core relational themes, irrational beliefs, and their relations to emotion. *Journal of Cognitive and Behavioral Psychotherapies, 5,* 1–42.

David, D., Schnur, J., DiGiuseppe, R., Szentagotai, A., Macavei, B., & Kallay, E. (2005). The organization and the nature of irrational beliefs: Schemas or appraisal. *Journal of Cognitive and Behavioral Psychotherapies, 5,* 139–158.

David, D., Szentagotai, A., Kallay, E., & Macavei, B. (in press). A synopsis of rational emotive behaviour therapy (REBT): Fundamental and applied research. *Journal of Rational-Emotive & Cognitive-Behavior Therapy.*

Davison, G. C., Feldman, P. M., & Osborn, C. E. (1984). Articulated thoughts, irrational beliefs, and fear of negative evaluations. *Cognitive Therapy and Research, 8,* 349–362.

Davison, G. C., Robins, C., & Johnson, M. K. (1983). Articulated thoughts during simulated situations: A paradigm for studying cognition in emotion and behavior. *Cognitive Therapy and Research, 7,* 17–40.

Deffenbacher, J. L., Zwemer, W. A., Whisman, M. A., Hill, R. A., & Sloan, R. D. (1986). Irrational beliefs and anxiety. *Cognitive Therapy and Research, 10,* 281–292.

Dendato, K. M., & Diener, D. (1986). Effectiveness of cognitive/relaxation therapy and study-skills training in reducing self-reported anxiety and improving the academic performance of test-anxious students. *Journal of Counseling Psychology, 33,* 131–135.

DeRogatis, L., & Cleary, P. (1977). Confirmation of the dimensional structure of the SCL-90: A study in construct validation. *Journal of Clinical Psychology, 33,* 981–987.

Ellis, A. (1962). *Reason and emotion in psychotherapy.* New York: Stuart.

Ellis, A. (1987). A sadly neglected element in depression. *Cognitive Therapy and Research, 11,* 121–146.

Ellis, A. (1994). *Reason and emotion in psychotherapy* (rev. ed.). Secaucus, NJ: Birch Lane.

Ellis, A. (1997). Must musturbation and demandingness lead to emotional disorders? *Psychotherapy: Theory, Research, Practice, Training, 34,* 95–98.

Ellis, A., & Dryden, W. (1997). *The practice of rational emotive behavior therapy.* New York: Springer.

Engels, G. I., Garnefski, N., & Diekstra, R. F. W. (1993). Efficacy of rational-emotive therapy: A quantitative analysis. *Journal of Consulting and Clinical Psychology, 61,* 1083–1090.

Friedman, M., & Rosenman, R. H. (1974). *Type A behavior and your heart.* New York: Knopf.

Gambrill, E., & Ritchey, C. (1975). An assertion inventory for use in assessment and research. *Behavior Therapy, 6,* 550–561.

Gormally, J., Sipps, G., Raphael, R., Edwin, D., & Varvil-Weld, D. (1981). The relationship between maladaptive cognitions and social anxiety. *Journal of Consulting and Clinical Psychology, 49,* 300–301.

Himle, D., Thyer, B., & Papsdorf, J. (1982). Relationships between rational beliefs and anxiety. *Cognitive Therapy and Research, 6,* 219–223.

Hirschfeld, R. M. A., Klerman, G. L., Lavori, P., Keller, M. B., Griffith, P., & Coryell, W. (1989). Premorbid personality assessments of major depression. *Archives of General Psychiatry, 46,* 345–350.

Jakubowski, P., & Lange, A. J. (1978). *The assertiveness option.* Champaign, IL: Research Press.

Jenkins, C. D., Zyzanski, S. J., & Rosenman, R. H. (1979). *Jenkins Activity Survey.* New York: The Psychological Corporation.

Jones, R. (1968). *A factored measure of Ellis' irrational belief system with personality and maladjustment correlates.* Unpublished doctoral dissertation, Texas Technical College, Lubbock.

Kassinove, H., Crisci, R., & Tiegerman, S. (1977). Developmental trends in rational thinking. *Journal of Community Psychology, 5,* 266–274.

Kelly, W. E., & Miller, M. J. (1999). A discussion of worry with suggestions for counselors. *Counseling and Values, 44,* 55–65.

Lange, A., & Jakubowski, P. (1976). *Responsible assertive behavior: Cognitive/behavioral procedures for trainers.* Champaign, IL: Research Press.

Leahy, R. L. (2004). Pessimism and the evolution of negativity. In P. Gilbert (Ed.), *Evolutionary theory and cognitive therapy* (pp. 91–118). New York: Springer.

Lipsky, M. J., Kassinove, H., & Miller, N. J. (1980). Effects of rational-emotive therapy, rational role reversal, and rational-emotive imagery on the emotional adjustment of community mental health center patients. *Journal of Consulting and Clinical Psychology, 48,* 366–374.

Lorcher, P. S. (2003). Worry and irrational beliefs: A preliminary investigation. *Individual Differences Research, 1,* 73–76.

Lyons, L. C., & Woods, P. J. (1991). The efficacy of rational-emotive therapy: A quantitative review of the outcome research. *Clinical Psychology Review, 11,* 357–369.

Malouff, J. M., & Schutte, N. S. (1986). Development and validation of a measure of irrational beliefs. *Journal of Consulting and Clinical Psychology, 54,* 860–862.

McDermut, J. F., Haaga, D. A. F., & Bilek, L. A. (1997). Cognitive bias and irrational beliefs in major depression and dysphoria. *Cognitive Therapy & Research, 21,* 459–476.

Muran, J. C., Kassinove, H., Ross, S., & Muran, E. (1989). Irrational thinking and negative emotionality in college students and applicants for mental health services. *Journal of Clinical Psychology, 45,* 188–193.

Nelson, E. (1977). Irrational beliefs in depression. *Journal of Consulting and Clinical Psychology, 45,* 1190–1191.

Newmark, C. S., Frerking, R. A., Cook, L., & Newmark, L. (1973). Endorsement of Ellis' irrational beliefs as a function of psychopathology. *Journal of Clinical Psychology, 29,* 300–302.

Prud'homme, L., & Barron, P. (1992). The pattern of irrational belief associated with major depressive disorder. *Social Behavior and Personality, 20,* 199–212.

Rosenbaum, M., Lewinsohn, P. M., & Gotlib, I. H. (1996). Distinguishing between state-dependent and non-state-dependent depression-related psychosocial variables. *British Journal of Clinical Psychology, 35,* 341–358.

Schwartz, R., & Gottman, J. (1976). Toward a task analysis of assertive behavior. *Journal of Consulting and Clinical Psychology, 44,* 910–920.

Shorkey, C. T., & Whiteman, V. L. (1977). Development of the Rational Behavior Inventory: Initial validity and reliability. *Educational and Psychological Measurement, 37,* 527–534.

Siegman, A. W., Anderson, R., Herbst, J., Boyle, S., & Wilkinson, J. (1992). Dimensions of anger-hostility and cardiovascular reactivity in provoked and angered men. *Journal of Behavioral Medicine, 15,* 257–272.

Smith, T. W. (1983). Change in irrational beliefs and the outcome of rational-emotive psychotherapy. *Journal of Consulting and Clinical Psychology, 51,* 156–157.

Smith, T. W. (1989). Assessment in rational-emotive therapy: Empirical access to the ABCD model. In M. E. Bernard & R. DiGiuseppe (Eds.), *Inside rational-emotive therapy: A critical appraisal of the theory and therapy of Albert Ellis* (pp. 135–153). San Diego, CA: Academic Press.

Smith, T. W., & Brehm, S. S. (1981). Cognitive correlates of the Type A coronary-prone behavior pattern. *Motivation and Emotion, 5,* 215–223.

Solomon, A. (1998). *The Specific Demands on Self Scale.* Unpublished manuscript, Stanford University.

Solomon, A., Arnow, B. A., Gotlib, I. H., & Wind, B. (2003). Individualized measurement of irrational beliefs in remitted depressives. *Journal of Clinical Psychology, 59,* 439–455.

Solomon, A., Haaga, D. A. F., Brody, C., Kirk, L., & Friedman, D. G. (1998). Priming irrational beliefs in recovered-depressed people. *Journal of Abnormal Psychology, 107,* 440–449.

Spielberger, C. D., Gorsuch, R. L., & Lushene, R. E. (1970). *The State-Trait Anxiety Inventory (STAI) manual.* Palo Alto, CA: Consulting Psychologists Press.

Tallis, F., Davey, C. G. I., & Bond, A. (1994). The Worry Domains Questionnaire. In G. Davey & F. Tallis (Eds.), *Worrying: Perspectives on theory, assessment, and treatment* (pp. 286–297). New York: Wiley.

Thyer, B. A., Papsdorf, J. D., & Kilgore, S. A. (1983). Relationships between irrational thinking and psychiatric symptomatology. *The Journal of Psychology, 113,* 31–34.

Watson, D., Clark, L. A., & Tellegen, A. (1988). Development and validation of brief measures of positive and negative affect: The PANAS scales. *Journal of Personality and Social Psychology, 54,* 1063–1070.

Whiteman, V., & Shorkey, C. (1978). Validation testing of the rational behavior inventory. *Educational and Psychological Measurement, 38,* 1143–1149.

Woods, P. J. (1987). Reductions in Type A behavior, anxiety, anger, and physical illness as related to changes in irrational beliefs: Results of a demonstration project in industry. *Journal of Rational-Emotive Therapy, 5,* 213–237.

9

Rational and Irrational Beliefs in Primary Prevention and Mental Health

Donald A. Caserta, E. Thomas Dowd, Daniel David, and Albert Ellis

REBT theory argues that a philosophy of relativism or "desiring" is a central feature of psychologically healthy humans. This philosophy acknowledges that humans have a large variety of desires, wishes, wants, preferences, and so forth; but if they refuse to escalate these nonabsolute values into grandiose dogmas and demands, they will become less psychologically disturbed (Ellis & Dryden, 1997, p. 17).

Given the evidence that irrational beliefs (IBs) are associated with psychopathology and maladaptive functioning, as summarized in Chapter 8 (this volume), it follows, at least conceptually and theoretically, that rational beliefs (RBs) have the potential to protect against the development of pathological disturbance and to foster resilience during times of emotional distress. However, as outlined in more detail later in this chapter, the preventive nature of RBs is difficult to support via statistical and empirical data, especially because the research methodologies and the associated statistical techniques necessary to draw such conclusions have not been consistently applied in the REBT literature and because of the historical problem of valid measures of rationality and irrationality (Kendall et al., 1995). Additionally, the literature on prevention inherently suffers from confounding variables, and theories explaining such factors often vary in the amount of weight provided to environmental or interpersonal factors versus individual or intrapersonal determinants. Despite these challenges, there are several examples from the empirical literature that have, to varying degrees, accounted for some of these complexities and that bolster the general position that RBs can act as protective factors in stressful situations.

This chapter will review the research on the relationship between RBs and indicators of emotional wellness, the predictive utility of RBs when identifying healthier adaptive functioning in children, adolescents, and adults, and the current status of RBs in the prevention literature. However, in order to narrow the focus of this review to the most relevant empirical research, we begin by reviewing the key constructs of rational psychological health, including the evolution of the REBT ABC model, the operational characteristics of RBs and IBs, and the inherent obstacles to studying adequately the role of RBs and IBs in mental health outcomes.

Introduction to Rational Psychological Health

The central goal of REBT is to assist clients in improving their functioning by means of introspective identification and direct challenging of the maladaptive beliefs that interfere with their ability to pursue and fulfill goals. Since its inception, the theory and practice of REBT has been successfully applied outside the traditional psychotherapy office, including REBT derivatives such as rational-emotive behavioral consultation (REBC; for review, see Bernard & DiGiuseppe, 2000) and rational-emotive education programs (REE; for review, see DiGiuseppe & Bernard, 1990). The REBT ABC framework fundamentally holds that individuals tend to allow their beliefs (Bs) about certain circumstances, or activating events (As), to influence unduly their emotional and behavioral responses, or consequences (Cs).

These constructs are interrelated, however, and none exist in a purely monolithic state, since each construct can create the context for the others (for review, see Ellis & Dryden, 1997, ch. 1). Indeed, Ellis (2004) claims that this complex interconnection has historically been a part of his early writings on rational-emotive theory and notes that "human thinking, feeling, and behaving are all distinctly interrelated, not disparate, and include important aspects of the other two processes" (p. 86). Furthermore, the REBT model does not deny the potential influence of biological factors in the organism that may actually create a predisposition for emotional disturbance, nor does it ignore cases in which severe environmental conditions appear to propel otherwise healthy individuals into dysfunctional states of mental illness.

However, proponents of REBT usually view these influences within the context of the ABC model. For example, powerful activating events do not usually occur in isolation and therefore an individual's resulting cognitive, affective, and behavioral consequences are the result of both the actual event and the beliefs that were brought to the situation. Typically an individual has already developed IBs prior to being exposed to an undesirable event or stressor, such that the beliefs predisposed a negative response to the activating event. When considering the interactions of these potential influences on the development of unhealthy emotional regulation, the extension of REBT as a clinical approach into the realm of prevention and expression of resilience makes theoretical and therapeutic sense. More specifically, if IBs tend to further an individual's dysfunctional and maladaptive behavior through dogmatic and unconditional *musts* and *shoulds*, then it logically follows that RBs contribute to an individual's overall psychological and emotional health because balanced, logical reasoning allows for adaptive responses to privation. For operational clarification, and borrowing from Dryden (2003), RBs are generally considered flexible and/or nonextreme, consistent with reality, logical or sensible, and largely constructive to each person.

Furthermore, REBT theory holds that those engaging in chronic, irrational thought processes tend to perpetuate unknowingly such thinking by means of flawed feedback loops that elicit more IBs as a function of being reinforced by ignoring any evidence to the contrary. Conversely those who eschew dogmatic thinking in favor of more flexible RBs are more likely to experience healthy negative emotions in the face of such adversity. As Ellis and Dryden (1997) note, rather than insisting that someone act a certain way, for example, or that a situation should or must not happen, individuals empowered by RBs express their desires, wants, or preferences, such that if their desires are not fulfilled, then they are able to move forward and reformulate their goals in a productive and logical manner.

Ellis and Dryden (1997) offer three derivatives of this *desiring* that allow psychologically healthy individuals to manage stressors; rating or evaluating badness, tolerance, and acceptance. Rating or evaluating badness is equivalent to avoiding the tendency to rate unpleasant events or unexpected failures on an exaggerated level of awfulness. Tolerance involves one's appreciation that undesirable events occur and, in the event that one does occur, rating the event on the badness continuum (as opposed to *awfulizing*), attempting to change the situation if possible, and, if that is not possible, turning attention and action to achieving other goals. Acceptance involves the ability to recognize that all humans are fallible and that assigning global or fixed rating of oneself is unhealthy, especially since the world is a complex place governed by rules that are outside of one's control. Building on the importance of these three main derivatives, Ziegler (2003) claims that the "essence of psychological health in REBT theory is rational acceptance of reality" (p. 28). In summary, REBT theory holds that RBs are central to adaptive responses to stressors and preclude negative mental health outcomes through the acceptance of reality as it is, rather than demanding that reality not be so as in IBs, and by acting on preferences rather than demands.

Although the efficacy and effectiveness of REBT has been well established (for reviews, see Lyons & Woods, 1991; Solomon & Haaga, 1995; Terjesen, DiGiuseppe, & Gruner, 2000), empirical support for several core features of REBT theory is difficult to produce given the introspective nature of beliefs and emotions, the inherent problems in measuring and assessing beliefs (Bond & Dryden, 1996a; Haaga & Davison, 1993), and the statistical challenge of testing for the directionality and causality between beliefs and emotions. Furthermore, because the constructs of irrationality and negative emotionality are, by REBT definition and by statistical examination, intercorrelated, researchers have had a difficult time parsing out the individual and collective contributions of IBs and negative emotions to dysfunctional mental health outcomes (Kendall et al., 1995) and determining whether and which one is primary over the other (Raimy, 2004).

Likewise, testing the role of RBs in the development of adaptive, resilient functioning during times of stress appears to also be complicated by the entanglement of RBs with the construct of positive affectivity. In addition to the difficulties inherent in measuring individuals' internal belief systems, measurement problems specific to the differentiation between RBs and IBs, or rationality and irrationality more generally, also exist. It is incorrect to assume the presence of a rational belief system based solely on an individual's low scores on a measure of irrationality (Haaga & Davison, 1993). As a consequence, many of the conclusions drawn from the empirical literature on the protective nature of RBs are limited by virtue of nonspecific operational definitions and measurement of RBs.

Furthermore, equivocal empirical evidence exists in determining whether dysfunctional and functional emotions are qualitatively different, quantitatively different, or both. To clarify, REBT theory posits that individuals operating from RB systems tend to hold more functional positive and negative emotions, while those thinking and behaving out of IBs tend to hold more dysfunctional positive and negative emotions. For example, according to Ellis (1994), functional negative emotions may include "disappointment, sorrow, regret, and frustration" whereas dysfunctional negative emotions may include "panic, depression, and rage" (p. 82). Although Cramer and Fong (1991) offer evidence that functional, or appropriate, and dysfunctional, or inappropriate, emotions that follow from RBs and IBs vary quantitatively (i.e., via level of intensity) rather than qualitatively, Ellis and DiGiuseppe (1993) challenge these conclusions and claim that these two types of emotional responses, or Cs, are qualitatively different.

Most notably, although all of these authors would probably agree that both functional and dysfunctional feelings can have varying intensities, Ellis and DiGiuseppe (1993) posit that dysfunctional emotions "tend to be more intense, more profound, more pervasive, and more physiologically arousing, and have more enduring consequences" (p. 472). Furthermore, Ellis and DiGiuseppe argue that Cramer and Fong (1991) failed to consider that one can have both functional and dysfunctional emotions concurrently, that intense negative feelings are not always dysfunctional, and that their measure of emotions only involved intensity and therefore did not provide evidence that the words used to describe either functional or dysfunctional emotions differed qualitatively. Finally, proponents of REBT theory see the RBs and IBs that tend to precede emotional responses as also varying qualitatively, where dysfunctional negative emotions tend to be the product of IBs that add demands and musts on to what may have begun initially as preferential RBs. As D. David (2003) elucidates, it is the *adaptiveness*, not the intensity, of an emotional response that is the critical distinction between functional and dysfunctional emotions, and therefore these constructs are viewed as being qualitatively distinct.

More recently and partly in response to the findings of Cramer and Fong (1991), several researchers have further investigated the relationships between RBs and IBs and functional and dysfunctional emotions. Research from two areas provides clarification and support for the REBT model of emotion formation. One focuses on a new avenue of research exploring the relationships between REBT and appraisal theory and the potential for each to be complemented by the other (A. David, Ghinea, Macavei, & Kallay, 2005; D. David, Schnur, & Belloiu, 2002; D. David, Schnur, & Birk, 2004) while the other focuses more on parsing out the effects that IBs and RBs have on subsequent *functionality of inferences* (Bond & Dryden, 1996b, 1997; Bond, Dryden, & Briscoe, 1999; McDuff & Dryden, 1998).

D. David et al. (2002) and A. David et al. (2005) extend previous research on the REBT theory of emotion formation into the research that has been conducted on the appraisal theory of emotion formation by Lazarus and Smith (as cited in D. David et al., 2002). These authors claim that although previous research has noted the relationships between the constructs of IBs and appraisal, most lacked empirical support (for discussion, see D. David, 2003). These two studies collectively provide support for the hypothesized relationships between appraisal, dysfunctional affectivity, and IBs. Specifically, these data appear to validate the initial theory of REBT that dysfunctional emotions seem to correspond with primary appraisal that involve irrational demands/ musts, whereas functional emotions appear to involve primary appraisal associated with rational preferences.

In another study (D. David et al., 2004), after subjects were primed with either RBs or IBs, they participated in a physiologically arousing activity and were given randomly assigned time to recover from this activity. For some subjects, the time was not sufficient, and these subjects are referred to as having explained arousal; however, other subjects were given sufficient time to recover and are referred to as having unexplained arousal (assumed to be present due to the priming of beliefs. Because the findings suggest that subjects in the IB-unexplained arousal condition produce feelings that are different from those mediated by RBs, D. David et al. conclude that "it is the quality (negative vs. positive) and cognitive content (IBs vs. RBs) of the feelings, and not their intensity (arousal) that differentiates them" (p. 878). These findings challenge those reported by Cramer and Fong (1991).

Despite a history of conflicting empirical evidence for the construct validity of RBs and IBs that appears to be a function of improper measurement, ill-specified operational definitions, and inadequate application of statistical techniques, more recent data support the legitimacy of these two constructs and their role in the development of dysfunctional patterns of behavior and emotion. For example, a factor analysis of the Attitude and Belief Scale conducted by Burgess (as cited in DiGiuseppe & Leaf, 1990) identified one factor, called irrationality, that accounted for 83% of the variance in scores collected from 201 outpatients in a general clinical population. DiGiuseppe and Leaf also provide evidence in support of the REBT theory that dysfunctional irrationality is associated with a few core IBs, namely demandingness, awfulizing, self-worth, and low frustration tolerance, especially demandingness.

Silverman and DiGiuseppe (2001) conducted a study investigating the relationships between children's internalizing and externalizing emotional and behavioral problems across four dominant CBT constructs, including irrationality. Based on cut-off scores determined from teacher ratings scales, 126 children between the ages of 9 and 13 were included and identified as expressing internalized, externalized, or mixed emotional and behavioral problems or no problems. Children identified as having behavioral and emotional problems, regardless of type, scored higher on IBs than children with no problems on the self-downing and demandingness subscales of the Child and Adolescent Scale of Irrationality (CASI; Bernard & Laws, 1988; as cited in Silverman & DiGiuseppe), and the low frustration tolerance subscale differentiated the children identified as having internalized problems from those with no problems.

Finally, above and beyond data supporting the validity of RBs and IBs via better measurement and statistical design, evidence from the field of cognitive neuroscience is mounting that offers validation for RBs and IBs in REBT theory. For example, a pilot study conducted by Tiba (2003) indicates different neurological systems are associated with Ellis's concepts of preferential RBs and demanding IBs. Specifically, these data support the conclusion that individuals who score high on measures of demandingness tend to exhibit both low updating and inhibitory abilities, both of which are correlated with unhealthy emotional ratings.

Rational Beliefs in the Empirical Literature

In order to narrow the scope of this chapter to empirical evidence that supports RBs as providing a protective factor against stress, we excluded research studies of general cognitive-based and prevention interventions that do not specifically measure or target aspects of RBs. Therefore this review targets the literature that provides evidence for the protective functions of RBs both directly and indirectly. More specifically, the remaining sections describe generally what has been ascertained from child and adult research on the role of rationality in two domains: (a) healthy adjustment to and coping with common life stressors and general measures of well-being and (b) prevention of negative mental health outcomes. Although much literature indicates that healthy cognitions and belief structures can reduce physiological symptoms or assist in the prevention of certain diseases such as coronary heart disease (for review, see Gallo, Ghaed, & Bracken, 2004), this review will focus almost exclusively on mental health outcomes.

Rational Beliefs, Adjustment to Stressors, and General Well-Being

This section reviews prospective and retrospective research on the relationships between beliefs (both RBs and IBs) and adaptive responses to actual, perceived, and hypothetical stressors as well as general outcome measures of well-being and adaptive functioning. More specifically, features related to healthy management of stress have been demonstrated to be associated with rational ways of thinking, or less overall irrationality, in several areas of functioning, including general response to negative life events (A. David et al., 2005; Master & Miller, 1991; Ziegler & Leslie, 2003), job-related stress (Tan, 2004), disagreements or problems in marital and close relationships (Addis & Bernard, 2002; Cramer, 2004, 2005a, 2005b), bereavement (Boelen, Kip, Voorsluijs, & van den Bout, 2004), anticipation of surgery (D. David, Montgomery, Macavei, & Bovbjerg, 2005), dealing with chronic medical disabilities (Greaves, 1997), adjustment to imprisonment in adolescent offenders (Ireland, Boustead, & Ireland, 2005), and adjustment in high school students (Lee, Sohn, & Park, 2004). Similarly, empirical support has linked RBs and IBs to outcomes of general functioning (Ciarrochi, 2004; Day & Maltby, 2003) and trait (Ziegler & Smith, 2004) and state (Tafrate & Kassinove, 1998) anger.

Although primarily investigating the cognitive antecedents to both dysfunctional maladaptive feelings and functional adaptive feelings, two studies by A. David et al. (2005) provide evidence that individuals' beliefs about past negative events are associated with functional and dysfunctional negative emotions. Specifically, they found that although both dysfunctional and functional negative emotions are associated with an individual's appraisal and core relational themes, only IBs are only associated with dysfunctional negative emotions. Since these studies separately sampled both clinical and nonclinical populations, these findings seem to indicate that those who endorse more IBs will tend to respond to stressful events with a number of dysfunctional negative emotions that perpetuate maladaptive functioning while those who endorse fewer IBs will engage in more adaptive responses due to the presence of functional negative emotions.

In a separate study investigating IBs and RBs and their relationships to physiological arousal in a mood induction task, Master and Miller (1991) separated subjects into one of three groups. Subjects in one group were instructed to repeat rational self-statements, those in the second group were instructed to repeat irrational self-statements, and those in the last group were instructed to repeat neutral self-statements. After being presented with statements that were highly arousing and provocative for each subject, measures on physiological arousal were collected using a measure of skin resistance. Findings support the protective role of RBs during times of elevated mood and arousal, because only subjects in the rational self-statement group evidenced decreases on measures of physiological arousal over time. Furthermore, subjects in the irrational self-statement group reported more subjective anxiety, more negative thinking, and greater physiological arousal than did either the rational or neutral self-statement groups.

Similar evidence for the utility of RBs in responding positively to negative life stress was documented by Ziegler and Leslie (2003), in their investigation of a hypothesis that was born out of a core tenet of the REBT ABC model, namely that those who report more IBs will report responding to stress with more dysfunctional behaviors than those who report fewer IBs. A sample of 192 college students completed self-report measures assessing their level of irrational thinking and their perceptions of the intensity and frequency of their daily hassles. They found significant differences between students with higher and lower levels of overall irrationality, as measured by the Survey of Personal Beliefs; the former group reported more frequent hassles or stressors, as measured by the Hassles Scale. Furthermore, students scoring higher on two specific types of IBs measured, namely "awfulizing" and low frustration tolerance, reported significantly more intense hassles than those who scored lower on the same types of IBs. These results support the conclusion that individuals who report less irrationality, and possibly those who maintain more RBs, will experience fewer life stressors and perceive actual life stress as less intense and problematic than those espousing more irrational thinking.

In another study of belief systems and their relationship to management of work-related stress, Tan (2004) investigated the following two research questions: *(1)* what is the relationship between the intensity of IBs and perceived levels of stress, and *(2)* what are the relationships between certain types of IBs and various sources of stress? Occupational therapists (OTs) practicing in Singapore were targeted for this study, and potential participants were able to respond to self-report questionnaires that were received either through posted material or via electronic mailing of surveys. Results indicated that although the reported intensity of IBs was not related to perceived levels of stress, some beliefs were associated with certain sources of stress. Low frustration tolerance was significantly correlated with reports of stress related to patient contact while IBs about self-worth were associated with stress concerning rewards and recognition for work and with stress regarding the value of their profession. Despite being quite limited in terms of their generalizability, especially since there was no control for the selection of participants, these results offer useful insights into the possible utility of assessing the presence or absence of these IBs while managing the specific types of stressors, as doing so would appear to increase the likeliness of adaptive responses.

Similar attempts at identifying the types of RBs and IBs that are associated with maladaptive versus adaptive functioning in response to stress has been examined in both marital and close relationships. In one report concerning married couples, Addis and Bernard (2002) attempted to identify the aspects of IBs that allow differentiation between *(1)* status of marital therapy (i.e., attending or not attending), and *(2)* self-reported satisfaction with the marriage, as measured by the Locke-Wallace Marital Adjustment Test. Of the 60 participating married couples, 18 were actively attending marriage counseling, while the other 43 couples were not enrolled in marriage counseling. After each partner completed self-report measures of RBs, IBs, emotional traits (e.g., anger, anxiety), and communication skills, they conducted correlational and multiple regression analyses on these data and found overall support for the REBT propositions that high levels of IBs interfere with healthy marital adjustment and overall marital satisfaction and that certain negative emotional traits contribute to maladaptive interpersonal functioning. Specifically, Addis and Bernard identified *irrational self-downing* and *need for support* as the specific aspects of IBs that interfere most with, or are correlated strongest with, general marital dysfunction and the negative emotional traits of anger and anxiety were both able to sort out couples who are or are not experiencing significant problems in their relationship.

In a series of studies, Cramer (2004, 2005a, 2005b) manipulated subjects' beliefs associated with imagining having a serious disagreement with a romantic partner or closest friend. In the first study, Cramer (2004) randomly assigned subjects to one of the following five conditions: *(a)* rational (i.e., imagining believing that disagreement is not destructive), *(b)* rational with a counterdemand (i.e., imagining believing the RB and that believing in this RB may result in feeling worse about the relationship), *(c)* control (i.e., imagining believing neutral, factual statements about the disagreement, void of beliefs about destructiveness), (d) irrational (i.e., imagining believing that disagreement is destructive), and *(e)* irrational with a counterdemand (i.e., imagining believing the IB and that believing in this IB may result in feeling better about the relationship). The counterdemand conditions were supposed to assess for potential demand characteristics on the effect of belief condition. Participants included 150 undergraduate students who also completed pre- and posttest measures of relationship satisfaction.

Cramer (2004) reported findings that are consistent with his hypothesis, namely that individuals imagining the RB report less dissatisfaction with their relationships than those who imagined the IB. Furthermore, scores on the posttest relationship satisfaction measure were significantly higher in the RB group than in the control or the IB groups. These findings, although strongly limited by the contrived conditions, provide evidence that beliefs can be successfully manipulated and that RBs do appear to result in more functional responses to potential stress that is experienced in important interpersonal relationships.

In a subsequent study, Cramer (2005a) reported a related, but distinct finding in an examination of the aspects of RBs that serve to decrease the likelihood of dissatisfaction with close relationships after imagining a serious disagreement. He found that significant differences on posttest relationship satisfaction ratings between subjects in the RB condition and those in the control condition were only present when all four of the main aspects of RBs were used in combination. This cumulative or additive effect again supports the proposition of REBT that RBs act as buffers when managing stressful inter-personal situations, such as when disagreements or arguments ensue with significant others. Continuing the study of the destructive disagreement belief, Cramer (2005b) again investigated whether verbalizations of IBs about the destructiveness of disagreement with one's closest friend result in less relation-ship satisfaction. Conversely, he hypothesized that subjects instructed to repeat RBs that disagreement with one's closest friend is not destructive would lead to more positive ratings of relationship satisfaction. Indeed, after controlling for demand characteristics, subjects who were repeating RBs reported more satis-faction in their relationship and those verbalizing IBs scored significantly lower on measures of relationship satisfaction.

Applying similar questions about the relationships between IBs and responses to the significant stress associated with the death of a loved one, Boelen et al. (2004) compared the bereavement responses, as well as their related beliefs and basic assumptions, of a group of 30 college students to a matched group of 30 nonbereaved students. Although not testing any specific aspect of the role of RBs, results supported the researchers' hypothesis that the students forced to deal with the death of a parent or sibling, when compared to students not suffering such loss, would report less positive views about the meaningfulness of the world as well as self-worth. Similarly, bereaved students exhibited significantly higher levels of IBs than their nonbereaved counter-parts, thus confirming the hypothesis that levels of IBs increase after a stressful life events. Given that bereaved individuals' IBs were also significantly asso-ciated with self-ratings on the intensity of traumatic grief symptoms, it is apparent that the presence of high levels of IBs when dealing with such significant life events may contribute to dysfunctional assessments of the perceived intensity and, as a consequence, lower levels of adaptive responses.

In an investigation of the utility of a binary model of distress, in which distress is comprised of two constructs, functional negative affect and dysfunc-tional negative affect, D. David et al. (2005) report on two studies of female breast-cancer patients preparing for upcoming breast surgery. The binary model was investigated in light of the contrary and more traditional unitary model of distress, where individuals described as highly distressed are viewed as high on negative affect and those described as not highly distressed are considered low on negative affect. Subjects included 55 patients from the United States and 45 patients living in Romania, and, when comparing hypotheses that were developed for both the unitary model and the binary model, results provide support for the binary over the unitary model. Specifically, for individuals from both the United States and Romania, while higher scores on IBs were associated with both functional and dysfunctional negative emotions, lower scores on measures of IBs were significantly associated with low levels of dysfunctional negative feelings and high levels of functional negative emotions.

Although a detailed discussion of the negative effect that diagnosed medical illness and developmental disabilities can have on children's healthy adjustment and development is well beyond the scope of this chapter (for discussion, see Harbeck-Weber, Fisher, & Dittner, 2003; Wallander, Thompson, & Alriksson-Schmidt, 2003), it suffices to note that dealing with the chronic stressors related to daily management of the special needs of an ill or disabled child can create significant distress for the child and for family members, especially primary caregivers. In an examination of the effect of an REE parent group designed for mothers of children with Down Syndrome, Greaves (1997) provides evidence that stress of this kind can be better managed via more rational ways of coping. Fifty-four mothers were randomly assigned to an intervention group, a comparative-treatment control group, and a no-treatment control group. Mothers in the experimental group showed significant reductions on measures of parenting stress when compared to both control groups. Although not a direct test of the role of rational beliefs in reducing the stress associated with parenting a child with a disability, this finding appears to support the conclusion that parental stress can be effectively reduced by learning the strategies associated with disputing core IBs and replacing them with preferential RBs.

In a study investigating the coping strategies used by incarcerated adolescent offenders, Ireland et al. (2005) apply the work of Roger, Jarvis, and Najarian (as cited in Ireland et al.) who describe four types of coping: rational, detached, emotional, and avoidant. The first two are considered to be effective and the last two are considered to be ineffective, especially in the long term. Of particular interest, Ireland et al. expected the rational coping style, defined generally as a problem-focused technique and, as an effective strategy, to "maintain the psychological health of an individual at times of stress" (p. 412).

Using multiple regression analysis in a model building format, Ireland et al. (2005) discovered that rational coping predicted decreased scores on overall psychological distress and scores on all psychological health subscales, including somatic symptoms, social dysfunction, anxiety and insomnia, and depression for the offenders between the ages of 18 and 21. Following previous developmental research discussed earlier about the increased use of cognitive coping strategies with age, for offenders between the ages of 15 and 17 detached coping, not rational coping, predicted decreased scores on overall psychological distress.

REBT theory would likely predict that high school student who are rated by their peers as more mentally healthy would also think more rationally and be more accepted by their peers. Lee et al. (2004) tested this hypothesis in a sample of 476 Korean adolescents, who were rated by peers as mentally healthy based on five aspects of overall mental health, one of which involved the ability to cope with stressful situations, and general social acceptance, and who all completed self-report measures of level of IBs. Although the results are based on a small effect size, the findings suggest that adolescents rated higher on overall mental health, when compared with adolescents low on overall mental health, tended to have higher ratings on social acceptance; however, similar results were not found with levels of IBs.

Beyond empirical support for the adaptive nature of RBs in adjusting to life stressors, research on the associations between RBs, or low levels of IBs in some cases, and general factors of well-being have provided additional support for the contention that belief systems can either nurture or reduce positive outcomes on measures of well-being. One example involves a study conducted by Ciarrochi (2004) in which he examined the relationships between the dysfunctional belief subscales of the Common Beliefs Survey-III and positive and negative measures of well-being. College student participants completed self-report measures that provided scores on various aspects of dysfunctional belief, negative well-being (i.e., depression, anxiety, stress, guilt, hostility, hope-lessness, suicidal thinking), positive well-being (i.e., life satisfaction, joviality, state self-assurance), and social desirability, as a control variable. Results showed that lower scores on well-being were related to certain IBs; specifically self-worth beliefs were dependent on success and on approval and demand beliefs, such as holding unrealistically high expectations for events and individuals. In fact, scores on the IBs were found to predict 14% of the variance in negative well-being scores, yet this decreased by about half for the amount of variance explained in positive well-being scores. Stepwise regression revealed that the optimal set of belief predictors depended on the type of well-being predicted.

In an examination of the potential relationships between having a belief in good luck and various cognitive and personality variables that are commonly used to explain mental health outcomes, Day and Maltby (2003) administered a number of relevant self-report measures to a sample of college students. Results of correlational analyses identified significant relationships between belief in good luck and both optimism and IBs. Various models were evaluated to determine the mediational relationships among these variables on negative mental health outcomes (i.e., depression and anxiety), and the resulting negative relationship between belief in good luck and negative mental health outcome appeared to be best explained by the model in which high scores on belief in good luck resulted in increased optimism scores and decreased scores on IBs that would otherwise interfere with healthy outcomes.

For some individuals, anger management is problematic, which can lead to intense distress and is generally associated with overall maladaptive coping with various stressors. Difficulties with managing anger as an indicator of poor mental health involve both state and trait characteristics. Ziegler and Smith (2004) examined the REBT theory of trait anger, which predicts that individuals who demonstrate more irrational ways of thinking will exhibit greater symptoms of trait anger than those who think more rationally. Consistent with this prediction, they found that subjects who scored higher on a composite measure of irrational thinking and on a measure of low frustration tolerance scored significantly higher on a measure of trait anger than subjects with lower scores on the same measures of irrationality.

Tafrate and Kassinove (1998) provide further evidence that RBs can assist individuals in more effective management of state anger, based on a study of 45 men with elevated scores on measures of trait anger. After collecting baseline data on all subjects, they were trained over 12 half-hour sessions to recite rational, irrational, or irrelevant self-statements in response to being provoked with a barb technique (in which the researchers leveled negative, aversive statements at them) or in response to imagined provocation. Results indicate that subjects in the rational self-statement group were less angry on posttreatment measures of state anger, expressions of anger, and both intensity and frequency of grip as measured by a hand dynamometer than were subjects in both the irrational and irrelevant self-statement group.

Rational Beliefs and Primary Prevention Programs

Prevention of certain health and mental health outcomes is of critical interest to professionals charged with meeting goals that are often outlined by government agencies and public interest groups. For example, mental health is one of the 10 leading health indicators that are being used to measure Americans' progress toward the goals for healthier living that have been outlined by the current *Healthy People 2010*, managed by the Office of Disease Prevention and Health Promotion (U.S. Department of Health and Human Services [DHHS], 2000). Consequently there is a growing body of literature that provides support for the potential prevention of certain health and mental health problems and that has developed more sophisticated terminologies for the various types of prevention activities.

A complete review of the prevention literature regarding programs with demonstrated potential for curtailing the negative impacts of stress on mental health outcomes is well beyond the scope of this chapter. Furthermore, given the comprehensive and multimodal approach used in many primary prevention programs, determining the individual effects that RBs may have on the prevention on negative mental health outcomes is nearly impossible, especially given that very few primary prevention programs adequately measure and track participants' RBs over the course of treatment.

Therefore, this section serves as a summary of research protocols that directly or indirectly involve therapeutic or educational strategies born out of REBT theory and that have been successfully applied in prevention programs. Such programs vicariously offer support for the assertion that RBs, or at least low levels of irrationality or low scores on measures of IBs, aid in the prevention of negative mental health outcomes. Although this discussion begins with a general review of specific prevention programs that have set out to reduce subjects' IBs via implementation of REBT or one of its derivatives (Jaycox, Reivich, Gillham, & Seligman, 1994; Kachman & Mazer, 1990; Nielsen et al., 1996), it concludes with a discussion of a few prominent literature and meta-analytic reviews of prevention programs that have demonstrated positive outcomes after rigorous evaluation (Durlak & Wells, 1997; Gillham, Shatte, & Freres, 2000). Although these reviews tend to review programs that are commonly based on cognitive-behavioral therapies, we pay particular attention to effective and/or efficacious prevention programs that explicitly include aspects of REBT.

Several prevention programs have been developed that do provide support for the utility of general cognitive-behavioral techniques in the prevention of maladaptive functioning, including those successfully applied to adult populations in reducing symptoms of depression and anxiety and increasing self-esteem (e.g., Schiraldi & Brown, 2001) and those successfully applied at the school-level that enhance children's adaptive coping skills, ability to develop and implement effective solutions in the face of stressors, and self-efficacy, and that reduce symptoms of anxiety in both at-risk and normal populations (e.g., Cowen, Wyman, Work, & Iker, 1995; Dubow, Schmidt, McBride, & Edwards, 1993; Misfud & Rapee, 2005). However, far fewer prevention programs have specifically targeted the modification of RB and IBs as a core component of the therapeutic or educational intervention.

One such program, The Penn Prevention Program, was evaluated by Jaycox et al. (1994) for its potential to reduce depressive symptoms in school children between the ages of 10 and 13 who were identified as at-risk for depression and related problems with conduct, low academic achievement, and poor peer relations. According to Jaycox et al., this program's cognitive component is based on the REBT ABC model and "emphasizes that it is beliefs about events rather than the events themselves that generate feelings" (p. 806). They found that by targeting the modification of IBs in children identified as at-risk for maladaptive depressive symptoms, significant improvement on measures of classroom behavior and significant reductions of depressive symptoms are possible at posttreatment when compared to controls. More robust findings were evidenced at six-month follow-up, where subjects in the intervention group continued to exhibit significant reductions in depressive and conduct symptoms when compared to those in the control group. Similar findings have been reported for the positive effects of REE in significantly increasing adolescents' use of more adaptive defense mechanisms and grades on academic effort (Kachman & Mazer, 1990) and for significant improvements on adolescent's self-esteem after participation in a prevention program that targeted specific IBs known to correlate with low self-esteem (Nielsen et al., 1996).

Additional support for the positive impact that REBT interventions have on the prevention of negative mental health outcomes is provided by extant literature reviews. For example, Durlak and Wells (1997) conducted a meta-analytic review of 177 primary prevention programs that targeted prevention of childhood and adolescent behavioral and psychosocial problems. Programs were grouped by types, including environment-centered, transition programs, and person-centered, the last of which is most relevant for our purposes. Notably, Durlak and Wells write that person-centered programs were further subdivided into three types, those that primarily involved affective education, those that adhered to an interpersonal problem-solving approach, and those that "were more difficult to categorize because of the diversity of their procedures and objectives" (p. 131), which were labeled as *other person-centered approaches*. Within this group, a prevention program implemented by DiGiuseppe and Kassinove (as cited in Durlak & Wells) targeted the modification of irrational beliefs in order to reduce symptoms of anxiety. This program was one of 26 *other person-centered approaches* that was further categorized as employing behavioral or cognitive behavioral interventions, and Durlak and Wells found that these types of programs were nearly twice as effective (i.e., mean effect size of 0.49) than the 16 *other person-centered approaches* that employed nonbehavioral interventions (i.e., mean effect size of 0.25).

Another review, conducted by Gillham et al. (2000), focused on the empirical literature providing support for interventions that utilize cognitive-behavioral and family techniques in the prevention of depressive symptoms in children and adults. Only one prevention program by Peterson's group (as cited in Gillham et al.) specifically mentioned that the intervention included a focus on the reduction of irrational thinking and increasing self-affirming beliefs. Peterson et al. randomly assigned 486 7th-grade students to either an intervention group or a no-intervention, control group, and the intervention involved 16 40-minute group sessions that were conducted by psychologists and clinical psychology graduate students. Although there was no intervention effect for diagnosis of depression at posttreatment or at follow-up, students in the intervention group, compared to those in the control group, evidenced significant improvements at posttreatment on measures of internalizing and externalizing symptoms and effective coping.

Conclusion

REBT theory holds that rational beliefs serve a protective function during times of stress and prevent or attenuate dysfunctional behaviors and emotions. While the theory and practice regarding the role and function of irrational beliefs has been well developed and empirically tested, the same cannot be said about the role and function of rational beliefs. Much more work needs to be done to fully elucidate the conditions under which rational beliefs may enhance mental health. Furthermore, one cannot simply assume that rational beliefs will arise in the absence of irrational beliefs. The two domains are to a large extent independent constructs.

The review of the research described in this chapter provides evidence for the associations between indicators of rational beliefs and adaptive responses to general negative life events and stressors, such as job-related stress, anticipation of surgery, adolescents' general adjustment in high school, relationship problems, and frustration/anger management, as well as more significant or chronic adversities, including loss of a loved one, imprisonment, management of a disability, and childhood maltreatment. What is less clear is what types of rational beliefs provide psychological protection against what kinds of problems.

Although not numerous, there are studies that have also provided support less directly for the role of RBs in effective prevention programs that have adopted specific aspects of REBT. These are a subset of the more general prevention programs that have appeared in the literature. However, these programs tend to be directed toward the reduction or elimination of irrational beliefs rather than the inculcation of rational beliefs. Further research should be conducted on the prophylactic effects of specifically teaching rational beliefs at an early age. A good place to begin might be the reduction of *desiring* (Ellis & Dryden, 1997), and its three derivatives of *rating or evaluating badness, tolerance,* and *acceptance* from absolutism to relativism. Curiously these attitudes come close to a Buddhist conceptualization of cognitive therapy (Dowd, 2005, 2006), although Buddhism advocates the extinction of desire, and there are extant techniques in Buddhist practice for achieving these attitudes. Books and manuals of REBT practice contain techniques as well. Likewise explicit early training in preferential attitudes rather than absolutist attitudes might be useful.

REFERENCES

Addis, J., & Bernard, M. E. (2002). Marital adjustment and irrational beliefs. *Journal of Rational-Emotive & Cognitive-Behavior Therapy, 20,* 3–13.

Bernard, M. E., & DiGiuseppe, R. (2000). Advances in the theory and practice of rational-emotive behavioral consultation. *Journal of Educational & Psychological Consultation, 11,* 333–355.

Boelen, P. A., Kip, H. J., Voorsluijs, J. J., & van den Bout, J. (2004). Irrational beliefs and basic assumptions in bereaved university students: A comparison study. *Journal of Rational-Emotive & Cognitive-Behavior Therapy, 22,* 111–129.

Bond, F. W., & Dryden, W. (1996a). Why two, central REBT hypotheses appear untestable. *Journal of Rational-Emotive & Cognitive-Behavior Therapy, 14,* 29–40.

Bond, F. W., & Dryden, W. (1996b). Testing an REBT theory: The effects of rational beliefs, irrational beliefs, and their control or certainty contents on the functionality of interference: 2. In a personal context. *International Journal of Psychotherapy, 1,* 55–77.

Bond, F. W., & Dryden, W. (1997). Testing an REBT theory: The effects of rational beliefs, irrational beliefs, and their control or certainty contents on the functionality of inferences: 1. In a social context. *Journal of Rational-Emotive & Cognitive-Behavior Therapy, 15,* 157–188.

Bond, F. W., Dryden, W., & Briscoe, R. (1999). Testing two mechanisms by which rational and irrational beliefs may affect the functionality of inferences. *British Journal of Medical Psychology, 72,* 557–566.

Ciarrochi, J. (2004). Relationships between dysfunctional beliefs and positive and negative indices of well-being: A critical evaluation of the common beliefs survey: 3. Journal of *Rational-Emotive & Cognitive-Behavior Therapy, 22,* 171–188.

Cowen, E. L., Wyman, P. A., Work, W. C., & Iker, M. R. (1995). A preventive intervention for enhancing resilience among highly stressed urban children. *Journal of Primary Prevention, 15*, 247–260.

Cramer, D. (2004). Effect of the destructive disagreement belief on relationship satisfaction with a romantic partner or closest friend. *Psychology and Psychotherapy: Theory, Research, and Practice, 77*, 121–133.

Cramer, D. (2005a). Effect of four aspects of rational statements on expected satisfaction with a close relationship. *British Journal of Guidance & Counselling, 33*, 227–238.

Cramer, D. (2005b). Effect of the destructive disagreement belief on satisfaction with one's closest friend. *The Journal of Psychology, 139*, 57–66.

Cramer, D., & Fong, J. (1991). Effect of rational and irrational beliefs on intensity and "inappropriateness" of feelings: A test of rational-emotive theory. *Cognitive Therapy & Research, 15*, 319–329.

David, A., Ghinea, C., Macavei, B., & Kallay, E. (2005). A search for "hot" cognitions in a clinical and a non-clinical context: Appraisal, attributions, core relational themes, irrational beliefs, and their relations to emotion. *Journal of Cognitive & Behavioral Psychotherapies, 5*, 1–42.

David, D. (2003). Rational emotive behavior therapy (REBT): The view of a cognitive psychologist. In W. Dryden (Ed.), *Rational Emotive Behaviour Therapy: Theoretical Developments* (pp. 130–159). London: Brunner-Routledge.

David, D., Montgomery, G. H., Macavei, B., & Bovbjerg, D. H. (2005). An empirical investigation of Albert Ellis's binary model of distress. *Journal of Clinical Psychology, 61*, 499–516.

David, D., Schnur, J., & Belloiu, A. (2002). Another search for the "hot" cognitions: Appraisal, irrational beliefs, attributions, and their relation to emotion. *Journal of Rational-Emotive & Cognitive-Behavior Therapy, 20*, 93–130.

David, D., Schnur, J., & Birk, J. (2004). Functional and dysfunctional feelings in Ellis' cognitive theory of emotion: An empirical analysis. *Cognition & Emotion, 18*, 869–880.

Day, L., & Maltby, J. (2003). Belief in good luck and psychological well-being: The mediating role of optimism and irrational beliefs. *Journal of Psychology: Interdisciplinary & Applied 137*, 99–110.

DiGiuseppe, R., & Bernard, M. E. (1990). The application of rational-emotive theory and therapy to school-aged children. *School Psychology Review 19*, 268–286.

DiGiuseppe, R., & Leaf, R. C. (1990). The endorsement of irrational beliefs in a general clinical population. *Journal of Rational-Emotive & Cognitive-Behavior Therapy, 8*, 235–247.

Dowd, E. T. (2005, June). Elements of compassion in cognitive therapy: The role of cultural specifics and universals. Invited Address at the International Congress of Cognitive Psychotherapy, Gothenburg, Sweden.

Dowd, E. T. (2006). Cognitive hypnotherapy and the management of anger. In R. Chapman (Ed.), *The clinical use of hypnosis in cognitive behavioral therapy: A practitioners' casebook*. New York: Springer.

Dryden, W. (2003). "The cream cake made me eat it": An introduction to the ABC theory of REBT. In W. Dryden (Ed.), *Rational Emotive Behaviour Therapy: Theoretical Developments* (pp. 1–21). Hove, UK: Brunner-Routledge.

Dubow, E. F., Schmidt, D., McBride, J., & Edwards, S. (1993). Teaching children to cope with stressful experiences: Initial implementation and evaluation of a primary prevention program. *Journal of Clinical Child Psychology, 22,* 428–440.

Durlak, J. A., & Wells, A. M. (1997). Primary prevention mental health programs for children and adolescents: A meta-analytic review. *American Journal of Community Psychology, 25,* 115–151.

Ellis, A. (1994). *Reason and emotion in psychotherapy: Revised and updated.* New York: Carol Publishing Group.

Ellis, A. (2004). Why rational emotive behavior therapy is the most comprehensive and effective form of behavior therapy. *Journal of Rational-Emotive & Cognitive-Behavior Therapy, 22,* 85–92.

Ellis, A., & DiGiuseppe, R. (1993). Are inappropriate or dysfunctional feelings in rational-emotive therapy qualitative or quantitative? *Cognitive Therapy & Research, 17,* 471–477.

Ellis, A., & Dryden, W. (1997). *The practice of rational emotive behavior therapy* (2nd ed.). New York: Springer Publishing Company.

Gallo, L. C., Ghaed, S. G., & Bracken, W. S. (2004). Emotions and cognitions in coronary heart disease: Risk, resilience, and social context. *Cognitive Therapy & Research, 28,* 669–694.

Gillham, J. E., Shatte, A. J., & Freres, D. R. (2000). Preventing depression: A review of cognitive-behavioral and family interventions. *Applied & Preventive Psychology, 9,* 63–88.

Greaves, D. (1997). The effect of rational-emotive parent education on the stress of mothers of young children with down syndrome. *Journal of Rational-Emotive & Cognitive-Behavior Therapy, 15,* 249–267.

Haaga, D. A., & Davison, G. C. (1993). An appraisal of rational-emotive therapy. *Journal of Consulting and Clinical Psychology, 61,* 215–220.

Harbeck-Weber, C., Fisher, J. L., & Dittner, C. A. (2003). Promoting coping and enhancing adaptation to illness. In M. C. Roberts (Ed.), *Handbook of pediatric psychology* (3rd ed., pp. 99–118). New York: Guilford Press.

Ireland, J., Boustead, R., & Ireland, C. (2005). Coping style and psychological health among adolescent prisoners: A study of young and juvenile offenders. *Journal of Adolescence, 28,* 411–423.

Jaycox, L. H., Reivich, K. J., Gillham, J., & Seligman, M. E. P. (1994). Prevention of depressive symptoms in school children. *Behaviour Research & Therapy, 32,* 801–816.

Kachman, D. J., & Mazer, G. E. (1990). Effects of rational emotive education on the rationality, neuroticism, and defense mechanisms of adolescents. *Adolescence, 25,* 131–144.

Kendall, P. C., Haaga, D. A. F., Ellis, A., Bernard, M., DiGiuseppe, R., & Kassinove, H. (1995). Rational-emotive therapy in the 1990s and beyond: Current status, recent revisions, and research questions. *Clinical Psychology Review, 15,* 169–185.

Lee, D. Y., Sohn, N. H., & Park, S. H. (2004). Adolescents' peer-rated mental health, peer-acceptance, and irrational beliefs. *Psychological Reports, 94,* 1144–1148.

Lyons, L. C., & Woods, P. J. (1991). The efficacy of rational-emotive therapy: A quantitative review of the outcome research. *Clinical Psychology Review, 11,* 357–369.

Master, S., & Miller, S. (1991). A test of RET theory using an RET theory-based mood induction procedure: The rationality of thinking rationally. *Cognitive Therapy & Research, 15,* 491–502.

McDuff, A. C., & Dryden, W. (1998). REBT and emotion: 1. A role-play experiment using a shame/disappointment scenario to investigate the effects of rational, irrational, and indifference beliefs on inferences and action tendencies. *Journal of Rational-Emotive & Cognitive-Behavior Therapy, 16,* 235–254.

Misfud, C., & Rapee, R. A. (2005). Early intervention for childhood anxiety in a school setting: Outcomes for an economically disadvantaged population. *Journal of the American Academy of Child and Adolescent Psychiatry, 44,* 996–1004.

Nielsen, D. M., Horan, J. J., Keen, B., Cox-St. Peter, C., Dyche-Ceperich, S., & Ostlund, D. (1996). An attempt to improve self-esteem by modifying specific irrational beliefs. *Journal of Cognitive Psychotherapy: An International Quarterly, 10,* 137–149.

Raimy, V. (2004). Misconceptions and the cognitive therapies. In A. Freeman, M. J. Mahoney, P. DeVito, & D. Martin (Eds.), *Cognition and psychotherapy* (2nd ed., pp. 165–184). New York: Springer.

Schiraldi, G. R., & Brown, S. L. (2001). Primary prevention for mental health: Results of an exploratory cognitive-behavioral college course. *Journal of Primary Prevention, 22,* 55–67.

Silverman, S., & DiGiuseppe, R. (2001). Cognitive-behavioral constructs and children's behavioral and emotional problems. *Journal of Rational-Emotive & Cognitive-Behavior Therapy, 19,* 119–134.

Solomon, A., & Haaga, D. A. F. (1995). Rational emotive behavior therapy research: What we know and what we need to know. *Journal of Rational-Emotive & Cognitive-Behavior Therapy, 13,* 179–191.

Tafrate, R., & Kassinove, H. (1998). Anger control in men: Barb exposure with rational, irrational, and irrelevant self-statements. *Journal of Cognitive Psychotherapy: An International Quarterly, 12,* 187–211.

Tan, B.-L. (2004). Irrational beliefs and job stress among occupational therapists in Singapore. *British Journal of Occupational Therapy, 67,* 303–309.

Terjesen, M. D., DiGiuseppe, R., & Gruner, P. (2000). A review of REBT research in alcohol abuse treatment [Special Issue]. *Cognitive-behavioral treatment of addictions 18*(3, Pt. 1), 165–179.

Tiba, A. (2003). Rational and irrational beliefs from a neuroscience framework. *Romanian Journal of Cognitive & Behavioral Psychotherapies, 3,* 61–78.

U.S. Department of Health and Human Services (2000, November). *Healthy People 2010: Understanding and improving health.* Retrieved December 20, 2005, from http://healthypeople.gov/Document/pdf/uih/2010uih.pdf.

Wallander, J. L., Thompson, R. J., & Alriksson-Schmidt, A. (2003). Psychosocial adjustment of children with chronic physical conditions. In M. C. Roberts (Ed.), *Handbook of pediatric psychology* (3rd ed., pp. 141–158). New York: Guilford Press.

Ziegler, D. J. (2003). The concept of psychological health in rational emotive behavior therapy. *Journal of Rational-Emotive & Cognitive-Behavior Therapy, 21,* 21–36.

Ziegler, D. J., & Leslie, Y. M. (2003). A test of the ABC model underlying rational emotive behavior therapy. *Psychological Reports, 92,* 235–240.

Ziegler, D. J., & Smith, P. N. (2004). Anger and the ABC model underlying rational-emotive behavior therapy. *Psychological Reports, 94,* 1009–1014.

10

Rational and Irrational Beliefs: Implications for Mechanisms of Change and Practice in Psychotherapy

Daniel David, Arthur Freeman, and Raymond DiGiuseppe

According to the ABC(DE) model (Ellis, 1994), reviewed in Chapter 1 of this volume, people experience both positive and negative activating events (A), and hold rational and irrational beliefs/cognitions (B), in relation to these events that influence a broad range of their personal and interpersonal experiences. Beliefs have emotional, behavioral, and cognitive consequences (C). Rational beliefs (RBs) generally promote adaptive and healthy behaviors and emotions, whereas irrational beliefs (IBs) typically instigate maladaptive and unhealthy consequences, typically labeled psychopathology, as recognized and classified by various diagnostic systems (e.g., DSM).

Clients who engage in cognitive-behavioral and rational-emotive behavior therapy (CBT/REBT) are encouraged to actively dispute or challenge (i.e., restructure) (D) their IBs and to assimilate more efficient (E) rational beliefs, with a resultant positive impact on their emotional, cognitive, and behavioral responses (Ellis, 1994). Once generated, a consequence (C) may become an (A), about which the individual may have other beliefs (B; meta-beliefs) generating secondary emotional consequences

(C; metaconsequences. For example, people whose depression is the product of highly negative irrational beliefs may be depressed about their depression. Thus, according to this cognitive perspective, the relation between A and C— a particular event and its consequences—is cognitively mediated. However, rational and irrational beliefs are only one type of cogniton, albeit an important and central one, that mediates emotional and behavioral disturbance. For example, cognitions can also be processed at an unconscious level, as acknowledged by the recent emphasis on the study of the so-called cognitive unconscious (see Culhane & Watson, 2003; David, 2003). We will examine the interactions between various types of cognition (B) in mediating the relation between A and C later in this chapter.

Having said that the relation between A and C is almost always mediated by B, one might ask whether this means that all emotions occur on a postcognitive basis? According to the cognitive perspective, this is exactly the case. Obviously, an emotion can be an A and thus, is apparently, precognitive (i.e., emotions appear before the belief). However, this is just a misinterpretation. In order to have an emotion at A, it must have been generated before that point in time, and thus, the computational (i.e., information processing) component involved in its generation makes it postcognitive.

The ABC(DE) model is not just a model for understanding psychopathology and a platform for psychotherapy, but a general model of human functioning. Therefore, it can be used to understand and explain human functioning and disturbance in a broad range of settings such as educational, industrial, pastoral, and other contexts in which it is important to be able to understand, predict, describe, and explain human activity.

In summary, according to this model, irrational beliefs are important causal mechanisms involved in psychopathology, whereas rational beliefs are important health promoting mechanisms. We will explore the role of irrational beliefs in stressful and nonstressful situations in health promoting behaviors, cognitive-behavioral therapy, and psychotherapy in general.

Irrational Beliefs as Etiopathogenetic Mechanisms in (Psycho) Pathology (based on David, Szentagotai, Kallay, & Macavei, 2005)

As we noted, REBT maintains that beliefs mediate the relation between environmental events and emotional distress (CBT/REBT diathesis-stress model). Simply stated, the diathesis-stress model proposes that the clinical symptoms are generated by the interaction between stress and vulnerability, be it psychological and/or biological. IBs are hypothesized to engender "cognitive vulnerability" in stressful situations, whereas RBs are "protective factors." We will first analyze the role of irrational beliefs as etiopathogenetic (causal) mechanisms. Three lines of research have been employed to provide support for this assumption (David et al., 2005).

Correlational and Cross-Sectional Studies (The B–C Connection)

Measures of IBs are reliably associated with, or co-occur with, measures of emotional disorders and symptoms in both nonclinical and clinical populations. For example, high levels of IBs have been shown to be associated with general anxiety (Jones, 1968), social phobia, speech anxiety, test anxiety (e.g., Goldfried & Sobocinski, 1975), self-reported depression (Nelson, 1977), general psychiatric symptoms (Jones, 1968), assertiveness deficits (Alden & Safran, 1978), and type-A coronary-prone behavior (Smith & Brehm, 1981). On admission to an inpatient psychiatric unit, individuals diagnosed as neurotic (based on MMPI scores) showed higher levels of IBs than nonhospitalized nonsymptomatic individuals (Newark, Frerking, Cook, & Newark, 1973).

However, researchers have criticized many of these studies for confounding the assessment of IBs with predicted outcomes (e.g., emotional distress). In addition, many of the studies were contaminated by a "context effect," as IBs and other correlated variables were measured in the same context, a procedure that may have inflated the correlations, as suggested by the finding that some of these correlations reached values around 0.7 (Smith, 1989).

As a result of these critiques, a new generation of IBs scales was undertaken in which contamination with emotional items was avoided. Research using these new measures (e.g., Bernard, 1998) has consistently indicated that high levels of IBs are reliably associated with a variety of indicators of emotional distress (measured in the same or in a different context), in both clinical and nonclinical populations. For example, IBs are associated with anxiety and/or depressive symptoms in both college populations (e.g., Chang & Bridewell, 1998; Montgomery et al., 2007; Muran, Kassinove, Ross, & Muran, 1989) and clinical samples (e.g., David, Szentagotai, Lupu, & Cosman, 2008; Nottingham, 1992; Muran & Motta, 1993).

Unfortunately, the correlational nature of these research designs precludes inferences regarding the causal role of IBs in distress. Do these studies and their results support the CBT/REBT theory? Supposing that one did not find an association between high IBs and various symptoms, would using this methodology constitute a disconfirmation of CBT/REBT theory and of the diathesis-stress model? The answer is no (see also David, Szentagotai, & Kallay, 2007).

Although the results of these correlational and cross-sectional designs are interesting, they fail to test directly CBT/REBT theory, insofar as IBs and symptoms are hypothesized to be correlated only in stressful situations. People can have high levels of IBs, but if they have not encountered stressful situations they are not predicted to experience symptoms. Therefore, a less than perfect or low correlation does not disconfirm CBT/REBT theory, unless irrational thoughts are sampled during a stressful event that is hypothesized to activate available IBs. A more comprehensive test is needed, taking into account the presence/absence of activating events and their influence on the associations found in these studies.

Correlational and Cross-Sectional Studies during Stressful Events (A–B–C)

By including all three hypothesized factors (i.e., events, beliefs, and responses) correlational and cross-sectional studies during stressful events have provided a more complete test of the CBT/REBT theory and of the diathesis-stress model. IBs have been found to be associated with negative mood during stressful situations in formerly depressed persons (Solomon et al., 1998), emotional adjustments in marital separation (Munoz-Eguileta, 2007), and in college students with state and trait anxiety experiencing both high and low stress (Chang, 1997).

The overall picture of this research is that IBs are associated with measures of psychological disturbance. In this case, too, the correlational nature of the design precludes inferences about (1) the causal role of IBs or (2) the moderating or mediating role (for a distinction between moderation and mediation see Baron & Kenny, 1986) of IBs on the impact of stressful events and on emotional/psychological disturbance. It is possible, for example, that both stressful events and IBs are correlated with psychological disturbance, but IBs do not mediate the impact of stressful events on psychological disturbance, as the CBT/REBT diathesis-stress model would predict.

The diathesis-stress model of CBT/REBT (i.e., in stressful situations, IBs produce cognitive vulnerability, whereas RBs are protective) can be empirically investigated using a 2x2 factorial design with stress and IBs as independent variables. Research along this line, with stressful events being induced experimentally (e.g., by imagining various stressful situations), has produced mixed findings. Whereas Goldfried and Sobocinski (1975) found support for the CBT/REBT diathesis-stress model, Craighead et al. (1979) did not. Craighead et al. (1979) found, however, that participants exhibiting high levels of IBs produced more negative self-statements while imagining negative events. This finding is consistent with the CBT/REBT diathesis-stress model when the outcome measures are cognitions rather than feelings. Smith et al. (1984) found no evidence for the diathesis-stress model of anxiety in a college population when the stressful event was taking part in an intelligence test.

Researchers have criticized these studies for assuming they test the CBT/REBT diathesis-stress model, as they often relied on artificially induced stressful situations (e.g., by imagery) rather than real ones. Ellis (1994) has noted that generic events may not be relevant primers for IBs. Rather, it is necessary to test the hypothesis in relation to specific events that thwart personal goals or represent meaningful losses or failures. Because activating events are idiosyncratic, it difficult to identify situations that induce stress in all participants. Consequently, laboratory studies with limited generalizability have provided only a minimal test of the CBT/REBT diathesis-stress model.

Other researchers have evaluated the CBT/REBT diathesis-stress model by focusing on real stressful events on a retrospective basis (e.g., in the last six months to one year). For example, Hart, Turner, Hittner, Cardozo, and Paras (1991) found support for the CBT/REBT diathesis-stress model for hostility but not for anxiety, whereas Chang (1997) found no support for the CBT/REBT model in explaining depressive symptoms in college students. However, measuring stressful events after long periods of time (six months to one year), significantly reduces the likelihood of arriving at meaningful conclusions insofar as over time, stressors and emotional problems may diminish as individuals employ effective coping mechanisms or the stressor is no longer present. When researchers have used rigorous methods, the results have generally supported the CBT/REBT diathesis-model, as in the case of Malouff, Schutte, and McClelland, (1992) who studied real stressful events prospectively (e.g., immediately before a final exam), and found support for the CBT/REBT diathesis-stress model of anxiety; namely, irrational beliefs were strong predictors of anxiety before the exam.

To conclude, studies investigating the CBT/REBT diathesis-stress model do not permit decisive conclusions. Rather, they suggest that the model can predict some outcomes (e.g., hostility) but not others (e.g., trait anxiety). However, when prospective designs and real stressful events are incorporated into the design, hypotheses generated from the model are empirically supported.

Studies of Self-Referent Speech and Self-Statements

Some researchers have directly manipulated cognitions to establish a causal role of IBs/RBs in generating various emotions. Studies have systematically shown that self-referent speech or self-statements—based on experimentally manipulated IBs/RBs—(e.g., Cramer, 2005; Cramer & Fong, 1991; Cramer & Kupshik, 1993) are associated with physiological and emotional indices of stress and decreased task performance (e.g., Schill, Monroe, Evans, & Ramanaiah, 1978). Also, studies based on other types of negative self-referent speech (e.g., cognitions not directly expressing IBs/RBs) (e.g., Hollon & Kendall, 1980) have provided indirect support for the CBT/REBT theory, as IBs are reliably correlated with such negative self-statements (Harrel, Chamless, & Calhoun, 1981). The main limitations of these studies are that they do not address: *(1)* the conceptual difference between viewing IBs/RBs as core beliefs or as self-statements produced during experimental manipulations (e.g., the transitory nature of self-statements versus the stability of IBs); *(2)* the fact that some self-statements (e.g., cognitions not directly expressing IBs/RBs) could be involved in emotional disorders without core IBs playing a direct role; and *(3)* the demand characteristics of the tasks (but see Cramer & Buckland, 1996).

In summary, results based on these three lines of research tentatively support some aspects of the CBT/REBT diathesis-stress model. The three main criticisms of studies investigating the causal role of IBs in pathology (based on the diathesis-stress model) are:

1. A diathesis-stress model can only be tested rigorously in a prospective design involving *(a)* the need for repeated measures for IBs as mediators, using a variety of other outcome variables (e.g., distress); and *(b)* the need to rely more on real stressful situations. Because only a few studies (e.g., Malouff et al., 1992) are based on methodologically adequate designs, the results supporting the CBT/REBT diathesis-stress model require further replication.

2. Most previous studies have assumed that a high RBs score indicates a low IBs score; however, as discussed above, IBs and RBs load on two different factors and should be measured independently. Unfortunately, previous studies investigating the CBT/REBT diathesis-stress model have failed to follow this recommendation.

3. Researchers have often assumed that all outcome measures (e.g.,cognitive, behavioral, physiological, emotional) should confirm the CBT/REBT diathesis-stress model. A more pertinent question would be: to what extent are different outcomes supported by the CBT/REBT diathesis-stress model? For example, some outcomes (e.g., galvanic skin response) may be more related to unconscious information processing (e.g., conditioning) than to consciously held beliefs.

Rational Beliefs as Health and Well-Being Promoting Mechanisms

Few studies directly investigate the role of rational beliefs in health (see also Chapter 12, this volume), and in those studies that do, often, rational beliefs are conceptualized as low levels of irrational beliefs. Most of the studies are correlational in nature, and/or have used imaginal exposure to activating events and to rational beliefs. For example, Froh and his colleagues (Froh et al., 2007) determined that rational beliefs (measured as a low score of irrational beliefs) are related to life satisfaction and meaning. Vandervoort (2006) found that irrational beliefs play a mediating role between hostility and health. However, these relations do not seem very strong. For example, Ciarrochi (2004) found that irrational beliefs predicted 14% of the variance in negative indices of well-being (depression, anxiety, stress, quilt, hostility, hope-lessness, suicidal thinking), and only 7.3% of variance in the positive indices (e.g., life satisfaction, joviality, state self-assurance). Pekarik (1986) found that rationality seemed to prevent distress and illness when there were few stres-sors, but did not have this effect in the case of major stressors. Försterling (1985), on the other hand, ascertained that rational beliefs were strongly asso-ciated with adaptive emotions. Taken as a whole, these results are not sufficient for an empirically supported conclusion regarding the health-promoting role of rational beliefs (for further details see Chapter 7). Rational thinking, as mea-sured by low scores on IB measures, may not reflect the true nature of RBs. Future research in this area should focus on the use of measures of RBs that contain items reflecting rational statements.

Rational and Irrational Beliefs in Cognitive-Behavioral Therapies

Based on the ABC model, we exclude from the CBT family approaches that employ cognitions to control behavior without acknowledging their importance in generating feelings and behaviors. CBT also assumes that most complex human responses (e.g., emotional, cognitive, behavioral, and some physiolo-gical) are cognitively penetrable. Cognitive penetrability means two things (David, Miclea, & Opre, 2004): *(a)* that a response (e.g., behavior) is an out-come of cognitive processing (i.e., computation), be it conscious or uncon-scious; and *(b)* that a change in cognition (e.g., by cognitive and behavioral techniques) will induce a change in the expressed response (e.g., behavior). It is important to note that the limits of cognitive penetrability reflect the limitations of CBT. In other words, because some basic human responses are not cognitively penetrable, (e.g., some basic behaviors are genetically determined), they are not typically considered within the realm of CBT.

CBT professionals have ascribed greater importance to one type of cognition without necessarily excluding the others. Some differences therefore exist in the theory of disturbance each has proposed, and in the identification of the crucial cognitions that are the target of intervention. For example, whereas REBT (CBT/REBT) pivots around the concept of rational and irrational beliefs (Ellis, 1994), cognitive therapy (CT) is organized around the concepts of automatic thoughts and schemas (Beck, 1995). Kuehlwein and Rosen (1993) have identified more than ten types of CBT approaches (e.g., cognitive therapy, cognitive-behavioral modifications, dialectic behavioral therapy, meta-cognitive therapy, rational-emotive behavior therapy, schema-focused therapy, multimodal therapy etc.). Each approach argues that the level or type of cognition it focuses on is more important than other types or levels of cognition. Accordingly, researchers typically only assess the type or level of cognition deemed central by their respective approach, thereby stalling progress in understanding whether different types of cognitions have explanatory value, or whether diverse treatments produce more or less effective changes in psychopathology, regardless of the type of cognition hypothesized as central to change. It is possible that one or several of the cognitions identified by the various CBT schools provide a stronger causal link with maladaptive functioning, or that seemingly disparate cognitions can be understood in terms of a more encompassing latent variable.

This state of affairs is indicative of a pre-paradigmatic phase of science (Kuhn, 1996). Because CBT itself is not coherent, we doubt that, at present, this modality can accomplish its ambitious goal of being the platform for psychotherapy integration. Moreover, professionals who define themselves as cognitive-behavioral therapists often neglect to attend to the hypothesized theory of change, and instead practice what we call "a cocktail school of cognitive-behavioral therapy" (David et al., 2004). More precisely, CBT therapists often combine different cognitive and behavioral techniques in a cocktail-like process while ignoring the hypothesized theory of change, or fail to propose an overarching theory of change. Although such a cocktail might prove effective, and even be manualized, it fails to inform the science of cognitive-behavioral therapy (CBT), rendering treatment a potpourri of procedures. Indeed, it could be argued that CBT as a science is withering, if not "dying" as a consequence of the proliferation of cocktail-like manuals for all conceivable disorders. Without a clearly hypothesized theory of change (e.g., precisely which cognition to restructure by using which specific techniques) accompanied by manualized treatments, CBT can hardly lay claim to the status of a rigorous scientific therapeutic system. In our discussion that follows, we will describe and attempt to organize the main cognitive constructs used in various cognitive-behavioral therapies.

Any statement referring to one's cognitions—and scientists work with statements about cognitions and not cognitions themselves—can be categorized according to whether it is evaluative (hot) or nonevaluative (cold), general (semantic) or specific (autobiographic), conscious or nonconscious, and available or accessible (see David & Szentagotai, 2006, and Chapter 1 this volume). These categories can be described as continua as well as dichotomies.

Cold versus Hot Cognitions (based on David & Szentagotai, 2006)

Cold cognitions refer to how we represent (B) activating events in our mind. Hot cognitions refer to how we evaluate or appraise (B) the cold cognitions to generate feelings. Put another way, cold cognitions represent what "is," whereas hot cognitions represent how desirable what we think "is." Most cognitive theories of various disorders focus on cold cognitions while ignoring hot cognitions. For example, influential cognitive therapy models (Clark, 1999) of panic emphasize the fact that the basic cognition in panic is catastrophizing, expressed by the thought, "I will die!" However, this thought is a cold cognition that might generate no negative feelings in a hypothetical society in which dying is desirable because one makes contact with God. According to new developments in cognitive psychology (see David, 2003) (even if there is still a lack of empirical investigation on this topic in the case of clinical disorders) hot cognitions like "I must not die; It is awful to die," are the sorts of cognitions that are more likely to generate panic. Researchers could profitably initiate an entire research program in CBT/REBT based on a clear distinction between hot and cold cognitions (for details, see David & McMahon, 2001).

We will briefly detail some possible avenues of investigation of such a program. According to the appraisal theory of emotions (Lazarus, 1991), emotional problems will only emerge in the event of (1) distorted representations that are negatively appraised, and (2) nondistorted representations negatively appraised. In the first case, if one changes this distorted representation (e.g., "He hates me") into an accurate one (e.g., "He does not hate me" or "he hates me far less than I thought") one may change the negative emotion (e.g., anxiety) into a generally more positive one (e.g., satisfaction or even happiness). However, the individual may still be prone to emotional problems because the tendency to make negative appraisals (e.g., "It is awful that he hates me") is still present. If one changes a negative appraisal (e.g., "It is awful that he hates me" or "it is terrible to be hated by anyone") into a less irrational and personally relevant one (e.g., "It is bad that he hates me but I can stand it and survive") one will likely change dysfunctional emotions (e.g., anxiety) into negative, but more functional ones (e.g., concern).

The presence of cold cognitions bears some similarity to the actual presence of stressful life events. To elaborate, if one erroneously predicts death, rejection, or failure, for example, it may have the same effect on emotional arousal as the actual occurrence of the aversive event. In terms of REBCT (CBT/REBT), the presence of a cold cognition may serve the same function as a real-life stressor. Thus, the theory could be amended to say that an activating event A can be the occurrence of a negative life event or the erroneous thought that the event has occurred or will occur. In CBT/REBT practice, interventions aimed at modifying cold cognitions are often referred to as "changing the A" (Wallen, DiGiuseppe, & Dryden, 1992).

Some people may argue that by changing negative appraisal, we indirectly change the probability that distorted representations will arise as well (Ellis, 1994). This outcome is possible, although experimental evidence for this hypothesis is mixed (Bond & Dryden, 2000; Dryden, Ferguson, & McTeague 1989). Supposing that distorted, cold cognitions are initially influenced by negative appraisal, subsequently they may become functionally autonomous from appraisal by rehearsal or practice and occur more or less automatically (for details about "functional autonomy," see Allport, 1958). Therefore, a strategy that would change both distorted, cold representations, and negative, hot appraisals seems to be appropriate. *Moreover,* it is likely that if one changes the negative appraisal, one will generate a positive (e.g., happiness) or a negative (e.g., concern) functional emotion. Another possibility, however, would be to reframe the nondistorted representation into a positively distorted one (e.g., "His negative comments about me are a way of communicating that he considers me strong enough to withstand his criticism"). This type of intervention changes the attribution for the event and is a common CBT intervention (Seligman & Csikszentmihalyi, 2000). Positive psychology, which is focused on the role of positive thoughts and positive illusions, may offer ways to help people make this kind of change (see Seligman & Csikszentmihalyi, 2000).

To conclude, although CBT/REBT theorists make the distinction between cold and hot cognitions (Ellis & Dryden, 1997), this distinction is insufficiently explored experimentally. By incorporating a more clear distinction between hot and cold cognitions in their studies, CBT/REBT researchers could significantly enrich their fund of knowledge. For example, one could study how different

CBT/REBT strategies impact cold vs. hot cognitions to generate functional vs. dysfunctional emotions, cognitions, and behaviors.

Hot cognitions are emphasized in Ellis's approach to psychotherapy, but receive less attention in other cognitively oriented psychotherapies. A number of cold cognitions are discussed in cognitively oriented psychotherapies. Among these are anticipation of events (Kelly, 1955), expectancies (Rotter, 1954), anticipated outcomes (Bandura, 1969), attributions (Seligman, 1994), core beliefs and automatic thoughts (Beck, 1995), and more recently response expectancies (Kirsch, 1999). Other cold cognitions include attributions or hypotheses people create to explain their own and others' behavior (Försterling, 1980), and conclusions based on logic (Beck, 1976).

Researchers have examined the link between rational and irrational beliefs and various cold cognitions in numerous studies (see for a review David et al., 2002). Here we discuss two major cognitive constructs, namely inferential cognitions (e.g., automatic thoughts) and response expectancies, and their relations with hot cognitions (i.e., rational and irrational beliefs).

In a series of programmatic studies Dryden and his collaborators (Bond & Dryden, 1996, 1997, 2000; Bond, Dryden, Briscoe, 1999; Dryden, Ferguson, & Clark 1989; Dryden, Ferguson, & Hylton, 1989; Dryden, Ferguson, & McTeague, 1989; McDuff & Dryden, 1998) documented that functional and dysfunctional inferences are generated by rational and irrational beliefs. Civitci (2007) found that an external locus of control is related to demand for comfort and demand for success on four dimensions of control (i.e., family relationships, peer relationships, superstition, and fate). Participants with an internal locus of control exhibited more demand for comfort and respect than did participants with an external locus of control on the achievement dimension of locus of control. Szentagotai and Freeman (2007) found that the impact of irrational beliefs on depressed mood was mediated by automatic thoughts (i.e., distorted inferences).

Taken as a whole, these data suggest the following picture. The way we represent (descriptions and inferences—cold cognitions) activating events depends on the interaction between activating events and our rational and irrational beliefs (hot cognitions); rational beliefs favor functional descriptions and inferences; whereas irrational beliefs disfavor functional descriptions and inferences (see Dryden's programmatic research mentioned above). Cold cognitions may, in turn, generate various operant behaviors, and then both cold cognitions and operant behaviors may be further appraised in a rational/irrational manner, producing feelings and psychophysiological responses (see David & Szentagotai, 2006; Szentagotai & Freeman, 2007). Further, the degree of conviction in beliefs is an important variable. For example, if a person were to believe, "no woman would want me," he might be reluctant or fearful to seek contact with women. If, however, the belief was held but only accepted or believed with 20% conviction, it would likely be far less inhibiting than if the beliefs were accepted at a level of 98%.

A robust literature (see Kirsch, 1999) illustrates the impact of response expectancies (i.e., what individuals expect regarding nonvolitional responses) on nonvolitional outcomes (e.g., pain, anxiety, depressed mood). However, few researchers have investigated the relation between response expectancies and rational and irrational beliefs. In fact, only one study has addressed this important topic (Montgomery, David, DiLorenzo, & Schnur, 2007). The authors found that the impact of general irrational beliefs on emotional disturbance was completely mediated by response expectancies, whereas the impact of specific irrational beliefs on distress was partially mediated by response expectancies. Whereas rational and irrational beliefs are initial, and then latent causes of nonvolitional outcomes, following practice and repetition, the relation between A and C comes under the control of response expectancies. For example, when confronted with a stressor, the irrational belief "It is awful that I am in this situation" might generate anxiety. However, confronting the same stressor repeatedly may result in anxiety because of the response expectancy "I expect to be anxious when I encounter the stressor."

In sum, cognitive behavior therapy research has failed to disambiguate cold and hot cognitions, with negative implication for theoretical and practical developments. Cold and hot cognitions may influence each other. Because they are studied separately, we have little knowledge of their reciprocal relationships. The new ABC model must explicitly address and incorporate this interaction. Accordingly, research provides little guidance regarding when therapy is best aimed at the level of hot or cold cognitions. Because hot cognitions are more closely associated with emotions, this area of research is critically important to understanding psychological disturbance and intervention.

Conscious versus Unconscious Cognition

Unfortunately, some in the psychotherapeutic community have misunderstood the distinction between conscious and unconscious thought (discussion based on David & Szentagotai, 2006). For example, Mahoney (1993) used Beck's (1976) concepts of automatic thoughts and schema to exemplify his point that the construct of the cognitive unconscious had already penetrated the field of psychotherapy. Mahoney (1993) seemed to refer to that aspect of information processing that functions unconsciously, but can potentially become conscious, thus representing a kind of "functional dissociation" between conscious and unconscious processes, determined by the automatization of some conscious processes and/or by coping and defense mechanisms (e.g., suppression, Wegner & Smart, 1997). We believe that Mahoney over-represented the impact of the cognitive unconscious in CBT.

Modern work in cognitive psychology (e.g., Reber, 1993; Schacter, 1987; Seger, 1992) argues for a "structural dissociation" between conscious and unconscious processes (i.e., as two different psychological and neurobiological structures). This concept has nothing to do with the Freudian concept of the dynamic unconscious (which is functionally separated from consciousness). We might speculate that Freud did not discover the unconscious but rather invented it. Freud the scientist found that there were gaps in the data flow in memory for ordinary events or during psychoanalytic sessions. As a scientist, Freud needed to make the data flow continuous, so he invented the unconscious as a construct to account for the gaps in data he observed. He then could explore these gaps to make data flow more smoothly.

In our view, in the best case, the dynamic unconscious should or could be reinterpreted in the light of modern research regarding the cognitive unconscious (for details, see Kihlstrom, 1999). Some types of information processing (including both perceptual and semantic processing), by their nature, cannot be made conscious because they are represented in our memory in a format (e.g., nonverbal associations) that is not consciously accessible (Schacter & Tulving, 1994). Few workers in the field have assimilated this line of cognitive unconscious research in psychotherapy.

Contrary to Mahoney (1993) and others, we argue that the "unconscious revolution in cognitive behavior therapy" has not yet begun. Such a revolution would require a clear understanding of the construct of the cognitive unconscious. We further suggest that a more important and helpful development would be to incorporate the distinction between nondeclarative and implicit memory processing into psychotherapy and CBT/REBT theory. Nondeclarative/implicit memory processes (i.e., nonconsciously accessible) are structurally separated from consciousness and not consciously accessible. Nevertheless, these processes exert a major impact on interpersonal experiences, emotions, cognitions, and behaviors, independent of beliefs, and they need to be analyzed on their own terms. Implicit processes should not be mistakenly viewed as forms of repressed memories or as mere automatizations (functionally separated from consciousness and consciously accessible) of explicit memory processes (e.g., beliefs) (Tobias et al., 1992).

Some "Cs" (consequences) in REBT terms, are not mediated by beliefs at all, but are mediated instead by unconscious information processing, structurally separated from consciousness (e.g., nonverbal associations). It remains an empirical question whether these Cs generated by unconscious information processing are intense enough to have clinical significance, or whether they will become new "As" and subject to evaluation by conscious rational and/or irrational beliefs, thus generating clinical outputs. The concepts of implicit memory and cognitive unconscious could relate CBT theory to recent research in the neurobiology of memory and emotion (e.g., LeDoux, 2000; Schacter & Tulving, 1994). This development would bring CBT/REBT further into the mainstream of current psychological research. In addition, the assimilation of the cognitive unconscious construct could contribute to a better integration of some behaviorist constructs (e.g., associations) into CBT/REBT theory. So far, behaviorism has only been assimilated into CBT at the level of technique, rather than at the level of clinical conceptualization. The concept of implicit memory (e.g., Schacter, 1987), combined with Rescorla's (1990) work on classical conditioning, which suggests that classical conditioning can be described in terms of information processing and computation, might lead to a better assimilation of behaviorist principles into CBT/REBT theory. Assimilation of these views might also stimulate the development of new techniques to deal with unconscious information processes that are structurally separated from consciousness. Thus, the new ABC model must explicitly address and incorporate the construct of unconscious information processing (i.e., cognitive unconscious).

Autobiographical versus Semantic Cognitions (based on David &
Szentagotai, 2006)

Cognitions can range from broad and pervasive (semantic; not related to time and location) to situation-specific (autobiographic). Ellis distinguishes between elegant and inelegant solutions to emotional problems (Ellis, 1962). Elegant solutions involve pervasive philosophical change, (i.e., change in one's general evaluative thinking regarding values, namely general irrational beliefs). Inelegant solutions involve either a change in a situation-specific evaluation or in a cold cognition, but not pervasive philosophical change. Thus, the distinction between elegant and inelegant CBT/REBT has important consequences for CBT/REBT clinical strategies. We suggest that all CBT theories address the extent to which an intervention will provide a strategy to cope with or effect a wide range of triggering stimuli or activating events (As), creating the potential for more pervasive personal changes. Thus, the new ABC model must explicitly address and incorporate the distinction between autobiographical versus semantic cognitions.

Available versus Accessible Cognitions (based on David &
Szentagotai, 2006)

If we represent cognitions in our thinking, it means that they are available; if they are activated so as to have an impact on our responses, we say that they are accessible. Cognitions targeted by the various schools of CBT differ in terms of both availability and accessibility. Most prior CBT/REBT research has not investigated or controlled for differences in availability and accessibility. Typically, researchers assess availability. Measuring available cognitions is analogous to choosing research samples of convenience. This is to say, the data are easy data to obtain, but might not address particularly important research questions. For example, researchers often use scales to evaluate IBs (at time Tn) and later evaluate how IBs (measured at time Tn) impact various dependent variables measured at time Tn + 1. In our opinion, such research is relatively meaningless due to the confusion between available and accessible IBs. For example, IBs measured by various scales might be both accessible (they are activated by reading the scale) and available at time Tn. However, at time Tn + 1 they might be available (still exist in our mind) but not accessible (deactivated). Therefore the lack of impact of IBs on various dependent variables may be caused by the lack of their accessibility, despite their availability.

As we noted earlier, Ellis (1994) argued that irrational beliefs are often latent and inaccessible during nonstressful or low stressful periods. Most prior studies did not use relevant stressful situations, and, therefore, it is debatable that they adequately tested the CBT theory regarding the impact of IBs on various dependent variables. Just as stress in the form of strenuous exercises is sometimes necessary for the accurate interpretation of electrocardiogram results, relevant stressful situations may be necessary to identify the effect of cognitive vulnerability (Solomon et al., 1998). Strategies that make IBs accessible need to be developed. Once we have methods to achieve accessibility, research can progress to answer other questions proposed by CBT theory. Thus, the new ABC model must explicitly address and incorporate the dictinction between available versus accessible cognitions.

Rational and Irrational Beliefs in Psychotherapy

If Ellis's theory of change is valid, than changes in irrationality would account for changes produced by many forms of psychotherapy. A comprehensive theory needs to account for all of the facts relevant to the domain of inquiry.

To pursue this argument further, a momentus psychotherapy debate centers on the fact that outcome studies suggest that all major forms of psychotherapy can produce treatment gains. Wampold (2001, 2007) has argued that most of the variance in psychotherapeutic change can be accounted for by common factors, including the therapeutic alliance, therapist provision of a viable treatment rationale, and elaborate rituals for change with a caring person. Wampold further suggests that variance in outcome due to theoretical orientation is trivial or nonexistent.

Most schools of psychotherapy tend to neglect Wampold's data, focusing instead on their preferred theory of change and the mediating variables hypothesized to produce change. Each of the more than 400 psychotherapies has, at heart, two components: *(1)* a theoretical framework; and *(2)* a practical package of techniques. For each therapy we can ask whether the treatment package works, and whether it works for the reasons stipulated by the theory of change allied to the therapy. Even well-designed clinical trials that provide evidence of a particular therapy's effectiveness do not necessarily validate the theory that underpins the treatment. Rather, it is necessary to validate the theory during the clinical trial by evaluating the hypothesized mechanisms of change or independent of the clinical trial by evaluating the etiopathogenetic mechanisms. Various theories may account for treatment success, not only the original theory associated with the particular treatment.

One possibility is that the success of many psychotherapies can be attributed to the fact that they all incorporate the same or similar common factors. However, another possibility is that they all have some unique mechanism of change. The latter hypothesis seems unlikely, and is far from parsimonious. For this hypothesis to be true, or even partly true, there would have to be hundreds of different mechanisms of behavior change at play.

Yet another possibility is that therapies "work," but not for the reason the theories say they do. Perhaps, psychoanalysis and Rogerian therapy are successful because they influence clients' irrational beliefs, although less efficiently than REBT. In fact, Abrams and Abrams (1997) have made just such a claim. They demonstrate through an analysis of therapy transcripts that some prominent psychodynamic therapists succeeded in changing client's irrational beliefs, albeit in a less direct and forceful way than does Ellis, for example. Of course, theorists from each persuasion could maintain that their favored mechanism of change could account for the change in other therapies as we have done.

Indeed, we contend that REBT provides a unifying construct (i.e., changes in rational and irrational beliefs) for explaining change across diverse psychotherapies. CBT theorists, in particular, have largely ignored Wampold's challenge, and have minimized or ignored data suggesting that other forms of therapy often yield positive outcomes. Perhaps cognitive-behavior therapies are effective because they produce cognitive change proposed by their respective models of psychopathology. Or perhaps cognitive-behavior therapies are effective because they influence some common latent cognitive variable responsible for treatment gains. From our perspective, we believe that IBs represent such a latent variable.

One way to investigate the strength of the connection between IBs and emotional disturbance is to investigate the the the extent to which IBs are modified in successful treatment interventions. Typically, a psychotherapy package of techniques is derived from a particular theoretical framework. For example, free associations are used to access allegedly past repressed conflicts in therapies that are based on the idea that present conflicts are generated by childhood repressed conflicts. Similarly, the use of Gestalt techniques to close a gestalt is justified by the belief that an open gestalt is the cause of suffering. However, the efficacy of free associations could be interpreted as a modification of semantic networks, rather than the uncovering and repairing of a repressed conflict.

Practical eclecticism, in which therapists combine interventions from different therapeutic approaches in the hopes of modifying relevant variables such as IBs can be better justified than theoretical eclecticism. Theoretical eclecticism is more difficult to justify insofar as two different and incompatible theories cannot be simultaneously true. Which theory or set of variables best explains or predicts the efficacy of various treatment packages should be resolved by empirical data.

We have demonstrated that whereas irrational beliefs are important etiopathogenetic (causal) mechanisms, rational beliefs are important sanogenetic (health promoting) mechanisms. Accordingly, we suggest that an effective treatment package must produce a change in irrational and rational beliefs. If it does not produce a change in rational and irrational beliefs but still ameliorates the clinical condition, we suggest that the intervention results in *feeling better* (i.e., symptomatic treatment), rather than *getting better* and *staying better* (i.e., causal treatment) because important etiopathogenetic and/or sanogenetic mechanisms were not targeted. Unfortunately, few studies have investigated this conclusion empirically.

Conclusion

Our discussion suggests that irrational beliefs are important causal factors in psychopathology, and that rational beliefs are an important health promoting mechanism. This hypothesis pertains to both cognitive-behavioral therapies and psychotherapy in general. The role of irrational beliefs, as a central cognitive mechanism in psychopathology, is better established than the role of rational beliefs, warranting a research focus on this latter topic. The contribution of rational beliefs in health promotion has important social and public health implications. However, rational beliefs do not invariably generate positive feelings, which are typically experienced during a positive activating event such as passing an important test. During a negative event, such as the loss of a loved one, rational beliefs generate negative feelings (e.g., sadness), that are healthy and that allow positive feelings to emerge later. However, when irrational beliefs generate dysfunctional negative feelings, such as a prolonged depressed mood, it may be difficult to experience positive feelings under such circumstances. Thus, CBT/REBT can nicely complement the research and theory in the burgeoning field of positive psychology (see David, 2003).

Finally, future research examining the role of rational and irrational beliefs as etiopathogenetic and sanogenetic mechanisms should focus on:

1. Endorsement of rational and irrational beliefs and physiological, behavioral, cognitive, and emotional responses in individuals exposed to real-life stressful situations in the context of longitudinal and randomized designs.
2. Treatment outcome studies with experimental manipulations of sufficient magnitude and duration to influence both core beliefs and self-statements.
3. Changes in rational and irrational beliefs associated with *(a)* feeling better-getting better-and staying better and *(b)* clinical interventions that are not CBT/REBT in nature.

REFERENCES

Abrams, M., & Abrams, L. D. (1997). The paradox of psychodynamic and Cognitive-Behavioral Psychotherapy. *Journal of Rational Emotive and Cognitive Behavior Therapies, 15*(2), 133–156.
Alden, L., & Safran, J. (1978). Irrational beliefs and nonassertive behavior. *Cognitive Therapy and Research, 2,* 357–364.
Allport, G. W. (1958). *The nature of prejudice.* Garden City, NY: Doubleday Anchor Books.
Avrahami, E. (2003). Cognitive-behavioral approach in psychodrama: Discussion and example from addiction treatment. *The Arts in Psychotherapy, 30,* 209–216.
Bandura, A. (1969). *Principles of behavior modification.* New York: Holt.
Baron, R. M., & Kenny, D. A. (1986). The moderator-mediator variable distinction in social psychological research: Conceptual, strategic, and statistical considerations. *Journal of Personality and Social Psychology, 51,* 1173–1182.

Beck, A. T. (1976). *Cognitive therapy and the emotional disorders.* New York: International Universities Press.

Beck, J. S. (1995). *Cognitive therapy: Basics and beyond.* New York: Guilford Press.

Bernard, M. E. (1998). Validations of General Attitude and Beliefs Scale. *Journal of Rational-Emotive & Cognitive-Behavior Therapy, 16,* 183–196.

Bond, F. W., & Dryden, W. (1996). Testing an REBT theory: The effects of rational beliefs, irrational beliefs, and their control or certainty contents on the functionality of inferences: 2. In a personal context. *International Journal of Psychotherapy, 1,* 55–77.

Bond, F. W., & Dryden, W. (1997). Testing an REBT theory: The effects of rational beliefs, irrational beliefs, and their control or certainty contents on the functionality of inferences: 1. In a social context. *Journal of Rational-Emotive and Cognitive-Behaviour Therapy, 15,* 157–188.

Bond, F. W., & Dryden, W. (2000). How rational beliefs and irrational beliefs affect people's inferences: An experimental investigation. *Behavioural and Cognitive Psychotherapy, 28,* 33–43.

Bond, F. W., Dryden, W., & Briscoe, R. (1999). Testing two mechanisms by which rational and irrational beliefs may affect the functionality of inferences. *British Journal of Medical Psychology, 72,* 557–566.

Chang, E. C. (1997). Irrational beliefs and negative life stress: Testing a diathesis-stress model of depressive symptoms. *Personality and Individual Differences, 25,* 117–155.

Chang, E. C., & Bridewell, W. B. (1998). Irrational beliefs, optimism, pessimism, and psychological distress: A preliminary examination of differential effects in a college population. *Journal of Clinical Psychology, 54,* 137–142.

Ciarrochi, J. (2004). Relationships between dysfunctional beliefs and positive and negative indices of well-being: A critical evaluation of the Common Beliefs Survey-III. *Journal of Rational-Emotive & Cognitive-Behavior Therapy, 22,* 171–188.

Civitci, A. (2007). The adaptation of multidimensional students' life satisfaction scale into Turkish: Validity and reliability studies. *Eurasian Journal of Educational Research, 26,* 51–60.

Clark, D. M. (1999). Anxiety disorders: Why they persist and how to treat them. *Behaviour Research and Therapy, 37*(Suppl. 1), S5–S57.

Craighead, W. E., Kimball, W., & Rehak, P. (1979). Mood changes, physiological responses, and self-statements during social rejection imagery. *Journal of Consulting and Clinical Psychology, 47,* 385–396.

Cramer, D. (2005). Effect of four aspects of rational statements on expected satisfaction with a close relationship. *British Journal of Guidance & Counselling, 33,* 227–238.

Cramer, D., & Buckland, N. (1996). Effect of rational and irrational statements and demand characteristics on task anxiety. *The Journal of Psychology, 129,* 269–275.

Cramer, D., & Fong, J. (1991). Effect of rational and irrational beliefs on intensity and "inappropriateness" of feelings: A test of rational-emotive theory. *Cognitive Therapy and Research, 4,* 319–329.

Cramer, D., & Kupshik, G. (1993). Effect of rational and irrational statements on intensity and "inappropriateness" of emotional distress and irrational beliefs in psychotherapy patients. *British Journal of Clinical Psychology, 32,* 319–325.

Culhane S. E., & Watson P. J. (2003). Alexithymia, irrational beliefs, and the rational-emotive explanation of emotional disturbance. *Journal of Rational-Emotive and Cognitive-Behavior Therapy, 21,* 57–72.

David, D. (2003). Rational Emotive Behavior Therapy (REBT): The view of a cognitive psychologist. In W. Dryden (Ed.), *Rational emotive behavior therapy: Theoretical developments.* New York: Brunner-Routledge.

David, D., & McMahon, J. (2001). Clinical strategies in cognitive behavioral therapy: A case analysis. *Romanian Journal of Cognitive and Behavioral Psychotherapy, 1,* 71–86.

David, D., Miclea, M., & Opre, A. (2004). The information processing approach to the human mind: Basic and beyond. *Journal of Clinical Psychology, 4,* 353–369.

David, D., Schnur, J., & Belloiu, A. (2002). Another search for the "hot" cognition: Appraisal irrational beliefs, attribution, and their relation to emotion. *Journal of Rational-Emotive & Cognitive-Behavior Therapy, 20,* 93–131.

David, D., & Szentagotai, A. (2006). Cognition in cognitive-behavioral psychotherapies: Toward an integrative model. *Clinical Psychology Review, 26,* 284–298.

David, D., Szentagotai, A., & Kallay, E. (2006). The faster you move the longer you live—A test of rational emotive behavior therapy. *Journal of Cognitive and Behavioral Psychotherapies, 6,* 69–80.

David, D., Szentagotai, A., Kallay, E., & Macavei, B. (2005). A synopsis of rational emotive behaviour therapy (REBT): Fundamental and applied research. *Journal of Rational-Emotive & Cognitive-Behavior Therapy, 3,* 175–221.

David, D., Szentagotai, A., Lupu, V., & Cosman, D. (2008). REBT versus cognitive therapy versus medication in the treatment of major depressive disorder: Oucomes study and six months follow-up. *Journal of Clinical Psychology, 64,* 728–746.

Dryden, W., Ferguson, J., & Clark, T. (1989). Beliefs and inferences: A test of rational-emotive hypothesis: 1. Performing in an academic seminar. *Journal of Rational-Emotive & Cognitive-Behavior Therapy, 7,* 119–129.

Dryden, W., Ferguson, J., & Hylton, B. (1989). Beliefs and inference: A test of rational-emotive hypothesis: 3. On expectations about enjoying a party. *British Journal of Guidance and Counseling, 17,* 68–75.

Dryden, W., Ferguson, J., & McTeague, S. (1989). Beliefs and inferences: A test of rational-emotive hypothesis: 2. On the prospect of seeing a spider. *Psychological Reports, 64,* 115–123.

Ellis, A. (1962). *Reason and emotion in psychotherapy.* New York: Lyle Stuart.

Ellis, A. (1994). *Reason and emotion in psychotherapy* (rev. ed.). Secaucus, NJ: Birch Lane.

Ellis, A., & Dryden, W. (1997). *The practice of rational emotive behavior therapy.* New York: Springer Publishing Co.

Försterling, F. (1980). Attributional aspects of cognitive behavior modification: A theoretical approach and suggestions for modification. *Cognitive Therapy and Research, 4,* 27–37.

Försterling, F. (1985). Attributional retraining: A review. *Psychological Bulletin, 98,* 494–512.

Froh, J. J., Fives, C. J., Fuller, J. R., Jacofsky, M. D., Terjesen, M. D., & Yurkewicz, C. (2007). Interpersonal relationships and irrationality as predictors of life satisfaction. *The Journal of Positive Psychology, 1*, 29–39.

Goldfried, M., & Sobocinski, D. (1975). Effect of irrational beliefs on emotional arousal. *Journal of Consulting and Clinical Psychology, 43*, 504–510.

Harrel, T. H., Chamless, D. L., & Calhoun, J. F. (1981). Correlational relationships between self-statements and affective states. *Cognitive Therapy and Research, 5*, 159–173.

Hart, K. E., Turner, S. H., Hittner, J. B., Cardozo, S. R., & Paras, K. C. (1991). Life stress and anger: Moderating effects of Type A irrational beliefs. *Personality and Individual Differences, 12*, 557–560.

Hollon, S. D., & Kendall, P. C. (1980). Cognitive self-statements in depression: Development of an automatic thoughts questionnaire. *Cognitive Therapy and Research, 4*, 109–143.

Jones, R. A. (1968). A factored measure of Ellis' irrational belief system with personality and maladjustment correlates. *Dissertation Abstracts International, 29*, 4379–4380.

Kelly, G. A. (1955). *The psychology of personal constructs.* New York: Norton.

Kihlstrom, J. F. (1999). Conscious versus unconscious cognition. In R. J. Sternberg (Ed.), *The concept of cognition* (pp. 173–204). Cambridge, MA: MIT Press.

Kirsch, I. (Ed.). (1999). *How expectancies shape experience.* Washington, DC: American Psychological Association.

Kuehlwein, K. T., & Rosen, H. (Eds.). (1993). *Cognitive therapies in action: Evolving innovative practice.* San Francisco: Jossey-Bass.

Kuhn, T. (1996). *The structure of scientific revolutions* (3rd ed). Chicago: University of Chicago Press.

Lazarus, R. S. (1991). *Emotion and adaptation.* New York: Oxford University Press.

LeDoux J. E. (2000). Emotion circuits in the brain. *Annual Review of Neuroscience, 23*, 155–184.

Mahoney, M. J. (1993). Introduction to special section: Theoretical developments in the cognitive psychotherapies. *Journal of Consulting and Clinical Psychology, 61*, 187–194.

Malouff, J. M., Schutte, N. S., & McClelland, T. (1992). Examination of the relationship between irrational beliefs and state anxiety. *Personality and Individual Differences, 4*, 451–456.

McDuff, A., & Dryden, W. (1998). REBT and emotion I: A role playing experiment using a shame/disappointment scenario to investigate the effects of rational, irrational, and indifference beliefs on inferences and action tendencies. *Journal of Rational Emotive and Cognitive Behavior Therapy, 4*, 235–254.

Montgomery, G., David, D., DiLorenzo, T., Schnur, J. (2007). Response expectancies and irrational beliefs predict exam-related distress. *Journal of Rational-Emotive & Cognitive-Behavior Therapy, 25*, 17–34.

Munoz-Eguileta, A. (2007). Irrational beliefs as predictors of emotional adjustment after divorce. *Journal of Rational-Emotive & Cognitive-Behavior Therapy, 1*, 1–15.

Muran, E. M., & Motta, R. W. (1993). Cognitive distortions and irrational beliefs in post-traumatic stress, anxiety, and depressive disorders. *Journal of Clinical Psychology, 49,* 166–176.

Muran, J. C., Kassinove, H., Ross, S., & Muran, E. (1989). Irrational thinking and negative emotionality in college students and applicants for mental health services. *Journal of Clinical Psychology, 45,* 188–193.

Nelson, R. (1977). Irrational beliefs and depression. *Journal of Consulting and Clinical Psychology, 45,* 1190–1191.

Newark, C., Frerking, R., Cook, L., & Newark, L. (1973). Endorsement of Ellis' irrational beliefs as a function of psychopathology. *Journal of Clinical Psychology, 29,* 300–302.

Nottingham, E. J. (1992). Further validation of a measure of irrational beliefs with psychiatric inpatients. *Journal of Rational-Emotive & Cognitive-Behavior Therapy, 10,* 207–217.

Pekarik, G. (1986). Rationality as a moderator between life events and illness. *Journal of American College Health, 4,* 170–173.

Reber, A. S. (1993). *Implicit learning and tacit knowledge: An essay in the cognitive unconscious.* Oxford: Oxford University Press.

Rescorla, R. A. (1990). Evidence for an association between the discriminative stimulus and the response-outcome association in instrumental learning. *Journal of Experimental Psychology: Animal Behavior Processes, 16,* 326–334.

Rotter, J. B. (1954). *Social learning and clinical psychology.* Englewood Cliffs, NJ: Prentice-Hall.

Schacter, D. L. (1987). Implicit memory: History and its current status. *Journal of Experimental Psychology: Learning, Memory and Cognition, 3,* 501–518.

Schacter, D. L., & Tulving, E. (1994). *Memory systems.* Cambridge, MA: MIT Press.

Schill, T., Monroe, S., Evans, R., & Ramanaiah, N. (1978). The effects of self-verbalization on performance: A test of the rational-emotive position. *Psychotherapy: Theory, Research, and Practice, 15,* 2–7.

Seger, C. A. (1992). *Implicit learning.* UCLA Cognitive Science Research Program Technical Report #UCLA-CSRP-92-3.

Seligman, M. E. P. (1994). *What you can change and what you can't.* New York: Knopf/ Random House.

Seligman, M. E. P., & Csikszentmihalyi, M. (2000). Positive psychology. *American Psychologist, 55,* 5–15.

Smith, T. (1989). In M. E. Bernard & R. DiGiuseppe (Eds.), *Inside rational-emotive therapy: A critical appraisal of the theory and therapy of Albert Ellis.* San Diego: Academic Press.

Smith, T. W., & Brehm, S. S. (1981). Cognitive correlates of the Type A coronary-prone behavior pattern. *Motivation and Emotion, 5,* 215–223.

Smith, T. W., Houston, B. K., & Zurawski, R. M. (1984). Irrational beliefs and the arousal of emotional distress. *Journal of Counselling Psychology, 31,* 190–201.

Solomon, A., Haaga, D. A. F., Brody, K., Kirk, K., & Friedman, D. G. (1998). Priming irrational beliefs in formerly depressed individuals. *Journal of Abnormal Psychology, 107,* 440–449.

Szentagotai, A., & Freeman, A. (2007). An analysis of the relationship between irrational beliefs and automatic thoughts in predicting distress. *Journal of Cognitive and Behavioral Psychotherapies, 7*, 1–9.

Tobias, B. A., Kihlstrom, J. F., & Schacter, D. L. (1992). Emotion and implicit memory. In S.-A. Christianson (Ed.), *Handbook of emotion and memory* (pp. 67–92). Hillsdale, NJ: Erlbaum.

Vandervoort, D. J. (2006). Hostility and health: Mediating effects of belief systems and coping styles. *Current Psychology: Developmental, Learning, Personality, Social, 25*, 50–66.

Walen, S. R., DiGiuseppe, R., & Dryden, W. (1992). *A practitioner's guide to rational-emotive therapy* (2nd ed.). New York: Oxford University Press.

Wampold, B. E. (2001). *The great psychotherapy debate: Models, methods, and findings.* Mahwah, NJ: Lawrence Erlbaum Associates.

Wampold, B. E. (2007). Psychotherapy: The humanistic (and effective) treatment. *American Psychologists, 62*(8), 857–873.

Wegner, D. M., & Smart, L. (1997). Deep cognitive activation: A new approach to the unconscious. *Journal of Consulting and Clinical Psychology, 6*, 984–995.

II

Mindfulness and Irrational Beliefs

David I. Mellinger

More than two thousand years ago, the Buddha taught mindfulness as a means of counteracting the deep-seated distress that fills people's lives. He attributed suffering to the tendency to cling to certain thoughts, feelings, and ingrained perceptions of reality and habitual ways of acting in the world while engaging in habits of aversion to direct, open, and unguarded contact with what is unpleasant. Mindfulness eases suffering by enabling people to "know things as they are" (A. Munindra, personal communication, cited in Goldstein, 2002) by devoting purposeful attention, without judging, to the unfolding of present-moment experience (Kabat-Zinn, 2005). With so many functions that it has been likened to a great executive's chief of staff, mindfulness helps people distinguish good from bad, worthy from unworthy, and enables them to connect with their inherent goodness. Mindfulness can keep different wholesome states of mind in balance and working in harmony, clear people's mental confusion and contribute to thinking wisely (Goldstein, 2002). In concert with compassion and wisdom, mindfulness is a powerful means of easing emotional distress.

In Western terms, mindfulness is a traditional meditation practice originating in Asia that serves to raise people's awareness of the role of dysfunctional thinking in their emotional suffering and to alter processes that feed into the pain and confusion of psychological disorders. After the Second World War, interest in Eastern spiritual practices quickened when multitudes became fascinated by the writings of philosophers like Alan Watts and Zen master Suzuki Roshi, and a flood of Buddhist teachers and teachings started arriving in the West in the 1950s and 1960s. By the early 1970s, Tibetan Buddhist master Chogyam Trungpa Rinpoche and Suzuki Roshi began a dialogue about the best means of working with the many emotionally unstable students who presented for training at meditation centers, and they developed a Buddhist therapeutic community and a graduate program in Buddhist psychology (Lief, 2005) as a result. Trungpa described mindfulness practice as a way of "making friends with one's own neurosis" and the practice of meditation as "a way to make us more acceptable to ourselves." His descriptions might be reframed in cognitive-behavioral terms as desensitizing to one's disturbing thoughts and becoming more self-accepting and compassionate. This chapter will examine the ways that mindfulness has been integrated into contemporary therapeutic approaches to the treatment of irrational thinking in emotional disorders. In Buddhist psychology, mindfulness is considered the method for cultivating the ability to perceive reality accurately, so the cognitions and feelings of a person who attains mindfulness would represent a very sound basis for arriving at truth through rational thinking. Mindfulness will be discussed in the contexts of rational and irrational thinking, and its role in acceptance-based behavioral approaches, mindfulness-based therapies, and information processing-based metacognitive therapies will be examined.

Buddhist psychology occupies an unusual position in Western thought, because Buddhism is actually a philosophy, not a religion, and mindfulness is a spiritual practice integral to the philosophy. Without the practice, the philosophical principals will not get you far: Buddhist teacher Joseph Goldstein (2002) observed that mindfulness is of central importance in every Buddhist path. Mindfulness is a bridge between Buddhist and Western psychology that rests on pylons of compassion and acceptance.

Here are typical instructions for mindfulness meditation practice. After choosing a quiet place, sit comfortably upright in a chair, or kneel, or assume the half- or full-lotus posture with your hands resting on your lap or legs and your eyes shut or half-shut. Turn your attention to your breathing by keeping quiet and alert and finding your breath in your body. Practice keeping your attention steady at the place where you experience the strongest sensation of your breathing, and concentrate on the breathing process and the sensations— the movement of air through your airway, the sound of breathing, the coolness of the air going in, the warmth of exhaled breath, and the motion of your nostrils, mouth, chest, diaphragm, and stomach. Be aware of each inhalation and exhalation, perhaps by counting each in-breath or softly saying "in" and "out" in the back of your mind. When you notice different sensations arising, whether pleasant or unpleasant, "let [each] sensation become the object of meditation, making a soft mental note to help keep the mind receptive and nonreactive . . . When it is no longer predominant, let your attention return to the breath" (Goldstein, 2002, p. 94).

Our minds wander naturally, so when thoughts or images appear to your mind during practice, make a mental note like "wandering," "thinking," "hearing," or "remembering." The content of the thought or image, while sometimes fascinating or absorbing, is unimportant; and when it fades, return your awareness to your body, sounds, or the breath. The key to the art of mindfulness meditation is cultivation of full, steady attention with a grateful and tender heart—the gentle returning of your attention again and again to the practice you have chosen (Kornfield, 1993).

Acceptance and Change

A variety of clinical methods may be employed to help clients develop the sense of a transcendent, consistent sense of themselves, separate from the myriad transient mental experiences that are experienced from moment to moment, and to promote a compassionate stance toward these internal experiences. Mindfulness-based practice is consistent with emerging trends in contemporary psychology that: (a) recognize the importance of exposure to what is feared, (b) heighten awareness of subjective experiences, and (c) promote unconditional acceptance of thoughts, feelings, and actions—an acceptance that does not preclude choice, preferences, plans, or sincere efforts to make changes for the better.

Mid-twentieth-century scholars of acceptance-based approaches focused on self-acceptance and acceptance of others, defined, respectively, as a positive attitude toward the self and others (e.g., Berger, 1952; Rogers, 1961). More recently, a wealth of acceptance-based approaches to treatment have developed that encourage a shift from a controlling, judgmental stance toward internal experiences to an accepting, compassionate stance. Those practiced most widely today couch acceptance as a learnable skill (e.g., ACT—Hayes, 1994; Hayes, Strosahl, & Wilson, 1999; DBT—Linehan, 1993) and teach clients strategies for mastering their particular brands of acceptance in order to achieve therapeutic change (Hayes, 1994; Hayes et. al.,1999). From humanistic-existentialist approaches (Greenberg, 1994) to rational-emotive therapy (Ellis & Robb, 1994), solution-focused therapy (Fish, 1996), behavior therapy (Koerner & Jacobson, 1994), and acceptance and commitment therapy (ACT; Hayes, et. al., 1999), acceptance seems to be an idea whose time has come.

Classic Cognitive and Rational Therapies

Because there is neither a consensus about the meaning of acceptance nor well-substantiated information processing pathways that link acceptance to change of irrational beliefs, contemporary acceptance-based perspectives differ in crucial qualitative and technical ways. In his classic formulations of CBT, Beck discusses acceptance less as a value to be woven into the fabric of treatment than a core issue underlying maladaptive assumptions and beliefs to be targeted in cognitive-behavioral therapy, such as fear of rejection, the absence of love, or abandonment if one is not accepted by significant others (e.g., Beck, Emery, & Greenberg, 1985). Acceptance is integral to rational-emotive behavior therapy (REBT), but with the assumption that acceptance and change should co-occur *simultaneously* (Ellis & Robb, 1994). The focus of acceptance in REBT is on actively and willingly accepting the presence of disturbing aspects of one's life, acknowledging the unmitigated facts of particular situations, and then modifying one's irrational beliefs in accordance with one's current values and intentions. As Ellis elaborates that REBT helps enable clients to accept "obnoxious conditions that they can't change" (p. 98), his use of the descriptor "obnoxious" illustrates the *judgmental* quality of REBT, in contrast with the *nonjudgmental awareness* that is fundamental to more explicitly acceptance-based behavioral approaches.

The contrasts between the various therapeutic approaches' conceptualizations of acceptance also represent important differences between their methodologies for changing irrational beliefs. Semantic cognitive-behaviorists like Beck and Ellis advocate identification and challenge of irrational thoughts and beliefs through forms of the Socratic method in which the central technique, referred to in Greek as *elenchus*, may conform to the Wikipedia (2007) definition—"*cross-examination* for the purpose of *refutation.*" Although superficially similar to other acceptance-based behavioral approaches that espouse active willingness of clients to change, classic REBT actually encourages therapists to press clients "to forcefully dispute their own non-acceptance," questioning and challenging their beliefs through "verbal and behavioral counter-propagandizing activity" (Ellis, 2007). These passages further distinguish between REBT and the newer, acceptance-based approaches that share the Buddhist emphasis on "stopping the war," rather than getting caught up in futile wranglings with ourselves.

In treatment of panic and phobias, the successes of these and other adversarial approaches, such as ferociously challenging irrationality through standing up to one's fears in phobic situations, roaring battle cries like "Bring it on!" or "Do your worst!" may owe their effectiveness less to challenging specific irrational thoughts than to the paradox of assuming a hawkish stance when facing fear. As renowned Buddhist teacher Jack Kornfield observes (1993, p. 25), "trying to change through *struggle* [with ourselves; emphasis mine] only continues the patterns of self-judgment and aggression that ultimately strengthen the . . . denial we intend to change."

A middle ground has developed in classic CBT since the beginning of the twenty-first century. For instance, a key training tape for prospective cognitive therapists offered in the 1990s by Christine Padesky's prestigious Center for Cognitive Therapy was titled "Socratic Questioning," whereas the comparable compact disc offered by the Center today is titled "Guided Discovery." The emphasis has shifted from *refutation* of irrational beliefs to *acceptance: Acceptance* of clients' beliefs and *willingness* to change as a starting point, *imparting the knowledge* they need to grasp their conditions and recognize their irrational beliefs, and *guidance* through directive questioning until they ultimately arrive at more realistic perspectives.

Similar to guided discovery—but in contrast to rational-emotive approaches—acceptance-based behavioral treatments carefully avert strategies that might inadvertently fuel judgmentalism and negative reactivity toward one's internal experiences, such as labeling one's thoughts as "irrational." Utilizing paradoxes, metaphors, and experiential exercises, dialectical behavior therapy (DBT—Linehan, 1993) emphasizes dialectics as the means of resolving the apparent contradiction between acceptance and change (Mennin, 2005). Like DBT, acceptance and commitment therapy (ACT—Hayes, Strosahl, & Wilson, 1999) encourages therapeutic action promoting both acceptance and change, favoring metaphors and cognitive and behavioral exercises including mindfulness practice over the logical, disputational style of the Socratic method. According to the ACT model of psychopathology (Hayes et al., 1999; Hayes, Wilson, Gifford, Follette, & Strosahl, 1996), irrational beliefs are held in a matrix of linguistic constructs, so "certain internal experiences including feeling, thoughts, and bodily sensations are judged to be pathological, threatening, or impairing, which triggers escape and avoidance responses." Experiential avoidance is the target of ACT: Mennin asserts that ACT training enables clients to overcome avoidance, allows greater flexibility to both internal and external possibilities, and promotes behavioral action in accordance with their values (Mennin, 2005). Despite the remarkable track record of classic cognitive-behavioral therapies built on semantic cognitive-behavioral models of irrational beliefs, automatic thoughts, and schemata, a surprisingly high proportion of individuals presenting with generalized anxiety disorder (Brown, Barlow, & Liebowitz, 1994; Ninan, 2001) and social anxiety disorder (Brown, Heimberg, & Juster,1995; Hope et. al., 1995; Turner, Beidel, & Wolff, 1994) are partial or nonresponders to empirically supported, classic CBT. Recent perspectives on the role of irrational beliefs in psychopathology (Harvey et. al., 2004; Depression—Ingram & Hollon, 1986; Segal, Williams, & Teasdale, 2002; Teasdale, 1999, Teasdale, Segal, & Williams, 1995. GAD—Borkovec et. al., 2002; Newman et. al., 2004; Roemer & Orsillo, 2005. SAD—Herbert & Cardaciotto, 2005; Vassilopoulos, 2008) help to illuminate the nature of these shortfalls. Cognitive-behavioral therapies that modify paradigms of psychotherapy with mindfulness-based strategies appear to have strong potential for augmenting the helping power of CBT in a variety of ways.

At first blush, one might question the basis for favoring treatments that utilize metaphors and paradoxes over classic cognitive-behavioral therapies built on models of irrational beliefs, automatic thoughts, and schemata as vehicles for modifying irrational thinking. We can briefly analyze this profound issue by contrasting the target mental states of these two models. The cognitive-behavioral model guides clients in challenging thinking errors that underlie the core irrational assumptions and beliefs of their emotional distress so that their maladaptive, erroneous beliefs can be weakened. Using paradoxes, metaphors, and mindfulness exercises as therapeutic vehicles, mindfulness- and acceptance-based approaches focus clients on learning to contend with the nuances, uncertainties, and inherent contradictions in their emotional thinking, the ambiguity of their perceptions, and the ambivalence and conflicts that their feelings represent.

Acceptance-Based CBT Treatments

Herbert and Cardaciotto (2005) discuss distinctions between classic and acceptance-based CBT programs for social anxiety, observing that classic programs propose modification of the content and/or frequency of dysfunctional cognitions as a necessary antecedent to anxiety reduction and improved social performance. In contrast, the acceptance paradigm shifts radically away from utilization of modification of irrational beliefs or reduction of anxious discomfort as criteria for therapeutic progress. "In acceptance-based approaches, the specific content or frequency of thoughts is essentially irrelevant. Adopting a stance of nonjudgmental acceptance instead allows one to be willing to experience whatever occurs regardless of its emotional valence. One can have physiological arousal, negative social-evaluative thoughts, or both, and nevertheless continue to perform effectively" (202–203).

Acceptance-based behavioral treatments share with mindfulness practice the common ground of nonjudgmental acceptance of internal experiences, as opposed to judgmentalism and experiential avoidance, while training clients in the active use of innovative, flexible behavioral techniques validated by the clinical experience and empirical research characteristic of traditional cognitive-behavioral therapies. A number of concepts integral to the acceptance-based approaches are also applicable to other mindfulness-based techniques.

Common Elements of Acceptance-Based and Mindfulness-Based Approaches

Acceptance- and mindfulness-based approaches practices differ distinctively from classic cognitive therapies in their emphasis on *changing the context, rather than the content,* of irrational thinking.

Experiential Avoidance

Experiential avoidance refers to the cognitive and behavioral strategies that people unconsciously or consciously employ that are aimed at reducing the intensity of or eliminating emotionally distressing internal experiences. According to ACT, experiential avoidance obscures reality, feeds irrational thinking, and compounds an individual's suffering. Experiential avoidance also refers to the cognitive habits of aversion, identified by the Buddha, to direct, open, and unguarded contact with that which is unpleasant.

Research indicates that efforts to suppress thoughts and actions, especially those linked with strong affect, actually *increase* the propensity to engage in the thought or action. (Polivy & Herman, 1987; Strauss, Doyle, & Kreipe, 1994; Wegner, Schneider, Carte, & White, 1987). When emotions are suppressed or concealed, rather than fully experienced and expressed, memory (pleasant and unpleasant slides; Bonanno, Papa, Lalande, Westphal, & Coifman, 2004; recall of what was said in a social interaction; Richards, Butler, & Gross, 2003) and problem solving (anagram problem-solving task; Baumeister, Bratslavsky, Muraven, & Tice, 1998) are compromised. Moreover, physiological markers of stress increase (e.g., electrical conductivity of the skin, constriction of blood vessels; Richards & Gross, 1999, Study 2) during instances of emotional suppression. Relatively poor clinical outcomes accompany avoidance or suppression of negative emotions or thoughts (Amir et al., 2001; Hayes et al., 1999; Teasdale et al., 1995). From an ACT perspective, the more vigorously a person engages in experiential avoidance, the more distressing things get.

Hayes (in Hayes & Smith, 2005) equates this kind of suffering with getting stuck in quicksand and struggling to get out: the harder you try, the deeper you sink.

In contrast, a high level of acceptance and experiencing of emotions is associated with positive psychotherapeutic outcomes (e.g., Greenberg & Safran, 1987). Foa and Kozak (1986) asserted that active experiencing of emotion is integral to emotional processing of fear. Bach and Hayes (2002) demonstrated that rehospitalization rates decreased among psychotic patients who were taught to accept unavoidable events such as auditory hallucinations. Finally, therapies that promote exposure to negative as well as positive feelings and directly confront experiential avoidance have an important role in the treatment of anxiety and posttraumatic stress disorders (see Lynn et al., 2006; Mellinger & Lynn, 2003).

ACT designates experiential avoidance as a primary target, and clients learn to counteract it by practicing experiential acceptance (Foreman, 2007) through promoting intentional awareness of emotional suffering coupled with training in nonjudgmental acceptance. Although mindfulness practice does not expressly target experiential avoidance, it does endeavor to free people through radical acceptance from the suffering engendered by attachments, aversions, and illusions. In modern, Western Buddhist psychology, "radical acceptance" (Brach, 2003, p. 26) consists of "clearly recognizing what is happening inside us and regarding what we see with an open, kind, and loving heart." Developers of acceptance-based treatments find that mindfulness provides individuals with an opportunity to observe their internal dialogue in a nonjudgmental way that ultimately eases inner turmoil and negative emotions and promotes enhanced behavioral flexibility.

Cognitive Fusion and Defusion

In ACT and other cognitive-behavioral therapies, cognitive fusion is the process of treating thoughts and feelings as if they were facts, or inappropriately and excessively identifying with one's thoughts and feelings. A number of contemporary models of learning and cognition in the anxiety disorders associate cognitive fusion with increased anxious distress and impairment in functioning (**Orsillo, Roemer, & Holowka**, 2005). Thought-action fusion, or the belief that thoughts have direct influence on external events (e.g., "If I imagine my wife crashing her car, it will happen.") and that having negatively evaluated intrusive thoughts (e.g., "I wish my grandfather would die so I could inherit his fortune") is morally equivalent to carrying out a prohibited action, has been implicated in the development and maintenance of OCD (Shafran, Thordarson, & Rachman, 1996). Interoceptive conditioning, the learning of associations that link internal cues and false alarms, has been proposed as an important factor in the development of panic disorder (Bouton et. al, 2001; Goldstein & Chambless, 1978). Anxiety sensitivity, the fear of anxiety-related symptoms (Reiss, 1991), and the fear of other emotional states (Williams, Chambless, & Ahrens, 1997) have been identified as prominent factors in anxiety disorders. Through CBT, clients can heighten their awareness of the temporal or psychological fusing of thoughts and beliefs to emotional disturbance or disorders and create the potential to modify them. Anxiety sensitivity has recently been demonstrated also to be a mechanism of change in CBT of panic disorder (Smits, Powers, Cho, & Telch, 2004): by modifying subjects' "fear of fear"[1] of acute stress symptoms, the researchers succeeded in reducing the frequency of panickers' attacks, agoraphobic avoidance, and anxiety. Hayes et al. (1999) use the term *defusion* to describe the process in ACT of learning to separate thoughts from their antecedents and referents. Defusion can enable clients to develop an observer perspective on their thoughts so they can begin to grasp the illusory nature of propositional reality and begin progress toward the achievement of emotional liberation from the distorted worldview of experiential avoidance.

Letting Go

Buddhist teacher Jack Kornfield defines letting go as "allowing the changing mystery of life to move through us without our fearing it, without holding and grasping" (1993, p. 15). In mindfulness practice, letting go can start with the release of each breath and continue as the individual works on "the art of surrender"—moving from controlling the breathing (e.g., by breathing deeply or slowing and regulating the breath) to simply being aware and accepting of the breathing. A "softer" version of letting go, "letting be"—as in "There will be an answer, Let it be." (Lennon & McCartney, 1970)—refers to "releasing one's feelings, thoughts, judgments, aversions, and yearnings—not getting rid of them or avoiding them, but allowing what is present to arise and pass like the waves of an ocean" (Kornfield, 1993, p. 112). In Buddhist tradition, letting go is referred to as "nonclinging" or "nonattachment." The ability to let go can be cultivated through acceptance-based approaches and meditation practice. Mindfulness of breathing can serves as a starting point for this

---

[1] "Fear of fear," a term brought into the parlance of psychology by the late Albert Ellis, was coined by semantic theorist Alfred Korzybski [e.g., A. Korzybski (1958). *Science and sanity: An introduction to non-Aristotelian systems and general semantic* (5th ed.). Fort Worth, TX: Institute of General Semantics].

process: "If we can learn to allow the breath to unfold naturally, without tampering with it, then in time we may be able to do that with other aspects of our experience: we might learn to let the feelings be, to let the mind be" (Rosenberg, 1998, p. 21). A person who can let go as he or she moves through life from one mode of experience to the next, from one mode of cognition to the next, from one major change to another, and can function with grace, wisdom, and compassion. On the other hand, the consequence of clinging and attachment to feelings and experiences is equated to rope burn—"the suffering that comes from trying to hold on as the rope is inexorably pulled through our hands" (Goldstein, 2002, p. 134).

Decentering

Decentering is defined as the process of cultivating an altered relationship between oneself and one's cognitions and feelings, through shifting from a stance of personal identification with thoughts, feelings, and experiences with the self in the center to a wider context of awareness in which they are viewed as ceaseless, transient mental events, that can be differentiated from "self" or "reality." Decentering relates to a Buddhist perspective on cognition that holds that thoughts and moods, including the sense of a constant self, have no permanency and no inherent potency (Toneatto, 2002). Mindfulness teaches individuals to relate to thoughts and feelings in the context of a wider perspective, not governed by negative or positive reactions. Training to achieve this perspective is an integral part of acceptance-based behavioral treatments, as well.

Externalizing

Externalizing is a strategy of conceptualizing a quality, emotional feeling, or mood as separate from or outside of oneself. When therapist Michael White talked with children who had not yet mastered bowel control, he coined the term "Sneaky Poo" to refer to encopresis in order to help relieve their feelings of excessive responsibility. Therapist and child collaboratively talked about the problem as an entity separate from the child and externalized it so that it eventually was thought of as Sneaky Poo's problem, not the child's. As a result, the parents had less reason to criticize and blame the child or themselves (Tomm, 1989). By saying "I am not my depression" or talking about one's "angry self" as if it occupies its own chair in the therapy room, the disturbing feeling or mood is no longer locked in a rigid framework as if caged inside the person, the sense of responsibility becomes less onerous, and the individual may be liberated to creatively employ different therapeutic strategies. Externalization resembles the ACT concept of defusion, in that objectifying subjective feelings places them into a more realistic and perhaps more accessible perspective.

A small but powerful externalization technique for dealing with persistent worry is postponement. Theorists believe that intense, persistent worry, nebulous, disconcerting, and difficult to control, is a driving force of GAD. Postponement consists of monitoring when specific persistent worries arise and engaging in a metacognitive plan of worrying them at a specific future time—treating them, in effect, as unwelcome visitors. Multiple postponements are perfectly acceptable. When the right time arrives to think about the worry, it is dealt with actively and intensively. Through use of postponement, worry is treated like a misbehaving puppy that has to learn to wait for treats and goes through intensive obedience training every evening.

Mindfulness-based techniques can be effective means of externalizing emotional feelings and dealing with them more flexibly. By applying the doctrine of impermanence, for instance—that thoughts and feelings are not permanent and pass through our minds and bodies like water coursing along a riverbed—individuals can deal with irritable moods or an irrational sense of threat in different, nonhabitual ways, by thinking of them as temporary states of discomfort that pass in and out of their minds and lives.

Focus on the Present

Another variable distinguishing the various psychological approaches that include mindfulness meditation techniques is *present-moment focus*. Classic CBT and REBT involve recording recently passed, emotionally disturbing events in order to identify salient irrational or erroneous thoughts and beliefs and then reframing or challenging them so that clients can respond differently to similar occurrences in the future—in essence, using the present to reconsider the past in order to modify future responses. Mindfulness practice differs distinctively from classic cognitive therapies in its emphasis on training the mind to focus intentionally and preeminently on the present while concurrently expanding awareness and acceptance, so that the present becomes the principal arena for change. The present can also become a precious, spacious refuge: when focus on the past draws an individual into dwelling, ruminating, and regretting, and the future, though illusory, stirs fears or anger, by learning to return to the present and feel emotions and sensations willingly, directly, and with immediacy, she can gain the liberty to make emotional progress.

Awareness

Half a century ago, Carl Rogers discussed awareness as a key piece in therapeutic change and emotional dysfunction, arguing in 1959 that therapy produces change as a function of the client experiencing acceptance by the therapist, which in turn facilitates emotional self-awareness and self-acceptance. Emphasis on both acceptance and awareness has rebounded in contemporary acceptance-based approaches. Herbert and Cardaciotto (2005) observed that most descriptions of mindfulness in CBT incorporate both components of present-moment awareness—the continual monitoring of present-moment inner experience and external perceptions—and nonjudgmental acceptance. Enhanced awareness of maladaptive thought patterns and attachments to habitual ways of thinking may provide early warning of indicators of maladaptive responses (Baer, 2003; Linehan, 1993; Marlatt, 1994) and of tendencies to relapse from disorders such as depression (Teasdale et al., 1995). This advanced notice or grace period may afford the individual greater flexibility to shift to more adaptive responses. The practice of mindful awareness may, in itself, serve to dilute or nullify the malign influence of irrational beliefs. By appraising troubling irrational thoughts as they arise as nothing more than chains or cascades of mental events and detaching, decentering, or disidentifying from such thoughts (e.g., Just because I think I will die if I do not wash my hands, does not mean I actually will die), thus changing the context or perceived relationship between the self and mental activity, it is possible to achieve a degree of freedom from habitual or conditioned reactions (Lynn, Das, Hallquist, & Williams, 2006).

Attention

Attention is an integral factor in both mindfulness-based and cognitive conceptualizations of mental disorders, as well as acceptance-based approaches. Scant, bare, and naked mindful attention are other terms for mindfulness in Buddhist tradition. Bare attention is implemented by "paying precise attention, moment by moment, to exactly what you are experiencing, right now, *separating out your reactions from the raw sensory events*" (Epstein, 1995, p. 110). According to Toneatto (2002), mindful attention is a metacognitive control strategy—an effort, intentional or automatic, that individuals devote to controlling the activities of their cognitive systems: He asserts that mindful attention applied to cognition is the primary and most effective tool taught by the Buddha for reducing or correcting people's tendency to engage in irrational beliefs and attitudes.

In Rapgay's and his colleagues' (2007) model of treatment of generalized anxiety disorder with "classical mindfulness-based integrative cognitive-behavioral therapy," they deem anxiety to be a narrow-minded, rigid, hyperattentive state characterized by intense, worrisome self-talk. Treatment begins with training in bare attention, which they maintain can inhibit implicit verbal and thinking processes. Once sustainable, bare attention can enable the dehabituation of judgmentalism and the incessant mental verbalization integral to GAD-type worry. The faculty for focusing attention is trained separately from awareness, defined by Rapgay as a state of expanded spatiality. Clients are then trained to divide their focus between direct attention on their anxiety and awareness of the context of the anxiety—and thus ultimately to "reinstate the[ir] thinking and conceptual processes within the premise of direct experience." Vassilopoulos (2008) recently studied the utility of distinguishing between two modes of self-focused attention in the maintenance of social anxiety. He determined that rumination, described as an active, analytic focus on the meanings and causes of one's symptoms, does not relieve social anxiety, whereas the "experiential form of self-focus" on the direct experience of one's feelings, symptoms, and mental events decreased ratings of anxious mood and was associated with more positive thoughts. The experiential self-focus condition in his study closely resembles mindfulness practice.

In 1994, Wells and Mathews published *Attention and Emotion*, in which they proposed a framework to integrate cognitive psychology and information processing—the self-regulatory executive function (S-REF) model—as a basis for understanding the mechanisms of the regulation of attention, beliefs, and thinking in emotional disorders. Elsewhere, Wells (2002) has identified possible limitations and weaknesses of classic CBT and mindfulness-based techniques. He asserts that a pattern of spiraling psychological disturbance that he labels the cognitive attention syndrome (CAS—2000) is activated in all emotional disorders. The CAS consists of the narrowing and redirection of attention, particularly intense, threat-directed attention and perseverative, self-focused attention. He has proposed metacognitive treatment strategies based on the S-REF model to help overcome the alterations of the attentional faculty that occur in psychopathology, including an attention training technique (Papageorgiou & Wells, 1998; Wells, 2000), as well as a technique of attention training plus mindfulness (Wells, 2005). Evidence from recent neuroscientific research strengthens the links between the practice of meditation and improvement in attentional performance. Lazar (Lazar et al., 2005; Lazar, 2007) has determined that extended practice in mindfulness meditation results in a greater volume of gray matter, leading to improved attention and memory. Zen meditation, a related technique, appears to slow the shrinking of gray matter due to age and specifically the decline of the putamen, a structure strongly implicated in attentional processing (Pagnoni & Cekic, 2007). Jha, Klein, Krompinger, & Baime (in press) have demonstrated that individuals provided with eight weeks' training in mindfulness-based stress reduction (MBSR; Kabat-Zinn, 2003) improve in orienting and selectivity of attention, and consequently in the ability to focus attention. Evidence is mounting that mindfulness practice has important effects on attentional factors that are likely to bear on the capacity for rational thinking.

Clinical Applications of Mindfulness

Baer (2003) concluded that mindfulness-based interventions and mindfulness combined with cognitive-behavioral therapy significantly improved a variety of problems and medical conditions. These include depression, stress, anxiety, chronic pain, psoriasis, binge eating, fibromyalgia, and mood disturbance in cancer patients. Baer reported an effect size range at post-treatment of .15 to 1.65 and medium mean effect size follow-up of .59. She also concluded after evaluation of the limited number of controlled studies of mindfulness-based stress reduction (MBSR), an eight-week course of mindfulness-meditation training, that it is "probably efficacious" (according to the standards of the APA Division 12 Task Force on Promotion and Dissemination of Psychological Procedures; see Chambless et al., 1998). Preliminary results from randomized clinical trials of mindfulness-based cognitive therapy (MBCT—Segal et al., 2002) suggest that nospecific effects of this program may reduce the incidence of relapse by as much as two-thirds among clients with multiply-relapsing depression. Mindfulness can be used to promote cognitive and behavioral change, problem-solving, and acceptance of a wide array of emotions and thoughts (Baer, 2003; Teasdale et al., 2003). As Lynn et al. (2006) have observed, utilizing mindfulness-based models of mental disorders, acceptance-based approaches have offered novel solutions to vexing problems—such as relapse, application of therapeutic learning to real-life coping, and increasing satisfaction with life—in personality disorders (Linehan, 1993), depression (Segal et al., 2002), and anxiety disorders (Eifert & Forsyth, 2005; Hayes et al., 1999; Mennin, 2005; Orsillo et al., 2005). Nonspecific metacognitive strategies that include mindfulness-based techniques have shown promise for treatment of anxiety disorders including panic disorder (Germer, 2005; Karekla et al., 2004), social anxiety disorder (Herbert & Cardaciotto, 2005), generalized anxiety disorder (Roemer & Orsillo, 2005), and obsessive-compulsive disorder (Hannan & Tolin, 2005; Papantonio, 2008).

Mindfulness and Response Set Theory

The response set theory of Kirsch and Lynn (1997, 1998) highlights the
role of automaticity of thoughts and reactions in developing and maintaining a wide variety of clinical conditions (e.g., anxiety and depression),
and provides an understanding of the way mindfulness approaches enable
the deautomatization of metacognitions that underpin mental disorders.
Response sets are conditioned patterns of associations composed of expectancies, intentions, and cognitive representations or constructions of the
self. Expectancies and intentions are temporary states of readiness to
respond in particular ways to particular stimuli (e.g., mindfulness techniques, hypnotic suggestions) under particular conditions. Response sets
prepare cognitive and behavioral schemas (i.e., knowledge structures) or
scripts for efficient activation and can be triggered or automatically activated by environmental and internal stimuli, such as physical sensations
and moods (see Lynn et al., 2006). Widespread cultural beliefs in the
calming and liberating effects of meditation in general and mindfulness in
specific facilitate their salutary effect on emotional and spiritual well-
being. People anticipate that mindfulness practice will enable them to
alter the course of disturbing thinking patterns by "disengaging their
mental clutches," and mindfulness approaches have been advanced as a
promising means of deautomatizing habitual response sets (e.g., Lynn
et al., 2006). The following examples, described by Lynn and his colleagues (Lynn et al., 2006), suggest that the deautomatizing response sets of
mindfulness meditation can be valuable in a variety of contexts:

> Marlatt (2002): Meditation helps clients with addictive behavior problems
> to monitor urges and cravings without "overidentifying" with them and
> reacting in automatic, habitual ways—by "surfing the wave" of the urge
> without being "submerged."
> Groves and Farmer (1994): "Mindfulness might mean becoming
> aware of triggers for alcohol, smoking, depression, and choosing to
> do something else—weakening the habitual, relatively automatic,
> patterns of reaction into more intentional, considered choices of
> response" (p. 159).
> Lama Surya Das (1997): "Mindful awareness in structured meditation
> sessions is the practice of freedom. It intentionally reconditions and
> eventually deconditions the mind, liberating it from unfulfilling
> reaction patterns and inculcating broader present awareness
> conducive to creative proactivity rather than habitual reactivity."

These ideas are consistent with the notion that mindfulness training and meditation practice attention can play a pivotal role in modifying response sets (Lynn & Hallquist, 2004), giving clients greater flexibility in dealing with emotional disturbance, more effective capacity to engage in metacognitive strategies, and a more accepting and willing attitude.

Metacognition and Mindfulness

Mindfulness, cognition, and psychological disturbance will now be examined at the level of *metacognition* in order to arrive at a deeper understanding of ways that people are capable of modifying their irrational thinking in order to overcome emotional disorders. Metacognition is defined by Wells (2000) as any beliefs, cognitive processes, or strategies that are engaged in the appraisal, monitoring, or control of other cognitions, and by Toneatto (2002), who considers metacognition a bridge between Buddhist psychology and CBT, as the body of beliefs and attitudes about cognition. Both mindfulness-based treatments and classic cognitive-behavioral therapy share common ground as metacognitive control strategies, because they consist of intentional and automatic efforts that individuals devote to controlling their cognitive activities and for distinguishing and separating rationality from irrationality. Both distinguish adaptive from maladaptive metacognitions on the basis of their accuracy in perceiving the external and internal environment, and both emphasize the importance of correcting erroneous perceptions and conceptions.

In Buddhist psychology, cognitions are categorized as either conceptual or perceptual (Komito, 1987). *Conceptual cognitions* are the stream of descriptive, analytic, or evaluative cognitions that occur concomitant with present-moment awareness of physical sensations and emotional feelings. When an individual is not fully mindful, and particularly when he or she is actively suffering from emotional distress, conceptual cognitions arise almost immediately along with perceptions of internal and external sensations, fuse with them, and become virtually inseparable.

Perceptual cognition is synonymous with *nonjudgmental awareness* of the world within and without us and of bodily and interoceptive sensations. As Toneatto observes, "when the metacognition is perfectly accurate and without distortion or bias, [it] is equivalent to awareness" (Toneatto, 2002, pp. 73–74). In Indian tradition, mindfulness is actually thought of as an additional sensory modality, a virtual lens for perceptual cognition. Viewed in this light, practice in mindfulness is kindred to a visually impaired person learning to use a bionic eye, a visual detector-transducer device that restores sight by feeding electrical signals that accurately represent the real world directly into the optical nerves and thence to the brain. Thus, a fully mindful person with clear perceptual cognition would perceive both physical sensations and emotional feelings nonjudgmentally and without any compulsion to act on them.

Naming or labeling of cognitions is an important strategy often incorporated into the practice of mindfulness for augmenting the capacity for perceptual cognition. When a practitioner notices that her focus has shifted from the anchoring activity of meditation—usually breathing or walking—she would simply name the type of activity to which her mind has wandered—for example, thinking, itching, imagining, fidgeting, or feeling edgy, impatient, or annoyed. If she discovers her effort to label has become perfectionistic, she should either accept the first label that comes to mind or name her latest activity "self-criticizing" or "obsessing." Through practice and determination, an individual can become skilled at noticing and naming the mental activity engaged in during each mental shift and guiding (or nudging, or easing) the attention back to the breathing in an increasingly effortless fashion.

The following summary of Buddhist propositions about metacognitive experience, based on Toneatto (2002), further articulates the nature of mindful appraisal of cognition:

- *Objects of awareness do not necessarily mirror reality accurately.* Valid perceptions are inextricably entwined with beliefs, feelings, assumptions, and attitudes about perception.
- *We can't stop thinking,* regardless of whether our thoughts are pleasant or disconcerting, because cognitive phenomena are unavoidable. Although pleasant cognitions are preferable, unpleasant cognitions will regularly occur, despite our best efforts to avoid, suppress, or eliminate them. Thoughts and feelings appear to arise, abide, and leave awareness without any apparent conscious involvement of the individual. The cessation of each cognition creates the necessary condition for the arising of another. Although we can label cognitions, we cannot summon or prevent them.
- *Cognitive events are impermanent.* Thoughts and feelings continually enter our awareness, evolve into other thoughts, or cease just as quickly.
- *Cognitive states have no independent existence.* They are insubstantial or illusory. Imagining each thought as a ripple on the moving river of awareness and each feeling as a wave on an ocean of emotion or sensation is more valid than believing that a critical perspective is set in stone or a monument to bravery or ignominy is inherently fraught with meaning.

- *Cognitions have no inherent potency,* no direct power or influence over an individual's behavior or the environment. Unpleasant cognitive states are not inherently dangerous or harmful, and pleasant cognitions are fundamentally neither harmless nor helpful.

These statements can be thought of as propositions that facilitate understanding of the Buddhist perspective cognition and experience. Within Buddhism, however, they are known as contemplations—objective statements about human nature and the nature of the universe that can be arrived at through the practice of meditation.

Metacognition and Information Processing

Wells (2000) has identified three types of metacognition—metacognitive knowledge, metacognitive experiences, and metacognitive control strategies. Metacognitive knowledge refers to individuals' beliefs and theories about their own cognitions, such as beliefs about the meaning of particular types of thoughts, the efficiency of memory, and the efficacy of cognitive control. Metacognition can be divided into two categories—implicit (i.e., normally not conscious or verbally expressible) and explicit (i.e., conscious and verbally expressible).

Implicit metacognitive knowledge includes positive and negative beliefs about emotional states. Regarding a tendency to get angry, for example, a positive implicit belief might hold that it keeps annoying people at a distance from the angry person, while an example of a negative belief would be the conviction that the person who acts angriest in a situation will always receive the greatest blame. Many individuals with perfectionistic tendencies, as well as people with OCD who check compulsively, share the implicit negative belief that their working memories are defective in recalling details about their most worrisome concerns. Commonly held *explicit* metacognitive beliefs include the adages, "better to be safe than sorry" and "better to do too much than too little." An example of explicit metacognitive knowledge reflective of a Buddhist psychological perspective is the belief that thoughts and feelings are passing events in the mind rather than inherent aspects of the self or accurate reflections of reality.

Metacognitive experiences are conscious, moment-to-moment interpretations of cognitions, including appraisals of and judgments about the meaning of specific thoughts and feelings and the status of cognition (Wells, 2000) that correspond to conceptual cognitions in Buddhist psychology. Catastrophizing is an important metacognitive, experiential component of anxiety (Ellis, 2000) and depression—the tendency to greatly exaggerate the frequency, danger, or unpleasantness of a negative feeling or aspect of the environment one dislikes (see Beck, Emery, & Greenberg, 1985; Mellinger & Lynn, 2003). According to Teasdale (1999), another metacognitive experience, the "conceptualising/doing mode of mind," may perpetuate depression by supporting ruminative, conceptually dominated emotional processing. Fear of fear and worry about worry are other examples of metacognitive experiences. An example of a mindful metacognitive experience would be a person feeling intense disgust while thinking concurrently that feelings have no inherent potency and do not have direct influence over her behavior or the environment, and then choosing not to act disgusted.

Metacognitive Control Strategies

Metacognitive control strategies consist of the intentional and/or automatic efforts that individuals devote to controlling the activities of their cognitive systems. These strategies may intensify or suppress thinking strategies and may be directed toward increasing monitoring of thoughts or feelings. The strategies we use in everyday life may be functional or dysfunctional, helpful or damaging. Coping techniques, cognitive therapies, and mindfulness-based practice are all examples of metacognitive control strategies. Experiential avoidance is an automatic metacognitive control strategy. In psychological disorders, control strategies often consist of attempts to stem the stream of consciousness, such as by suppression of particular thoughts (like blasphemous images or thoughts of harming others in OCD) or thinking in special ways in an attempt to prevent catastrophe or reduce a sense of threat, like entertaining positive beliefs about worry in GAD (Wells, 2000).

Metacognitive therapies are intentional metacognitive control strategies. Wells and Matthews's S-REF-based model (1994) and Teasdale and colleagues' metacognitive model (1995) are examples of process-oriented theories and techniques, based on information processing theory, that have evolved to augment the effectiveness of traditional, content-focused cognitive-behavioral approaches. The focusing of attention is a central feature of both models, and awareness and attentional processes are deemed to be key variables mediating psychopathology. Based on their interactive cognitive systems model of psychopathology (ICS; Barnard & Teasdale, 1995), Teasdale and his colleagues propose that *the context or mode of thinking, rather than the content of irrational thoughts or beliefs*, is at the root of much of emotional disturbance. At times of potential depressive relapse, cognitive processes are activated and maintained through mood-congruent thinking that focuses on the self, depression, and its causes and consequences. In process-oriented terms, as a person relapses into depression, her mind switches into a mental mode that attenuates present-moment external awareness and shifts attention to internal processing, characterized by the "conceptualizing/doing mode." After completing clinical trials of their program melding CBT with mindfulness-based techniques aimed at preventing relapse from depression, Williams Teasdale, Segal, and Kabat-Zinn (2007) developed mindfulness-based cognitive therapy (MBCT). MBCT is intended to help individuals learn to deautomatize their depressive responses by disengaging from the depressive lockup of the conceptualizing/doing mode and entering the more liberating "mindful/being mode of thinking" (Segal et al., 2002). Clients train for eight weeks in mindfulness-based stress reduction (Kabat-Zinn, 2003), learn to meditate, and practice for forty-five minutes a day. Presumably this practice strengthens the orienting response, the "flashlight" of their attentional faculties, and enhances their facility at detecting early signs of the emergence of depressogenic themes. They are taught to engage in a "three-minute breathing space," a brief mindfulness practice for decentering themselves by widening the scope of their attention, and to implement an array of other mindfulness and acceptance strategies, including labeling thoughts, learning to let them be, and reminding themselves that thoughts are mental events, not facts. By dealing with depressive thoughts and feelings repeatedly through MBCT, Teasdale and his colleagues find that clients learn to respond more adaptively to depressogenic cognitions by more readily and intentionally shifting from doing mode to mindful being mode.

Wells (2000) critiques the ICS model, contending that it is limited in its capacity for increasing the accuracy of metacognition by a lack of precision in its methods of appraisal, monitoring, and controlling cognitions. He asserts that a pattern of spiraling psychological disturbance is activated in emotional disorders that he dubs the cognitive attention syndrome (CAS), a mode of thinking that consists of the narrowing and redirection of attention, particularly intense attention directed toward threats and perseverative, self-focused attention. Wells (2007) proposes the attention training technique (ATT) for contending with the CAS, a metacognitive control strategy that consists of training in selective attention, attention switching, and divided attention aimed at increasing control over processing and reducing self-focus of attention. Instead of questioning or striving to modify irrational beliefs or automatic thoughts (following the semantic model) or monitoring thought patterns and striving to modify their mode of thinking (following MBCT), individuals using the ATT *intentionally alter their attention strategies* during negative emotional states. In other words, ATT is a metacognitive control strategy for developing adeptness at attentional control in order to shift attention from the CAS to present-moment awareness (Papageorgiou & Wells, 1998; Wells, 1990).

The ATT has been used effectively for treatment of panic disorder and social phobia (Wells, 1990; Wells, White, and Carter, 1997), hypchondriasis (Papageorgiou & Wells, 1998; Cavanagh & Franklin, 2000), major depression (Papageorgiou & Wells, 2000; Siegle et al., 2007), and auditory hallucinations (Ensum & Morrison, 2003; Valmaggia et al., 2007). Like mindfulness meditation, ATT is a metacognitive strategy for working with the attentional faculty to shift focus to present-moment awareness during episodes of mental disturbance; unlike mindfulness, it implements a plan for monitoring and selecting attentional focus based on a model of the pathogenic qualities of the CAS. A caveat: Neither ATT nor mindfulness meditation is intended to be used as a form of distraction or anxiety management lest it becomes a means of experiential avoidance.

Limitations of Mindfulness-Based Techniques

Mindfulness-based techniques may facilitate modification of the response sets that lead to some forms of emotional disturbance, but they do not afford strong or lasting relief from every kind of psychological disorder. Their limitations are due in part to individuals' expectations and in part to the nature of their disorders. A desire for training in mindfulness might be motivated by deep emotional distress and thus can inadvertently serve as a method of experiential avoidance, an effort to smooth the rough edges of raw emotions. Conversely, emotional disturbance may interfere with individuals' capacity to respond to mindfulness-based practice. Renowned insight meditation teacher and psychologist Jack Kornfield has observed that at least half of the students at extended insight meditation retreats find themselves unable to do traditional meditation because they encounter so much unresolved emotional pain and unfinished developmental business "that this becomes their meditation." Upon their return to everyday life, problems of daily living, family issues, or even falling in love trigger old patterns of suffering, as neurosis, attachment, and delusion reassert themselves as irresistibly as ever. "Because [these patterns] are often the source of our greatest suffering . . . we fear them and may unconsciously use spiritual practice to avoid dealing with them" (1993, pp. 246–247). Parameters of technique may enable individuals to utilize mindfulness-based practice to overcome some of these limitations. For example, if a person discovers that he is engaging in unhealthy worrying or rumination—dwelling on his inadequacies, or worrying actively and struggling hard to refocus on his breathing—following the mindfulness agenda, he should simply continue to meditate and observe where his attention goes. To sustain mindfulness, he should not abort the meditation, shift from the present moment, nor judgmentally fixate on potentially negative future outcomes of the stream of negative automatic thoughts, such as the possibility of it turning into a full-blown anxious or depressed mood. Better that he should simply label the cognitions—for example, "thinking," "worrying," "ruminating," "judging," or "remembering," continue to label while devoting scant attention to the cognitions themselves; and gently restore attention to the anchoring activity, such as breathing or walking. In this instance, mindfulness would in itself be a metacognitive process, a plan involving appraisal, monitoring, and control of cognitions.

To deal with the fear, judgment, anger, and ambition that may be encountered repeatedly during mindfulness meditation, a committed mindfulness meditator might also practice placing his difficulties into the center of his meditations, and embark on the often arduous spiritual path of practicing strategies devised for contending with painful emotions through learning of compassion and loving kindness toward himself and others. Mindfulness is, after all, but one of a triumvirate of spiritual practices that make up the Buddhist *dharma*, the spiritual path to free the mind from suffering. As Joseph Goldstein explains, "in the One Dharma of emerging Western Buddhism, the method is mindfulness—the key to the present; the expression is compassion; the essence is wisdom." (Goldstein, 2002, p. 13) Buddhist teacher Tara Brach observes: "The two parts of genuine acceptance—seeing clearly and holding our experience with compassion—are as interdependent as the two wings of a great bird. Together, they enable us to fly and be free" (2003, p. 27).

The Problem of Active Worry and Rumination

Despite the fact that active worry and rumination feed into states of emotional disturbance (e.g, Nolen-Hoeksma & Morrow, 1991; Wells, 2000; Teasdale et al., 2003), neither mindfulness meditation in itself nor classic CBT for weakening irrational beliefs provides an effective means of preventing their development or overcoming them. Classic CBT is not very effective in relieving the active worry component of generalized anxiety disorder (e.g., Newman et al., 2004); nor is it strongly effective in alleviating depressive, angry (Nolen-Hoeksma, 2007), or socially anxious rumination (Clark, 2001). In his analysis of this shortfall, Wells (2002) holds that Beck's schematic model of cognition (e.g., Beck, 1976, Beck, Emery, & Greenberg, 1985) fails to adequately describe and account for appraisals occurring when these disturbing realms of thinking hold sway. He asserts that negative beliefs about the self are implicit and metacognitive in nature (e.g., "Worrying actively will protect me from harm"), rather than consisting of explicit negative propositions (e.g., "I'm incapable of protecting myself") as Beck proposed. According to schema theory, activation of irrational negative beliefs precipitates the emergence of automatic negative thoughts in a rapid, telegraphic fashion that must be challenged one by one in order to defuse emotional distress. Isn't it difficult to imagine a course of Socratic questioning or guided discovery that would enable clients to tease apart the mindstorm of irrational beliefs inherent in their ruminating, obsessing, or active worrying, and then implementing effective strategies that would modify irrational beliefs they uncover and thus allay their emotional disturbance? Wells reframes active worry and rumination as defective metacognitive control strategies and posits that effective worry prevention should aim at replacing the classic CBT treatment plan of modifying particular beliefs or assumptions with alternative strategies for thinking, paying attention, and behaving during episodes of active worry or rumination. Commenting on the potential for mindfulness as an alternative to or enhancement of CBT, Wells (2000) asserts that unless the parameters of technique are modified, mindfulness training is likely to backfire by strengthening self-consciousness and morbid self-preoccupation and thus *increasing* vulnerability to psychological disturbance. In his discussion of treatment for GAD, for example, he observes that while mindfulness may unbind locked-in perseverative processing such as active worry or rumination, it may also introduce misleading or counterproductive factors into metacognitive therapy. For instance, worry in GAD is locked in by both positive post hoc beliefs (e.g., "worry helps me maintain my responsibilities") and negative post hoc beliefs (e.g., "my worrying is incessant because my mind is out of control"). Mindfulness-based strategies do not contain information that can lead to unambiguous disconfirmation of such erroneous beliefs (Wells, 2002). On the other hand, mindfulness may be construed as the means by which an individual succeeds in controlling or escaping from *nonexistent* threats because "the nonoccurrence of catastrophe could be attributed to use of mindfulness and not the fact that catastrophe would not have occurred" (p. 97). Wells recently proposed augmenting his ATT technique (see pp. 29–30) with "detached mindfulness" (DM; Wells, 2000, 2005), a technique combining mindfulness-based precepts, acceptance-based techniques, and select experiential exercises that he maintains could facilitate change in core underlying pathological processes and act as the antithesis of CAS. Clients are taught decentering and trained to keep mindful that thoughts are events, not facts; to switch their attention or engage it selectively, so they can ultimately modulate and refocus their attention away or outward from their disturbing self-talk; and to refrain from overfocusing on the illusory goals of removing or avoiding threat. In sum, when events occur that could trigger a client's cognitive affective state, DM offers a way to disengage from or prevent full activation of the CAS.

A number of mindfulness-based techniques also offer egress through this quandary. Lynn and his colleagues (Lynn et al., 2006) have suggested that a meditator could gently redirect attention to what is transpiring in the environment in order to control mental activities such as rumination or apprehension. L. W. Sushinsky (personal communication, June, 2007) has proposed *overfocusing*, a related metacognitive strategy through which the worrier or ruminator would actively, intentionally shift his attention away from illusory, distressing thoughts and onto concrete aspects of external reality. However, classic mindful awareness does not aim to control cognitions as much as to observe them, insofar as the goal is to remain decentered from cognitions and related emotions as they arise. From this perspective, it is more productive to appraise thoughts in terms of categories than to label them as good or bad, which is contrary to the goal of nonjudgmental awareness. Of course, one may also employ the strategy of redirecting one's attention to the intention to be mindful in the present. Advanced practitioners of mindfulness may also adopt a strategy along the lines of the Zen concept of no mind, cultivating thought-free or nonconceptual awareness, which is not merely mindlessness or stupor but actually a lucid and vivid presence of mind.

Conclusion

Over the past 15 years, the techniques and conceptualizations of mindfulness have been integrated into innovative cognitive-behavioral therapies that diverge from classic, schema-based CBT in technique, philosophy, and conceptualization of the role of irrational beliefs. Contemporary cognitive-behavioral therapies, augmented by mindfulness- and acceptance-based strategies, trend increasingly toward the Buddhist direction of "stopping the war" with irrationality. As a product of the influence of mindfulness on contemporary CBT, greater emphasis is placed on changing of the context in which disorders occur, rather than targeting the irrational beliefs themselves.

Advocates of acceptance and commitment therapy (ACT) argue that therapists and clients alike have traditionally been buying into a sort of therapeutic illusion, most notably in the case of generalized anxiety, social phobia, and depression, by selecting elimination of irrational beliefs and eradication of emotional distress as principal targets. This choice of targets constitutes a kind of *experiential avoidance*—a dynamic that often feeds irrational thinking rather than modifying it, obscures reality, and compounds emotional pain. By cultivating mindfulness, willingness to change, and nonjudgmental awareness in clients, mindfulness and acceptance-based approaches attempt to circumvent this quandary. Straddling the boundary between CBT and mindfulness and enriched by both traditions, these approaches seek to empower clients to refrain from judgmentally rejecting their own feelings or moods while learning to function in less constricted, disturbed ways that are more in accord with their values.

Metacognitions are discussed in this chapter from the vantage points of Buddhist psychology and cognitive behavior theory, and metacognitive therapy strategies based on CBT and mindfulness practice are described. From the metacognitive perspective, both mindfulness and CBT are metacognitive control strategies; but so are states intrinsic to psychopathology, such as experiential avoidance and perseverative, refractory, self-focused negative states like rumination and active worry. Teasdale and his colleagues and Wells have developed distinctive cognitive models of emotional disturbance that involve modification of the *process* of emotional thinking rather than challenging the *content* of irrational beliefs, and both utilize fundamental concepts of mindfulness in their models of treatment.

Mindfulness-based techniques and Buddhist psychology are reshaping and augmenting contemporary cognitive-behavioral therapy in far-reaching ways. Acceptance- and mindfulness-based approaches are increasing the versatility and robustness of CBT. The cross-pollination of process-based cognitive theory with content-based theories shows promise for fortifying the power of cognitive-behavioral therapy to contend with pervasive problems of rumination and active worry. Mindfulness-based theories are modifying traditional perspectives on the role of irrational beliefs in psychopathology and contributing to the scope and power of CBT to address refractory problems in a new era.

REFERENCES

Amir, N., Coles, M. E., Brigidi, B., & Foa, E. B. (2001). The effect of practice on recall of emotional information in individuals with generalized social phobia. *Journal of Abnormal Psychology, 110,* 76–82.

Bach, P., & Hayes, S. C. (2002). The use of acceptance and commitment therapy to prevent the rehospitalization of psychotic patients: A controlled trial. *Journal of Consulting and Clinical Psychology, 75,* 1129–1139.

Baer, R. A. (2003). Mindfulness training as a clinical intervention: A conceptual and empirical review. *Clinical Psychology: Science and Practice, 10,* 125–143.

Barnard, P. J., & Teasdale, J. D. (1995). *Affect, cognition, and change: Remodelling depressive thought.* Hove, UK: Lawrence Erlbaum.

Baumeister, R. F., Bratslavsky, E., Muraven, M., & Tice, D. M. (1998). Ego depletion: Is the self a limited resource? *Journal of Personality and Social Psychology, 74,* 1252–1265.

Beck, A. T. (1976). *Cognitive therapy and the emotional disorders.* New York: International Universities Press.

Beck, A. T., Emery, G., & Greenberg, R. (1985). *Anxiety disorders and phobias: A cognitive perspective.* New York: Basic Books.

Berger, E. M. (1952). The relation between expressed acceptance of self and expressed acceptance of others. *Journal of Abnormal and Social Psychology, 47,* 778–782.

Bonanno, G. A., Papa, A., Lalande, K., Westphal, M., & Coifman, K. (2004). The importance of being flexible: The ability to both enhance and suppress emotional expression predicts long-term adjustment. *Psychological Science, 15,* 482–487.

Borkovec, T. D., Newman, M. G., Pincus, A. L., & Lytle, R. (2002). A component analysis of cognitive behavioral therapy for generalized anxiety disorder and the role of interpersonal problems. *Journal of Clinical Psychiatry, 62*(Suppl. 11), 37–45.

Bouton, M. E., Mineka, S., & Barlow, D. H. (2001). A modern learning theory perspective on the etiology of panic disorder. *Psychological Review, 108,* 4–32.

Brach, T. (2003). *Radical acceptance: Embracing your life with the heart of a Buddha.* New York: Bantam Dell.

Brown, T. A., Barlow, D. H., & Liebowitz, M. R. (1994). The empirical basis of generalized anxiety disorder. *American Journal of Psychiatry, 151,* 1272–1280.

Brown, E. J., Heimberg, R. G., & Juster, H. R. (1995). Social phobia subtype and avoidant personality disorder: Effect on severity of social phobia, impairment, and outcome of cognitive behavioral treatment. *Behavior Therapy, 26,* 467–486.

Cavanagh, M., & Franklin, J. (2000). *Attention training and hypochondriasis: Preliminary results of a controlled treatment trial.* Paper presented at the World Congress of Cognitive and Behavioral Therapy, Vancouver, Canada.

Chambless, D., Baker, M., Baucom, D., Beutler, L., Calhoun, K., Crits-Christoph, P., et al. (1998). Update on empirically validated therapies, 2. *The Clinical Psychologist, 51*(1), 3–16.

Clark, D. M. (2001). A cognitive perspective on social phobia. In W. R. Crozier & L. E. Alden (Eds.), *Social phobia: Diagnosis, assessment, and treatment.* New York: Guilford.

Das, Lama Surya. (1997). *Awakening the Buddha within.* New York: Broadway Books.

Eifert, G. H., & Forsyth, J. P. (2005). *Acceptance and commitment therapy for anxiety disorders: A practitioner's treatment guide to using mindfulness, acceptance, and values-based behavior change strategies.* Oakland, CA: New Harbinger.

Ellis, A. (2000). *How to control anxiety before it controls you.* New York: Carol Publishing.

Ellis, A. (2007). Albert Ellis Institute Website. Retrieved July 3, 2007, from www.albertellisinstitute.org.

Ellis, A., & Robb, H. (1994). Acceptance in rational-emotive therapy. In S. C. Hayes, N. S. Jacobson, V. M. Follette, & M. J. Dougher (Eds.), *Acceptance and change: Content and context in psychotherapy*. Reno, NV: Context Press.

Ensum, I., & Morrison, A. P. (2003). The effects of focus of attention on attributional bias in patients experiencing auditory hallucinations. *Behaviour Research and Therapy, 41,* 895–907.

Epstein, M. (1995). *Thoughts without a thinker: Psychotherapy from a Buddhist perspective.* New York: HarperCollins.

Fish, J. M. (1996). Prevention, solution-focused therapy, and the illusion of mental disorders. *Applied and Preventive Psychology, 5*(1), 37–40.

Foa, E. B., & Kozak, M. J. (1986). Emotional processing of fear: Exposure to corrective information. *Psychological Bulletin, 99,* 20–35.

Foreman, E. (2007, November). *Not all dimensions of mindfulness are created equally.* Paper presented at the meeting of the ABCT Conference, Philadelphia, PA.

Germer, C. K. (2005). Anxiety disorders: Befriending fear. In C. K. Germer, R. D. Siegel, & P. R. Fulton (Eds.), *Mindfulness and psychotherapy*. New York: Guilford Press.

Goldstein, A. J., & Chambless, D. L. (1978). A reanalysis of agoraphobia. *Behavior Therapy, 9,* 47–59.

Goldstein, J. (2002). *One Dharma: The emerging western Buddhism.* New York: HarperCollins.

Greenberg, L. (1994). Acceptance in experiential therapy. In S. C. Hayes, N. S. Jacobson, V. M. Follette, & M. J. Dougher (Eds.), *Acceptance and change: Content and context in psychotherapy*. Reno, NV: Context Press.

Greenberg, L., & Safran, J. D. (1987). *Emotion in psychotherapy.* New York: Guilford.

Groves, P., & Farmer, R. (1994). Buddhism and addictions. *Addiction Research, 2,* 183–194.

Hannan, S. E. & Tolin, D. F. (2005). Mindfulness- and acceptance-based behavior therapy for obsessive-compulsive disorder. In S. M. Orsillo & L. Roemer (Eds.), *Acceptance and mindfulness-based approaches to anxiety: Conceptualization and treatment*. New York: Springer.

Harvey, A. G., Watkins, E., Mansell, W., & Shafran, R. (2004). *Cognitive behavioural processes across psychological disorders*. Oxford: Oxford University Press.

Hayes, S. C. (1994). Content, context, and the types of psychological acceptance. In S. C. Hayes, N. S. Jacobson, V. M. Follette, & M. J. Dougher (Eds.), *Acceptance and change: Content and context in psychotherapy*. Reno, NV: Context Press.

Hayes, S. C., & Smith, S. (2005). *Get out of your mind and into your life: The new acceptance and commitment therapy.* Oakland, CA: New Harbinger.

Hayes, S. C., Strosahl, K. D., & Wilson, K. G. (1999). *Acceptance and commitment therapy: An experiential approach to behavior change.* New York: Guilford.

Hayes, S. C., Wilson, K. G., Gifford, E. V., Follette, V. M., & Strosahl, K. (1996). Experiential avoidance and behavioral disorders: A functional dimensional approach to diagnosis and treatment. *Journal of Consulting and Clinical Psychology, 64,* 1152–1168.

Herbert, J. D., & Cardaciotto, L. (2005). An acceptance and mindfulness-based perspective on social anxiety disorder. In S. M. Orsillo & L. Roemer (Eds.),

Acceptance and mindfulness-based approaches to anxiety: Conceptualization and treatment. New York: Springer.

Hope, D. A., Herbert, J. D., & White, C. (1995). Social phobia subtype, avoidant personality disorder, and psychotherapy outcome. *Cognitive Therapy and Research, 19*, 339–417.

Ingram, R. E., & Hollon, S. D. (1986). Cognitive therapy for depression from an information processing perspective. In R. E. Ingram (Ed.), *Information processing approaches to clinical psychology.* Orlando, FL: Academic Press.

Jha, A. P., Klein, R., Krompinger, J., & Baime, M. J. (in press). The effects of mindfulness training on attentional subsystems. *Cognitive, Affective, and Behavioral Neuroscience.*

Kabat-Zinn, J. (2003). Mindfulness-based interventions in context: Past, present, and future. *Clinical Psychology: Science & Practice, 10,* 144–156.

Kabat-Zinn, J. (2005). *Full catastrophe living.* New York: Random House.

Karekla, M., Forsyth, J. P., & Kelly, M. (2004). Emotional avoidance and panicogenic responding to a biological challenge procedure. *Behavior Therapy, 35*(4), 725–746.

Kirsch, I., & Lynn, S. J. (1997). Hypnotic involuntariness and the automaticity of everyday life. *American Journal of Clinical Hypnosis, 40,* 329–348.

Kirsch, I., & Lynn, S. J. (1998). Social-cognitive alternatives to dissociation theories of hypnotic involuntariness. *Review of General Psychology, 2,* 66–80.

Koerner, K., & Jacobson, N. S. (1994). Emotional acceptance in integrative behavioral couple therapy. In S. C. Hayes, N. S. Jacobson, V. M. Follette, & M. J. Dougher (Eds.), *Acceptance and change: Content and context in psychotherapy.* Reno, NV: Context Press.

Komito, D. R. (1987). *Nagarjuna's "Seventy Stanzas": A Buddhist psychology of emptiness.* Ithaca, NY: Snow Lion Publications.

Kornfield, J. (1993). *A path with heart: A guide through the perils and promises of spiritual life.* New York: Bantam.

Lazar, S. W. (2007, October). The neurobiology of meditation. Talk given at the Mindfulness and Psychotherapy Conference: Contemplating Wellbeing in the Present Moment, Lifespan Learning Institute, UCLA, Westwood, CA.

Lazar, S. W., Kerr, C., Wasserman, R. H., Gray, J. R., Greve, D., Treadway, M. T., McGarvey, M., Quinn, B. T., Dusek, J. A., Benson, H., Rauch, S. L., Moore, C. I., & Fischl, B. (2005). Meditation experience is associated with increased cortical thickness. *NeuroReport, 2005*(16), 1893–1897.

Lejeune, C. (2007) *The worry trap: How to free yourself from worry and anxiety using acceptance and commitment therapy.* Oakland, CA: New Harbinger Publications.

Lennon, J., & McCartney, P. (1970). Let it be. On *Let it be* [record]. London: Apple Records, Inc.

Lief, J. L. (2005). Transforming psychology: The development of maitri space awareness practice. In F. Midal (Ed.), *Recalling Chogyam Trungpa.* Boston: Shambala Publications.

Linehan, M. M. (1993). *Cognitive behavioral treatment for borderline personality disorder.* New York: Guilford.

Lynn, S. J., Das, L., Hallquist, M., & Williams, J. (2006). Mindfulness, acceptance, and hypnosis: Cognitive and clinical perspectives. *International Journal of Clinical and Experimental Hypnosis, 54*(2), 143–166.

Lynn, S. J., & Hallquist, M. N. (2004). Toward a scientifically based understanding of Milton H. Erickson's strategies and tactics: Hypnosis, response sets, and common factors in psychotherapy. *Contemporary Hypnosis, 21,* 63–78.

Marlatt, G. A. (1994). Addiction, mindfulness, and acceptance. In S. C. Hayes, N. S., Jacobson, V. M. Follette, & M. J. Dougher (Eds.), *Acceptance and change: Content and context in psychotherapy* (pp. 175–197). Reno, NV: Context Press.

Marlatt, G. A. (2002). Buddhist philosophy and the treatment of addictive behavior. *Cognitive and Behavioral Practice, 9,* 44–49.

Mellinger, D. I. & Lynn, S. J. (2003). *The monster in the cave: How to face your fear and anxiety and live your life.* New York: Berkley.

Mennin, D. S. (2005). Emotion and the acceptance-based approaches to the anxiety disorders. In S. M. Orsillo & L. Roemer (Eds.), *Acceptance and mindfulness-based approaches to anxiety: Conceptualization and treatment.* New York: Springer.

Newman, M. G., Castonguay, L. G., Borkovec, T. D., & Molnar, C. (2004). Integrative psychotherapy. In R. G. Heimberg, C. L. Turk, & D. S. Mennin (Eds.), *Generalized anxiety disorder: Advances in research and practice.* New York: Guilford Press.

Ninan, P. T. (2001). Generalized anxiety disorder: Why are we failing our patients? *Journal of Clinical Psychiatry, 62*(Suppl. 19), 3–4.

Nolen-Hoeksma, S. (2007, November). Rethinking rumination. Talk given at the National Conference of the Association for Behavioral and Cognitive Therapy, Philadelphia, PA.

Nolen-Hoeksma, S., & Morrow, J. (1991). A prospective study of depression and post-traumatic stress symptoms following a natural disaster: The 1989 Loma Prieto earthquake. *Journal of Personality and Social Psychology, 61,* 115–121.

Orsillo, S., Roemer, L., & Holowka, D. W. (2005). Acceptance-based behavioral therapies for anxiety using acceptance and mindfulness to enhance traditional cognitive-behavioral approaches. In S. M. Orsillo & L. Roemer (Eds.), *Acceptance and mindfulness-based approaches to anxiety: Conceptualization and treatment.* New York: Springer.

Pagnoni, G., & Cekic, M. (2007, July 25). Age effects on gray matter volume and attentional performance in zen meditation. *Neurobiology of Aging.*

Papageorgiou, C., & Wells, A. (1998). Effects of attention training on hypochondriasis: A brief case series. *Psychological Medicine, 28,* 193–200.

Papageorgiou, C., & Wells, A. (2000). Treatment of recurrent major depression with attention training. *Cognitive and Behavioral Practice, 7,* 407–413.

Papantonio, A. (2008, March). The misuse and use of mindfulness meditation in the treatment of OCD. Talk given at the 40th Annual Conference of the Anxiety Disorders Association of America, Savannah, GA.

Polivy, J., & Herman, C. P. (1987). Diagnosis and treatment of normal eating. *Journal of Consulting & Clinical Psychology. Special Issue: Eating Disorders, 55,* 635–644.

Rapgay, L. (2007, October 5). Classical mindfulness and MBCT for generalized anxiety disorders. Conference on Mindfulness and Psychotherapy: Cultivating Well-being in the Present Moment, UCLA, Westwood, CA.

Reiss, S. (1991). Expectancy theory of fear, anxiety, and panic. *Clnical Psychology Review, 11,* 141–153.

Richards, J. M., Butler, E. A., & Gross, J. J. (2003). Emotion regulation in romantic relationships: The cognitive consequences of concealing feelings. *Journal of Social and Personal Relationships, 20,* 599–520.

Richards, J. M., & Gross, J. J. (1999). Composure at any cost? The cognitive consequences of emotion suppression. *Personality and Social Psychology Bulletin, 25,* 1033–1044.

Roemer, L., & Orsillo, S. M. (2005). An acceptance-based behavior therapy for generalized anxiety disorder. In In S. M. Orsillo & L. Roemer (Eds.), *Acceptance and mindfulness-based approaches to anxiety: Conceptualization and treatment.* New York: Springer.

Rogers, C. R. (1959). A theory of therapy, personality, and interpersonal relationships as developed in the client-centered framework. In S. Koch (Ed.), *Psychology: A study of a science*: Vol. 3. *Formulations of the person and the social context.* New York: McGraw Hill.

Rogers, C. R. (1961). *On becoming a person.* Boston: Houghton Mifflin.

Rosenberg, Larry (1998). *Breath by breath: The liberating practice of insight meditation.* Boston, MA: Shambala.

Segal, Z. V., Williams, J. M. G., & Teasdale, J. D. (2002). *Mindfulness-based cognitive therapy for depression: A new approach to preventing relapse.* New York: Guilford Press.

Shafran, R., Thordarson, D. S, & Rachman, S. (1996). Thought-action fusion in obsessive compulsive disorder. *Journal of Anxiety Disorders, 10,* 379–391.

Siegle, G. J., Ghinassi, F., Thase, M. E. (2007). Neurobehavioral therapies in the 21st century: Summary of an emerging field and an extended example of cognitive control training for depression. *Cognitive Therapy and Research, 31*(2).

Smits, J. A. J., Powers, M. B., Cho, Y., & Telch, M. J. (2004). Mechanism of change in cognitive-behavioral treatment of panic disorder: Evidence for the fear of fear meditational hypothesis. *Journal of Consulting and Clinical Psychology, 72,* 646–652.

Strauss, J., Doyle, A. E., & Kreipe, R. E. (1994). The paradoxical effect of diet commercials on reinhibition of dietary restraint. *Journal of Abnormal Psychology, 103,* 441–444.

Teasdale, J. D. (1999). Emotional processing, three modes of mind and the prevention of relapse in depression. *Behaviour Research and Therapy, 37,* S53–S77.

Teasdale, J. D., Segal, Z., & Williams, J. M. G. (1995). How does cognitive therapy prevent depressive relapse and why should attentional control (mindfulness) training help? *Behaviour Research & Therapy, 33,* 25–39.

Teasdale, J. D., Segal, Z., & Williams, J. M. G. (2003). Mindfulness training and problem formulation. *Clinical Psychology: Science and Practice, 2,* 157–160.

Tomm, Karl. (1989). Externalizing the problem and internalizing personal agency. *Journal of Strategic and Systemic Therapies 8*(1), 54–59.

Toneatto, T. (2002). Metacognitive therapy for anxiety disorders: Buddhist psychology applied. *Cognitive and Behavioral Practice, 9,* 72–78.

Turner, S. M., Beidel, D. C., & Wolff, P. L. (1994). A compositive measure to determine improvement following treatment for social phobia: The Index of Social Phobia Improvement. *Behaviour Research & Therapy, 4,* 471–476.

Valmaggia, L. R., Bouman, T. K., & Schuurman, L. (2007). Attention training with auditory hallucinations: A case study. *Cognitive & Behavioral Practice 14,* 127–133.

Vassilopoulos, S. P. (2008). Social anxiety and ruminative self-focus. *Journal of Anxiety Disorders, 22,* 860–867.

Wegner, D. M., Schneider, D. J., Carter, S. R., & White, T. L. (1987). Paradoxical effects of thought suppression. *Journal of Personality and Social Psychology, 53,* 5–13.

Wells, A. (1990). Panic disorder in association with relaxation induced anxiety: An attentional training approach to treatment. *Behavior Therapy, 21,* 273–280.

Wells, A. (2000). *Emotional disorders and metacognition.* New York: Wiley.

Wells, A. (2002). GAD, metacognition, and mindfulness: An information processing analysis. *Clinical Psychology: Science and Practice, 9*(1), 95–100.

Wells, A. (2005). Detached mindfulness in cognitive therapy: A metacognitive analysis and ten techniques. *Journal of Rational-Emotive & Cognitive Behavior Therapy, 23*(4), 340.

Wells, A. (2007). The attention training technique: Theory, effects, and a metacognitive hypothesis on auditory hallucinations. *Cognitive and Behavioral Practice 14,* 134–138.

Wells, A., & Matthews, G. (1994). *Attention and emotion: A clinical perspective.* Hove, UK: Lawrence Erlbaum.

Wells, A., White, J., & Carter, K. E. P. (1997). Attention training: Effects on anxiety and beliefs in panic and social phobia. *Clinical Psychology and Psychotherapy, 4,* 226–232.

Wikipedia (2007). Socratic method. Retrieved July 14 from en.wikipedia.org/wiki/Socratic_method.

Williams, K. E., Chambless, D. L., & Ahrens, A. (1997). Are emotions frightening? An extension of the fear of fear construct. *Behaviour Research and Therapy, 35,* 239–248.

Williams, M., Teasdale, J., Segal, Z., & Kabat-Zinn, J. (2007). *The mindful way through depression: Freeing yourself from chronic unhappiness.* New York: Guilford.

PART IV

Physical Health and Pain

12

Irrational and Rational Beliefs and Physical Health

Julie B. Schnur, Guy H. Montgomery, and Daniel David

For centuries, philosophers and scientists have recognized the relationship between psychological factors and physical health. Both cognitive (e.g., response expectancies) and emotional (e.g., depression, anxiety) variables have been shown to contribute to physical sensations, symptoms, and suffering (Kirsch, 1990; Trief, Grant, & Fredrickson, 2000). However, a psychological variable that has been too frequently neglected as a predictor of health outcomes is irrational beliefs, which are the lynchpin of rational-emotive behavior therapy (REBT) (Ellis, 1994).

Currently, irrational beliefs are defined as a combination of psychological process and thought content. Irrational beliefs are believed to consist of four categories of cognitive processes: *(1)* demandingness; *(2)* awfulizing/catastrophizing; *(3)* frustration intolerance; and *(4)* global evaluation/self-downing (GE/SD). Each category covers various content areas (e.g., achivement, affiliation, comfort; Walen, DiGiuseppe, & Dryden, 1992; Ellis, 1994). The counterparts to irrational beliefs are rational beliefs, which cover the same content areas, but involve different cognitive processes; that is, *(1)* preferences rather than demandingness; *(2)* the appropriate evaluation of the negative aspects of a situation rather than awfulizing; *(3)* statements of frustration tolerance rather than frustration intolerance; and *(4)* evaluation of specific actions and acceptance of fallibility (non-GE/SD) rather than global evaluation of human worth and self-downing.

REBT holds that it is not the activating events we experience that cause our suffering, but rather our beliefs about those events. Two individuals can experience the same activating event, and yet respond completely differently due to the discrepant beliefs they hold. This basic tenet justifies the application of REBT theory to understanding health outcomes, where the activating event (e.g., being diagnosed with an illness) may be impossible to control, but one's reaction to it is not. For example, consider two individuals that have been diagnosed with cancer, and are scheduled to receive external beam radiation treatment. Person A might *irrationally* think in response to this event, "This is AWFUL! This treatment will ruin my life! I can't stand it," whereas Person B might *rationally* think, "I wish I didn't have to deal with this treatment, but it is only a part of my life. It will not dominate 100% of my life. And even though I don't like having to go through this, I will be able to stand it."

Based on their varying beliefs, these two individuals (Persons A and B) might experience very different emotional, behavioral, and physical responses to cancer and its treatment. Person A, who holds irrational beliefs, may well experience dysfunctional negative emotions (e.g., rage, depression), engage in unhelpful health-related behaviors (e.g., refuse or delay treatment), and suffer from various stress-related physical complaints (e.g., nausea, fatigue, head-aches). On the other hand, as a result of holding more rational beliefs, Person B might fare considerably better than Person A emotionally (e.g., annoyance, mild sadness), behaviorally (e.g., maintain treatment compliance), and physi-cally (e.g., reduced physical complaints).

Although many clinicians may regard the links between beliefs (rational and irrational) and a wide variety of health-related outcomes as obvious, scien-tifically sound research is needed to support this clinical intuition. Unfortunately, there is a dearth of empirical clinical data in this area. What literature exists can be divided into two primary categories: *(1)* studies that directly examine the relationship between beliefs and health outcomes, and *(2)* studies that examine the effects of REBT on health outcomes.

The Relationship between Irrational Beliefs and Health Outcomes

A limited number of studies examine the direct effects of irrational beliefs on health outcomes. Papageorgiou and colleagues (2006) discuss the role of depression in the development of coronary vascular disease. They theorized that depressed mood can lead to inflammation of tissue, which in turn may lead to coronary vascular disease. If their hypothesis is accurate, then factors that contribute to depressed mood may also predict inflammation. Accordingly, the authors tested the association of irrational beliefs with plasma inflammatory markers, hypothesizing that higher levels of irrational beliefs predict higher levels of plasma inflammatory markers. In a sample of 853 healthy individuals, the authors found that irrational belief scores were positively correlated with plasma inflammation markers, after controlling for age, sex, body mass, physical activity, and depressed mood.

In a sample of 203 adolescents (129 with asthma and 74 without), Silverglade and his colleagues (Silverglade, Tosi, Wise, & D'Costa, 1994) reported that irrational beliefs were significantly related to severity of disease. Participants who scored significantly higher on a measure of irrational thoughts (i.e., the importance of approval and the need to control emotions) experienced more severe asthma than patients who scored lower on the irrational thoughts measure. Consistent with the idea that irrational beliefs are important predictors of health outcomes, McNaughton and associates (McNaughton, Patterson, Smith, & Grant, 1995) demonstrated that irrational beliefs were related to depression and poor health in Alzheimer's disease caregivers. Specifically, the researchers found that decreased adherence to irrational beliefs was related to improved subjective health in 89 caregivers over a period of six months.

Catastrophizing: An Exemplar of Irrational Beliefs Research

One area of research has focused on the effects of a specific type of irrational health belief, commonly known as catastrophizing. Catastrophizing has most often been examined in the context of pain. Pain catastrophizing has been conceptualized as a negative mental set that can be activated in anticipation of and during painful experiences (Sullivan et al., 2001). In REBT terminology, catastrophizing is most similar to awfulizing about discomfort (e.g., This pain is AWFUL!).

Research has indicated that catastrophizing is associated with patients' experiences of pain. For example, patients undergoing knee surgery who tend to catastrophize before surgery are at greater risk for postsurgical pain (Pavlin, Sullivan, Freund, & Roesen, 2005). Additionally, greater catastrophizing predicts greater pain in patients with rheumatic disease (Edwards, Bingham III, Bathon, & Haythornthwaite, 2006). More broadly, review articles support the important role of catastrophizing in determining pain outcomes (see Ehde & Jensen, Chapter 13 this volume; Keefe, Rumble, Scipio, Giordano, & Perri, 2004; Tang & Crane, 2006; Zaza & Baine, 2002).

The Relationship between Irrational Beliefs and Health Behaviors

Irrational beliefs are not only associated with physical symptoms like pain, but also with health behaviors. For example, eating disordered populations show a greater tendency toward catastrophizing, low frustration tolerance, and negative self-rating when compared to control patients (Moller & Bothma, 2001). Phillips and her colleagues (Phillips, Tiggemann, & Wade, 1997) demonstrated that bulimics tend to have levels of irrational beliefs on par with depressed patients, and greater than those of healthy controls. Consistent with these data, the literature also suggests that increased levels of irrational beliefs are linked to inappropriate eating attitudes in nonclinical samples of young women (Tomotake, Okura, Taniguchi, & Ishimoto, 2002).

Further supporting the generalizability of the connection between irrational beliefs and health behaviors, Christensen and colleagues (Christensen, Moran, & Wiebe, 1999) demonstrated that higher levels of irrational beliefs were predictive of self-reported diabetic regimen, as well as objective levels of hemoglobin HbA1. Irrational beliefs have also been linked to alcohol problems, such that higher levels of irrational beliefs predict higher levels of alcohol problems in college students (Camatta & Nagoshi, 1995).

In summary, the empirical evidence supporting links between irrational beliefs, health outcomes, and behaviors is growing. Additional work is needed in this area to both refine our conceptual understanding of the effects of irrational beliefs on health outcomes and the underlying mechanisms responsible for these effects.

The Effects of REBT on Health Outcomes

The above literature indicates that irrational beliefs predict health outcomes and behaviors in a variety of contexts. Below, we will review literature suggesting that REBT, which is designed to reduce irrational beliefs, can affect health outcomes and behaviors as well.

Drazen and his colleagues (Drazen, Nevid, Pace, & O'Brien, 1982) found that REBT was effective for reducing blood pressure in mild hypertensives. REBT was administered in 40-minute sessions, once weekly, for 10 weeks. Following participation in this intervention program, patients in the REBT group showed significant decreases in their systolic and diastolic pressures at a two-month follow-up. Maes and Schlosser (1988) demonstrated that REBT resulted in patients being less preoccupied with their asthma and less emotionally distressed in their daily lives using a pre-post study design. However, the study relied on a small sample of patients, and did not focus on asthma symptoms per se (e.g., dyspnea). The generalizability of treatment effects also needs to be further substantiated in a randomized clinical trial.

More recently, Montgomery and colleagues (2009) demonstrated that an intervention combining an REBT-based intervention with hypnosis had a significant effect on the rate of change in fatigue in breast cancer radiotherapy patients over the course of radiotherapy treatment. On average, patients randomized to receive the psychological intervention did not show increased fatigue over the typically six-week course of treatment, whereas patients randomized to the control group showed a linear increase in fatigue over the same six weeks. The results suggest that an REBT-based intervention is an effective means for controlling and potentially preventing fatigue in breast cancer radiotherapy patients, although future researchers would do well to tease apart the independent and interactive effects of REBT and hypnosis.

In summary, existing data on the effects of REBT on health outcomes are consistent with the hypothesized link between irrational beliefs and health outcomes. However, insufficient empirical data exist to draw definitive conclusions concerning the role of irrational beliefs in REBT effectiveness.

There is growing support for the influence of irrational beliefs on health outcomes, and for positive effects of REBT on health outcomes. However, none of the studies we reviewed have conducted a comprehensive formal analysis including an REBT treatment, assessments of irrational beliefs, and evaluations of health outcomes within the same study. Overall, more empirical research is needed in this area.

Theoretical Model

Considering the literature reviewed above, and REBT theory, there appear to be at least three possible pathways through which irrational beliefs might affect health outcomes. First, irrational beliefs may influence health outcomes directly. Second, irrational beliefs may influence health outcomes indirectly through their effect on psychological distress. Third, irrational beliefs may influence health outcomes indirectly through their effect on response expectancies. We will elaborate on each of these possibilities in turn, using the outcome of pain as an illustrative example.

First, irrational beliefs, such as catastrophizing, may directly contribute to increased experiences of pain. In other words, a thought, like "The pain will be horrible," could lead to more intense pain experiences. This pathway does not assume further psychological mediation, and suggests that reducing irrational beliefs should directly improve health outcomes.

Second, the relationship between irrational beliefs and pain may be mediated by psychological distress. In other words, increased irrational beliefs result in increased distress, which in turn results in increased pain. For example, the thought, "The pain will be horrible," leads to anxiety, and anxiety increases pain. This notion is supported by studies which have found that emotional factors, particularly anxiety, depression, and hostility are related to *both* irrational thoughts and health outcomes (i.e., the severity of asthma) (Silverglade et al., 1994). However, other literature suggests that emotional distress may not account for all the effects of irrational beliefs on health (Papageorgiou et al., 2006). This mediational pathway suggests that reducing either irrational beliefs or psychological distress should improve health outcomes.

Third, the relationship between irrational beliefs and pain may be mediated by response expectancies. Response expectancies are defined as expectations for nonvolitional outcomes. For example, an expectation that one will experience pain is a response expectancy; expectations that one can lift one's arm or that it will rain today are not. Response expectancies are viewed as automatic and self-reinforcing (Kirsch, 1990). There is now strong empirical evidence supporting the association of response expectancies with a wide variety of health outcomes in experimental and clinical samples (Roscoe et al., 2006; Kirsch, 1999). This pathway would suggest that increased irrational thoughts result in increased expectancies for pain, which in turn result in increased pain. For example, the thought, "The pain will be horrible," leads to an expectancy of more intense pain, and this expectancy leads to increased experienced pain. This mediational pathway suggests that reducing either irrational beliefs or response expectancies should improve health outcomes.

Each of these pathways can potentially be tested through correlational or experimental designs. For example, a correlational design would examine relations between irrational beliefs, psychological distress and response expectancies. Using such a design, our own research has supported the hypothesis that irrational beliefs in part may operate through response expectancies (Montgomery, David, DiLorenzo, & Schnur, 2007). We investigated the contribution of response expectancies and irrational beliefs (both general and exam-specific) to exam-related distress in college students using a prospective design. In a sample of 105 undergraduates, our findings revealed that both response expectancies and general irrational beliefs separately predicted exam-related distress. Observed effects of general irrational beliefs were perfectly mediated by response expectancies, and observed effects of exam-specific irrational beliefs were partially mediated by response expectancies. Though the study was not focused on health outcomes, these data support the view that response expectancies may mediate the effects of irrational beliefs. In a study of 120 undergraduates, response expectancies partially mediated the effects of catastrophizing on experimentally induced pain (immersing one's arm in ice water) (Sullivan, Rodgers, & Kirsch, 2001).

Experimental manipulation could also be used to test all three pathways described above simultaneously. In the future, a randomized controlled trial of REBT effects on pain, which assessed irrational beliefs, psychological distress, and response expectancies following the intervention, would allow for statistical modeling of both direct and indirect effects. That is, inclusion of all of the pathways in a single study should result in a more thorough understanding of the role of irrational beliefs on physical health, and will provide insights for modifying and improving REBT theory and practice.

A Brighter Future

As we have demonstrated, emerging evidence suggests that irrational beliefs may play a role in both directly influencing health outcomes, as well as perhaps indirectly affecting those outcomes through mediators such as psychological distress or response expectancies. However, on a broader level, perhaps the most important revelation generated by our literature review was the overall lack of literature to review. This is a critical point, as without empirical justification, additional areas of study and clinical practice (e.g., medicine) will not accept the real-world relevance of these constructs, and will not move to incorporate psychotherapeutic strategies to combat irrational beliefs into routine clinical practice. Consequently, the population at large—for it is the rare individual who escapes entirely from health problems or physical discomfort—may be deprived of the benefit of an intervention that could improve both health as well as the ability to cope with illness or discomfort.

This raises the question of, why? Why have irrational beliefs largely been ignored within the broader domains of physical health and health psychology? Below, we will discuss our views as to why the constructs of rational and irrational beliefs have failed to translate into the broader health psychology literature, and possible solutions to the issues we raise.

Issue #1: Lack of rigorous empirical data within the health domain. As can be seen from the literature reviewed above, very few empirical studies have been conducted focused specifically on the relationship between irrational beliefs and health. Additionally, of the few relevant papers, some seem to focus on REBT, and to make the assumption that if REBT is effective in improving health that irrational beliefs must consequently be implicated in this change. Although this is possible, and in fact quite likely, we cannot take this assumption as fact without data to back it up.

Possible Solution #1: Initially, rigorous studies must be conducted to test either the explicit hypothesis that: *(1)* IBs and RBs prospectively predict health-related symptoms, behaviors, and/or quality of life; or that *(2)* IBs and RBs significantly mediate the relationship between REBT and improvements in health status, health behaviors, and/or health-related quality of life. Subsequently (as will be discussed in greater detail below), the results of these studies must be published in a variety of health-focused journals (e.g., *Health Psychology, Annals of Behavioral Medicine, Pain*) and disseminated to a wide audience of health-care professionals to promote interdisciplinary awareness.

Issue #2: Bad Press. In the health-care-related fields, REBT may have an undeserved poor reputation as a "rough" intervention. This may be particularly true in the cancer setting. Clinicians on the front lines of cancer patient care have expressed concern that the perceived confrontational approach of REBT may be inappropriate for use with cancer patients. We believe it possible that the view of REBT as harsh and antagonistic may discourage the study or practice of irrational belief change in physically ill patients.

Possible Solution #2: Research, education, and advertising (i.e., good press). We suggest that REBT incorporate some strategies used by proponents of other psychotherapeutic techniques who have experienced bias. First, one must identify the sources and types of bias held against REBT. For example, surveys of health professionals (e.g., American Medical Association, American Psychological Association, American Psychiatric Association, Society of Behavioral Medicine) would be helpful in identifying misconceptions and barriers to the study of REBT and its influence on irrational beliefs. Once misconceptions have been clearly identified, they can be combated through education. The community of health-care professionals needs to be made aware of the "facts" of REBT perhaps through the following avenues: *(a)* case reports and papers published in journals with a wide audience; *(b)* videotapes of REBT sessions (either with medically ill patients, or directed at physical symptom management) distributed through larger psychology and/or behavioral medicine organizations (e.g., SBM, APA); and *(c)* perhaps participation by REBT researchers and clinicians in grand rounds or other lecture series in medical centers.

More specifically, in the course of this public/professional education campaign, it must be made clear that disrespect for patients runs distinctly counter to the central tenets of REBT. As REBT practitioners know, REBT is a therapeutic orientation that: *(1)* is supremely focused on human worth. All human beings, no matter how irrational or how fallible they might be are recognized as possessing worth, and of being deserving of care and validation; and *(2)* recognizes that all humans are fallible and that no one is rational every second of every day. Consequently, a skilled REBT practitioner will not disparage patients for holding irrational beliefs, but rather, will work to change those beliefs in a respectful manner, recognizing that no one (including therapists) is exempt from such beliefs.

On a related note, REBT is an inherently validating form of therapy, in that it does not adopt as its primary focus revising the patient's view of reality. Unlike other forms of CBT, which ask patients to find the evidence to support their view of reality, REBT practitioners generally begin by accepting the patient's view of reality, and asking "what now" or "what if." For example, in the case of chronic pain, the message may be conveyed that "While the pain itself cannot be taken away, the psychological consequences can be altered so that the pain becomes less intrusive and the person can move in new directions" (Rothschild, 1993). This validation of the patients' view of their reality (i.e., their illness and/or symptoms) may be particularly important for medically ill patients, who often receive unsupportive reactions from others when they try to disclose their illness experience (e.g., Peters-Golden, 1982; Dunkel-Schetter, 1984; Wortman & Lehman, 1985; Wortman & Dunkel-Schetter, 1979). If a psychotherapist were to repeat this invalidating behavior, it could be especially destructive to both the patients' well-being, as well as to their relationship and alliance with the therapist (see Ackerman & Hilsenroth, 2003).

To summarize, researchers interested in irrational beliefs will be of great service to the field not only by producing high-quality research, but also by educating the lay and professional public about REBT and its effects on irrational beliefs. Just as one might begin a psychotherapy case by setting appropriate expectations for what the therapy will entail, so must we as dedicated researchers, set appropriate expectations for the public about what rational and irrational beliefs are, and what the study and shaping of them can accomplish.

Conclusion

Although the literature on irrational beliefs and physical health is not as developed as one might like it to be, the situation is not AWFUL (à la REBT); there is enough evidence to encourage and support further investigation in this area. In this chapter, we propose a theoretical model that if rigorously tested, could potentially increase our understanding of the effects of irrational beliefs on health outcomes.

To conclude, it has been written that REBT "is perhaps the only therapeutic system that directly tackles our confrontation with reality" (Rothschild, 1993). And as humans cannot help but be all too aware, physical suffering is an inextricable part of reality. REBT arms us in our struggle with this aspect of reality by providing us with two weapons: a willingness to accept reality, combined with an unwillingness to accept our irrational interpretations of that reality. In other words, "it is far better to focus on how to have inner control rather than decry the reality that events occur without our permission" (Rothschild, 1993).

REFERENCES

Ackerman, S. J., & Hilsenroth, M. J. (2003). A review of therapist characteristics and techniques positively impacting the therapeutic alliance. *Clinical Psychology Review, 23*, 1–33.

Camatta, C. D., & Nagoshi, C. T. (1995). Stress, depression, irrational beliefs, and alcohol use and problems in a college student sample. *Alcoholism: Clinical and Experimental Research, 19*, 142–146.

Christensen, A. J., Moran, P. J., & Wiebe, J. S. (1999). Assessment of irrational health beliefs: Relation to health practices and medical regimen adherence. *Health Psychology, 18*, 169–176.

Drazen, M., Nevid, J. S., Pace, N., & O'Brien, R. M. (1982). Worksite-based behavioral treatment of mild hypertension. *Journal of Occupational Medicine, 24*, 511–514.

Dunkel-Schetter, C. (1984). Social support and cancer: Findings based on patient interviews and their implications. *Journal of Social Issues, 40*, 77–98.

Edwards, R. R., Bingham, C. O., III, Bathon, J., & Haythornthwaite, J. A. (2006). Catastrophizing and pain in arthritis, fibromyalgia, and other rheumatic diseases. *Arthritis & Rheumatism, 55*, 325–332.

Ellis, A. (1994). *Reason and emotion in psychotherapy*. Secaucus, NJ: Birch Lane.

Keefe, F. J., Rumble, M. E., Scipio, C. D., Giordano, L. A., & Perri, L. M. (2004). Psychological aspects of persistent pain: Current state of the science. *Journal of Pain, 5*, 195–211.

Kiecolt-Glaser, J. K., Page, G. G., Marucha, P. T., MacCallum, R. C., & Glaser, R. (1998). Psychological influences on surgical recovery: Perspectives from psychoneuroimmunology. *American Psychologist, 53*, 1209–1218.

Kirsch, I. (1990). *Changing expectations: A key to effective psychotherapy*. Pacific Grove, CA: Brooks/Cole.

Kirsch, I. (1999). *How expectancies shape experience* (1st ed.). Washington, DC: American Psychological Association.

Maes, S., & Schlosser, M. (1988). Changing health behaviour outcomes in asthmatic patients: A pilot intervention study. *Social Science & Medicine, 26*, 359–364.

McNaughton, M. E., Patterson, T. L., Smith, T. L., & Grant, I. (1995). The relationship among stress, depression, locus of control, irrational beliefs, social support, and health in Alzheimer's disease caregivers. *Journal of Nervous and Mental Disease, 183*, 78–85.

Moller, A. T., & Bothma, M. E. (2001). Body dissatisfaction and irrational beliefs. *Psychological Reports, 88*, 423–430.

Montgomery, G. H., & Bovbjerg, D. H. (2004). Pre-surgery distress and specific response expectancies predict post-surgery outcomes in surgery patients confronting breast cancer. *Health Psychology, 23*, 381–387.

Montgomery, G. H., David, D., DiLorenzo, T. A., & Schnur, J. B. (2007). Response expectancies and irrational beliefs predict exam-related distress. *Journal of Rational-Emotive & Cognitive-Behavior Therapy, 25*, 17–34.

Montgomery, G. H., Kangas, M., David, D., Hallquist, M. N., Green, S., Bovbjerg, D. H., et al. (2009). Fatigue during breast cancer radiotherapy: An initial randomized study of CBT plus hypnosis. *Health Psychology, 28(3)*.

Nicholson, A., Fuhrer, R., & Marmot, M. (2005). Psychological distress as a predictor of CHD events in men: The effect of persistence and components of risk. *Psychosomatic Medicine, 67*, 522–530.

Papageorgiou, C., Panagiotakos, D. B., Pitsavos, C., Tsetsekou, E., Kontoangelos, K., Stefanadis, C., et al. (2006). Association between plasma inflammatory markers and irrational beliefs; The ATTICA epidemiological study. *Progress in Neuro-Psychopharmacology and Biological Psychiatry, 30*, 1496–1503.

Pavlin, D. J., Sullivan, M. J., Freund, P. R., & Roesen, K. (2005). Catastrophizing: A risk factor for postsurgical pain. *Clinical Journal of Pain, 21*, 83–90.

Pembroke, T. P., Rasul, F., Hart, C. L., Davey, S. G., & Stansfeld, S. A. (2006). Psychological distress and chronic obstructive pulmonary disease in the Renfrew and Paisley (MIDSPAN) study. *Journal of Epidemiology and Community Health, 60*, 789–792.

Peters-Golden, H. (1982). Breast cancer: Varied perceptions of social support in the illness experience. *Social Science and Medicine, 16*, 483–491.

Phillips, L., Tiggemann, M., & Wade, T. (1997). Comparison of cognitive style in bulimia nervosa and depression. *Behaviour Research and Therapy, 35*, 939–948.

Roscoe, J. A., Jean-Pierre, P., Shelke, A. R., Kaufman, M. E., Bole, C., & Morrow, G. R. (2006). The role of patients' response expectancies in side effect development and control. *Current Problems in Cancer, 30*, 40–98.

Rothschild, B. H. (1993). RET and chronic pain. In *Innovations in rational-emotive therapy* (pp. 91–115). Thousand Oaks, CA: Sage Publications.

Silverglade, L., Tosi, D. J., Wise, P. S., & D'Costa, A. (1994). Irrational beliefs and emotionality in adolescents with and without bronchial asthma. *Journal of General Psychology, 121*, 199–207.

Sullivan, M. J., Rodgers, W. M., & Kirsch, I. (2001). Catastrophizing, depression, and expectancies for pain and emotional distress. *Pain, 91*, 147–154.

Sullivan, M. J., Thorn, B., Haythornthwaite, J. A., Keefe, F., Martin, M., Bradley, L. A., et al. (2001). Theoretical perspectives on the relation between catastrophizing and pain. *Clinical Journal of Pain, 17*, 52–64.

Tang, N. K., & Crane, C. (2006). Suicidality in chronic pain: A review of the prevalence, risk factors, and psychological links. *Psychological Medicine, 36*, 575–586.

Tomotake, M., Okura, M., Taniguchi, T., & Ishimoto, Y. (2002). Traits of irrational beliefs related to eating problems in Japanese college women. *Journal of Medical Investigation, 49*, 51–55.

Trief, P. M., Grant, W., & Fredrickson, B. (2000). A prospective study of psychological predictors of lumbar surgery outcome. *Spine, 25*, 2616–2621.

Walen, S. R., DiGiuseppe, R., & Dryden, W. (1992). *A practitioner's guide to rational-emotive therapy* (2nd ed.). New York: Oxford University Press.

Wortman, C. B., & Dunkel-Schetter, C. (1979). Interpersonal relationships and cancer: A theoretical analysis. *Journal of Social Issues, 35*, 120–155.

Wortman, C. B., & Lehman, D. R. (1985). Reactions to victims of life crises: Support attempts that fail. In I. G. Sarason & B. R. Sarason (Eds.), *Social support: Theory, research, and applications* (pp. 463–489). Dordrecht, The Netherlands: Martinus Nijhoff.

Zaza, C., & Baine, N. (2002). Cancer pain and psychosocial factors: A critical review of the literature. *Journal of Pain and Symptom Management, 24*, 526–542.

Acknowledgments: The project described was supported by Award Number K07CA131473 from the National Cancer Institute and by RSGPB CPPB-108036 from the American Cancer Society. The content is solely the responsibility of the authors and does not necessarily represent the official views of the National Cancer Institute, the National Institutes of Health, or the American Cancer Society.

13

Coping and Catastrophic Thinking: The Experience and Treatment of Chronic Pain

Dawn M. Ehde and Mark P. Jensen

Pain is a common chronic health condition that contributes to disability and suffering throughout the world (Fejer, Kyvik, & Hartvigsen, 2006; Luime et al., 2004; Svendsen et al., 2005; Verhaak, Kerssens, Dekker, Sorbi, & Bensing, 1998; Volinn, 1997). For example, arthritis afflicts an estimated 21% of adults in the United States and has been described as a leading cause of disability in the United States (Centers for Disease Control and Prevention [CDC], 2001). The second leading cause of disability in the United States, back/spine problems, is also associated with pain (CDC, 2001). Pain has been reported to be the most common presenting problem to primary care clinics (Deyo, 1998; Turk & Melzack, 2001), as well as a common problem in persons with cancer (Liu et al., 2001) and physical disabilities such as cerebral palsy, limb loss, multiple sclerosis, spinal cord injury, and stroke (Benrud-Larson & Wegener, 2000; Ehde et al., 2003).

Despite the recent explosion of knowledge concerning the physiological mechanisms that contribute to pain, the biomedical treatment approaches that are currently available for pain treatment and management are often inadequate. For example, opioids are considered the most powerful analgesics available, yet significant controversy exists concerning their efficacy for chronic pain treatment (Eriksen, Sjøgren, Bruera, Ekholm, & Rasmussen, 2006). A recent review noted, for example, that the average reduction in chronic pain in persons who receive opioids is only 32% (Turk, 2002); there appears to be no such thing as a "pain killer." Also, although there are a number of other medications that have shown some efficacy for the management of neuropathic pain, such as anticonvulsants and antidepressants, these treatments have provided a clinically meaningful reduction in pain (defined as a decrease of 50% or more) in only one out of three patients, on average (Turk, 2002). Other purely biomedical approaches, such as surgery and spinal cord stimulation, do not eliminate pain in the majority of patients treated (Turk, 2002). Moreover, the focus of all of these treatments is pain intensity; they do not address nor significantly impact the many other domains related to pain, such as mood and physical dysfunction. Furthermore, the use of only biomedical approaches to treatment is based on outmoded views of pain. Current thinking recognizes that pain and its effects are best viewed from more comprehensive biopsychosocial models, rather than views that focus only on biological, psychological, or social/environmental factors (Novy, Nelson, Francis, & Turk, 1995).

Among the many psychosocial factors that impact the experience of chronic pain, the thoughts people have about their pain are perhaps most salient to the experience and impact of pain. As we will describe in this chapter, maladaptive beliefs and thoughts about pain are strongly associated with greater pain severity, greater psychosocial distress, greater disability, and poorer quality of life; treatments that impact those thoughts, such as cognitive therapy, can provide important reductions in pain, pain-related suffering, and disability. The purpose of this chapter is to provide an overview of the theory, research, and practice of cognitive therapy for pain. It begins with a summary of cognitive-behavioral theory of pain, followed by a description of pain-specific beliefs thought to influence adaptation to chronic pain. Given the saliency of catastrophizing cognitions to the experience of pain, the "pain catastrophizing" literature will be emphasized, followed by a discussion of assessment of beliefs and cognitions. A description of cognitive therapy for pain is then provided, followed by ideas for future directions for advancing the theory, research, and practice of cognitive therapy for pain.

Cognitive-Behavioral Theory of Chronic Pain

Individuals with chronic pain differ markedly in their levels of psychological distress and pain-related disability, even when comparing individuals who report similar levels of pain intensity and present with similar types of physical pathology (Turk, 1996). Cognitive-behavioral theory of chronic pain is one of several biopsychosocial models of pain that hypothesizes a key role (but not an exclusive role) for psychological factors in explaining differences in how persons adjust to chronic pain (Novy et al., 1995). Cognitive-behavioral models have significantly advanced our understanding of some of this variability in individuals' responses to chronic pain (Boothby, Thorn, Stroud, & Jensen, 1999; Jensen, Turner, Romano, & Karoly, 1991).

Cognitive-behavioral theory hypothesizes that individuals' pain-related cognitions, beliefs, and coping behaviors play key causal roles in determining their adjustment to pain, including psychological distress, pain-related disability, and health-care utilization. Numerous studies have provided support for cognitive-behavioral models, having shown that pain-related cognitions and behaviors are indeed associated with patients' pain intensity, physical functioning, psychological functioning, and disability (Boothby et al., 1999; Edwards, Bingham, Bathon, & Haythornthwaite, 2006; Jensen, Romano, Turner, Good, & Wald, 1999; Keefe, Rumble, Scipio, Giordano, & Perri, 2004; Sullivan, Thorn, Rodgers, & Ward, 2004).

Further support for the cognitive-behavioral model of pain comes from studies that have examined the effectiveness of cognitive-behavioral therapy (CBT) for pain. CBT treatments for chronic pain are based on the theoretical assumption that decreasing maladaptive and increasing adaptive cognitive and behavioral responses to pain will result in improvements in pain and pain-related functioning. In research studies treating a range of chronic pain disorders, cognitive behavioral interventions have proven effective in improving physical and psychosocial functioning (e.g., Dixon, Keefe, Scipio, Perri, & Abernethy, 2007; Hoffman, Papas, Chatkoff, & Kerns, 2007; Morley, Eccleston, & Williams, 1999; Turner, Mancel, & Aaron, 2006). Studies have also shown that continued improvements in functioning occur for some patients as many as six months after completion of the active cognitive behavioral treatment (Bennett, Burckhardt, Clark, O'Reilly, Wiens, & Campbell, 1996; Peters, Large, & Elkind, 1992; Turner et al., 2006).

The Importance of Cognitions and Beliefs in the Adjustment to Chronic Pain

The extant literature documents a number of pain-specific beliefs, cognitions, and coping strategies that are associated with functioning among persons with chronic pain (Boothby et al., 1999; Jensen et al., 1991). Pain-specific beliefs are beliefs about the experience of pain; they encompass a variety of beliefs such as beliefs regarding the etiology of pain, treatment expectations, the meaning of pain, outcome expectations, and personal control over pain. Studies have consistently demonstrated the importance of pain-specific beliefs in adjustment to chronic pain as well as in adherence and response to pain treatment (Boothby et al., 1999; Jensen, Turner, & Romano, 2007; Keefe et al., 2004). Beliefs that one does not have control over pain, that pain signifies harm, and that one is disabled by pain are particularly problematic for persons with chronic pain (Engel, Schwartz, Jensen, & Johnson, 2000; Jensen et al., 2007; Turner, Jensen, & Romano, 2000). Increases in patient's self-efficacy beliefs for managing pain also appear beneficial (Keefe et al., 2004; Turner et al., 2007). Among the various coping strategies hypothesized to impact adjustment to chronic pain, both maladaptive strategies (e.g., guarding the pain site and responding to pain with rest) and adaptive strategies (ignoring pain) appear to be important.

Although a number of cognitions and attributions have demonstrated fairly consistent associations with important functioning variables in persons with chronic pain, "negative" beliefs or cognitions tend to stand out as most important (Boothby et al., 1999; Thorn, Rich, & Boothby, 1999). In particular, one type of maladaptive cognition—catastrophizing—has been the cognition most consistently and most strongly associated with poorer adjustment to pain. Pain catastrophizing can be defined as excessively negative and unrealistic thoughts or self-statements about pain. Examples of catastrophizing pain cognitions include "pain is awful and I feel that it overwhelms me," "I can't stand this," and "this pain is never going to get better." Pain catastrophizing is hypothesized to be an active cognitive process that occurs not only in response to pain but also to anticipated pain (Dixon, Thorn, & Ward, 2004).

Pain catastrophizing has been shown to be negatively associated with virtually all pain outcomes investigated. For example, studies utilizing correlational and regression analyses have shown pain catastrophizing to be positively associated with higher levels of pain intensity (Hanley et al., 2004; Jensen et al., 2002; Sullivan, Stanish, Waite, Sullivan, & Tripp, 1998), pain-related interference with activities (Lin & Ward, 1996; Osborne, Jensen, Ehde, Hanley, & Kraft, 2007; Robinson et al., 1997; Stroud, Thorn, Jensen, & Boothby, 2000); psychological distress (Robinson et al., 1997; Stroud et al., 2000; Turner, Jensen, Warms, & Cardenas, 2002); analgesic use (Jacobsen & Butler, 1996); and medical services utilization (Keefe & Williams, 1990). Studies have also shown that pain catastrophizing is negatively associated with individuals' vocational functioning (Lester, Lefebvre, & Keefe, 1996; Sullivan et al., 1998). In nearly every study, the strength of the relationships found between catastrophizing and measures of adjustment are moderate to strong (Boothby et al., 1999). Another commonality across studies is that the association between catastrophizing and outcomes remains strong even when controlling for variables that may influence the relationship such as demographics, pain severity, other pain beliefs, or depressive symptoms (Stroud et al., 2000; Sullivan et al., 1998).

Early studies examining the relationship between catastrophizing and pain suggested the possibility that these cognitions might best be considered merely a symptom of depression, as opposed to a distinct construct that contributes to depressive symptoms (Sullivan & D'Eon, 1990). However, research has since found that catastrophizing mediates the relationship between depression and pain, supporting the conclusion that catastrophizing is related to the experience of pain independent of its relationship to depression (Gatchel, Polatin, & Mayer, 1995; Geisser & Roth, 1998). Additional studies have provided support for the contention that catastrophizing is not merely a result of the depressive symptoms that often co-occur with pain. For example, in a prospective study of persons with osteoarthritic knee pain, Keefe et al. (1990) found that catastrophizing cognitions predicted depression at outcome, even when controlling for initial level of depression. Similarly, Sullivan et al. (1998) found that catastrophizing was positively related to pain intensity and disability even when controlling for depressive symptoms. Thus, although catastrophizing is related to depression and may contribute to the maintenance of depression, its influence on pain adjustment also appears to be independent of mood.

The construct of pain catastrophizing has received considerable empirical attention in recent years given its hypothesized role in adjustment to chronic pain. One of the few prospective studies to examine pain, catastrophizing, and other pain variables over time found that increases in pain were predictive of increases in catastrophizing, both concurrently as well as over the course of a day (Holtzman & DeLongis, 2007). These investigators also found that increases in catastrophizing in the morning were related to increases in pain intensity in the evening. Furthermore, individuals were likely fluctuate over the course of a day in the extent to which they catastrophize about pain (Holtzman & DeLongis, 2007).

Support for the Role of Catastrophizing in Treatment Research

There is also a growing body of research that suggests that changes in pain catastrophizing are associated with changes in functioning among persons with chronic pain. Evidence for this association has been drawn from a variety of treatment studies that, although not specifically targeting catastrophizing in isolation from other cognitive behavioral variables, have shown reductions in both catastrophizing and subsequent improvements in functioning, including decreased pain, disability, depressive symptoms, and health-care utilization (Burns, Johnson, Mahoney, Devine, & Pawl, 1998; Burns, Glenn, Bruehl, Harden, & Lofland, 2003; Jensen, Turner, & Romano, 1994; Jensen et al., 2007; Nielson & Jensen, 2004; Turner, Whitney, Dworkin, Massoth, & Wilson, 1995). These studies are promising in that they suggest that catastrophizing may be amenable to change. However, it is important to note that these studies evaluated cognitive behavioral treatments that were multimodal and, although including a cognitive restructuring component, did not specifically target or manipulate catastrophizing alone. It is not yet known if the associations among catastrophizing cognitions, pain, and adjustment to pain emerged in these studies because changes in catastrophizing cause changes in outcome (pain and pain interference), or if changes in outcome influence changes in catastrophizing beliefs.

Only one study (Turner, Holtzman, & Mancl, 2007) has formally tested the assumption that changes in the cognitive and behavioral processes targeted in CBT mediate change in pain outcomes within the context of a prospective randomized clinical trial of CBT for chronic pain. Turner et al. (2006) found that a brief (four sessions) CBT intervention, relative to an education/attention control condition, improved chronic temporomandibular disorder pain and disability in a randomized clinical trial. Turner et al. (2007) determined that pre- to posttreatment changes in beliefs (specifically, control, disability, and harm), catastrophizing, and self-efficacy mediated the effects of CBT on one-year pain intensity. These results support the CBT model of chronic pain and highlight the importance of targeting pain specific beliefs and cognitions in chronic pain treatment.

Assessment of Pain Catastrophizing and Maladaptive Beliefs

Clinical Interview

A thorough assessment of pain-specific beliefs and cognitions is vital to implementing cognitive therapy for pain. There are a number of ways a clinician can obtain information about adaptive and maladaptive pain beliefs as part of a clinical interview. Many patients with pain find it easier to describe their emotional responses to pain than to generate their automatic beliefs and thoughts specific to pain. Thus, one initial approach is to help patients elucidate the emotions that they experience when in pain. Persons with chronic pain often describe a variety of emotions such as frustration, anger, sadness, depression, hopelessness, discouragement, anxiety, and fear in response to pain and its impact on their lives. For those who find it difficult to identify emotions associated with pain, it may be helpful to ask them to specifically to describe a recent episode of pain, for example, "Tell me about the last time you were really in pain. What was going on? Where were you? What were you doing? What were you feeling?" As patients describe their feelings, specific pain beliefs, catastrophizing, and other negative thoughts will likely be described as part of the overall narrative of the experience. For example, in describing a recent episode of severe pain, a person might say "I was feeling so discouraged; my pain is never going to get better, and I don't think I can stand this." In this example, the emotion identified was discouragement, and the subsequent statements reflect catastrophizing thoughts about pain.

In addition to noting the beliefs and thoughts that patients generate while describing their emotions, it is also important to specifically ask patients what thoughts they have in response to or as a result of pain; for example, "What were you thinking about as you experienced pain and felt angry?" or "What was going through your mind when you were in pain?"

It is important during the initial interview that the clinician not challenge or modify any maladaptive thoughts or beliefs about pain, as such attempts, even though well-intended, may be perceived as invalidating. Persons with chronic pain are often subjected to questions about the validity of their pain complaints, and thus challenging maladaptive thoughts too early may be conterproductive. For a more detailed description of how to conduct an effective clinical interview of a person with pain, see Bradley and McKenree-Smith, 2001.

Psychometric Measures

A number of psychometrically validated measures are available that assess pain-specific beliefs and cognitions (c.f., DeGood & Tait, 2001). These measures have been used primarily as research tools, and as such, tend to be long and do not always have well-defined cutoffs for use in clinical practice. Nonetheless, clinicians may wish to consider examining them for ideas on measuring pain-specific beliefs, catastrophizing cognitions, or self-efficacy beliefs beyond the clinical interview. To illustrate the maladaptive pain-specific beliefs and cognitions commonly held by persons with chronic pain, several of the more commonly used instruments are described below.

The Survey of Pain Attitudes Scale (SOPA: Jensen, Turner, Romano, & Lawler, 1994) is one of the most extensively studied and used instruments assessing pain-specific beliefs. The SOPA has seven scales that assess pain beliefs that: *(1)* one has personal control over pain and its effects (Control); *(2)* one is unable to function due to and is disabled by pain (Disability); *(3)* pain signifies damage and that activity should be avoided to minimize damage (Harm); *(4)* emotions influence pain (Emotion); *(5)* medications are an appropriate treatment for chronic pain (Medication); *(6)* others should respond solicitously to pain (Solicitude); and *(7)* a medical cure is available for pain (Medical Cure). SOPA items are rated on a 0 ("This is very untrue for me") to 4 ("This is very true for me") scale, reflecting the extent to which respondents agree with each of the items. The range of possible responses for the scale is 0 to 4, with higher scores indicating a greater degree of endorsement of the pain beliefs. These scales from the SOPA have demonstrated good internal consistency, test-retest reliability, and criterion-oriented validity (Jensen et al., 1994). Studies have also provided support for the subscales' validity (Jensen et al., 1994; Strong, Ashton, & Chant, 1992). To illustrate the various pain-specific beliefs assessed by this measure, the abbreviated SOPA is presented in Table 13.1.

A limitation of the original SOPA is its length-57 items, and therefore shorter versions have been developed, including a 35-item version (Jensen, Turner, & Romano, 2000), a seven-item version (representing one item from each subscale: Jensen, Keefe, Lefebvre, Romano, & Turner, 2003), and a 14-item version (representing two items from each subscale: Jensen et al., 2003). The abbreviated SOPA, although less reliable, may be useful in screening patients for problematic beliefs or when the length of the original instrument is impractical.

Given the prominence of catastrophizing cognitions in poor adjustment to chronic pain, we recommend specifically assessing them in clinical practice as well as in research. Perhaps the most frequently used instrument in research for assessing catastrophizing is the six-item Catastrophizing scale of the Coping Strategies Questionnaire (CSQ: Rosenstiel & Keefe, 1983). This scale assesses the frequency with which persons respond to pain with catastrophizing thoughts (e.g., "It is terrible and I feel it is never going to get any better" and "I worry all the time about whether it will end"). Evidence of the scale's validity comes from its strong associations with measures of depression and psychosocial dysfunction (Keefe & Williams, 1990; Sullivan & D'Eon, 1990), as well as its sensitivity to change with treatments thought to alter catastrophizing (Jensen et al., 1994). It has excellent internal consistency (Rosenstiel & Keefe, 1983), and given its brevity, it is easy to obtain via self-report or interview. As the Catastrophizing Scale of the CSQ has primarily been used as a research tool, information regarding its clinical utility is lacking.

TABLE 13.1. One- and Two-Item Versions of the Survey of Pain Attitudes (SOPA)

Instructions: Please indicate how much you agree with each of the following statements about your pain problem by using the following scale:

0 = This is very untrue for me.
1 = This is somewhat untrue for me.
2 = This is neither true nor untrue for me (or it does not apply to me).
3 = This is somewhat true for me.
4 = This is very true for me.

Single-item SOPA:

1. There is little I can do to ease my pain*	0 1 2 3 4
2. My pain does not stop me from leading a physically active life*	0 1 2 3 4
3. The pain I feel is a sign that damage is being done	0 1 2 3 4
4. There is a connection between my emotions and my pain level	0 1 2 3 4
5. I will probably always have to take pain medications	0 1 2 3 4
6. When I am hurting, I deserve to be treated with care and concern	0 1 2 3 4
7. I trust that doctors can cure my pain	0 1 2 3 4

Two-item SOPA scales consist of the above plus the following:

8. I have learned to control my pain	0 1 2 3 4
9. My pain does not need to interfere with my activity level*	0 1 2 3 4
10. Exercise can decrease the amount of pain I experience*	0 1 2 3 4

TABLE 13.1. (Continued)

11. Stress in my life increases the pain I feel.	0 1 2 3 4
12. I will never take pain medications again*.	0 1 2 3 4
13. When I hurt, I want my family to treat me better.	0 1 2 3 4
14. I do not expect a medical cure for my pain*.	0 1 2 3 4

Scoring instructions: Items 1, 2, 3, 4, 5, 6, and 7 assess the SOPA Pain Control, Disability, Harm, Emotion, Medication, Solicitude, and Medical Cure scales, respectively. After reverse-scoring those items with an asterisk (i.e., subtract the response from 4 for each item with an asterisk), the respondent's rating for each item is the score for that SOPA scale. Items 8, 9, 10, 11, 12, 13, and 14 are the second items for each of the SOPA scales, respectively. Scores for the two-item SOPA scales are the averages of the two scale items, following the reversal of appropriate (asterisked) items.

One-item and two-item versions of the this scale have been psychometrically validated (Jensen et al., 2003) and may be useful when only one or two items can be included in an assessment or research protocol.

The Pain Catastrophizing Scale (PCS; Sullivan, Bishop, & Pivik., 1995) is an instrument that was developed specifically to examine pain catastrophizing. Research has suggested that pain catastrophizing may be multidimensional and comprised of rumination, magnification, and helplessness (Sullivan et al., 1995, 1998). Thus, this 13-item measure was developed, based in part on several items from the CSQ (described above), to reflect these three dimensions and has the following corresponding subscales: Rumination ("I keep thinking about how much it hurts"), Magnification ("I wonder whether something serious may happen"), and Helplessness ("There is nothing I can do to reduce the pain"). An advantage of the PCS over the CSQ Catastrophizing scale is that it captures ruminative thoughts, worry, and an inability to inhibit pain-related thoughts that are not captured by the CSQ (Sullivan et al., 1995). The PCS has shown good internal consistency, concurrent validity, criterion-related validity, and discriminant validity (Osman et al., 2000) and has been found to be associated with measures of pain and disability (Osman et al., 2000; Sullivan et al., 1998). Like the CSQ, little is known about its utilization in clinical settings. However, like the CSQ Catastrophizing scale, the PCS is brief and therefore could easily be administered in a clinical setting to provide information about the presence of catastrophizing cognitions.

At least two screening instruments, the Cognitive Risk Profile for Pain (Cook & DeGood, 2006) and the Pain Belief Screening Instrument (Sandborgh, Lindberg, & Denison, 2007), have recently been developed for use in identifying patients with maladaptive pain-specific beliefs in clinical practice. Preliminary evidence suggests that each may be useful in identifying patients at high risk for maladaptive beliefs and thoughts about pain, which may in turn facilitate treatment planning. Further research on the clinical utility of these measures and other existing measures of pain beliefs is needed.

It is important to assess other dimensions of the pain experience besides beliefs and catastrophizing thoughts, including pain onset, location, intensity, frequency, and duration of pain episodes, as well as the type of sensations (e.g., burning, aching, stabbing, tingling) experienced. Assessment of how people with pain respond to pain, including their coping strategies, is also important. We also encourage assessment of how pain interferes with a person's life in order to provide a clearer picture of the impact of pain on daily activities and general functioning. In a clinical evaluation, other aspects of the client's psychosocial functioning should be assessed such as their mood, sleep, and social support. For the practitioner new to treating persons with chronic pain, a number of reliable and valid standardized instruments for assessing multiple dimensions of pain are available in the pain literature. For more information on pain assessment, including psychological evaluation of persons with pain, the reader is referred to the *Handbook of Pain Assessment* by Turk and Melzack (2001); for guidance on selecting measures for clinical research on pain, see also Dworkin et al. (2005).

Cognitive Therapy for Chronic Pain

Cognitive therapy targeting pain catastrophizing and other maladaptive beliefs is modeled after empirically supported cognitive interventions developed for and used to treat a variety of medical and psychological disorders, including depression (e.g., Beck, 1995; Greenberger & Padesky, 1995; Persons, Davidson, & Tompkins, 2001). Typically, treatment manuals and workbooks for chronic pain briefly describe cognitive therapy as one of several treatment components (but see Thorn, 2004; and Winterowd, Beck, & Gruener, 2003, for the rare exception in which cognitive therapy for pain is the focus).

In our research program, we developed a cognitive therapy specific to persons with chronic pain and disability (spinal cord injury, amputation, or multiple sclerosis). After preliminary education in the first session about the prevalence and scope of chronic pain in the specific disabilities groups, for the remainder of the therapy the intervention provides: *(1)* education about the role of cognitions, particularly catastrophizing, in chronic pain and adjustment; *(2)* instruction in how to identify negative thinking and cognitive distortions about pain and its consequences; *(3)* instruction in thought-stopping techniques; *(4)* instruction in utilizing cognitive-restructuring techniques, including challenging negative thoughts and core beliefs about pain; and *(5)* instruction in utilizing positive coping self-statements (Ehde & Jensen, 2004).

The cognitive therapy can be delivered via individual or group therapy; currently there is no evidence in the pain literature to suggest that one mode of delivery is superior to the other. We have provided the therapy in both formats and have found that each approach has its advantages. For example, individually delivered therapy allows the therapist to focus solely on the client's specific thoughts, core beliefs, and coping strategies and thus allows more individually tailored attention and intervention. However, although providing less individual attention, group therapy allows opportunities for participants to learn from one another as well as to provide one another support and reinforcement. Group therapy is presumed to be more cost effective as well, although no research has examined this claim in the context of cognitive therapy for pain. When we have used a group format for our treatment, we conducted ten 45–60 minute sessions delivered over a five-week period (two sessions per week). We have also delivered our intervention to persons with spinal cord injury or limb loss via individual therapy, which entailed eight 45–60 minute sessions over a four-to-six-week period (averaging two sessions per week). See Table 13.2 for the table of contents for our individually delivered cognitive therapy for pain intervention.

Each treatment session begins with a review of the homework from the last session followed by presentation of new information relevant to the specific skill or skills being taught that session. For example, in the session in which thought-stopping is taught, participants are provided a rationale for the use of thought-stopping and how to utilize it in managing pain and pain-related cognitions. The bulk of the treatment session is then spent rehearsing the specific cognitive techniques using situations from the client's everyday life, often drawn from their homework. Participants are provided with handouts summarizing the main points from the session and strategies for imple-menting the techniques in between sessions. Each session concludes with a summary of the main points of the session's content, instruction in the home-work assignment for the following week, and time for answering participants' questions. For a sample session and the corresponding participant handout, see Table 13.3.

As in other forms of cognitive behavior therapy, a key component of the pain cognitive therapy is homework and rehearsal of specific cognitive techni-ques outside of the therapy session. Participants are asked to complete a Daily Record of Automatic Thoughts Concerning Pain on a daily basis throughout the duration of treatment. This form is adapted from ones used in the broader cognitive therapy literature. It includes identification of the situation, auto-matic thoughts, emotional responses, and physical responses, as well as ques-tions designed to challenge automatic thoughts and generate more reassuring, adaptive, and helpful thoughts in response to pain. Throughout treatment the therapist reviews the thought records to ensure completion and to utilize within treatment. As in other forms of therapy, participants sometimes have difficul-ties completing the thought records and other homework. Thus treatment includes discussion of potential difficulties and utilizes cognitive therapy tech-niques and problem-solving to address such barriers to full participation. Other less formalized homework assignments may also be assigned, including practi-cing other cognitive and behavioral skills learned in treatment (e.g., thought-stopping techniques). Participants are repeatedly encouraged to use their adap-tive cognitive strategies any time they experience bothersome pain, any time

TABLE 13.2. Overview of Sessions from the Individually Delivered Cognitive Therapy for Pain in Persons with Disabilities Treatment Manual (Ehde et al., unpublished)

Session 1:	**Introduction to Cognitive Therapy for Pain** • Treatment Overview • Expectations for therapist and client • Importance of homework to treating and managing pain • Prevalence and scope of pain in persons with disabilities • Biopsychosocial model for understanding pain • Introduction to cognitive aspects of pain • Rationale for cognitive therapy for pain
Session 2:	**Identifying Automatic Thoughts Related to Pain** • Review of Homework • Distinguishing situations, emotions, thoughts, and physical responses • Helpful, unhelpful, and neutral thoughts about pain • Common thinking traps related to pain • Strategies for identifying unhelpful (automatic) thoughts related to pain
Session 3:	**Evaluating Automatic Thoughts Related to Pain** • Review of Homework • Evaluating the helpfulness of automatic thoughts: labeling • Evaluating the accuracy of automatic thoughts: evidence gathering • Strategies for evaluating automatic thoughts
Session 4:	**Modifying Automatic Thoughts Related to Pain** • Review of Homework • Modifying inaccurate or unhelpful thoughts about pain • Generating alternative thoughts to pain • Generating helpful or more realistic thoughts
Session 5:	**Rehearsal of Cognitive Restructuring Skills** • Review of Homework • Putting it all together: repeated rehearsal of cognitive restructuring strategies (using all strategies learned in previous sessions) • Review of barriers to completing homework • Problem solving barriers to homework completion
Session 6:	**Thought Stopping and Coping Self-Statements** • Review of Homework • Thought stopping strategies • Generating coping self-statements specific to pain • Developing a "coping card"
Session 7:	**Recognizing and Modifying Core Beliefs about Pain** • Review of Homework • Role of core beliefs in pain • Overview of pain-specific core beliefs • Strategies for recognizing and modifying core beliefs
Session 8:	**Maintenance of Cognitive Coping Skills** • Review of Homework • Review of skills learned • Potential obstacles for using skills learned in the future • Relapse prevention plan • Discussion of progress and termination

TABLE 13.3. Example Participant Handout from Session 3 of the Individually Delivered Cognitive Therapy for Pain in Persons with Disabilities Treatment Manual (Ehde et al., unpublished)

Session 3—Participant Handout 3.1
Evaluating Automatic Thoughts Related to Pain

Session Goal
- To help you learn how to evaluate automatic thoughts.
- To help you learn how to tell whether automatic thoughts are helpful and accurate.

Review of Session 2
- Identifying your automatic thoughts is the first step in learning how to change thinking that can make pain worse.
- You can learn to become more aware of your own automatic thoughts by asking yourself, "What was going through my mind just then?" whenever you notice a change in your mood or how you feel physically.
- Writing down your automatic thoughts can help you become more aware of your thinking and make it easier to see patterns in your thinking.
- Sometimes when we are under stress, or don't feel well physically, we can fall into common thinking traps (Handout 2.2). Negative or unhelpful thoughts about pain can make pain worse.

Evaluating Automatic Thoughts
- Now that you have learned how to identify your automatic thoughts, the next step is to learn how to evaluate your automatic thoughts so that you can decide which ones you might want to work on changing.
- Evaluating your automatic thoughts can involve deciding: *(1)* whether a thought is helpful to you; and *(2)* whether a thought is 100% accurate or true.

Labeling Automatic Thoughts As Helpful or Unhelpful
- One way to begin evaluating your automatic thoughts is to label them as helpful, unhelpful, or neutral.
- **Helpful** thoughts are those that are reassuring to you or motivate you. They generally lead to positive feelings and make you feel hopeful.

  Examples: "I have been through difficult things before and I know I can get though this." "I know there are things I can do to manage my pain."

- **Unhelpful** thoughts are those that are distressing or discouraging to you. They generally lead to negative feelings, like sadness, anxiety, or frustration, and can make your pain feel worse. Unhelpful thoughts often involve the common thinking traps (Handout 2.2).

  Examples: "I can't stand this pain." "Now that I have pain I can't enjoy anything."

- **Neutral** thoughts are those that just state the facts. They usually don't have much of an impact on your mood or your pain.

  Examples: "I have a headache." "It is raining today."

- One goal of treatment is to help you increase your helpful thoughts and decrease your unhelpful thoughts.

TABLE 13.3. (Continued)

Gathering Evidence to Test whether a Thought Is True

- Most thoughts related to pain are either completely or partially based on facts. However, sometimes thoughts in response to stress or pain are not based on facts because when we are under stress we can easily overlook important information.
- Another strategy for evaluating your automatic thoughts is to gather evidence to see how accurate or true they are. This involves collecting all the facts you can think of that both support and do not support a specific thought.
- Evidence, or "the facts," means only information you know for sure to be true. This can include exactly what happened, what someone said, how many times something has happened, etc.
- Facts do not include thoughts, feelings, or interpretations of situations. If you are not sure whether something is a fact, ask yourself, "Would this stand up in court?" If the answer is no, it is probably not a fact.
- To begin the process of gathering evidence you can ask yourself: (1) "What is the evidence that supports this thought?"; and (2) "What is the evidence that does not support this thought?" You then write down the evidence you can think of to answer both questions.
- Gathering evidence works best when you select a specific thought about a specific situation to evaluate. Otherwise, it can be difficult to come up with evidence.
- You don't need to gather evidence for and against all of your automatic thoughts—just the ones that you believe are the most unhelpful or make you feel the worst.
- Gathering evidence that both supports and does not support a specific thought can help you look at a situation more objectively, or see "the big picture."

Summary

- Evaluating your automatic thoughts can help you decide which ones you might want to work on changing.
- You can evaluate the helpfulness of your automatic thoughts by labeling them as helpful, unhelpful, or neutral.
- You can evaluate how accurate or true your automatic thoughts are by gathering evidence that both supports and does not support a specific thought. Once you have the evidence for both sides you can determine whether a thought is 100% true.
- You can learn how to change thoughts that are unhelpful or not 100% true into thoughts that are more helpful and more accurate/true.
- It is important to practice the skills covered in treatment in order for the treatment to be helpful.

Practice Worksheet

- To help you practice evaluating your automatic thoughts, please complete Worksheet 3— Evaluating Automatic Thoughts before we meet for our next session. If you have difficulty completing the worksheet, feel free to look at the example worksheet or the worksheet that you completed during the session.
- Focus on a recent stressful situation in which you experienced pain.
- Write down anything you can think of, even if you are not sure about it. There are no "right" or "wrong" answers.
- Bring this worksheet with you to our next session so that we can review it and discuss any questions you might have.

they have a "negative" emotion, or anytime they notice negative thoughts about pain such as catastrophizing cognitions. An example of the daily pain diaries is included in Table 13.4.

We recently conducted a pilot study (Ehde & Jensen, 2004) examining the feasibility of this intervention for the treatment of pain in persons with chronic pain secondary to disability, and are now completing a larger-scale controlled trial of this same intervention. Chronic pain is common among persons with physical disabilities such as amputation, cerebral palsy, multiple sclerosis, and spinal cord injury (Ehde et al., 2003). In the preliminary study, the participants (N = 18) completed measures of pain intensity, pain interference, and psychological functioning at pre- and posttreatment, and also rated the helpfulness of the interventions at the end of the study. Participants were then randomly assigned to participate in either the cognitive therapy intervention (CT) or an education control condition (EC), both of which were delivered in eight 90-minute group sessions. Participants in the education control condition received eight 90-minute sessions of group education about chronic pain. This included information about the definition of chronic pain, the physiological processes underlying pain, theories of pain, sleep problems in pain, and common pain treatments. Participants in the education control condition were encouraged to ask questions about and discuss the information presented in the groups but were not instructed in any specific coping techniques. The education participants were also asked to think about the information they learned between sessions but not prescribed any specific homework activities between sessions.

The cognitive therapy group showed a decrease in average pain intensity from pre- (M = 5.4 on 0–10 NRS) to posttreatment (M = 4.4), and the education group did not (M = 5.0 & 5.0, respectively). Both groups also showed reductions in pain interference and distress from pre- to posttreatment. When asked if their pain problem had improved, worsened, or stayed the same from pre- to posttreatment, 40% of the EC participants and 71% of the CT participants rated their pain problem as improved. Interestingly, however, when asked to rate how helpful the group was on a scale from 0 (not helpful) to 10 (extremely helpful), the two groups were rated as equally helpful (M = 8.0 on 0–10 scale). In response to open-ended questions about what they found particularly helpful and not helpful about the interventions, each participant in the study reported that he or she benefited from the intervention and hoped similar treatments would be offered in the future. Only minor suggestions were made regarding the content of the interventions, primarily pertaining to the formatting of the participant workbooks.

TABLE 13.4. Thought Record Worksheet 2 (Example)

Situation	Automatic Thoughts	Emotions	Physical Reactions
Date: 3/15/05 Time: 9:00 AM I woke up late and realized that I was going to be late for my physical therapy appointment.	I'm not going to make it on time. (N) My physical therapist is going to be upset with me for being late. (U) My arm always hurts more during my physical therapy sessions. (U) I hate living with this pain. (U) I'm never going to get my life back. (U)	Frustrated Anxious Sad	Neck and shoulders getting tense Increased pain in arm Start to get a headache Feel tired, low energy
	Evidence for: I can't do all the things I used to be able to do. Rehab is taking longer than I thought it would. I probably won't regain everything that I lost after the accident. **Evidence against:** My doctor and my therapists are telling me that I am making progress. I can do more now than I could 2 months ago. There are a few things I am back to doing on my own again **Alternative thoughts:** Although I can't do everything I used to do, I am making progress. I can still find ways to enjoy my life even if I can't do everything I could before.	**Changes in emotions/physical reactions:** Hopeful Less anxious Motivated	Decreased tension in neck and shoulders Pain in arm decreasing Headache starting to go away Still feel tired

Questions to help generate alternative thoughts: (1) What does the evidence say? (2) Is there a more helpful way to think about this? (3) Are there other explanations or points of view? (4) What would I tell a friend in the same situation?

Future Directions

Although considerable evidence exists that psychological interventions are effective in reducing pain and suffering in persons with chronic pain, the mechanisms underlying their efficacy are not fully understood (Burns et al., 2003; Keefe et al., 2004; Morley and Keefe, 2007; Vlaeyen & Morley, 2005). Changes in cognitions and behaviors are thought to account for the benefits seen in clinical trials of CBT for pain. However, it remains possible that such changes are due to other reasons such as improvements in mood, physical condition, or other factors. Methodologically rigorous experimental studies are needed testing the assumption that catastrophizing cognitions cause poor outcomes in persons with chronic pain. Experimental studies examining this basic hypothesis of cognitive-behavioral models for chronic pain are needed to advance the field.

Both research studies on and clinical services for pain are typically aimed at treating pain once it becomes chronic. It would be interesting to determine if cognitive therapy provided early after the onset of a painful condition or an injury can prevent the development of pain catastrophizing in persons at risk for chronic pain. Little is known about the natural history of maladaptive beliefs and catastrophizing cognitions in chronic pain; further research in this area is clearly warranted.

A promising area for future research is the use of the telephone for conducting cognitive therapy for chronic pain. Telephone-delivered interventions (TDIs) are increasingly being used to provide a broad array of health behavior interventions targeting a range of issues such as obesity, smoking cessation, alcohol abuse, treatment adherence, and preventative behaviors (McBride & Rimer, 1999). A review of 74 studies evaluating the effectiveness of TDIs, McBride and Rimmer (1999) concluded that TDIs can be as effective as face-to-face interventions for target groups with psychosocial barriers or limited access to services. Given many persons with chronic pain—particularly those with disability-related pain such as spinal cord injury, limb loss, and multiple sclerosis—may have limited access to cognitive therapy for pain (Ehde et al., 2003), the use of the telephone to deliver cognitive therapy warrants exploration.

Conclusion

Given the salient role that maladaptive cognitions and beliefs play in the experience of pain, cognitive therapy has considerable potential to improve not only the sensory experience of pain but also the psychological suffering and reduced quality of life that too often accompany it. Pain-related catastrophizing cognitions and maladaptive pain belief appear to be particularly important targets for cognitive therapy and can be readily assessed with a number of psychometric measures and/or via clinical interview. As described in this chapter, cognitive therapy for pain resembles cognitive therapy for other conditions, with the emphasis, however, on pain-specific cognitions, beliefs, and cognitive coping skills. Although cognitive therapy is frequently a component of psychological interventions targeting chronic pain, its efficacy as a stand-alone intervention for pain remains untested. The chronic pain field needs theoretically driven intervention research evaluating the efficacy of and mechanisms underlying cognitive therapy for pain.

REFERENCES

Beck, J. S. (1995). Cognitive therapy: Basics and beyond. New York: Guilford Press.

Bennett, R. M., Burckhardt, C. S., Clark, S. R., O'Reilly, C. A., Wiens, A. N., & Campbell, S. M. (1996). Group treatment of fibromyalgia: A 6 month outpatient program. *Journal of Rheumatology, 23*, 521–528.

Benrud-Larson, L. M., & Wegener, S. T. (2000). Chronic pain in neurorehabilitation populations: Prevalence, severity, and impact. *Neurorehabilitation, 14*, 127–137.

Boothby, J. L., Thorn, B. E., Stroud, M. W., & Jensen, M. P. (1999). Coping with pain. In R. J. Gatchel & D. C. Turk (Eds.), *Psychosocial factors in pain* (pp. 343–359). New York: Guilford.

Bradley, L. A., & McKendree-Smith, N. L. (2001). Assessment of psychological status using interviews and self-report instruments. In D. C. Turk & R. Melzack (Eds.), *Handbook of pain assessment* (2nd ed., pp. 292–319). New York: Guilford.

Burns, J. W., Glenn, B., Bruehl, S., Harden, R. N., & Lofland, K. (2003). Cognitive factors influence outcome following multidisciplinary chronic pain treatment: A replication and extension of a cross-lagged panel analysis. *Behaviour Research and Therapy, 41*, 1163–1182.

Burns, J. W., Johnson, B. J., Mahoney, N., Devine, J., & Pawl, R. (1998). Cognitive and physical capacity process variables predict long-term outcome after treatment of chronic pain. *Journal of Consulting and Clinical Psychology, 66*, 434–439.

Centers for Disease Control and Prevention (2001). Prevalence of disabilities and associated health conditions among adults—United States, 1999. *Morbidity and Mortality Weekly Report, 50*, 120–125.

Cook, A. J., & DeGood, D. I. (2006). The cognitive risk profile for pain: Development of a self-report inventory for identifying beliefs and attitudes that interfere with pain management. *Clinical Journal of Pain, 22*, 332–345.

DeGood, D. E., & Tait, R. C. (2001). Assessment of pain beliefs and pain coping. In D. C. Turk & R. Melzack (Eds.), *Handbook of pain assessment* (2nd ed., pp. 320–345). New York: Guilford Press.

Deyo, A. R. (1998, August). Low back pain. *Scientific American*, 48–53.

Dixon, K. E., Keefe, F. J., Scipio, C. D., Perri, L. M., & Abernethy, A. P. (2007). Psychological interventions for arthritis pain management in adults: A meta-analysis. *Health Psychology, 26*, 241–250.

Dixon, K. E., Thorn, B. E., & Ward, C. L. (2004). An evaluation of sex differences in psychological and physiological responses to experimentally-induced pain: A path analytic description. *Pain, 112*, 188–196.

Dworkin, R. H., Turk, D. C., Farrar, J. T., Haythornthwaite, J. A., Jensen, M. P., Katz, N. P., et al. (2005). Core outcome measures for chronic pain clinical trials: IMMPACT recommendations. *Pain, 113*, 9–19.

Edwards, R. R., Bingham, C. O., III, Bathon, J., & Haythornthwaite, J. A. (2006). Catastrophizing and pain in arthritis, fibromyalgia, and other rheumatic diseases. *Arthritis and Rheumatology, 55*, 325–532.

Ehde, D. M., & Jensen, M. P. (2004). Feasibility of a cognitive restructuring intervention for treatment of chronic pain in persons with disabilities. *Rehabilitation Psychology, 49*, 254–258.

Ehde, D. M., Jensen, M. P., Engel, J. M., Turner, J. A., Hoffman, A. J., & Cardenas, D. D. (2003). Chronic pain secondary to disability: A review. *Clinical Journal of Pain, 19*, 3–17.

Engel, J. M., Schwartz, L., Jensen, M. P., & Johnson, D. R. (2000). Pain in cerebral palsy: The relation of coping strategies to adjustment. *Pain, 88*, 225–230.

Eriksen, J., Sjøgren, P., Bruera, E., Ekholm, O., & Rasmussen, N. K. (2006). Critical issues on opioids in chronic non-cancer pain: An epidemiologic study. *Pain, 125*, 172–179.

Fejer, R., Kyvik, K. O., & Hartvigsen, J. (2006). The prevalence of neck pain in the world population: A systematic critical review of the literature. *European Spine Journal, 15*, 834–848.

Gatchel, R. J., Polatin, P. B., & Mayer, T. G. (1995). The dominant role of psychosocial risk factors in the development of chronic low back pain disability. *Spine, 20*, 2702–2709.

Geisser, M. E., & Roth, R. S. (1998). Knowledge of and agreement with pain diagnosis: Relation to pain beliefs, pain severity, disability, and psychological distress. *Journal of Occupational Rehabilitation, 8*, 73–88.

Greenberger, D., & Padesky, C. A. (1995). *Mind over mood*. New York: Guilford.

Hanley, M. A., Jensen, M. P., Ehde, D. M., Hoffman, A. J., Patterson, D. R., & Robinson, L. R. (2004). Psychosocial predictors of long-term adjustment to lower limb amputation and phantom limb pain. *Disability and Rehabilitation, 26*, 882–893.

Hoffman, B. M., Papas, R. K., Chatkoff, D. K., & Kerns, R. D. (2007). Meta-analysis of psychological interventions for chronic low back pain. *Health Psychology, 26*, 1–9.

Holtzman, S., & DeLongis, A. (2007). One day at a time: The impact of daily satisfaction with spouse responses on pain, negative affect, and catastrophizing among individuals with rheumatoid arthritis. *Pain, 131*, 202–213.

Jacobsen, P. B., & Butler, R. W. (1996). Relation of cognitive coping and catastrophizing to acute pain and analgesic use following breast cancer surgery. *Journal of Behavioral Medicine, 19*, 17–29.

Jensen, M. P., Ehde, D. M., Hoffman, A. J., Patterson, D. R., Czerniecki, J. M., & Robinson, L. R. (2002). Cognitions, coping, and social environment predict adjustment to phantom limb pain. *Pain, 95*, 133–142.

Jensen, M. P., Keefe, F. J., Lefebvre, J. C., Romano, J. M., & Turner, J. A. (2003). One- and two-item measures of pain beliefs and coping strategies. *Pain, 104,* 453–469.

Jensen, M. P., Romano, J. M., Turner, J. A., Good, A. B., & Wald, L. H. (1999). Patient beliefs predict patient functioning: Further support for a cognitive-behavioural model of chronic pain. *Pain, 81,* 95–104.

Jensen, M. P., Turner, J. A., & Romano, J. M. (1994). Correlates of improvement in multidisciplinary treatment of chronic pain. *Journal of Consulting and Clinical Psychology, 62,* 172–179.

Jensen, M. P., Turner, J. A., & Romano, J. M. (2000). Pain belief assessment: A comparison of the short and long versions of the survey of pain attitudes. *Journal of Pain, 1,* 138–150.

Jensen, M. P., Turner, J. A., & Romano, J. M. (2007). Changes after multidisciplinary pain treatment in patient pain beliefs and coping are associated with concurrent changes in patient functioning. *Pain, 131,* 38–47.

Jensen, M. P., Turner, J. A., Romano, J. M., & Karoly, P. (1991). Coping with chronic pain: A critical review of the literature. *Pain, 47,* 249–283.

Jensen, M. P., Turner, J. A., Romano, J. M., & Lawler, B. K. (1994). Relationship of pain-specific beliefs to chronic pain adjustment. *Pain, 57,* 301–309.

Keefe, F. J., Caldwell, D. S., Williams, D. A., Gil, K. M., et al. (1990). Pain coping skills training in the management of osteoarthritic knee pain: 2. Follow-up results. *Behavior Therapy, 21,* 435–447.

Keefe, F. J., Rumble, M. E., Scipio, C. D., Giordano, L. A., & Perri, L. M. (2004). Psychological aspects of persistent pain: Current state of the science. *Journal of Pain, 4,* 195–211.

Keefe, F. J., & Williams, D. A. (1990). A comparison of coping strategies in chronic pain patients in different age groups. *Journal of Gerontology, 45,* 161–165.

Lester, N., Lefebvre, J. C., & Keefe, F. J. (1996). Pain in young adults: 3. Relationships of three pain-coping measures to pain and activity interference. *Clinical Journal of Pain, 12,* 291–300.

Lin, C. C., & Ward, S. E. (1996). Perceived self-efficacy and outcome expectancies in coping with chronic low back pain. *Research in Nursing and Health, 19,* 299–310.

Liu, Z., Lian, Z., Zhou, W., Mu, Y., Lü, X., Zhao, D., et al. (2001). National survey on prevalence of cancer pain. *Chinese Medical Sciences Journal, 16,* 175–178.

Luime, J. J., Koes, B. W., Hendriksen, I. J., Burdorf, A., Verhagen, A. P., Miedema, H. S., et al. (2004). Prevalence and incidence of shoulder pain in the general population: A systematic review. *Scandinavian Journal of Rheumatology, 33,* 73–81.

McBride, C. M., & Rimer, B. K. (1999). Using the telephone to improve health behavior and health service delivery. *Patient Education and Counseling, 37,* 3–18.

Morley, S., Eccleston, C., & Williams, A. (1999). Systematic review and meta-analysis of randomized controlled trials of cognitive behaviour therapy and behaviour therapy for chronic pain in adults, excluding headache. *Pain, 80,* 1–13.

Morley, S., & Keefe, F. J. (2007). Getting a handle on process and change in CBT for chronic pain. *Pain, 127,* 197–198.

Nielson, W. R., & Jensen, M. P. (2004). Relationship between changes in coping and treatment outcome in patients with Fibromyalgia Syndrome. *Pain, 109,* 233–241.

Novy, D. M., Nelson, D. V., Francis, D. J., & Turk, D. C. (1995). Perspectives of chronic pain: An evaluative comparison of restrictive and comprehensive models. *Psychological Bulletin, 118*, 238–247.

Osborne, T. L., Jensen, M. P., Ehde, D. M., Hanley, M. A., & Kraft, G. H. (2007). Psychosocial factors associated with pain intensity, pain-related interference, and psychological functioning in persons with multiple sclerosis and pain. *Pain, 127*, 52–62.

Osman, A., Barrios, F. X., Gutierrez, P. M., Kopper, B. A., Merrifield, T., & Grittman, L. (2000). The pain catastrophizing scale: further psychometric evaluation with adult samples. *Journal of Behavioral Medicine, 23*, 351–365.

Persons, J. B., Davidson, J., & Tompkins, M. A. (2001). *Essential components of cognitive-behavioral therapy for depression*. Washington, DC: American Psychological Association.

Peters, J., Large, R. G., & Elkind, G. (1992). Follow-up results from a randomised controlled trial evaluating in- and outpatient pain management programmes. *Pain, 50*, 41–50.

Robinson, M. E., Riley, J. L., III, Myers, C. D., Sadler, I. J., Kvaal, S. A., Geisser, M. E., et al. (1997). The Coping Strategies Questionnaire: A large sample, item level factor analysis. *Clinical Journal of Pain, 13*, 43–49.

Rosenstiel, A. K., & Keefe, F. J. (1983). The use of coping strategies in chronic low back pain patients: Relationship to patient characteristics and current adjustment. *Pain, 17*, 33–44.

Sandborgh, M., Lindberg, P., & Denison, E. (2007). Pain belief screening instrument: Development and preliminary validation of a screening instrument for disabling persistent pain. *Journal of Rehabilitation Medicine, 39*, 461–466.

Strong, J., Ashton, R., & Chant, D. (1992). The measurement of attitudes towards and beliefs about pain. *Pain, 48*, 227–236.

Stroud, M. W., Thorn, B. E., Jensen, M. P., & Boothby, J. L. (2000). The relation between pain beliefs, negative thoughts, and psychosocial functioning in chronic pain patients. *Pain, 84*, 347–352.

Sullivan, M. J. L., Bishop, S. R., & Pivik, J. (1995). The Pain Catastrophizing Scale: Development and validation. *Psychological Assessment, 7*, 524–532.

Sullivan, M. J., & D'Eon, J. L. (1990). Relation between catastrophizing and depression in chronic pain patients. *Journal of Abnormal Psychology, 99*, 260–263.

Sullivan, M. J., Stanish, W., Waite, H., Sullivan, M., & Tripp, D. A. (1998). Catastrophizing, pain, and disability in patients with soft-tissue injuries. *Pain, 77*, 253–260.

Sullivan, M. J., Thorn, B., Rodgers, W., & Ward, L. C. (2004). Path model of psychological antecedents to pain experience: Experimental and clinical findings. *Clinical Journal of Pain, 2004*, 164–173.

Svendsen, K. B., Andersen, S., Arnason, S., Arnér, S., Breivik, H., Heiskanen, T., et al. (2005). Breakthrough pain in malignant and non-malignant diseases: A review of prevalence, characteristics, and mechanisms. *European Journal of Pain, 9*, 195–206.

Thorn, B. E. (2004). *Cognitive therapy for chronic pain: A step-by-step guide*. New York: Guilford.

Thorn, B. E., Rich, M. A., & Boothby, J. L. (1999). Pain beliefs and coping attempts. *Pain Forum, 8,* 169–171.

Turk, D. C. (1996). Biopsychosocial perspective on chronic pain. In R. J. Gatchel & D. C. Turk (Eds.), *Psychological approaches to pain management: A practitioner's handbook* (pp. 3–32). New York: Guilford Press.

Turk, D. C. (2002). Clinical effectiveness and cost-effectiveness of treatments for patients with chronic pain. *Clinical Journal of Pain, 18,* 355–365.

Turk, D. C., & Melzack, R. (Eds.). (2001). *Handbook of pain assessment* (2nd ed.). New York: Guilford Press.

Turner, J. A., Holtzman, S., & Mancl, L. (2007). Mediators, moderators, and predictors of therapeutic change in cognitive-behavioral therapy for chronic pain. *Pain, 127,* 276–286.

Turner, J. A., Jensen, M. P., & Romano, J. M. (2000). Do beliefs, coping, and catastrophizing independently predict functioning in patients with chronic pain? *Pain, 85,* 115–125.

Turner, J. A., Jensen, M. P., Warms, C. A., & Cardenas, D. D. (2002). Catastrophizing is associated with pain intensity, psychological distress, and pain-related disability among individuals with chronic pain after spinal cord injury. *Pain, 98,* 127–134.

Turner, J. A., Mancl, L., & Aaron, L. A. (2006). Short- and long-term efficacy of brief cognitive-behavioral therapy for patients with chronic temporomandibular disorder pain: A randomized, controlled trial. *Pain, 121,* 181–194.

Turner, J. A., Whitney, C., Dworkin, S. F., Massoth, D., & Wilson, L. (1995). Do changes in patient beliefs and coping strategies predict temporomandibular disorder treatment outcomes? *Clinical Journal of Pain, 11,* 177–188.

Verhaak, P. F., Kerssens, J. J., Dekker, J., Sorbi, M. J., & Bensing, J. M. (1998). Prevalence of chronic benign pain disorder among adults: A review of the literature. *Pain, 77,* 231–239.

Vlaeyen, J. W. S., & Morley, S. (2005). Cognitive behavioral treatments for chronic pain: What works for whom? *Clinical Journal of Pain, 21,* 1–8.

Volinn, E. (1997). The epidemiology of low back pain in the rest of the world: A review of surveys in low- and middle-income countries. *Spine, 22,* 1747–1754.

Winterowd, C., Beck, A. T., & Gruener, D. (2003). Cognitive therapy with chronic pain patients. New York: Springer Publishing Company.

Acknowledgments: Supported by grants from: (1) the National Institutes of Health, National Institute of Child Health and Human Development, National Center for Medical Rehabilitation Research (grant P01 HD33988); (2) the National Institutes of Health, National Institute of Child and Health, National Center for Medical Rehabilitation Research (grant R01 HD42838); and (3) the Centers for Disease Control and Prevention (CDC: grant R49 CE000483); support was also provided from the Hughes M. and Katherine G. Blake Endowed Professorship in Health Psychology. Contents are solely the responsibility of the authors and do not necessarily represent the official views of the CDC or NIH.

PART V

Judgment Errors and Popular Myths and Misconceptions

14

Irrational Beliefs Stemming from Judgment Errors: Cognitive Limitations, Biases, and Experiential Learning

John Ruscio

In the *New York Times* best-selling book *Word Freak*, Stefan Fatsis (2001) chronicles his journey into the world of competitive Scrabble players. The tale he tells about the development of expert judgment holds lessons that extend well beyond the realm of Scrabble. Players must memorize a tremendous amount of information, beginning with game rules and the frequencies and point values of the letters in a set of Scrabble tiles. This much is fairly simple, but studying the lists of acceptable words presents more daunting task: There are about 120,000 words allowed in U.S. tournaments, and the addition of about 40,000 British words yields a total of 160,000 words allowed in international tournaments. It takes many years of devoted study to approach complete word knowledge, and even the leading experts engage in a continual struggle to retain this information and create multiple, complex interconnections so that as many words as possible can be retrieved quickly in different game scenarios.

As impressive as these feats of memory may seem, successful expert-level play also demands sophisticated information processing. Increasingly thorny judgments and decisions must be made as one learns to master such strategic issues as rack and board management and the handling of the end game. Experts do much more than scan their memory stores for possible word plays. For example, many of the words played by experts are unrecognizable to laypersons, and even competitive players can be uncertain whether a particular play is an allowable word. This raises the question of whether to gamble a challenge of an opponent's play: If the word is invalid, it is removed and the opponent forfeits that turn. If the word is valid, one loses his or her own turn. If one opts not to challenge, another decision is whether to play a word or exchange one or more tiles. Particularly if no high-scoring or defensively important plays can be identified, it can be wise to forfeit a turn to exchange some unwanted letters for new ones. If one opts to make a play, this forces the decision of when to terminate the search for the best available play. These decisions, along with many others, must be made using limited information. One's retrievable word knowledge is incomplete, and information regarding an opponent's tiles and those that remain in the bag is bounded by probabilistic constraints. Likewise, decisions must be made rapidly, as there is a penalty for running over the 25-minute limit each player is allotted per game. With massive amounts of study and practice, some Scrabble players achieve a state in which their command of strategic decisions and generation of optimal or near-optimal plays appears effortless. Through a rigorous course of training and experience, the deliberative, short-sighted, and relatively foolhardy style of play exhibited by novices is replaced by the wisdom and automaticity characteristic of experts.

The process by which Scrabble players hone their judgment provides many useful clues about how to improve clinical judgment. Clinical practitioners must acquire and retain a wealth of factual knowledge as well as decision-making strategies for applying this knowledge effectively. Learning and using the full breadth and depth of theory and research related to the assessment, classification, and treatment of mental disorder within the constraints of applicable ethical and legal codes certainly does not constitute a game, yet many of the challenges of clinical work are analogous to those of an intricate game. A broad array of potentially relevant client characteristics, alternative interventions, and therapeutic goals constitutes the panoply of variables to consider. Relations among variables, especially causal relations, are seldom established unequivocally by previous research or experience. In light of available assessment tools and techniques, it can be difficult to obtain pertinent information in a reliable and valid manner. For a number of reasons, one will often have to make probabilistic inferences regarding gaps or apparent inconsistencies in the data. The nature of the judgments and decisions to be made, and the available options, are often open-ended. Ethical and legal codes proscribe some courses of action, but the breadth of tolerable practices remains vast. Tough choices must be made, and they can have significant consequences.

The complexity of the situation faced by clinical practitioners often demands the use of shortcuts to make critical judgments and decisions. Otherwise, the cognitive limits of human information processing could easily be exceeded. Likewise, inattention to potential cognitive biases can lead to judgment errors that might otherwise have been prevented. Although people vary in their aptitude for memorization and strategic thinking, the formidable knowledge base and skill set involved in competitive Scrabble or clinical practice must be built through training and experience. In what follows, suggestions for the development of expert clinical judgment will be drawn from an examination of cognitive limitations and biases, the disproportionate influence of personal experience, and the requirements for successful experiential learning.

Before proceeding, it is worth underscoring the approach and emphases of this chapter as well as the definition of irrational beliefs that is adopted. Dawes (2001) identified irrationality using the criterion of self-contradiction. For example, Dawes reviewed preferences for surgery versus radiation in the treatment of a 60-year-old man with lung cancer. When evidence bearing on the effectiveness of these alternative techniques was presented in terms of mortality rates, both doctors and potential patients preferred radiation. However, when the same evidence was presented in the mathematically equivalent form of survival rates (i.e., probability of survival = 1.00 − probability of death), doctors and potential patients preferred surgery. This preference reversal is irrational because it is self-contradictory: For the same decision problem and evidence base, one cannot simultaneously prefer surgery to radiation and prefer radition to surgery. In addition to preference reversals due to framing effects (Kahneman & Tversky, 1984), Dawes examined many potential causes and consequences of irrational, self-contradictory beliefs.

This chapter includes—but is not limited to—judgment errors that would meet the self-contradictory standard of irrationality. Rather than examining whether this criterion is satisfied or introducing another, the emphasis is on the many ways that judgment errors can lead to suboptimal decisions and ways to prevent this from happening. The link between judgment errors and irrationality is implicitly based on the notion that, to the greatest extent possible, a rational decision-maker should follow guidelines prescribed for scientific research. Among the cardinal principles of sound research, investigators are instructed to design studies that will afford the most informative comparisons by controlling extraneous variables, obtain large and random samples from populations of interest, measure variables reliably and validly, and evaluate data objectively using appropriate statistical techniques. To the extent that a mental health professional violates one or more of these principles, the expected accuracy of judgments and decisions will be compromised, increasing the chances of forming and retaining irrational beliefs.

In the space of a single chapter it would be impossible to catalog exhaustively the types of errors that have been identified in the judgment literature, any of which might lead to irrational beliefs. Instead, I have selected a handful of exemplars based on their applicability to clinical practice. Likewise, I have presented illustrative instances of judgment errors and irrational beliefs instead of descriptions of relevant research studies. I have provided citations for readers interested in pursuing additional reading, but the emphasis here is on the detection and prevention of judgment errors in clinical practice.

Finally, and perhaps most important, this chapter's treatment of judgment errors and irrationality is not intended in a pejorative sense. Human fallibility stems from universal cognitive limitations and biases, not from foibles unique to mental health practitioners. As Dawes (2001) and many others have observed, clinicians are prone to the *same* judgment errors as everyone else. In everyday life, individuals are relatively free to use flawed reasoning. In the role of an expert, however, one assumes an added responsibility to "get it right." Training and experience are expected to correct errors in experts' intuitive understanding of their disciplines, including both the factual knowledge base and the implementation of appropriate techniques through sound reasoning. The goal of this chapter is to provide an overview of the sources, types, and prevention of common judgment errors and irrational beliefs to which everyone is susceptible but that can adversely impact clinical work.

Cognitive Limitations and Biases

One of the most fundamental principles guiding research on judgment and decision making is that human information processing is constrained by certain cognitive limitations. For example, there are limits to the amount of information that can be retrieved into and held in working memory (e.g., Miller, 1956), the complexity of the operations that can be performed on this information (e.g., Halford, Baker, McCredden, & Bain, 2005; Ruscio & Stern, 2006), and the speed with which information can be processed (e.g., Sternberg, 1969). Whereas a computer will be unable to solve a problem when its memory capacity is exhausted, or will spend as long as necessary to work out a solution when its memory is sufficient and its processing speed is the limiting factor, clinicians seldom have the option of either reaching no judgment or taking longer to make a decision. When working with a client, many provisional judgments must be made rapidly, on the basis of a wealth of information of mixed or ambiguous validity, to proceed with an assessment or treatment during an ongoing session.

When a judgment must be reached, cognitive limitations often necessitate the use of mental shortcuts, or *heuristics* (Turk & Salovey, 1988; Tversky & Kahneman, 1974). By simplifying the task, these strategies afford a judgment—even if a normatively suboptimal one. Usually, there is an inherent trade-off between accuracy and efficiency (but see Gigerenzer, Todd, and the ABC Research Group, 1999, for possible exceptions in which both accuracy and efficiency might be improved). Of particular interest is that the errors resulting from the use of heuristics are not always random. Predictable types of mistakes are sometimes observed, in which case the use of a mental shortcut can be understood as causing a cognitive bias.

Representativeness and Availability Heuristics

Two heuristics have received the lion's share of attention in the literature, as they manifest themselves in myriad judgment errors. The *representativeness heuristic* produces similarity-based judgments made on the superficial basis of "like goes with like" (Kahneman & Tversky, 1972). For instance, effects are presumed to resemble their causes. Such relationships often, but not always, hold. Consider the popular notion that mental disorders with a "biological basis" are more appropriately treated with medication than with psychotherapy, whereas psychotherapy should be reserved for disorders with no biological basis. Setting aside the often vague meaning of "biological basis"— here it will be used to signify that biological factors play a role in the etiology of a disorder—the underlying assumption appears to be that a biological problem suggests the need for a biological solution (and vice versa). This clear case of representative thinking gives rise to a number of logical problems and conceptual puzzles.

Pitting interventions against one another in this way creates a false dichotomy between different levels of analysis (biological and psychological) at which one can conceptualize and test theories of psychopathology. There is no logical inconsistency between the existence of biological bases for a disorder and an understanding of that disorder in terms of psychological mechanisms. Unless one is a mind-body dualist, it should be easy to see that all mental functioning, normal or abnormal, must have a basis in the brain. However, even though all mental disorders are biologically *mediated* (i.e., situated somewhere in neural tissue), this does not guarantee that either the original cause(s) or the successful treatment of a disorder is biological in nature. Thus, the notion that some disorders have a biological basis whereas others do not is logically flawed. Instead, it is more appropriate to ask about the nature of the biological basis for each disorder and to pursue possible treatments based on promising knowledge at any level of analysis.

In addition, the apparent correlation between the existence of biological bases for disorders and the availability of biological treatments may be spurious. Whereas the discovery of biochemical anomalies among individuals suffering from a particular mental disorder often prompts the development and testing of new medications, the absence of known biological anomalies prohibits such focused research on biological interventions. Thus, present *knowledge* of biological bases may be associated with the availability of biological treatment options, with no causal connection between the nature or extent of biological bases and the utility of biological interventions. In the end, of course, efficacy and effectiveness research are required to evaluate the appropriateness of any treatment. The naïve, "like goes with like" belief that disorders with known biological bases are most appropriately treated using medications may hinder the search for fruitful treatments.

Whereas representative thinking uses similarity as a cue, the *availability heuristic* produces judgments of frequency or probability on the basis of the ease with which instances can be retrieved from memory (Tversky & Kahneman, 1973). Whereas the ease of recall generally provides a useful clue to how common or rare a class of events is, this heuristic can sometimes lead to biased or erroneous judgments. Unusual occurrences often attract greater attention than more mundane happenings, with the result that one might be able to retrieve instances of these relatively rare events more easily than objectively more frequent events. This can be especially true of vivid, emotionally compelling events that seem noteworthy in large part because of their rarity (Nisbett & Ross, 1980). For example, when Schreiber (1973) published *Sybil*, few (if any) individuals diagnosed with multiple personality disorder (MPD, now listed in *DSM-IV* as dissociative identity disorder) had reported childhood abuse or as many as 16 alternate personalities. Highly unusual features such as these not only helped to captivate a large audience, but served as models for future reports because many people—including professionals and laypersons—formed an MPD schema on the basis of this exceptional case. Many (if not most) subsequent MPD reports included childhood abuse and increasing numbers of alters (Spanos, 1996). Despite the absence of compelling evidence that childhood abuse is correlated with diagnoses of MPD (Lilienfeld et al., 1999; Spanos, 1996)—let alone etiologically relevant—when clinicians rely on the availability heuristic in evaluating this putative association, they can retrieve many instances consistent with an abuse-MPD link.

Even if there is no statistical association between abuse and MPD, such an *illusory correlation* (Chapman & Chapman, 1967) may persist due to the operation of the availability heuristic. A clinician who specializes in the diagnosis and treatment of MPD can expect to encounter a number of patients who report incidents of childhood abuse during a life history interview. After all, childhood abuse is not uncommon among clinical patients (or, for that matter, among mentally healthy individuals; Renaud & Estess, 1961). The availability of these instances in memory may be mistaken as evidence to support the abuse-MPD link. What is *not* available in memory are the frequencies with which individuals not diagnosed with MPD do and do not report abuse. Potentially available in memory, but not especially salient, is the frequency with which individuals diagnosed with MPD do not report abuse. Without comparing the relative frequencies of abuse histories among individuals diagnosed with MPD to individuals not diagnosed with MPD, one cannot determine whether these variables covary.

The operation of the availability heuristic explains how illusory correlations can be formed from equivocal observations, and additional research suggests that such illusions can persist in the face of contradictory evidence. Chapman and Chapman (1967) demonstrated that laypersons and clinical psychologists share many false beliefs about relations between characteristics of human figure drawings and the personality traits of the individuals who drew them. For example, the empirically unfounded belief that people who draw large or exaggerated eyes tend to be suspicious or paranoid is one illusory correlation used in the Chapmans' work. When provided with evidence of a *negative* relationship (e.g., a series of drawings and personality traits paired such that paranoid individuals tend to be less likely to draw large or exaggerated eyes), individuals still reported that they "learned" from these data that a *positive* relationship holds. The fact that laypersons and clinicians share many illusory correlations regarding projective tests, coupled with the fact that these illusions can persist despite experience with contradictory evidence, may help to explain the popularity of projective test indices of limited validity (Chapman & Chapman, 1969; Wood, Nezworski, Lilienfeld, & Garb, 2003).

Bad Habits: Confirmation and Hindsight Biases

The representativeness and availability heuristics are mental shortcuts that sacrifice accuracy for efficiency, yet they only result in biased judgment under certain circumstances. Other aspects of the normal cognitive repertoire, however, include more intrinsically biased ways of thinking, which Faust (1986) labeled "bad habits." One such bad habit, known as *confirmation bias*, involves selectively seeking, attending to, and attaching greater weight to information that supports rather than refutes one's own beliefs (Nickerson, 1998). For example, some clinicians who work with victims of trauma use techniques to recover allegedly repressed memories (Poole, Lindsay, Memon, & Bull, 1995), and Sagan (1995) suggests that the nature of the material obtained using these techniques often bears an uncanny resemblance to the expectations of the practitioner. There are at least three specializations within this niche, each of which involves belief in the high frequency and pathogenicity of a particular type of trauma: child sexual abuse, satanic ritual abuse, and alien abduction. Patients whose therapists emphasize alien abduction tend to recover memories of being abducted by aliens, seldom of being sexually abused as a child or of being abused by satanic cults. To the extent that a similar correspondence holds for clinicians in each of these specializations, this would place considerable strain on coincidence as an explanation, even after one acknowledges the potential influence of referral biases (i.e., patients may seek out or be referred to practitioners who share their core beliefs). The most parsimonious explanation may be that confirmation bias guides the memory recovery process, which proceeds in the service of strongly held preconceptions rather than in a more objective search for veridical information (Lynn, Lock, Loftus, Krackow, & Lilienfeld, 2003).

When confirmation bias goes unchecked, open-minded consideration of multiple perspectives can become the exception rather than the rule: Support for a single working hypothesis is sought and incoming information passes through filters that operate to distort or remove potentially troublesome data. Whether intentionally or not, we expose ourselves to situations and environments favoring our prior beliefs. For example, we tend to associate with people who think as we do, read books and articles that support our views, and join professional organizations and attend conferences to interact with others who share our beliefs. Information is often packaged in ways that will most appeal to people who hold certain beliefs—and that will not challenge those beliefs. Different chapters in the same edited book, like different presenters within a symposium at a conference, seldom take opposing positions. By choosing which book to read or which session to attend, one can avoid dissonance-provoking confrontations with alternative viewpoints. More generally, consumers of information are increasingly able to select information sources that share their preconceptions. Although it can be comforting to experience agreement on positions regarding important issues, there are serious drawbacks to consider.

First, one might mistake a carefully selected survey of opinion—a highly biased sample—for genuine, generalizable agreement. It is easy to overestimate the extent of support for a position, or the expertise of fellow supporters, when one only consults articulate, like-minded individuals. For example, in the fall of 2004, *National Public Radio* aired a story on the skyrocketing sales of political books during the U.S. presidential campaign. A number of book publishers observed that sales were brisk, yet none believed that these books were influencing readers' political views. Instead, they suspected that people were buying and reading books by authors that shared their views to gain ammunition—in the form of the authors' credentials as well as the readers' favorite anecdotes or factoids—for political discussions and debates.

Second, to avoid discrepant views is to squander valuable opportunities to learn, especially when one holds mistaken beliefs that are correctable. Often, one stands to benefit far more from engaging rather than evading the expertise of those with whom one disagrees. If the best arguments and evidence, presented in the most compelling fashion, fail to adequately support an opposing position, one can place greater confidence in one's own. In contrast, the case for an alternative stance may warrant changing one's position. Without giving a fair hearing to those who hold different views, one might foolishly cling to misguided or irrational beliefs.

The bad habit of confirmation bias manifests itself in many judgments and decisions that clinicians are called on to make routinely. For instance, when gathering information to reach a diagnosis, a preliminary hypothesis is often formed remarkably quickly (Garb, 1998). This working hypothesis can steer one toward a search for supportive information rather than the more normatively appropriate testing of competing hypotheses (Faust, 1986). Assessment performed in a confirmatory mode is likely to yield information that is consistent with an initial hunch, but this consistency is interpretationally ambiguous because the same information may be equally consistent with other, unconsidered hypotheses. The failure to adequately consider alternative hypotheses is known as *premature closure*. A clinician aware of this danger could pose multiple hypotheses and determine how to tease them apart most effectively. Performing assessment in a more explicitly hypothesis-testing mode is more likely to yield evidence that genuinely supports correct ideas and contradictory evidence that serves to rule out false ones.

Another bad habit of human judgment, *hindsight bias,* involves mistaking a perceived understanding of the past for an ability to predict or control future events (Hawkins & Hastie, 1990). Once knowledge of an event's outcome becomes available, one has a feeling of having "known it all along" (Fischhoff, 1975). This phenomenon has also been described as "creeping determinism" (Fischhoff, 1980), as a chain of events can appear to have unfolded in an inevitable sequence. Because it is easy to construct plausible explanations for events after they have occurred, it is unwise to place much confidence in such accounts, much less to deem an outcome inevitable. The remarkable ability to recognize patterns, which enables us to craft a good story by imposing order on chaos, is a perceptual skill of inestimable adaptive value. However, an apparatus adept at organizing information into coherent patterns carries with it the liability of occasional mistakes, patterns that are only apparent and not real. Given the survival imperative of successfully learning environmental contingencies, one might expect human beings to be imbued with a positive bias toward the recognition of potential patterns even when this entails frequent false positive identifications. The frequency with which people commit the *post hoc ergo propter hoc* fallacy (B follows A, therefore B was caused by A) attests to such a hypersensitivity of our pattern recognition faculties. For example, reasoning that "I tried this treatment and felt better, therefore the treatment works" is to commit this fallacy. Beyerstein (1997) describes many alternative explanations that cannot be ruled out when attempting to draw conclusions on the basis of personal experience, testimonials, or other anecdotal evidence.

Similarly, Meehl (1973) described as a common fallacy observed in clinical case conferences the "assumption that content and dynamics explain why this person is abnormal" (p. 244). Engaging the services of a clinical practitioner establishes that the client is currently experiencing problems that, even if not diagnosable as mental disorder, involve at least some of the symptoms. The individual's present mental state constitutes an outcome in need of an explanation, and one's therapeutic orientation often guides the conceptualization of the case. For example, clinicians who believe that traumatic exposure is the root cause of most mental anguish tend to search for trauma in a life history interview. Because even most mentally healthy individuals have experienced events that can be described—whether by client or therapist—as traumatic, a sufficiently effortful search will nearly always yield information that is consistent with the clinician's etiological theory. Confirmation bias can be influential in guiding the selective search for this information, but hindsight bias is the culprit when one concludes that the uncovered trauma explains the client's current mental problems. This outcome only seems inevitable in hindsight, and there may be either no causal connection between the trauma and present mental state or a connection that is more subtle or complicated than presumed. Either way, the premature acceptance of the first plausible narrative may preclude a more thorough assessment of other factors necessary for the most accurate case formulation or the best treatment plan. The true test of understanding is not the construction of a plausible explanation for past events, but the successful prediction of future events (Dawes, 1993).

The Disproportionate Influence of Personal Experience

Mental health disciplines such as psychology, psychiatry, and social work grant professional degrees that certify expertise in clinical practice. In an article aptly titled "Credentialed Persons, Credentialed Knowledge," Meehl (1997) considered the evidential support required to substantiate such claims to expertise. Any field of study necessarily begins with the anecdotal evidence of its practitioners' personal experiences. In clinical work, experience can include training exercises as well as supervised and independent practice; the term "personal experience" does not mean "single case" (see Chapter 7 for a discussion of the inferential value of single cases). Of course, anecdotes all too readily suggest faulty conclusions and unwarranted generalizations, especially when parsed impressionistically (Faust, 1984; Meehl, 1992). To overcome the shortcomings of human judgment, pioneers of a new discipline must promote a balance between open-minded speculation and skeptical inquiry within an atmosphere of dispassionate investigation. Recognizing that scientific methodology— including research design and data analysis—has been crafted to counter cognitive limitations and biases in teasing apart fact and fiction, Meehl (1997) emphasized the importance of collecting data systematically and testing relationships between variables using appropriate statistical analyses.

For a variety of reasons, clinicians' personal experience often exerts a strong influence on their judgments even when more reliable and valid information is available. Because it is acquired first-hand, knowledge gained through personal experience in clinical practice is often more emotionally resonant than the comparatively pallid reporting of research results that one encounters in the literature. Because more vivid information is more easily retrieved from memory, the application of the availability heuristic provides one avenue by which personal experience can be assigned substantial weight in reaching clinical judgments and decisions.

To grant center stage to one's personal experience, however, can be to devalue the more informative collective experience of many other clinicians who have worked with a much larger and broader sample of clients. Acknowledging the informational value of clinical experience does not give privileged status to *personal* experience relative to the experience of everyone else. Systematic research, for example, constitutes the synthesis of many people's experiences, often a much larger and more representative sampling of pertinent experiences than one has encountered first-hand. In addition, knowledge obtained through personal experience is seldom subjected to adequate statistical testing. As a result, illusory correlations may take root and actual relationships that are in any way subtle or counterintuitive may escape notice. Although theory and research on mental health are far from satisfactory—much less complete—in many important respects, the extant literature can often provide sounder guidelines for practice than a comparatively narrow consideration of one's personal experiences. An exercise such as the following might reveal a double standard of evidence skewed toward the acceptance of one's own experience and the rejection of others' experience:

Suppose that rather than having had certain experiences and reached a certain judgment myself, someone else presented me with the same conclusion on the basis of the same evidence. That is, the haphazard nature of the sampling, the unavailability of an unknown portion of the original data due to memory limitations and biases, the nonrandom assignment of clients to conditions that vary nonsystematically, the reliability and validity of objective and subjective outcome data (as it is recalled, not as it was initially assessed), and the steps in the reasoning process would be identical to what is going through my mind right now. The only difference would be that I did not personally experience any of this. Rather, I would be learning about the fully equivalent experiences of someone else, stated in unambiguous detail. Would I accept the judgment on these terms?

Through an exercise of this sort, which draws attention to normative and prescriptive principles of scientific reasoning, one might remove the *personal* aspect of the relevant experiences and more objectively accord them the weight they merit in the judgment process.

In addition to the potential roles that availability bias and evidential double standards may play, a widespread misunderstanding within the mental health community can serve—intentionally or otherwise—to dismiss the knowledge available from research literature. When the collective experience of clinical investigators is discredited in this way, practitioners are forced to rely more heavily on the anecdotal evidence of their personal experience.

The misunderstanding at issue is captured in the maxim that "probability is irrelevant to the unique individual." Variants of this claim involve the substitution of "statistics" or "research" for "probability." The idea is that knowledge of the long-run frequency of occurrence for many similar people, under similar circumstances, is of no bearing in a specific situation that is not to be repeated. For example, statistics reported in the research literature suggest that the probability of successfully alleviating an individual's specific phobia is maximized through exposure-based treatment (Barlow, 2002). It is not unusual, however, for a mental health expert to disregard this finding, administering some other treatment on the grounds that a particular client's case is special—that the probability/statistics/research do not apply to this unique individual. There are two ways of understanding such a claim.

First, one might interpret this as a claim that, despite the clinician's awareness that exposure therapy best addresses specific phobias, he or she perceives something sufficiently probative *in this instance* to countervail the prescribed treatment. Following Meehl's (1954) classic treatise on prediction, this is referred to this as a "broken leg" case: An otherwise sound statistical prediction that a certain professor is likely to attend a movie one evening *should* be modified in light of the fact that the professor had just broken a leg. Despite the existence of such cases, research has revealed that practitioners overidentify "broken leg" counterexamples, departing too frequently from the predictions of a statistical formula and making more errors in the process (Grove, Zald, Lebow, Snitz, & Nelson, 2000). Meehl (1998) noted that this fact is predictable from the more general finding that, when given the same pool of valid information and evaluated against the same criteria, statistical predictions are as or more accurate than clinical predictions *even when when the clinicians are provided with the statistical predictions and are allowed to copy them.* If clinicians adopted the statistical predictions except in those instances where they could correctly identify exceptions, then their accuracy would be higher than that of the formula. Because this does not happen, the clinicians must be identifying too many exceptions. It is important to recognize what this means: Appeals to the uniqueness of the individual as grounds for countervailing the dictates of probability will, on balance, *increase* judgment errors.

Second, one might interpret this as a claim that, *in general,* probability is irrelevant to understanding or predicting the behavior of an individual. A simple thought experiment, originally presented by Meehl (1973), exposes the speciousness of this interpretation. Suppose that you are to play Russian roulette once, meaning that you will put a revolver to your head and pull the trigger. Would you prefer that there be one bullet and five empty chambers in the revolver, or five bullets and one empty chamber? You are, after all, a unique person who will either live or die, and this event will not be repeated. The only basis for preferring that there be just one bullet is that the *probability* of death is 1/6 rather than 5/6. Clearly, probability is extremely relevant despite any unique aspects of this event.

The same reasoning applies when making clinical judgments—present knowledge (based on personal experience or more systematic research) can only establish the conditional probabilities of various outcomes given a certain decision. The most appropriate way to reach important judgments is to choose the option with the best probability of success. Granted, actual clinical work complicates the subjective assessment of probabilities, as it is extremely challenging to identify, gather, and integrate the wealth of information pertinent to making many of the important decisions that arise, and knowledge of the relations between predictors and outcomes is usually quite modest. Nonetheless, the obstacles faced by practitioners do not negate the basic principle—carefully considering probability is *essential* for minimizing the chance of making a judgment error in each unique case.

The Challenge of Experiential Learning

Expertise in any endeavor requires, among other things, a considerable amount of dedicated practice. Some skills, such as the motor coordination involved in playing a musical instrument, can be improved through repetitive practice exercises. Over time, the automaticity of performance increases and less effort is required to avoid making amateurish mistakes. Other types of skills, such as the creativity involved in composing new works of music, would not benefit from the same sort of repetitive practice. Instead, useful exercises might incorporate trial-and-error explorations of potential melodies, harmonizing, instrumentation, tempo, and so forth. With tasks as multifaceted and open-ended as this, there is no guarantee that experiential learning will occur. Certain requirements must be met, and there may be ways to structure practice sessions to maximize the rewards reaped for a fixed commitment of effort.

Some aspects of the earliest stages of clinical practice, when a large volume of information must be memorized, may bear greater similarity to the development of motor coordination than the development of musical creativity. An aspiring practitioner must learn about the signs and symptoms of a large number of mental disorders, an ever-expanding collection of assessment tools and treatment techniques (and, ideally, the empirical support for each), and the ethical and legal codes that apply to practitioners in a given locale, for example. Whereas the working vocabulary of mental health practice is acquired through rote learning, many interpersonal skills are honed through experiential learning in supervised training with actual clients and (later) through independent practice. With respect to the development of expert clinical judgment, how effective is experiential learning?

Reducing judgment errors by learning through experience requires attention to concrete, immediate, and unambiguous feedback on the accuracy (or inaccuracy) of prior judgments. Much of the feedback typically available to practitioners, however, is intrinsically ambiguous and temporally distal. For example, if a client does not arrive at several scheduled appointments and remains unreachable thereafter, one could interpret this outcome as a personal failure to form a strong therapeutic alliance. Or, one could assume that the client moved away on short notice and either lost his or her therapist's contact information or forgot to contact the therapist's office. Or, perhaps the client was cured. In either case, the feedback accumulates long after the sessions with this client have ended, and it becomes increasingly difficult to draw firm conclusions about what specific actions may have led to the early termination of therapy.

Practitioners also are exposed to and attend to more positive than negative feedback. Because it can be considerably more interpersonally awkward and difficult, displeased clients can be less likely to communicate blame to their therapists than pleased clients are to express gratitude. At least as important, even when feedback is available, the normal self-serving biases of human judgment can mount a variety of defenses against ego-threatening information while allowing more flattering information to arrive unfettered (Faust, 1986). Moreover, hindsight bias can make poor outcomes seem inevitable rather than the result of judgment errors. Even if a case is handled badly and therapeutic change is either nil or negative, there are many ways that a clinician can deflect this otherwise negative feedback. For instance, one might console oneself with the fact that the prognosis is poor for individuals suffering from chronic posttraumatic stress disorder, and especially poor for those with a comorbid substance abuse disorder. Even the most honestly self-critical therapist may not be able to distinguish the effects of some subtle errors in judgment from the effects of prior difficulties that ordinarily are not amenable to treatment. The net result of ambiguous feedback, time delay in the receipt of feedback, the scarcity of negative feedback, and hindsight bias is that there may be precious few opportunities to learn through experience.

Given these factors, it should not be surprising that research fails to support the belief that the accuracy of clinical judgment improves with clinical experience (Garb, 1989). Dawes (1994) characterizes this belief as the *myth of expanding expertise*. Many people—clinicians included—simply assume that skills improve with experience and fail to consider the requirements for such learning to occur. Whereas skills acquired through rote memorization can be assessed relatively directly and easily, those built through experiential learning are considerably more difficult to assess. In place of reliable and valid measures of genuine improvement in clinical judgment, the myth of expanding expertise may fill the void with the presumption of gains attributable to experiential learning.

Promoting Experiential Learning

A return to the world of competitive Scrabble suggests some strategies that might be adapted to promote more effective experiential learning in clinical practice. As in chess, Scrabble players are provided with numerical ratings of their skill level. These ratings, updated with each game played, are calculated based on such factors as the outcome of the game and the skill level of the opposing player. Given the psychometric proficiency of psychologists and others in related disciplines, it is not inconceivable that a rating system could similarly be devised to quantify therapists' track records. Although clients are not directly analogous to opposing players, a good rating system could account for clients' current mental health, history, and complicating factors so that therapists who succeed with more difficult cases earn higher ratings. It is easy to imagine abuses of a rating scheme, but it also is possible to imagine beneficial uses of a well-constructed system, especially if access to ratings is appropriately restricted to those with educational, training, research, or other approved purposes. Clinical trainees and less effective therapists could seek opportunities to learn from expert mentors, and researchers could study expert therapists for clues about how they achieve their success. Particularly if such a system were developed and maintained by mental health professionals them-selves, much might be learned about therapeutic success and truly expert clinical judgment. At the same time, the increasing demand for health-care accountability (Cummings, 2006) suggests that the imposition of a rating system on therapists by insurers or government agencies is not out of the question. This possibility may provide some incentive for clinicians to devise a satisfactory system of their own before being forced into one that they find less palatable.

Perhaps more striking than the quantification of Scrabble players' exper-tise are some of the behavioral differences between Scrabble novices and experts observed by Fatsis (2001). Whereas beginners tend to clear a board and begin a new game quickly after one has ended, presumably believing that the best way to improve their play is through practice, experts study each game for opportunities to prevent the repetition of suboptimal plays in the future. In addition to studying the board itself at the end of the game, an expert takes meticulous notes on each play so that it can be evaluated in the context of the game at that moment. As Meehl (1997) and others argued, clinicians might learn more effectively if they tabulated and quantified their experiences. This practice could be useful for the generation and testing of hypotheses in real-world contexts. Even if not done formally as a research project, more informal tallies of the frequencies with which certain types of hunches or approaches do and do not bear fruit, or with which certain variables do and do not co-occur, could be highly informative for oneself or others.

Another tool that is increasingly used by current and aspiring Scrabble experts is to compare actual or hypothetical plays with the "optimal" plays generated by an expert system. These plays are optimal in the sense that a computer program—provided with complete Scrabble word knowledge and algorithms to score plays—can determine, probabilistically, what play is likely to yield the best final game score margin across a large number of games that all begin with precisely the same specifications (e.g., layout of tiles on the board, each player's current score, one or both players' racks of tiles). One can use such a program to ask whether a certain play is optimal or whether the computer can devise a better play, or one can compare two or more alternative plays (e.g., playing a word, playing a different word, exchanging certain tiles) to learn which would have been best. The ability to simulate follow-up data to evaluate every judgment is a powerful tool for Scrabble players to exploit. Clinicians do not have the same opportunity, but just as they could tally observations for subsequent analysis, they could take better advantage of opportunities to gather systematic data on various criterion measures with which to evaluate critical judgments retrospectively. Such criterion data could be collected on an ongoing basis, at termination, or subsequent to termination.

A final recommendation for improving judgment is not only consistent with observations of expert Scrabble players, but also strongly supported by the literature on correcting judgment errors and overconfidence (Arkes, 1991). Scrabble experts are continually searching for weaknesses in their own play, striving to grow as players through ruthless self-appraisal. A key component of their success in learning through experience is the use of hypothetical counter-factuals such as "What mistakes have I made?" and "How might I prevent similar errors in the future?" In clinical work, one could examine cases with especially poor outcomes (e.g., the death of Candace Newmaker during rebirthing therapy; Mercer, 2002) to formulate hypotheses about how to pre-vent harmful judgment errors. Janis (1972) used this approach to identify the groupthink phenomenon as a culprit in many disastrous foreign policy deci-sions and recommended the institutionalization of a "devil's advocate." Of course, one can adopt that role with regard to one's own judgment. Like everyone else, clinicians are in a position to learn more about their trade by habitually asking themselves "Why might I be wrong?"

Conclusion

An understanding of the cognitive biases and limitations discussed in this chapter, each of which might be addressed by stricter adherence to sound principles of scientific reasoning, suggests a number of concrete steps that can be taken to minimize judgment errors and irrational beliefs in clinical practice.

1. *Scrutinize similarity-based arguments.* Because the representativeness heuristic can make claims taking the form "like goes with like" appear quite reasonable, one must be especially careful to evaluate the logic and evidence bearing on such assertions.

2. *Conceptualize problems in multiple ways.* The availability heuristic can lead one astray when the instances most easily retrieved from memory provide a biased sample of data. Reconceptualizing an issue may provide new memory cues that elicit complementary information which reduces the initial bias and provides a firmer basis for reaching a judgment.

3. *Formulate and test multiple working hypotheses.* To prevent the premature closure that can result from the operation of confirmation and hindsight biases, it is important to generate multiple hypotheses and to tease them apart rigorously. Deliberately constructing and evaluating plausible alternative explanations can prevent many of the judgment errors resulting from a search for information to support an impression that was formed quickly.

4. *Recognize that personal experience is anecdotal evidence.* It is all too easy to allow personal experience to disproportionately influence clinical judgments. Whereas research systematically aggregates the experience of many practitioners with many clients, one's personal experience may involve a smaller, more haphazard, and less rigorously evaluated knowledge base. Considering whether one's own conclusions would be acceptable if presented by someone else may help to identify instances in which personal experience is being given undue weight.

5. *Learn and apply basic principles of probability.* Because clinical work involves probabilistic relationships between variables, practitioners need to recognize that probability, statistics, and research evidence do apply to unique individuals. At least as important is learning the basic rules of probability and knowing when and how to apply them (e.g., using Bayes' Theorem to combine base rates with individuating information).

6. *Identify exceptions to statistical trends with caution.* A statistical trend represents a "signal" that can be detected despite the "noise" of individual differences and contextual variables. Although judgments informed by such trends will not be accurate in all cases, the literature strongly suggests that practitioners identify too many exceptions. Judgment errors can result from attaching too much significance to a client's uniqueness, which is often of little predictive value precisely

because it is impossible to establish statistical associations involving truly unique characteristics. Discovering meaningful ways in which a client's case shares features with others enables a savvy practitioner to more successfully play the odds by taking advantage of statistical trends.

7. *Play "devil's advocate" to one's own judgments.* Finally, asking why one might be wrong can suggest the need for additional information, help to differentiate between relevant and irrelevant information, or lead to a more appropriate way to integrate the available information when reaching a judgment. The more one learns about the limitations and biases of human reasoning, the more opportunities are afforded to prevent judgment errors by actively checking for mistaken premises or faulty logic in one's own thinking.

REFERENCES

(Each of the five recommended readings is marked with an asterisk.)

Arkes, H. R. (1991). Costs and benefits of judgment errors: Implications for debiasing. *Psychological Bulletin, 110,* 486–498.

Beyerstein, B. L. (1997). Why bogus therapies seem to work. *Skeptical Inquirer, 21,* 29–34.

Barlow, D. H. (2002). *Anxiety and Its disorders: The nature and treatment of anxiety and panic* (2nd ed.). New York: Guilford.

Chapman, L. J., & Chapman, J. P. (1967). Genesis of popular but erroneous diagnostic observations. *Journal of Abnormal Psychology, 72,* 193–204.

Chapman, L. J., & Chapman, J. P. (1969). Illusory correlation as an obstacle to the use of valid psychodiagnostic observations. *Journal of Abnormal Psychology, 74,* 271–280.

Cummings, N. A. (2006). Psychology, the stalwart profession, faces new challenges and opportunities. *Professional Psychology: Research and Practice, 37,* 598–605.

Dawes, R. M. (1993). Prediction of the future versus an understanding of the past: A basic asymmetry. *American Journal of Psychology, 106,* 1–24.

Dawes, R. M. (1994). *House of cards: Psychology and psychotherapy built on myth.* New York: Free Press.

Dawes, R. M. (2001). *Everyday irrationality: How pseudo-scientists, lunatics, and the rest of us systematically fail to think rationally.* Boulder, CO: Westview Press.

Dawes, R. M., Faust, D., & Meehl, P. E. (1989). Clinical versus actuarial judgment. *Science, 243,* 1668–1674.

Fatsis, S. (2001). *Word freak: Heartbreak, triumph, genius, and obsession in the world of competitive Scrabble players.* Boston: Houghton Mifflin.

Faust, D. (1984). *The limits of scientific reasoning.* Minneapolis: University of Minnesota Press.

*Faust, D. (1986). Research on human judgment and its application to clinical practice. *Professional Psychology: Research and Practice, 17,* 420–430.

Fischhoff, B. (1975). Hindsight foresight: The effect of outcome knowledge on judgment under uncertainty. *Journal of Experimental Psychology: Human Perception and Performance, 1,* 288–299.

Fischhoff, B. (1980). For those condemned to study the past: Reflections on historical judgment. In R. A. Shueder & D. W. Fiske (Eds.), *New directions for methodology of behavioral science: Fallible judgment in behavioral research* (pp. 79–93). San Francisco: Jossey-Bass.

Garb, H. N. (1989). Clinical judgment, clinical training, and professional experience. *Psychological Bulletin, 105,* 387–396.

*Garb, H. N. (1998). *Studying the clinician: Judgment research and psychological assessment.* Washington, DC: American Psychological Association.

Gigerenzer, G., Todd, P. M., & the ABC Research Group (1999). *Simple heuristics that make us smart.* New York: Oxford University Press.

Grove, W. M., Zald, D. H., Lebow, B. S., Snitz, B. E., & Nelson, C. (2000). Clinical versus mechanical prediction: A meta-analysis. *Psychological Assessment, 12,* 19–30.

Halford, G. S., Baker, R., McCredden, J. E., & Bain, J. D. (2005). How many variables can humans process? *Psychological Science, 16,* 70–76.

Hawkins, S. A., & Hastie, R. (1990). Hindsight: Biased judgments of past events after the outcomes are known. *Psychological Bulletin, 107,* 311–327.

Janis, I. L. (1972). *Victims of groupthink: A psychological study of foreign-policy decisions and fiascos.* Oxford: Houghton Mifflin.

Kahneman, D., & Tversky, A. (1972). Subjective probability: A judgment of representativeness. *Cognitive Psychology, 3,* 430–454.

Kahneman, D., & Tversky, A. (1984). Choices, values, and frames. *American Psychologist, 39,* 341–350.

Lilienfeld, S. O., Lynn, S. J., Kirsch, I., Chaves, J. F., Sarbin, T. R., Ganaway, G. K., et al. (1999). Dissociative identity disorder and the sociocognitive model: Recalling the lessons of the past. *Psychological Bulletin, 125,* 507–523.

Lynn, S. J., Lock, T., Loftus, E. F., Krackow, E., & Lilienfeld, S. O. (2003). The remembrance of things past: Problematic memory recovery techniques in psychotherapy. In S. O. Lilienfeld, S. J. Lynn, & J. M. Lohr (Eds.), *Science and pseudoscience in clinical psychology* (pp. 205–239). New York: Guilford.

Meehl, P. E. (1954). *Clinical versus statistical prediction: A theoretical analysis and a review of the evidence.* Minneapolis: University of Minnesota Press.

*Meehl, P. E. (1973). Why I do not attend case conferences. In P. E. Meehl (Ed.), *Psychodiagnosis: Selected papers* (pp. 225–302). Minneapolis: University of Minnesota Press.

Meehl, P. E. (1992). Cliometric metatheory: The actual approach to empirical, history-based philosophy of science. *Psychological Reports, 71,* 339–467.

*Meehl, P. E. (1997). Credentialed persons, credentialed knowledge. *Clinical Psychology: Science and Practice, 4,* 91–98.

Meehl, P. E. (1998, May). *The power of quantitative thinking.* Invited address as recipient of the James McKeen Cattell Award at the annual meeting of the American Psychological Society, Washington, DC.

Mercer, J. (2002). Attachment therapy: A treatment without empirical support. *Scientific Review of Mental Health Practice, 1,* 105–112.

Miller, G. A. (1956). The magical number seven, plus or minus two: Some limits on our capacity for processing information. *Psychological Review, 63,* 81–97.

Nickerson, R. S. (1998). Confirmation bias: A ubiquitous phenomenon in many guises. *Review of General Psychology, 2,* 175–220.

Nisbett, R. E., & Ross, L. 1980. *Human inference: Strategies and shortcomings of social judgment.* Englewood Cliffs, NJ: Prentice-Hall.

Poole, D. A., Lindsay, D., Memon, A., & Bull, R. (1995). Psychotherapy and the recovery of memories of childhood sexual abuse: U.S. and British practitioners' opinions, practices, and experiences. *Journal of Consulting and Clinical Psychology, 63,* 426–437.

Renaud, H., & Estess, F. (1961). Life history interviews with one hundred normal American males: "Pathogenicity" of childhood. *American Journal of Orthopsychiatry, 31,* 786–802.

Ruscio, J., & Stern, A. R. (2006). The consistency and accuracy of holistic judgment: Clinical decision making with a minimally complex task. *Scientific Review of Mental Health Practice, 4,* 52–65.

Sagan, C. (1995). *The demon-haunted world: Science as a candle in the dark.* New York: Random House.

Schreiber, F. R. (1973). *Sybil.* Chicago: Henry Regnery.

Spanos, N. P. (1996). *Multiple identities and false memories: A sociocognitive perspective.* Washington, DC: American Psychological Association.

Sternberg, S. (1969). The discovery of processing stages: Extensions of Donders' method. In W. G. Koster (Ed.), *Attention and performance II* (pp. 276–315). Amsterdam: Elsevier-North Holland.

*Turk, D. C., & Salovey, P. (1988). *Reasoning, inference, and judgment in clinical psychology.* New York: Free Press.

Tversky, A., & Kahneman, D. (1973). Availability: A heuristic for judging frequency and probability. *Cognitive Psychology, 5,* 207–232.

Tversky, A., & Kahneman, D. (1974). Judgment under uncertainty: Heuristics and biases. *Science, 185,* 1124–1131.

Wood, J. M., Nezworski, M. T., Lilienfeld, S. O., & Garb, H. N. (2003). *What's wrong with the Rorschach? Science confronts the controversial inkblot test.* San Francisco: Jossey-Bass.

GLOSSARY OF KEY CONCEPTS

Availability heuristic: A mental shortcut for judging of the probability or frequency of an event by using the ease with which instances can be retrieved from memory as a guide.

Confirmation bias: The tendency to selectively seek, attend to, or attach greater weight to information that supports rather than refutes one's beliefs.

Experiential learning: The development of expert knowledge or judgment through a process that requires concrete, immediate, and unambiguous feedback.

Hindsight bias: The presumption that the ability to construct a plausible explanation of past events implies a causal understanding that can be used to successfully predict future events.

Representativeness heuristic: A mental shortcut for reaching judgments based on perceived similarity or "goodness of fit" rather than actual probabilistic or causal relationships.

Note: This is a revised draft of a chapter previously published in Lilienfeld, S. O., & O'Donohue, W. (Eds.) (2006), *The great ideas of clinical science: 17 principles that every mental health researcher and practitioner should understand* (pp. 27–45). New York: Brunner-Taylor. It has been adapted with permission. The author would like to thank Scott Lilienfeld for his helpful suggestions and guidance.

15

The Five Great Myths of Popular Psychology: Implications for Psychotherapy

Scott O. Lilienfeld, Steven Jay Lynn, and Barry L. Beyerstein

Central to rational-emotive behavior therapy (REBT) and allied cognitive-behavioral interventions is the notion that accurate information regarding human behavior is helpful, at times perhaps even necessary, for successful treatment planning and implementation. Without scientifically adequate knowledge about how their minds work, psychotherapy clients may be susceptible to a host of incorrect beliefs regarding themselves and the world. As a consequence, they may persist in well-meaning but misguided efforts to alter their behaviors. For example, clients who believe erroneously that the first few years of life exert a nearly unshakable stranglehold over long-term adjustment may engage in fruitless efforts to rectify their past; clients who believe erroneously that human memory operates like a video-camera or tape recorder may spend months or years attempting to unearth putative early memories of trauma; and clients who believe falsely that they must "process" painful emotions to overcome them may spend far more time wallowing in their feelings than attempting to restructure them constructively.

In this chapter, we argue that misconceptions concerning the human mind are legion even among highly intelligent and well-educated members of the general public (Della Salla, 2000; Lilienfeld, 2005; Lilienfeld, Lynn, Ruscio, & Beyerstein, in press), and that these misconceptions can interfere with effective treatment planning and execution. Moreover, we contend that these misconceptions can impede effective coping with everyday life problems outside of the therapy room and contribute to a search for futile solutions to psychological distress. We further maintain that the best remedy for combating these misconceptions in clinical settings is straightforward: education. Psychotherapists, we propose, must often do more than administer efficacious treatments. In many instances, they must also function as good *teachers* of psychology, disabusing their clients of misconceptions concerning the human mind and imparting correct information in its stead.

Pervasiveness of Misconceptions of Mind

Virtually all people, even those of us without formal psychological training, are armchair psychologists. As humans, we are as fascinated and intrigued as we are challenged by a panorama of psychological phenomena that we encounter in daily life: anxiety, depression, and anger; parenting practices; the effects of divorce on children; friendships and romantic relationships; memory lapses; sexual difficulties; work-related stress; sleep problems; and the inevitable ravages of aging. Indeed, if there is one certainty in life other than death and taxes, it the inevitability of confronting difficult and often crucial decisions that require accurate information about the operation of the human mind.

Nevertheless, precious few people possess the time, training, or both, to keep abreast of the rapidly expanding and often confusing psychological literature. As a consequence, most laypersons, even those who are highly educated, exhibit low levels of "psychological literacy" (Boneau, 1990), that is, familiarity with basic psychological facts and principles. Moreover, many people are not merely psychologically illiterate, but supremely confident in their beliefs concerning psychological "facts" that are actually fictions. For example, large minorities or even majorities of laypersons (see Lamal, 1979; Taylor & Kowalski, 2004) believe that:

- Most people use only about 10% of their brain power.
- Speed reading courses allow individuals to dramatically increase both the reading speed and reading comprehension.
- Most children who are abused grow up to become abusers themselves.
- Opposites tend to attract in interpersonal relationships.

- Full moons are associated with increased numbers of psychiatric hospital admissions and suicides.
- The polygraph test is a virtually infallible indicator of lying.
- People can accurately recall events dating back to birth.
- Memories recalled under hypnosis are usually accurate.
- Most people with schizophrenia have multiple personalities.
- People's responses to inkblots can reveal an enormous amount about their personalities.
- Most severely mentally ill people are violent.

Despite the popularity of these and a myriad of other "mind myths" (Della Salla, 2000, 2006), research evidence suggests that they are all largely or entirely false (Lilienfeld, 2005; Lilienfeld, Lynn, Namy, & Woolf, 2009).

The Popular Psychology Industry

Where do these prevalent but inaccurate beliefs originate? Although the genesis of mind myths is surely multifaceted, the principal source of psychological misconceptions on which we focus is the popular ("pop") psychology industry. This industry routinely dispenses large dollops of information in readily accessible outlets, including self-help and recovery books, newsstand magazines, Hollywood movies, television shows, and the Internet. Modern-day psychological knowledge is shaped as much, if not more, by supermarket tabloids, talk shows, and self-proclaimed "self-help gurus" as it is by the most recent scientific advances (Lilienfeld, Lynn, & Lohr, 2003). The central problem is that the information propagated by the popular psychology industry is a bewildering hodgepodge of accurate and inaccurate knowledge. Because this industry offers laypersons scant guidance for distinguishing the wheat from the chaff, most people are left to their own devices to sort out what is scientifically trustworthy from what is not.

To be sure, some popular psychology wisdom is helpful and accurate, and it would be grossly unfair to tar all of pop psychology with the same skeptical brush. For example, many pop psychology sources urge us to assume more responsibility for our actions and to avoid blaming others for our life difficulties. Such common-sense advice is well in keeping with that provided by proponents of REBT and numerous other psychotherapies (Ellis, 2004). Moreover, some popularly available sources provide the public with high quality and useful information concerning the signs and symptoms of major psychiatric disorders and the scientific status of efficacious psychotherapies (e.g., Frances & First, 2000; Seligman, 1994).

Nevertheless, the popular psychology industry probably generates at least as much misinformation as information regarding human behavior. For example, scores of popular self-help books assure us that adult children of alcoholics are prone to codependent behaviors, autistic disorder (infantile autism) is triggered by mercury-bearing vaccines, divorce almost invariably exacts a serious psychological toll on children, and high self-esteem is essential to psychological health. Yet carefully conducted psychological research disconfirms each of these assertions (Baumeister, Campbell, Krueger, & Vohs, 2003; Herbert, Sharp, & Gaudiano, 2002; Logue, Sher, & Frensch, 1992). Indeed, despite former American Psychological Association president George Miller's (1969) famous clarion call to academic psychologists to "give psychology away," that is, to shower the public with the fruits of hard-won psychological science, *psychology* has become increasingly synonymous with nonscientific psychology.

Moreover, the steady flow of misinformation emanating from the popular psychology industry gives scant indication of subsiding. Recent estimates suggest that upwards of 3500 self-help books appear in print annually (Arkowitz & Lilienfeld, 2006; Rosen, 1993). Most of these books base their advice on little more than popular wisdom, and some contain blatant misinformation. At the same time, an increasing number of prominent television and radio self-help personalities such as Dr. Laura, Dr. Phil, and Charles McPhee ("The Dream Doctor") dispense psychological advice that often contradicts research findings (Wilson, 2003). For example, Dr. Phil recently contributed to the public's misunderstanding of psychology by offering to administer polygraph tests as a means of determining whether some his guests were lying about their romantic relationships (Levenson, 2005). Regrettably, he did not mention the enormous body of scientific research on the marked limitations of the polygraph test as an indicator of dishonesty (Lykken, 1998).

Moreover, the number of Web sites that offer misleading psychological information is proliferating on a monthly basis. For example, typing the words "past life regression," "rebirthing," and "inner child (or inner child therapy)" into Google yields approximately 48,000, 64,000, and 160,000 Web page links, respectively, most of which provide little or no critical examination of the claims regarding these entirely unsubstantiated treatments. Compare these numbers with the approximately 7000 and 800 hits, respectively, one receives for the terms of the "token economy" and "Beck Depression Inventory," both of which refer to scientifically supported techniques (see Lilienfeld, 1998; Olatunji, Parker, & Lohr, 2006). If these admittedly crude numbers are any indication, the world of popular psychology, as least as operationalized by the Internet, is far more imbued with nonscientific than scientific techniques.

The Five Great Myths of Popular Psychology

In an ongoing project (Lilienfeld et al., in press), we have identified well over 200 widespread misconceptions about the human mind that emanate largely from the popular psychology industry. Nevertheless, we suspect that the lion's share of these misconceptions stem from a smaller number of more "fundamental" underlying myths.

Indeed, if we conduct an "armchair factor analysis" of these 200 or more "lower-order" misconceptions, we can readily discern certain "higher-order" recurring themes that cut across them. Hence, after surveying the large array of misconceptions that dot the popular psychology landscape, we have tentatively converged on what we term the "Five Great Myths of Popular Psychology."

We believe that these five myths, although by no means exhaustive, represent the core false beliefs imparted by the popular psychology industry that have most deeply penetrated popular consciousness. These beliefs, we contend, can be barriers to effective psychotherapy, because if not addressed explicitly they can lead clients to *(a)* resist certain scientifically supported interventions (e.g., behavioral interventions that do not depend on acquiring insight into one's problems) within sessions or *(b)* attempt to engage in scientifically unsupported interventions (e.g., outwardly expressing anger toward provoking individuals) outside of sessions. In addition, when firmly held, these beliefs can be hazardous to individuals' everyday psychological health.

We first introduce these five "Great Myths" in list form below. In the remainder of the chapter, we proceed to discuss each myth's content and manifestations in the landscape of everyday life. In several cases, we also discuss the "mythlets" or more specific misconceptions that appear to derive from each Great Myth. In addition, we will examine the implications of each myth for clinical practice and, when relevant, discuss potential strategies of "debiasing" clients against them.

> *Myth # 1. The Myth of Fragility:* the idea that most individuals require treatment for minor stressors.
>
> *Myth # 2. The Myth of the Critical Importance of Early Experience:* the idea that traumatic childhood events almost always cause mental illness in adulthood, and that these events must be addressed in psychotherapy.
>
> *Myth # 3. The Myth of Catharsis:* the idea that expressing negative emotions is usually therapeutic.

Myth # 4. The Myth of Unrealized Potential: the idea that we use only a very small part of our brains and that our brain is a huge untapped reservoir of mental capacities.

Myth # 5. The Myth of Self-Esteem: the idea that high self-esteem is essential to psychological health.

The Myth of Fragility

In his classic chapter, "Why I Do Not Attend Case Conferences," Paul Meehl (1973) delineated a variety of fallacies that contribute to muddled thinking in both the clinical case conference and therapy consulting room. He referred to one of these fallacies as the "spun glass theory of the mind": the notion that our psyches are so vulnerable to stress that they are at risk for shattering in response to even the mildest of psychological provocations. As Meehl noted, this doctrine posits that

> The human organism, adult or child (particularly the latter), is constituted of such frail material, is of such exquisite psychological delicacy, that rather minor, garden-variety frustrations, deprivations, criticisms, rejections, or failure experiences are likely to play the causative role of major traumas (p. 253).

To illustrate the spun-glass theory, Meehl (1973) related the story of a social worker who was slated to interview a deeply disturbed patient who was about to be discharged from an inpatient unit. The social worker had considered the patient's psychotherapy to be successful. The interview was initially scheduled to be conducted in the same room in which the patient was accustomed to being seen, but due to an unavoidable room conflict, the interview had to be moved to a new room. The social worker responded that she had no choice but to cancel the interview, because the patient might find the experience of being interviewed in a different room overly traumatic. The irony of releasing the patient into the real world with all of its attendant stressors while shielding him from the "trauma" of being interviewed in a new room was not lost on Meehl.

Indeed, few notions are more pervasive in popular psychology than the belief that many or most of us are highly susceptible to mental breakdown on exposure to stress. As Meehl (1973) observed, this notion is especially ubiquitous when it comes to children, whom mental health professionals and teachers frequently assume to be exquisitely vulnerable to trivial stressors. Sommers and Satel (2005) offered a plethora of disturbing and at times unintentionally comical illustrations of this "myth of the fragile child" in contemporary American schools: banning dodgeball and other sports that might harm children's self-esteem; inventing games of tag in which "nobody is ever 'out' "; declining to correct students' blatantly wrong answers in class; and giving all students (including those who perform poorly) equivalent academic awards, like gold stars, for "effort." They also presented evidence that such practices are becoming increasingly widespread in the American educational system (see also "The Myth of Self-Esteem").

Popular psychology views of adults' capacity to handle stress are scarcely different. Yet a large body of psychological research reveals that resilience, not fragility, is the rule rather than the exception when it comes to individuals' response to psychological stressors (Bonanno, 2004, 2005; Garmezy, 1991; Masten, 2001). Even among individuals exposed to extreme life-threatening stressors, such as front-line combat and natural disasters, only about 25% typically develop posttraumatic stress disorder (PTSD), with rape being a potential exception to this minority rule (McNally, Bryant, & Ehlers, 2003; Rosen & Lilienfeld, 2008). Moreover, although about 50% to 60% of Americans experience or witness traumatic stressors at some point in their lives, only about 5% to 10% ever meet criteria for PTSD (Ozer, Best, Lipsey, & Weiss, 2003).

For example, following the terrorist attacks of September 11, 2001, many mental health experts confidently forecasted a veritable epidemic of PTSD, even among people who had only heard about the attacks or witnessed them on television. Yet the predicted onslaught of traumatized patients arriving at inpatients and outpatient clinics never materialized (Sommers & Satel, 2005). Certainly, surveys indicated that an overwhelming majority—perhaps 90% or more—of Americans reported mild and psychologically understandable symptoms of distress, such as "feeling upset," "feeling angry," and experiencing difficulties with sleeping or concentrating, in the days immediately following the September 11th attacks (e.g., Schuster et al., 2001). Yet comparable surveys conducted two months later revealed that almost all Americans had returned to their baseline levels of adjustment (Schlenger et al., 2002). Indeed, a survey conducted four months following the September 11th attacks revealed that only 1.7% of Americans had developed PTSD; this number declined to only 0.6% by six months after the attacks (Galea et al., 2002). Taken together, most of the post–September 11th data suggest at most a modest increase in PTSD following the attacks, but only among individuals in lower Manhattan, where the major attacks occurred (comparable surveys revealed no increases in PTSD among individuals in Washington, DC, where one of the other planes hit the Pentagon). Moreover, even in lower Manhattan, the substantial majority of individuals did not develop full-fledged PTSD (Sommers & Satel, 2005).

Similarly, a large number of individuals who experience the deaths of their husbands or wives fare surprisingly well in the aftermath of these tragic losses. Approximately 50% of bereaved individuals suffer from significant emotional distress, health problems, and impairments in interpersonal functioning in the months following the death of their spouses. Nevertheless, these deficits become long-lasting in only about 10% to 15% of individuals. Although some psychologists maintain that individuals who remain resilient following the deaths of their spouses are especially callous or uncaring, there is no research support for this notion (Bonanno, 2004).

Even most children emerge from traumatic stressors in reasonably good shape. In 1976, 26 schoolchildren in Chowchilla, California, experienced a terrifying kidnapping. Along with their bus-driver, they were taken hostage on a school bus for 11 hours, and then buried underground in a van for 16 hours. Remarkably, all survived. Two years later, although most of the children were understandably haunted by memories of the incident, virtually all were well-adjusted (Terr, 1988).

To take still one more example, much of the popular psychology literature informs us that divorce frequently enacts a serious emotional toll on children. On September 25, 2000, *Time Magazine* featured a cover story entitled "What Divorce Does to Kids," accompanied by the ominous warning that "New research says the long-term damage is worse than you thought." This story was sparked by a widely publicized 25-year longitudinal investigation by Judith Wallerstein (1989), who tracked 60 families in California in which parents had divorced. Wallerstein reported that although the children in these families seemed initially to recover from their parents' divorces, the apparent effects of divorce were subtle but enduring. Many years later, these children appeared to experience difficulties with forming stable romantic relationships and establishing realistic career goals. Yet Wallerstein's study contained a serious flaw that most of the news media overlooked: she didn't include a comparison group of families in which one or both parents have been separated from their children for reasons other than divorce, such as death from accident or disease. As a result, it is unclear whether her findings reflect the consequences of divorce per se as opposed to those of any stressful disruption within the family. Indeed, most rigorously designed studies suggest that the substantial majority of children survive divorce with few or no long-term emotional damage (Hetherington, Cox, & Cox, 1985).

One probable reason why many psychotherapists fall prey to the myth of fragility can be traced to what Patricia Cohen and Jacob Cohen (1984) termed "the clinician's illusion." Most practitioners are exposed selectively to individuals who respond dysfunctionally to psychological stressors. In contrast, they rarely see clients who respond well to stress, because such clients do not typically seek psychological help. As a consequence, many practitioners may conclude erroneously that fragility, not resilience, is the modal response to stress.

Clinical Implications

Practitioners should not assume that their clients are incapable of handling stressors adaptively. They should also avoid implying to their clients that posttraumatic symptoms are virtually inevitable in the face of extreme stressors. Such assertions may inadvertently foster negative expectations that could make such symptoms more likely (Boisvert & Faust, 2002; Sommers & Satel, 2005). Nor should practitioners assume that mild psychological symptoms that emerge in the wake of severe stressors are prognostic of later psychopathology, because many of these symptoms wane over time. In addition, as we will discover later in the chapter (see "The Myth of Catharsis"), there is evidence that interventions administered in the immediate aftermath of traumatic stressors may actually increase the risk of posttraumatic symptoms in some individuals (McNally, Bryant, & Ehlers, 2003). As a consequence, clinicians should not assume that intervening early in the aftermath of stressors is invariably therapeutic. To the contrary, clinicians should typically allow clients to rely on their own preferred coping mechanisms, offering emotional support and problem-solving guidance as needed rather than direct symptomatic treatment.

The Myth of the Critical Importance of Early Experience

In a superb although unjustly neglected book, psychiatrist Joel Paris (2000) outlined a plethora of myths concerning early psychological development. Foremost among them, according to Paris, is the "primacy of early experience," the widespread notion that earlier psychological experiences are necessarily more impactful than later experiences. Similarly, Bruer (1999) discussed "the myth of the first three years," the popular notion that the first few years of life are so critical to later psychological adjustment that even slight deviations from the expected course can result in serious, even disastrous, disturbances in later life.

Much of the popular psychology literature assures us that early patterns of emotional adjustment "lock us" into later patterns. If we start out life troubled, we'll almost surely end up that way. "The child is father to the man," wrote nineteenth-century poet Gerard Manley Hopkins. As Jerome Kagan (1994) reminded us, the myth of infant determinism is among the most pervasive beliefs in all of psychology. Some popular psychology sources take this belief to an extreme. For example, some books claim that even the first few hours after birth are a critical period for bonding (Klaus & Kennell, 1976), and that the separation of the infant from the mother within these first few hours can produce potent negative consequences for emotional adjustment later in life. Some parents have heeded this doubtful advice, taking great pains to spend a large amount of time with their babies almost immediately following birth.

There is no question that early life experiences can sometimes shape later development. Yet there are many reasons to believe that popular psychology has overstated the staying power of these experiences (Bruer, 1999; Clarke & Clarke, 1976; Kagan, 1998). Neuroscience research in animals offers little or no support for the existence of abruptly ending critical periods in humans. Instead, such research suggests that the brain is considerably more plastic (malleable) than advocates of the myth of the critical importance of early experience imply. The brain clearly changes in significant ways in response to environmental inputs throughout childhood, adolescence, and even early adulthood (Greenough, 1997). For instance, neural pruning continues at least through puberty, and perhaps beyond, in humans. Our frontal lobes in particular continue to develop throughout the teenage years into early adulthood (Paris, 2000).

Classic research by Jerome Kagan (1975) examined Guatemalan infants whose parents had reared them in nearly total isolation throughout their first year of life. During this time, the babies lived in small (75 square feet) windowless huts, experienced minimal contact with other adults or children, and few or no toys with which to play. The parents did, this, incidentally, because of a widespread Guatemalan belief in the *mal ojo* ("evil eye"), namely, the superstition that adults who stare directly into the eyes of infants will cause them to become ill and die. These babies were delayed significantly in several of their developmental milestones; for example, they typically did not begin to speak until age two and a half. Yet by adolescence, these children had caught up with typical American middle-class adolescents in their cognitive and social development. Early deprivation often engenders negative psychological effects, to be sure, but these effects are not necessarily long-lasting or irreversible.

As Paris (2000) observed, there is surprisingly little research suggesting that early life experiences, especially negative life experiences (e.g., trauma) of the kind emphasized by some authors, exert more substantial long-term psychological effects than later life experiences. Nevertheless, because early adverse experiences often persist over time and accumulate to produce large effects (Rutter & Rutter, 1993), researchers and clinicians may be fooled into concluding that early events cause more long-term impairment than later events.

Often following from the belief that early psychological experiences are especially formative is the assumption that such experiences must be recalled and processed in psychotherapy for improvement to occur. The assumption that insight into one's early experiences is a prerequisite for progress in psychotherapy dates back at least to Freud, and remains a bedrock component of many psychodynamic therapies. Yet the impressive track record of cognitive-behavioral and behavioral therapies (Chambless & Ollendick, 2001; Wampold, 2001), most of which do not focus on early life experiences, falsifies the claim that insight into one's childhood is a necessary condition for improvement in therapy.

Moreover, as Paul Wachtel (1977) noted, the traditional Freudian view likens repressed memories of early experiences to woolly mammoths "so perfectly preserved after thousands of years that their meat could be eaten by anyone with a taste for such regressive fare" (p. 28). Hence, the Freudian narrative continues, therapists must disinter these memories in their original, pristine form. Yet this view runs counter to several decades of research on the reconstructive nature of memory (Loftus, 1993; Lynn, Lock, Loftus, Krackow, & Lilienfeld, 2003), which strongly suggest that later experiences can alter previous memories. Hence, it is unlikely that most, if any, childhood memories remain perfectly preserved in their original form, only to be "unfrozen" decades later in psychotherapy.

Of course, recalling early experiences in psychotherapy may sometimes be helpful, particularly because doing so can alert us to longstanding and problematic patterns of interpersonal interaction. Nevertheless, it does not necessarily follow that recalling such experiences is inherently therapeutic, nor that such recall per se is helpful in the absence of efforts to alter present maladaptive behavioral patterns (Wachtel, 1977).

Clinical Implications

Therapists need not assume that early psychological experiences will necessarily "lock" clients into enduring patterns of behavior. Nor need they assume that early life events are necessarily more influential than later life events. In this respect, therapists and clients can avoid the pessimism engendered by popular psychology assumptions regarding the primacy of early experience (Paris, 2000). To the extent that early behavioral patterns have persisted into the present, reviewing such patterns in psychotherapy may sometimes be helpful in offering clues to unhealthy interpersonal cycles (Wachtel, 1977). Nevertheless, there is no evidence that recollection of early memories is necessary for behavioral improvement, and considerable evidence to the contrary.

The Myth of Catharsis

Another deeply entrenched notion in popular psychology is the belief that we must "process" or "release" our troubling feelings to get over them. This concept dates at least as far back as Aristotle, who referred to the concept of "catharsis" in his *Poetics* when describing a cleansing of emotional turmoil following a powerful release of feelings.

The myth of catharsis is especially prevalent with respect to one emotion: anger. A great deal of popular psychology literature assures us that "bottling up" our rage is bad for our psychological and emotional health (Tavris, 1989). Indeed, many self-help books inform readers that to conquer their angry feelings they must express their hostility directly. For example, in *Facing the fire: Experiencing and expressing anger appropriately,* John Lee (1993) exhorts angry readers to hit furniture with plastic baseball bats, twist towels, and shatter glass.

A variety of popular psychotherapies are premised on the assumption that venting anger is healthy. Proponents of rage reduction therapy encourage clients to reenact emotionally painful episodes from their pasts, such as child abuse, and to release the angry affects associated with them (Mercer, 2002). Similarly, advocates of primal therapy (often colloquially called "primal scream therapy") instruct clients to discharge the anger associated with painful emotions experienced in infancy, during birth, and even in utero. To do so, clients must yell, shout obscenities, and kick and hit objects (Singer & Lalich, 1996).

One daytime television psychotherapy reality program, "Starting Over," routinely encourages its real life guests to express their anger directly. The events in one episode (aired on October 20, 2005) are typical:

Rhonda ["the life coach"] and Jessica [the client] meet out by the pool. There are bricks laid out beside the pool, and Rhonda tells Jessica to write something she is angry about on each brick and throw them into the pool. Jessica writes on the bricks that she says she is angry at her grandmother for being mean to her mom. She is angry with herself because she was supposed to travel with her mom that day, but decided not to at the last minute. She is angry with politicians, and angry that she had to witness her mom die a violent death. She is also angry at not having control. She throws all the bricks in the pool. Jessica starts crying and says there is no way to escape these things. She says her mother's death was used as justification for war, but that her mom stood for peace. Then Rhonda tells her she will have to go and get each brick. Rhonda says the bricks are submerged just like Jessica's anger is submerged, and asks her whether she is willing to go in and retrieve that anger. Jessica dives in and retrieves the bricks (retrieved from http://startingover. betaparticle.com/ on January 9, 2006).

Nevertheless, a large body of psychological research demonstrates that expressing anger openly is rarely psychologically helpful in the long run, although it may make people feel slightly better in the short run. Indeed, in most cases expressing anger actually results in more, not less, long-term anger, raising serious questions concerning the catharsis hypothesis (Lohr, Olatunji, Baumeister, & Bushman, 2006). In a variety of laboratory studies, participants who engage in verbal, written, or physical anger against an aggressor (for example, in a simulated game involving electric shocks) have been found to experience more hostility than participants who did not (Bushman, 2002; Lewis & Bucher, 1992; Warren & Kurlycheck, 1981). In a classic study, Patterson (1974) found that football players showed a signifi- cant increase, not a decrease, in aggression over the course of the football season. In contrast, a comparison group of physical education students measured over the same time period showed no significant changes in anger. On balance, the research literature suggests that catharsis per se tends to be ineffective for long-term psychological adjustment. The only cases in which the overt expression of anger is helpful are when such expression is accompanied by a positive cognitive restructuring of the meaning of the provoking situation (Littrell, 1998).

Moreover, to the extent that cathartic interventions appear effective, this seeming effectiveness may stem more from others' reactions to clients' emo- tional expression than to catharsis per se. That is, people who express strong negative emotions in individual or group therapies may often be reinforced with support and sympathy by therapists, group members, or both, giving rise to the illusion that catharsis is effective. Indeed, research on encounter group casualties (Lieberman, Yalom, & Miles, 1973) suggests that when cathartic expressions of clients are not followed by supportive reactions in group members, harmful outcomes may follow.

The catharsis hypothesis also found widespread currency in the domain of traumatology. In particular, some forms of early intervention for trauma are premised on the assumption that individuals exposed to extreme stressors must "process" the accompanying emotions lest they develop enduring symptoms of PTSD. For example, critical incident stress debriefing (CISD) is a popular and widely used treatment that was administered to hundreds, perhaps thousands, of traumatized New York victims of the September 11th terrorist attacks (Sommers & Satel, 2005). This treatment is typically performed in group sessions lasting several hours, and is administered shortly following traumatic events. During CISD sessions, trainers encourage trauma-exposed individuals to discuss their emotional reactions to the critical incident. Disturbingly, controlled research indicates that CISD does not prevent PTSD, and is at best ineffective and perhaps even harmful (Bisson, Jenkins, Alexander, & Bannister, 1997; Lilienfeld, 2007). Although the reasons for CISD's possible iatrogenic effects are unclear, this treatment may impede individuals' natural coping responses to stress (McNally et al., 2003).

In addition, research suggests that although "expressive-experiential therapies" (e.g., Gestalt therapy)—namely, those that encourage clients to process and release strong emotions—can be helpful in some circumstances (Wood, Crane, Schaalje, & Law, 2005), such therapies may also be associated with harmful effects in certain clients (Lilienfeld, 2007; Mohr, 1995). These findings, although preliminary and based on only a few studies, dovetail with other research suggesting that cathartic interventions should be used with caution. In particular, therapists should be circumspect about using such techniques when they provoke powerful negative emotions without resolving them adequately.

Clinical Implications

Therapists should typically avoid using cathartic interventions with clients, especially when these interventions are not accompanied by a healthy cognitive restructuring of the situation at hand. Cathartic interventions allow people to "blow off steam" and may therefore help them to feel slightly better in the short term, but they typically produce a paradoxical increase in long-term anger. Therapists should instead help clients to acquire behavioral and coping skills that help them to alter or reconceptualize ongoing anger-provoking situations.

The Myth of Unrealized Potential

One of the most pervasive beliefs in the popular psychology industry is the notion that our brains possess an enormous amount of unrealized mental potential. In many cases, this belief takes the form that most of us use only a small amount, such as 10%, of our brain capacity. Admittedly, few of us would turn down a hefty hike in brain power if it were attainable. Always on the lookout for a "feel-good" story, the media has played a big part in keeping this optimistic myth alive. Moreover, a great deal of advertising copy for self-improvement products continues to refer to the 10% myth as fact. Such advertisements help to fuel the popularity of various "gizmos" designed to improve brain capacity, such as "brain tuners" that purport to synchronize activity in various brain regions (Beyerstein, 1999).

Nevertheless, an expert panel convened by the U.S. National Research Council surveyed an assortment of commercial offerings of the "brain booster" genre and concluded that in this, as with other miraculous self-improvement claims, there's no good substitute for hard work and effort when it comes to getting ahead in life (Beyerstein, 1999; Druckman & Swets, 1988). This panel found scant evidence for the efficacy of brain tuners and related techniques. Nor is there much evidence that popular techniques designed to increase the brain's alpha waves produce heightened states of relaxation or other mental health benefits (Beyerstein, 1990; Druckman & Bjork, 1994).

Even more far-fetched are the widely available offerings of New Age entrepreneurs who propose to hone the psychic skills we allegedly all possess using various devices. The self-proclaimed psychic Uri Geller (1996) asserted that "In fact, most of us use only about 10 percent of our brains, if that." Promoters like Geller claim that it's obvious that paranormal powers reside in the 90% of the brain that the rest of us forced to subsist on the drudgelike 10% have not yet been taught to use.

Yet there are ample reasons to doubt the claim that 90% of the average brain lies perpetually silent. Plentiful evidence from clinical neurology and neuropsychology reveals that losing far less than 90% of the brain to accident or disease typically has disastrous consequences for intellectual functioning. Moreover, decades of research on individuals who have experienced head injuries reveal that there seems to be no area of the brain that can be destroyed by strokes or head trauma without leaving the patient with major functional deficits (Kolb & Whishaw, 2003; Sacks, 1985).

Two other well-established principles of neuroscience also create problems for the 10% myth. Regions of the brain that are unused because of injuries or disease tend to do one of two things. They either wither away, or "degenerate," as neuroscientists put it, or they are taken over by nearby areas that on the lookout for unused territory to colonize for their own purposes. Either way, perfectly good, unused brain tissue is unlikely to remain on the sidelines for long.

All told, the foregoing suggests that there's no cerebral spare tire waiting to be mounted, with a little help from the self-improvement industrial complex. So, if the 10-percent myth is so poorly supported, how did it arise? Attempts to track down the origins of this myth haven't uncovered any smoking guns, but a few tantalizing clues have emerged (Beyerstein, 1999). One stream leads back to the pioneering American psychologist William James in the late nineteenth and early twentieth centuries. In one of his writings for the general public, James stated that he doubted that the average person achieves more than about ten percent of his or her *potential*. James always talked in terms of under-developed potential, never relating it to a specific amount of gray matter engaged. A generation of "positive thinking" gurus who followed were not so careful, however, and gradually "10 percent of our capacity" morphed into "10 percent of our brain" (Beyerstein, 1999). The pervasiveness of the ten-percent myth probably also stems in part from popular authors' misunder-standing of scientific papers by early brain researchers. For example, in calling a huge percentage of the human cerebral hemispheres "silent cortex," early investigators may have created the mistaken impression that what is now referred to as "association cortex" had no function. Of course, what was once called "silent cortex" is vitally important for our ability to use language, think abstractly, and engage in intricate sensory-motor tasks. In a similar vein, early researchers' appropriately modest admissions that they didn't know what 90 percent of the brain was doing may have fostered the widespread miscon-ception that it does nothing.

The 10% percent myth has undoubtedly motivated many people to strive for greater creativity and productivity in their lives, which is hardly a bad thing. The comfort, encouragement, and hope that it has generated probably help to explain its longevity. But, as Carl Sagan (1995) reminded us, if something sounds too good to be true, it probably is.

Clinical Implications

If necessary, therapists should be prepared to disabuse clients of the notion that they possess vast reservoirs of untapped mental potential. That is not to imply that intelligent clients who are not recognizing their full mental potential cannot often achieve more; in many cases they can. But the best means of realizing one's full intellectual capacity is to work harder and focus on acquiring new cognitive skills. Despite what much of popular psychology tells us, there are few, if any, quick fixes.

The Myth of Self-Esteem

In 1986, the state of California commissioned a task force to examine the merits of boosting the self-esteem of its citizenry. This task force was initiated on the advice of state assemblyman John Vasconcellos, who was convinced that self-esteem was an essential ingredient for good mental health. In arguing for the creation of this $245,000-a-year task force, Vasconcellos went so far as to argue that increasing Californians' self-esteem would help to balance the state's budget. After several years of research, the efforts of this task force culminated in a book (Mecca, Smelser, & Vasconcellos, 1989).

The conclusions of the book were oddly self-contradictory (Dawes, 1994). The book's introduction asserts that "Low self-esteem is the causally prior factor in individuals (sic) seeking out kinds of behavior that become social problems ... We all know this to be true." Yet the book's conclusions paint a strikingly different story, as acknowledged by the editor: "One of the disappointing aspects of every chapter in this volume ... is how low the association between self-esteem and its consequences are in the research to date" (p. 15). As the editor observed correctly, "If the association between self-esteem and behavior is often reported to be weak, even less can be said for the causal relationship between the two" (p. 15).

Yet the notion that self-esteem is important, even vital, to psychological health has long been a virtual mantra of popular psychology. In his best-selling book, *The Six Pillars of Self-Esteem,* self-esteem guru Nathaniel Brandon insisted that one "cannot think of a single psychological problem—from anxiety and depression, to fear of intimacy or of success, to spouse battery or child molestation—that is not traceable to the problem of low self-esteem" (Branden, 1994, p. 12).

A search of Amazon.com reveals several dozen books, CDs, and other products with "self-esteem" in their titles, including *The Self-Esteem Workbook, Ten Days to Self-Esteem, How to Raise Your Self-Esteem, Breaking the Chain of Low Self-Esteem,* and *The Complete Self-Esteem Hypnosis Program.* On this Web site, you can even purchase a bright yellow self-esteem bowl for your kitchen, replete with such self-affirming phrases as "I'm talented," I'm good looking," and "I rule!"

Moreover, the National Association for Self-Esteem claims that: "A close relationship has been documented between low self-esteem and such problems as violence, alcoholism, drug abuse, eating disorders, school dropouts, teenage pregnancy, suicide, and low academic achievement" (Reasoner, 1994, see http://www.more-selfesteem.com/selfesteemexercise. htm).

So what does the research concerning the relations between self-esteem and psychological adjustment indicate? In a comprehensive review of over 15,000 published studies, Baumeister, Campbell, Krueger, and Vohs (2003) unearthed surprisingly scant evidence that self-esteem is associated with either interpersonal success or academic performance. Nor, they found, is self-esteem consistently related to smoking, alcohol abuse, or drug abuse (Baumeister et al., 2003). Moreover, contrary to popular misconception, low self-esteem is not necessarily linked to a heightened risk of violence. To the contrary, a subset of people with high self-esteem, namely narcissistic individuals, appear to be at elevated risk for violence when provoked by threats to their self-concept (Baumeister, 2001; Bushman & Baumeister, 1998; Cale & Lilienfeld, 2006).

Nevertheless, Baumeister and colleagues did find that self-esteem is positively associated with greater *(a)* initiative and persistence, that is, a willingness to attempt tasks and to persevere when frustrations arise, and *(b)* happiness and emotional resilience. Even here, however, even these findings are only correlational and do not demonstrate a direct causal link between self-esteem and these outcomes. Instead, the associations could be attributable to a third variable, such as high levels of positive emotionality, that is, a tendency to experience positive affects of many kinds (Tellegen & Waller, in press). Alternatively, the causal arrow in these cases may be reversed; for example, people who successfully complete difficult tasks while overcoming obstacles may end up with higher self-esteem as a consequence (Pajares & Schunk, 2001).

Finally, Baumeister et al. found that self-esteem is related to a tendency to perceive oneself more positively than others do. High self-esteem individuals tend to regard themselves as more intelligent, physically attractive, and likable than others. Yet high self-esteem individuals score no higher than do other individuals on relatively objective measures of intelligence, attractiveness, and popularity (Baumeister et al., 2003).

In sum, there is scant evidence that high self-esteem is necessary for positive psychological adjustment, although it may predispose individuals to somewhat greater enthusiasm and happiness. High self-esteem also tends to lead people to think more highly of themselves than is objectively warranted.

Clinical Implications

In general, clinicians should avoid making the attainment of high self-esteem per se a target of treatment. They should also avoid implying to their clients that they cannot achieve important life goals or adequate emotional adjustment without high self-esteem. Instead, in many cases high self-esteem may be more of an outcome than a cause of life successes. For clients whose self-esteem is low because of poor academic achievement, unsuccessful work performance, or failed interpersonal relationships, treatment should typically focus on providing clients with the cognitive and behavioral skills needed to remediate these deficits. In such cases, increases in self-esteem will often follow.

Conclusion

As we have discovered, the popular psychology industry is a sprawling mixture of information and misinformation. Regrettably, much of this industry has perpetuated widespread myths regarding human nature and potential, many of which have the potential to influence clients' and practitioners' approaches to psychotherapy.

Fortunately, most of the "news" imparted by this chapter is positive. Most clients are more resilient than most of the popular psychology literature gives them credit for, and clients need not fear that adverse childhood experiences will canalize them inevitably into longstanding patterns of maladjustment. Although the other lessons offered by this chapter may not seem quite as positive, they too have a positive side.

In particular, clients need not typically worry about expressing powerful negative emotions if they do not feel ready to do so, and many may be able to cope with these emotions on their own. Clients need not worry about seeking out or spending money on quick fixes for realizing their underdeveloped intellectual potential. And clients with self-esteem problems need not be concerned that they cannot attain at least a significant measure of happiness or achieve many of their significant life goals.

By aligning their beliefs more closely with scientific evidence, psychotherapists and their clients can develop more realistic and rational treatment goals, and make more informed decisions about treatment planning. Scientific and popular psychology need not be alien worlds (Lilienfeld, 1998), as there is no inherent reason why the best available scientific knowledge regarding human behavior cannot be disseminated to the general public. We view this chapter as a modest, but helpful, step in that direction.

REFERENCES

Arkowitz, H., & Lilienfeld, S. O. (2006). Do self-help books help? *Scientific American Mind*, 17 (5), 90–91.

Baumeister, R. F. (2001). Violent pride. *Scientific American*, 284 (4), 96–101.

Baumeister, R. F., Campbell, J. D., Krueger, J. I., & Vohs, K. D. (2003). Does high self-esteem cause better performance, interpersonal success, happiness, or healthier lifestyles? *Psychological Science in the Public Interest, 4,* 1–44.

Beyerstein, B. L. (1999) Pseudoscience and the brain: Tuners and tonics for aspiring superhumans. In, S. Della Sala (Ed.), *Mind myths: Exploring popular assumptions about the mind and brain* (pp. 59–82). Chichester, UK: John Wiley and Sons.

Beyerstein, B. L., & Beyerstein, D. F. (Eds.). (1992). *The write stuff: Evaluations of graphology—The study of handwriting analysis.* Amherst, NY: Prometheus.

Bisson, J., Jenkins, P., Alexander, J., & Bannister, C. (1997) Randomised controlled trial of psychological debriefing for victims of acute burn trauma. *British Journal of Psychiatry, 171* 78–81.

Boisvert, C. M., & Faust, D. (2002). Iatrogenic symptoms in psychotherapy: A theoretical exploration of the potential impact of labels, language, and belief systems. *American Journal of Psychotherapy, 56,* 244–259.

Bonanno, G. A. (2004). Loss, trauma, and human resilience: Have we underestimated the human capacity to thrive after extremely aversive events? *American Psychologist, 59,* 20–28.

Bonanno, G. A. (2005). Resilience in the face of potential trauma. *Current Directions in Psychological Science, 14,* 135–138.

Boneau, C. A. (1990). Psychological literacy: A first approximation. *American Psychologist, 47,* 891–900.

Branden, T. (1994). *The six pillars of self-esteem.* New York: Bantam Books.

Bruer, J. T. (1999). *The myth of the first three years: A new understanding of brain development and lifelong learning.* New York: Free Press.

Bushman, B. J. (2002). Does venting anger feed or extinguish the flame? Catharsis, rumination, distraction, anger, and aggressive responding. *Personality and Social Psychology Bulletin, 28,* 724–731.

Bushman, B. J., & Baumeister, R. F. (1998). Threatened egotism, narcissism, self-esteem, and direct and displaced aggression: Does self-love or self-hate lead to violence? *Journal of Personality and Social Psychology, 75,* 219–229.

Cale, E. M., & Lilienfeld, S. O. (2006). Psychopathy factors and risk for aggressive behavior: A test of the "threatened egotism" hypothesis. *Law and Human Behavior, 30,* 51–74.

Chambless, D. L., & Ollendick, T. H. (2001). Empirically supported psychological interventions: Controversies and evidence. *Annual Review of Psychology, 52,* 685–716.

Clarke, A. M., & Clarke, A. D. B. (1976). *Early experience: Myth and evidence.* New York: Free Press.

Cohen, P., & Cohen, J. (1984). The clinician's illusion. *Archives of General Psychiatry, 41,* 1178–1182.

Cromer, A. (1993). *Uncommon sense: The heretical nature of science.* New York: Oxford University Press.

Dawes, R. M. (1994). *House of cards: Psychology and psychotherapy built on myth.* New York: Free Press.

Della Salla, S. (Ed.). (2000). *Mind myths: Exploring popular assumptions about the mind and brain*. New York: John Wiley & Sons.

Della Salla, S. (Ed.). (2006). *Tall tales about the brain*. New York: Oxford University Press.

Druckman, D., & Bjork, R. J. (Eds.). (1994). *Learning, remembering, believing: Enhancing human performance*. Washington, DC: National Academy Press.

Druckman, D., & Swets. J. A., (Eds). (1988) *Enhancing human performance: issues, theories and techniques*. Washington, DC: National Academy Press.

Ellis, A. E. (2004). *The road to tolerance: The philosophy of rational-emotive behavior therapy*. Amherst, NY: Prometheus Books.

Frances, A., & First, M. B. (2000). *Am I ok? A layman's guide to the psychiatrist's bible*. New York: Scribner.

Galea, S., et al. (2002). Psychological sequelae of the September 11 terrorist attacks in New York City. *New England Journal of Medicine, 346,* 982–987.

Gardner, R. M., & Dalsing, S. (1986). Misconceptions about psychology among college students. *Teaching of Psychology, 13,* 32–34.

Gardner, R. M., & Hund, R. M. (1983). Misconceptions of psychology among academicians. *Teaching of Psychology, 10,* 20–22.

Garmezy, N. (1991). Resiliency and vulnerability to adverse developmental outcomes associated with poverty. *American Behavioral Scientist, 34,* 416–430.

Geller, U. (1996). *Uri Geller's mind power kit*. New York: Penguin USA.

Gilovich, T. (1991). *How we know what isn't so: The fallibility of human reason in everyday life*. New York: Free Press.

Greenough, W. T. (1997). We can't just focus on the first three years. *American Psychological Association Monitor on Psychology, 28,* 19.

Herbert, J. D., Sharp, I. R., & Gaudiano, B. A. (2002). Separating fact from fiction in the etiology and treatment of autism: A scientific review of the evidence. *Scientific Review of Mental Health Practice, 1,* 23–43.

Hetherington, E. M., Cox, M., & Cox, R. (1985). The long-term effects of divorce and remarriage on the adjustment of children. *Journal of the American Academy of Child Psychiatry, 24,* 518–530.

Kagan, J. (1975). Resilience in cognitive development. *Ethos, 2,* 231247.

Kagan, J. (1998). *Three seductive ideas*. Cambridge, MA: Harvard University Press.

Klaus, M. H. & Kennell, J. H. (1976). *Maternal-infant bonding*. St. Louis, MO: Mosby.

Kolb, B., & Whishaw, I. Q. (2003) *Fundamentals of human neuropsychology* (5th ed). New York: Worth Publishers.

Lamal, P. A. (1979). College students' common beliefs about psychology. *Teaching of Psychology, 6,* 155–158.

Lee, J. (1993). *Facing the fire: Experiencing and expressing anger appropriately*. New York: Bantam.

Levenson, R. W. (2005). Desperately seeking Dr. Phil. *Association for Psychological Science Observer, 18,* 2–3.

Lewis, A. W., & Bucher, A. M. (1992). Anger, catharsis, the reformulated frustration-aggression hypothesis, and health consequences. *Psychotherapy, 29,* 385–393.

Lieberman, M. A., Yalom, I. D., & Miles, M. B. (1973). *Encounter groups: First facts.* New York: Basic Books.

Lilienfeld, S. O. (1998). Pseudoscience in contemporary clinical psychology: What it is and what we can do about it. *Clinical Psychologist, 51,* 3–9.

Lilienfeld, S. O. (2005). Challenging mind myths in introductory psychology courses. *Psychology Teacher Network, 15*(3), 1, 4, 6.

Lilienfeld, S. O. (2007). Psychological treatments that cause harm. *Perspectives on Psychological Science, 2,* 53–70.

Lilienfeld, S. O., & Lynn, S. J. (2002). Multiple personality disorder. In M. Shermer (Ed.), *The skeptic encyclopedia of pseudoscience* (pp. 146–151). Santa Barbara, CA: ABC-CLIO, Inc.

Lilienfeld, S. O., Lynn, S. J., Ruscio, J.P., & Beyerstein, B. L. (in press). *The fifty great myths of popular psychology: Shattering commonplace assumptions about human nature.* New York: Blackwell.

Lilienfeld, S. O., Lynn, S. J., & Lohr, J. M. (2003). *Science and pseudoscience in clinical psychology.* New York: Guilford.

Lilienfeld, S. O., Lynn, S. J., Namy, L., & Woolf, N. (2009). *Psychology: From inquiry to understanding.* Boston: Allyn & Bacon.

Lilienfeld, S. O., Wood, J. M., & Garb, H. N. (2000). The scientific status of projective techniques. *Psychological Science in the Public Interest, 1,* 27–66.

Littrell, J. (1998). Is the reexperience of painful emotion therapeutic? *Clinical Psychology Review, 18,* 71–102.

Loftus, E. F. (1993). The reality of repressed memories. *American Psychologist, 48,* 518–537.

Logue, M. B., Sher, K. J., & Frensch, P. A. (1992). Purported characteristics of adult children of alcoholics: A possible "Barnum effect." *Professional Psychology: Research and Practice, 23,* 226–232.

Lohr, J. M., Olatunji, B. O., Baumeister, R. F., & Bushman, B. J. (2006). The psychology of anger venting and empirically supported alternatives that do no harm. *Scientific Review of Mental Health Practice, 4,* 54–65.

Lykken, D. T. (1998). *A tremor in the blood: Uses and abuses of the lie detector* (2nd ed). New York: Plenum.

Lynn, S. J., Lock, T., Loftus, E., Krackow, E., & Lilienfeld, S. O. (2003). The remembrance of things past: Problematic memory recovery techniques in psychotherapy. In S. O. Lilienfeld, S. J. Lynn, & J. M. Lohr (Eds.), *Science and pseudoscience in clinical psychology* (pp. 205–239). New York: Guilford.

Masten, A. (2001). Ordinary magic: Resilience processes in development. *American Psychologist, 56,* 227–238.

McCutcheon, L. E. (1991). A new test of misconceptions about psychology. *Psychological Reports, 68,* 647–653.

McNally, R. J., Bryant, R. A., & Ehlers, A. (2003). Does early psychological intervention promote recovery from posttraumatic stress? *Psychological Science in the Public Interest, 4,* 45–79.

Mecca, A. M., Smelser, N. J., & Vasconcellos, J. (Eds.). (1989). *The social importance of self-esteem.* Berkeley, CA: University of California Press.

Meehl, P. E. (1973). Why I do not attend case conferences. In P. E. Meehl (Ed.), *Psychodiagnosis: Selected papers* (pp. 225–302). Minneapolis: University of Minnesota Press.

Mercer, J. (2002). Attachment therapy: A treatment without empirical support. *Scientific Review of Mental Health Practice, 1*, 9–16.

Miller, G. A. (1969). Psychology as a means of promoting human welfare. *American Psychologist, 24*, 1063–1075.

Mohr, D. C. (1995). Negative outcome in psychotherapy: A critical review. *Clinical Psychology: Science and Practice, 2*, 1–27.

Myers, D. G. (2002). *Intuition: Its powers and perils.* New Haven, CT: Yale University Press.

Nash, M. R. (2001, July). The truth and the hype of hypnosis. *Scientific American, 285*, 46–55.

Nisbett, R., & Wilson, T. (1977). Telling more than we can know: Verbal reports on mental processes. *Psychological Review, 84*, 231–259.

Olatunji, B. O., Parker, L. M., & Lohr, J. M. (2006). Pseudoscience in contemporary clinical psychology: Professional issues and implications. *Scientific Review of Mental Health Practice, 4*, 19–36.

Ozer, J., Best, S. R., Lipsey, T. L., & Weiss, D. S. (2003). Predictors of posttraumatic stress disorder and symptoms in adults: A meta-analysis, *Psychological Bulletin, 129*, 52–73.

Pajares, F., & Schunk, D. H. (2001). Self-beliefs and school success: Self-efficacy, self-concept, and school achievement. In R. Riding & S. Rayner (Eds.), *Perception* (pp. 239–266). London: Ablex Publishing.

Paris, J. (2000). *Myths of childhood.* New York: Brunner/Mazel.

Patterson, A. H. (1974). Hostility catharsis: A naturalistic quasi-experiment. *Personality and Social Psychology Bulletin, 1*, 195–197.

Reasoner, R. (1994). *Building self-esteem: An elementary schools'.administrators guide.* Consulting Psychologists Press: Palo Alto, CA.

Rosen, G. M. (1993). Self-help or hype? Comments on psychology's failure to advance self-care. *Professional Psychology: Research and Practice, 24*, 340–345.

Rosen, G. M., & Lilienfeld, S. O. (2008). Posttraumatic stress disorder: An empirical analysis of core assumptions. *Clinical Psychology Review, 28*, 837–868.

Rutter, M., & Rutter, M. (1993). *Developing minds: Challenge and continuity across the life span.* New York: Harper Collins.

Sacks, O. (1985). *The man who mistook his wife for a hat and other clinical tales.* New York: Simon & Schuster/Summit.

Sagan, C. (1995). *The demon-haunted world: Science as a candle in the dark.* New York: Random House.

Schlenger, W. E., et al. (2002). Psychological reactions to terrorist attacks: Findings from the National Study of Americans' Reactions to September 11. *Journal of the American Medical Association, 288*, 581–588.

Schuster, M. A., et al. (2001). A national survey of stress reactions after the September 11, 2001, terrorist attacks. *New England Journal of Medicine, 345*, 1507–1512.

Seligman, M. (1994). *What you can change and what you can't.* New York: Knopf.

Singer, M. T., & Lalich, J. (1996). *Crazy therapies: What are they? Do they work?* San Francisco: Jossey-Bass.

Sommers, C. H., & Satel, S. L. (2005). One nation under therapy: How the helping culture is eroding self-reliance. New York: St. Martin's Press.

Tavris, C. (1989). *Anger: The misunderstood emotion* (Rev. ed.). New York: Touchstone.

Taylor, A. J., & Kowalski, P. (2004). Naïve psychological science: The prevalence, strength, and sources of misconceptions. *Psychological Record, 54*, 15–25.

Tellegen, A., & Waller, N.G. (in press). *Exploring personality through test construction: Development of the Multidimensional Personality Questionnaire.* Minneapolis, MN: University of Minnesota Press.

Teplin, L. A. (1985). The criminality of the mentally ill: A dangerous misconception. *American Journal of Psychiatry, 142,* 593–599.

Terr, L. C. (1988). What happens to early memories of trauma? A study of twenty children under age five at the time of documented traumatic events. *Journal of the American Academy of Child and Adolescent Psychiatry, 27,* 96–104.

Tversky, A., & Kahneman, D. (1974). Judgments under uncertainty: Heuristics and biases. *Science, 185,* 1124–1131.

Vaughan, E. D. (1977). Misconceptions about psychology among introductory psychology students. *Teaching of Psychology, 4,* 138–141.

Wachtel, P. L. (1977). *Psychoanalysis and behavior therapy: Toward an integration.* New York: Basic Books.

Wahl, O. (1995). *Media madness: Public images of mental illness.* Piscataway, NJ: Rutgers University Press.

Wallerstein, J. (1989). *Second chances: Men, women, and children a decade after divorce.* New York: Ticknor and Fields.

Wampold, B. E. (2001). *The great psychotherapy debate: Model, methods, and findings.* Mahwah, NJ: Lawrence Erlbaum Associates.

Warren R., & Kurlycheck, R. (1981). Treatment of maladaptive anger and aggression: Catharsis versus behavior therapy. *Corrective and Social Psychiatry, 27,* 135–139.

Watkins, C. E., Campbell, V. L., Nieberding, R., & Hallmark, R. (1995). Contemporary practice of psychological assessment by clinical psychologists. *Professional Psychology: Research and Practice, 26,* 54–60.

Widom, C. S. (1989). The cycle of violence. *Science, 244,* 160–166.

Williams, W. M., & Ceci, S. (1998). *Escaping the advice trap: 59 tough relationship problems solved by the experts.* Kansas City, MO: Andrews McMeel Publishing.

Wilson, N. (2003). Commercializing mental health issues: Entertainment, advertising, and psychological advice. In S. O. Lilienfeld, S. J. Lynn, & J. M. Lohr (Eds.), *Science and pseudoscience in clinical psychology* (pp. 425–459). New York: Guilford.

Wilson, L., Greene, E., & Loftus, E. F. (1986). Beliefs about forensic hypnosis. *International Journal of Clinical and Experimental Hypnosis, 34,* 110–121.

Wolpert, L. (1994). *The unnatural nature of science.* Cambridge, MA: Harvard University Press.

Wood, N. D., Crane, R. C., Schaalje, G. B., & Law, D. D. (2005). What works for whom: A meta-analytic review of marital and couples therapy in reference to marital distress. *American Journal of Family Therapy, 33,* 273–287.

PART VI

A Look to the Future

16

A Summary and a New Research Agenda for Rational-Emotive and Cognitive-Behavior Therapy

Daniel David and Steven Jay Lynn

The Current State of REBT Research and Practice: A Summary

This final chapter will provide an integrative summary of what is known and what is not known regarding irrational and rational beliefs, and proffer suggestions and recommendations for future research, clinical work, and theory construction.

Irrational Beliefs

WHAT WE KNOW.

1. Irrational beliefs—nonlogical, nonempirical, and/or nonpragmatic beliefs—are important pathogenetic mechanisms involved in clinical conditions.
2. A change in irrational beliefs is accompanied by reductions in a variety of clinical conditions, including anxiety and depression.
3. Irrational beliefs are a particular type of appraisal, best construed as so-called hot cognitions.
4. DEM (demandingness) seems to be an irrational primary appraisal mechanism, whereas AWF (awfulizing), LFT

(low frustration tolerance), and GE/SD (global evaluation/self-downing) are irrational secondary appraisal mechanisms.

5. DEM and GE/SD seem to be represented in the cognitive system as schemata, whereas AWF and LFT are represented as propositional networks.

6. During activating events, irrational beliefs generate (and then appraise) both distorted cold cognitions (descriptions and inferences), and various behavioral, emotional, and physiological concomitants and consequences.

7. Irrational beliefs are associated with dysfunctional feelings and behaviors.

WHAT WE DO NOT KNOW.

1. To what extent are rational beliefs biologically determined, and to what extent they are they socially and culturally influenced? Are irrational beliefs the product of evolutionary designs? An approach informed by evolutionary psychology is fundamental to resolving these questions.

2. What is the specific pattern of irrational beliefs in various disorders? This must be identified in conjunction with particular cold cognitions, whose specificity for various clinical conditions has been identified (see David & Szentagotai, 2006). Some preliminary data are available on this topic (e.g., DEM and LFT in anger; DEM and GE/SD in depressed mood; DEM and AWF in anxiety), but a coherent research program to address this question is of fundamental importance.

3. Are irrational beliefs really changed during cognitive restructuring, or do such interventions enhance the corresponding rational beliefs?

As we can see, most of what we know about irrational beliefs is at the computational (what their role is) and algorithmic-representational (how this role is carried out, step by step) levels. However, we know practically nothing about irrational beliefs at the implementational (biological) level. Future studies should be focused on the biological level in order to elucidate the relationship between REBT as a theory of psychopathology and biological psychiatry, and the relationships between REBT as an intervention and pharmacotherapy. For example, an interesting empirical question is whether cold cognitions are mainly related to the prefrontal cortex whereas irrational beliefs are related to both the prefrontal cortex and the amygdala. Given the fact that irrational beliefs are highly affective and are thought to have a strong biological (and even evolutionary) basis, this hypothesis has important implications for theory and practice (e.g., what techniques are useful for cognitive restructuring) and warrants serious consideration.

Rational Beliefs

WHAT WE KNOW.

1. Rational beliefs—logical, empirical, and/or pragmatic beliefs—are not bipolar opposites of irrational beliefs; rather, they refer to a separate construct.
2. Rational beliefs are a particular type of appraisal.
3. PRE (preferences) seems to be a rational primary appraisal mechanism, whereas non-AWF, FT (frustration tolerance), and non-GE/SD are rational secondary appraisal mechanisms.
4. During activating events, rational beliefs generate both nondistorted cold cognitions (descriptions and inferences) and various behavioral, emotional, and physiological concomitants and consequences.
5. Rational beliefs are associated with functional feelings and behaviors.

WHAT WE DO NOT KNOW.

1. What is the role of rational beliefs in health promotion and the prevention of disorders?
2. To what extent are rational beliefs biologically determined, and to what extent are they socially and cultural influenced? Are rational beliefs an evolutionary design? An approach informed by evolutionary psychology is of fundamental importance.

As we can see, we do no know enough about rational beliefs at the computational and algorithmic-representational levels. Obviously, we know practically nothing about them at the implementational level. Future studies should be focused on all these levels, in order to promote a better understanding of the role of rational beliefs in health promotion and the prevention of mental disorders, their relapse and recurrence.

A New Research Agenda for REBT

Rational-emotive behavior therapy (REBT) has been developed and mainly guided by programmatic research that both synthesized extant knowledge and suggested new ideas and avenues of research. Although there are, of course, isolated studies related to REBT that are not part of this trend, programmatic research is the core of REBT research. This strategy was made possible, in part, by the organization of REBT on a worldwide basis.

The Albert Ellis Institute is an influential center with many affiliates in different countries. Several hundred fellows and supervisors in REBT are members of the institute. An obvious advantage of centralized organization is that it facilitates systematic research by mobilizing large numbers of researchers. From time to time the results of this research are summarized and new agendas are developed. However, a downside of centralized organization is that aspects of programmatic research emanating from the institute and its affiliates often were challenged, casting the entire systematic enterprise in a negative light. Indeed, in the heyday of criticism of psychotherapy research in general and cognitive-behavioral psychotherapy in particular, REBT often received what might be construed as a disproportionate share of scrutiny. Nevertheless, as this volume indicates, research on irrational and rational beliefs has repeatedly illustrated the value of these constructs in understanding psychopathology and influencing a variety of psychological and behavioral responses.

The product of REBT programmatic research can be summarized in three types of publications. The first type is concerned with critical appraisals of theory and/or practice and establishing new research agendas. The publication of Ellis's article (1956) and book (1958) set the first agenda for programmatic research. Ellis (1973, 1987), Bernard and DiGiuseppe (1989), and David (2003) have critically appraised both the theory and practice of REBT, formulating methodological and technical refinements and new lines of research. Also, the special issue of the *Journal of Rational-Emotive & Cognitive-Behavior Therapy* in 1996, entitled "Rational emotive behavior therapy: Critiques from within" was a major vehicle for these efforts.

A second set of publications is represented by qualitative meta-analyses summarizing findings related to the efficacy and effectiveness of REBT. The main qualitative meta-analyses include those of Ellis (1973), DiGiuseppe, Miller, and Trexler, (1977), Zettle and Hayes, (1980), Haaga and Davidson (1989a; 1989b), and David, Szentagotai, Kallay, and Macavei (2005). These reviews have underlined the efficacy and effectiveness of REBT, and revealed methodological weaknesses in the available literature and new directions for research.

A third category of publications is represented by quantitative meta-analyses that have documented the efficacy and effectiveness of REBT. REBT studies have been often included in large-scale psychotherapy (e.g., Smith & Glass, 1977) and/or cognitive-behavioral therapy meta-analyses (e.g., Wampold, Mondin, Moody, et al., 1997). However, two major quantitative meta-analyses are specifically related to REBT (Lyons & Woods, 1991; Engels, Garnefski, & Diekstra, 1993), and several more specific (e.g., REBT for children; Gonzales, Nelson, Gutkin, et al., 2004) meta-analyses have been conducted. All of the reviews determined that the effect sizes associated with

REBT range from medium to a large in producing treatment gains. Again, these reviews succeeded in identifying methodological problems and formulating future lines of research.

A legitimate question to ask is: What happens next? We suggest that the agenda for REBT research should be organized at two levels: *(1)* theory development and *(2)* increasing the efficacy/effectiveness of REBT's clinical applications.

Theory Development

At a theoretical level, the following lines of research are well worth pursuing:

SPECIFIC MODELS FOR PSYCHOPATHOLOGY. REBT should develop specific etio-pathogenetic (causal) models for particular disorders. REBT has often been accused of being a monolithic therapy, focused mainly on a few beliefs and not flexible enough to provide differentiated accounts of cognitive processes underlying different forms of psychopathology. It is now time for rigorous research to carefully evaluate claims made by REBT and take the model in new directions. One possibility (see David et al., 2005) is to investigate how irrational beliefs interact to generate specific manifestations of psychopathology. Another option is to explicitly assume a reductionistic approach, similar to that sometimes adopted in neurosciences, in which various forms of psychopathology are related to the same few neurotransmitters and their interactions. In keeping with the latter position (see David et al., 2002), specific interactions between irrational beliefs generate particular cold cognitions (e.g., automatic thoughts) that are then involved in specific types of psychopathology.

IMPLEMENTATIONAL LEVEL ANALYSIS. Implementational level analyses address two main questions: *(1)* How are the psychological mechanisms described by REBT represented in the brain? and *(2)* What are the neurobiological consequences of REBT interventions? We were unable to locate a single study investigating these issues, which could inform clinical strategies in terms of managing specific conditions by addressing when to use psychotherapy, medication, or a combination of the two interventions. As we hypothesized in Chapter 1, it is possible that irrational beliefs are implemented prefrontally and subcortically (e.g., amygdala), whereas rational beliefs are implmented mainly prefrontally. Future studies should investigate how rational and irrational beliefs are represented in the brain, which will have important implications for the cognitive theory of emotions and for clinical practice.

UNCONSCIOUS INFORMATION PROCESSING. Mahoney (1993) was premature in claiming that the construct of the cognitive unconscious had largely penetrated theories of psychopathology theories in using the example of automatic thoughts that influence behavioral and emotional consequences without awareness. However, Mahoney was referring a functional view of the unconscious, in which information functions unconsciously, but can become conscious under specific conditions. Such unconscious functioning can be due to automatization, defense mechanisms, and so forth. However, our behaviors and feelings are influenced greatly by information processing that is structurally unconscious (David & Szentagotai, 2006). This is, coded in our cognitive system in such a way that renders it inaccessible to consciousness. REBT needs to explicitly assimilate recent research and structural theories of unconscious information processing into an expanded version of the ABC model in order to be in a position to explain, predict, and change a wide range of beliefs, feelings, and behaviors.

EVOLUTIONARY PSYCHOLOGY. Evolutionary psychology is one of the main forces in contemporary psychology. It challenges conventional knowledge and creates new opportunities for understanding adaptation and the diverse characteristics of human nature. As far as psychopathology is concerned, evolutionary psychology has produced several influential theories pertinent to major clinical problems (e.g., depression and anxiety) (see Dickinson & Eva, 2006; Watson & Andrews, 2002). REBT should continue to incorporate new ideas from emerging evolutionary science to fortify the cognitive theory of REBT, and extend tests of the validity and practical implications of evolutionary theory for REBT to the laboratory; this should be undertaken in conjunction with rigorous analyses at the implementational level (see above).

Increasing the Efficacy/Effectiveness of REBT's Clinical Applications

At a practical level, the REBT agenda should include the following lines of research.

EFFICACY AND EFFECTIVENESS RESEARCH. Two important meta-analyses (Engels, Garnefski, Diekstra, 1993; Lyons & Woods, 1991) have shown that REBT is probably an efficacious form of psychotherapy. However, clinical studies should be improved in the following directions:

- Clearly delineating efficacy (how REBT works in clinical trials) from effectiveness (how REBT works in real life settings) in studies of REBT, as both efficacy and effectiveness research are important. That is, whereas efficacy studies in the laboratory are most relevant to determining the internal validity of the findings, effectiveness studies in the clinical realm better inform us about the external validity of therapeutic outcomes. Accordingly, the combination of efficacy and effectiveness research can provide a useful gauge of how robust and influential a treatment package can be.

- Multicomponential analyses should investigate which components (e.g., cognitive restructuring vs. behavioral modification) of the REBT clinical package are active and relevant for achieving important therapeutic outcomes.

THEORY OF CHANGE. Even in the case of studies indicating REBT efficacy and/or effectiveness, we cannot be sure that the effects are due to the REBT theory, unless we have a clear analysis of the theory of change. Few studies have investigated theories and mechanisms of change with sufficient rigor to draw more or less definitive conclusions. David, Szentagotai, Lupu, and Cosman (2008), and Szentagotai, David, Lupu, and Cosman (2008) took a first step in integrating theory with a multicomponent analysis of treatment effects when they compared the efficacy of cognitive therapy (CT), REBT, and medication for major depressive disorder in a randomized clinical trial. Moreover, the authors not only investigated the theory of change across treatments, but they also conducted componential analyses insofar as in the REBT protocol, the focus was only on irrational beliefs and not on automatic thoughts. Basically, they found that REBT is as efficient as CT and medication post treatment, and more efficient than medication (on one of two measures of depression) at six-months follow-up. Moreover, a change in irrational beliefs was accompanied by changes in both depressed mood and automatic thoughts. Assessment protocols in REBT studies should determine whether irrational and rational beliefs mediate and moderate treatment outcomes when REBT is pitted against other psychotherapies in randomized controlled trials.

COST-EFFECTIVE ANALYSES. In the era of monolithic health insurance companies, cost-effectiveness analyses are fundamental to disseminating a psychological treatment. Even if research documents the efficacy or effectiveness of a particular therapy and the intervention is underpinned by a well-validated theory of change, if the treatment is too expensive in relation to the resources of the health system, it may not be implemented. Therefore, cost-effectiveness studies are fundamental to the wide dissemination of REBT in the clinical field. Importantly, Sava, Yates, Lupu, Szentagotai, David, (2008) have conducted a cost-analysis in their clinical trials, finding that REBT is more cost-effective then medication for major depressive disorder.

TECHNOLOGICAL DEVELOPMENT. State of the science technologies such as virtual reality should be incorporated into REBT research, for at least three reasons: *(1)* Virtual reality may increase the success of the treatment insofar as it may facilitate cognitive restructuring by immersing the patient in a stressful environment, in a controlled and safe way; *(2)* virtual reality may provide new insights into REBT theory by creating a context to test new hypotheses, considering the fact that activating events (the "A" in the "ABC" model) can be realistically represented in a virtual environment, under controlled conditions); and *(3)* virtual reality has an increased face validity in our technologically oriented world.

ONLINE THERAPY AND SELF-HELP. REBT was among the first therapies used in a self-help framework, and recently in online services. However, REBT will likely lose this competitive edge because no manuals have been developed for REBT interventions, and researchers have not evaluated its efficacy, effectiveness, cost-effectiveness, and theoretical mechanisms in a self-help context. Accordingly, if REBT is to be competitive in the popular marketplace, while retaining its values of rigorous evaluation of theoretical mechanisms and principles, effort should be invested to ensure REBT can be conducted on a rigorous effective basis in a self-help format.

Conclusion

In summary, we have attempted to embrace the complexity of the literature related to rational and irrational beliefs. Because rational-emotive and cognitive-behavioral therapy (REBT/CBT) and theory are based on these constructs, their nuanced analysis is fundamental, particularly considering that REBT/ CBT is one of the most influential forms of psychotherapy today.

A search of major international databases (e.g., PsycInfo), reveals that irrational and rational beliefs are among the most investigated psychological constructs, and definitely the most researched cognitive constructs in the field of cognitive-behavioral therapies. After examining this voluminous literature, we have tried to distinguish what we know about rational and irrational beliefs based on rigorous research, from what is pseudo-knowledge (e.g., we assume we know but we have no data to support our allegations), and what we do not know at this point in time.

A dichotomous thinking error has been typically applied to rational-emotive and cognitive-behavioral theory. That is, these therapies have either been promoted as evidence-based, when rigorous evidence was lacking (typically from the

'60s to the '80s, when Ellis was highly active and influential) or described as lacking evidence, although this judgment was an overgeneralization (typically in the '90s, when other forms of cognitive-behavioral theories and therapies started to become visible). Following this extensive analysis of publications dealing with rational-emotive and cognitive-behavioral theory and therapy and their main constructs—rational and irrational beliefs—our conclusion is that REBT/CBT theory and therapy have a strong evidence base and probably qualify as empirically validated, with more evidence for some aspects and disorders and less evidence for other aspects and disorders. In its elegant form, REBT has important heuristic value for theory and practice that must be further exploited. The thoughtful consideration of many issues raised in this volume will hopefully stimulate insightful and rigorous research, and more effective and efficacious applications for health promotion and treatment of psychological disorders. We truly hope that this volume represents a firm step in this direction, and will prove to be a valuable guide for clinicians and researchers alike.

REFERENCES

Bernard, M. E., & DiGiuseppe, R. (1989). Rational-emotive therapy today. In M. E. Bernard & R. D. DiGiuseppe (Eds.), *Inside rational-emotive therapy: A critical appraisal of the theory and therapy of Albert Ellis* (pp. 1–7). San Diego, CA: Academic Press, Inc.

David, D., Schnur, J., & Belloiu, A. (2002). Another search for the "hot" cognitions: Appraisal, irrational beliefs, attributions, and their relation to emotion. *Journal of Rational-Emotive & Cognitive-Behavior Therapy, 2,* 93–131.

David, D. (2003). *Castele de nisip: Ştiinţă şi pseudoştiinţă în psihopatologie.* Bucureşti: Editura Tritonic.

David, D., & Szentagotai, A. (2006). Cognition in cognitive-behavioral psychotherapies: Toward an integrative model. *Clinical Psychology Review, 26,* 284–298.

David, D., Montgomery, G., & Holdevici, I. (2003). Romanian norms for the Harvard group Scale of Hypnotic Susceptibility, Form A. *International Journal of Clinical and Experimental Hypnosis, 51,* 66–77.

David, D., Szentagotai, A., Kallay, E., & Macavei, B. (2005). A synopsis of rational emotive behavior therapy: Fundamental and applied research. *Journal of Rational-Emotive & Cognitive-Behavior Therapy, 23,* 175–221.

David, D., Szentagotai, A., Lupu, V., & Cosman, D. (2008). REBT versus cognitive therapy versus medication in the treatment of major depressive disorder: Outcomes study and six months follow-up. *Journal of Clinical Psychology, 64,* 728–746.

DiGiuseppe, R., Miller, N., & Trexler, L. (1977). A review of rational-emotive psychotherapy outcome studies. *Counseling Psychologist, 7,* 64–72.

Dickinson, M. J., & Eva, F. J. (2006). Anxiety and depression may have an evolutionary role as negative reinforcers, encouraging socialization. *Medical Hypotheses, 66,* 796–800.

Ellis, A. (1956). An operational reformulation of some of the basic principles of psychoanalysis. *Psychoanalytic Review, 43,* 163–180.

Ellis, A. (1958). Rational psychotherapy. *The Journal of General Psychology, 59,* 35–49.

Ellis, A. (1973). *Humanistic psychotherapy: The rational-emotive approach.* New York: McGraw-Hill.

Ellis, A. (1987). *Anger: How to live with and without it.* Sacramento, CA: Citadel Press.

Engels, G. I., Garnefski, N., & Diekstra, R. F. W. (1993). Efficacy of rational-emotive therapy: A quantitative analysis. *Journal of Consulting and Clinical Psychology, 61,* 1083–1091.

Gonzalez, J.E., Nelson, J.R., Gutkin, T.B., & Shwery, C.S. (2004). Rational-emotive therapy with children and adolescents: a meta-analysis. *Journal of Emotional and Behavioral Disorders, 12,* 32–56.

Haaga, D. A. F., & Davidson, G. C. (1989a). Slow progress in rational-emotive therapy outcome research: Etiology and treatment. *Cognitive Therapy and Research, 13,* 493–508.

Haaga, D. A. F., & Davidson, G. C. (1989b). Outcome studies of rational-emotive therapy. In M. E. Bernard & R. DiGiuseppe (Eds.), *Inside rational-emotive therapy: A critical appraisal of the theory and therapy of Albert Ellis.* New York: Academic Press.

Lyons, L. C., & Woods, P. J. (1991). The efficacy of rational emotive therapy: A quantitative review of the outcome research. *Clinical Psychology Review, 11,* 357–369.

Mahoney, M. J. (1993). Introduction to special section: Theoretical developments in the cognitive psychotherapies. *Journal of Consulting and Clinical Psychology, 61,* 187–193.

Sava, F., Yates, B., Lupu, V., Szentagotai, A., & David, D. (2008). Cost-effectiveness and cost-utility of cognitive therapy, rational emotive behavioral therapy and fluoxetine in treating depression: a randomized clinical trial. *Journal of Clinical Psychology, 65,* 36–52.

Smith, M. L., & Glass, G. V. (1977). Meta-analysis of psychotherapy outcome studies. *American Psychologist, 32,* 752–760.

Szentagotai, A., David, D., Lupu, V., & Cosman, D. (2008). Rational emotive therapy, cognitive therapy and medication in the treatment of major depressive disorder: theory of change analysis. *Psychotherapy: Theory, Research, Practice and Training, 4,* 523–538.

Wampold, B. E., Mondin, G. W., Moody, M., Stich, F., Benson, K., & Ahn, H. (1997). A meta-analysis of outcome studies comparing bona fide psychotherapies: Empirically, "All must have prizes." *Psychological Bulletin, 3,* 203–215.

Watson, P. J., & Andrews, P. W. (2002). Toward a revised evolutionary adaptationist analysis of depression: The social navigation hypothesis. *Journal of Affective Disorders, 72,* 1–14.

Zettle, R. D., & Hayes, S. C. (1980). Conceptual and empirical status of rational-emotive therapy. *Progress in Behavior Modification, 9,* 125–166.

Index

Note: In this Index, tables are indicated by "*t*", figures "*f*".

ABC(DE) model, 4, 5, 15, 106, 137*t*, 138*t*,
    140*t*, 150
  anomalies in, 40
  commonsense emotional theories and,
    106, 107–108
  core tenet of, 181
  described, 15, 46, 195–196
  discrat and, 39–40
  new strategy inclusion (E), 38
  REBT's reliance on, 15, 75, 76
  "shoulds" and, 39
  unconscious information processing
    inclusion, 107–108
Abrams, L. D., 210
Abrams, M., 210
Acceptance, 176. *See also* Unconditional
    self-acceptance
  in CBT treatments, 224–225
  in classic cognitive/rational therapies,
    222–224
  unconditional life-acceptance, 10
  unconditional other-acceptance, 10, 78, 222
  unconditional self-acceptance, 10, 87, 88,
    89, 121, 122, 221, 230
Acceptance and commitment therapy
    (ACT), 27, 45, 221, 223, 242–243
  cognitive fusion/defusion and, 226–227
  description of, 223
  experiential avoidance and, 225–226
  externalization and, 229
Acceptance-based behavioral treatments
  commonalities with mindfulness, 225–232
    attention, 230–232
    awareness, 230
    cognitive fusion/defusion, 226–227
    decentering, 228
    experiential avoidance, 225–226

    externalizing, 228–229
    focus on the present, 229
    letting go, 227–228
    guided discovery vs., 223
Acceptance-based CBT treatments,
    224–225
Active worry and rumination, 240–242
Adaptations
  to chronic pain, 266
  evolutionary psychology on, 344
  genetic, of biological species, 65–66
  of mental processes, distortions of, 65
  shifting of role, 54
  special purpose, of human mind, 71
  useful vs. nonuseful, 69
Adaptive/maladaptive pain beliefs, 270–271
Addis, J., 91, 181–182
Adler, A., 8
Albert Ellis Institute, 341–342
Alden, L., 161, 162
Algorithmic-Representational Level Theory,
    13–14
Almann, John, 64
Ambulatory biosensors (ABs), 135
American Psychological Association (APA),
    316
Anxiety, 6*t*, 7, 9*t*, 88. *See also* State-Trait
    Anxiety Inventory
  ABC(DE) model and, 39
  action tendency study, 79–80
  assessment process and, 125
  awfulizing and, 83
  awfulizing/catastrophizing and, 158,
    236–237
  binary model of distress and, 103
  CBT and, 116
  demandingness and, 79, 158

Anxiety (*Continued*)
    Evaluative Belief Scale and, 123
    irrational beliefs and, 8, 106, 150,
        157–160
    REBT and, 149, 160
    social anxiety, 129
    Survey of Personal Beliefs and, 120
    types of, 84
    unconscious information processing
        and, 108
    worry and, 159
Appraisal theory (of emotions), 12, 100, 104,
    105t, 177, 203
Arbuthnott, K. D., 128
Aristotle, 5, 30, 34, 35, 87, 324
Articulated Thoughts in Simulated
    Situations (ATSS), 124
Assertion Information Form (AIF), 161–162
Assertiveness deficits and irrational beliefs,
    160–163
The Assertiveness Option (Jakubowski &
    Lange), 163
Assessment process, 124–125, 135
Attention and Emotion (Matthews & Wells),
    231
Attitude and Belief Scale 2/General Attitude
    and Belief Scale (ABS 2/GABS),
    118–119, 178
Automatic thoughts (surface cognitions), 3,
    13, 202. *See also* Cognitive behavioral
    therapies
    described, 12
    identification techniques, 127, 128, 131
    irrational beliefs and, 38, 59
Automatic vs. semantic cognitions (CBT),
    208
Availability heuristic, 295–297, 301, 308, 311
Available vs. accessible cognitions (CBT),
    209
Awfulizing (AWF)/catastrophizing, 11, 13,
    76, 78, 149
    ABS 2/GABS and, 118
    anxiety and, 158, 236–237
    behavioral consequences of, 83–84
    depression and, 83
    evaluative cognitions and, 166
    irrational beliefs and, 159, 255
    tolerance vs., 175

Bach, P., 226
Bad habits. *See* Confirmation bias;
    Hindsight bias
Barlow, David, 10
Barron, P., 154
Bartley, W. W., 28
Baumeister, R. F., 330
Beck, Aaron, 10, 102–103, 206, 222. *See also*
    Cognitive behavioral therapies

on dysfunctional beliefs, 11
on guided discovery/Socratic
    questioning, 126
on unreflective, automatic thoughts, 38
Beck Depression Inventory (BDI), 102–103,
    109, 120, 153–154, 316
Behavior therapy (Watson), 8
Behavioral Assertiveness Test-Revised, 129
Behavioral consequences
    of awfulizing/catastrophizing, 84–87
    of demandingness, 78–83
    of global evaluation/self or
        other-downing, 87–89
    of irrational beliefs, 75–93
    of low frustration tolerance, 84
Belief systems. *See also* Common Beliefs
        Survey-III; Dysfunctional beliefs
    cultural, 68
    irrational, 33, 46
    measurement difficulties, 176
    symbolic, 65–66
    well-being and, 185
    work-related stress and, 181
Bereavement, 180, 183, 320
Bernard, M. E., 91, 119, 181–182, 342
Beyerstein, Barry L., 313–331
Biases
    availability, 295–297, 301, 308, 311
    cognitive limitations and, 294–300
    confirmation, 297–300, 311
    hindsight, 297–300, 305, 308, 312
    memory, 133
    observational, 39
    retrospective, 134
Binary model of distress (qualitative theory),
    103–104, 106, 183–184
Biological basis of irrationality, 52, 54–55
Birk, J., 106
Blame proneness, 159, 164
Blame proneness scale (CBS-III), 121
Board games (children's technique), 132
Bowlby, John, 69
Brach, Tara, 240
Brandon, Nathaniel, 329
Breast-cancer patients, 183–184, 257
Breath/breathing awareness. *See*
    Mindfulness/mindfulness
    techniques
Brehm, S. S., 163, 165
Browne, Christopher M., 149–168
Bruer, J. T., 321
Buddha/Buddhism, 5, 7, 11, 219. *See also*
    Chogyam Trungpa Rinpoche;
    Goldstein, Joseph; Kornfield, Jack;
    Mindfulness/mindfulness
    techniques; Suzuki Roshi
    CBT/REBT and, 11, 18, 190
    on desires, 7, 190

enlightenment concept, 7
experiential avoidance and, 225
Four Noble Truths, 5
psychology techniques, 220, 225, 226
Burgess, P., 118–119, 178
Buss, D. M., 52

Campbell, D. T., 31
Campbell, J. D., 330
Cardaciotto, L., 224, 230
Cardozo, S. R., 199
Carnegie, Dale, 17
CAS. See cognitive attention syndrome
Caserta, Donald A., 173–190
Catastrophizing scale of Coping Strategies
    Questionnaire, 272–273
Catastrophizing/awfulizing, 11, 13, 76, 78,
    149. See also Pain catastrophizing
  ABS 2/GABS and, 118
  anxiety and, 158, 236–237
  behavioral consequences of, 83–84
  depression and, 83
  evaluative cognitions and, 166
  irrational beliefs and, 159, 255
  tolerance vs., 175
Catharsis myth, 324–326
CBTs. See cognitive behavioral therapies
Center for Cognitive Therapy, 223
Cerebral palsy, 265
Chang, E. C., 199
Chapman, J. P., 297
Chapman, L. J., 297
Child and Adolescent Scale of Irrationality
    (CASI), 86, 179
Children
  attachment styles, 69
  internalizing/externalizing emotional/
    behavioral problem study, 178–179
  irrational beliefs of, 51, 60, 82–83
  methods used with, 131–132
  REBT strategies, 9, 33
  self-downing and, 89
Chogyam Trungpa Rinpoche, 220
Christensen, A. J., 256
Christianity, 35
Chronic pain. See also Pain catastrophizing
  biomedical approaches, 266
  CBT theory of, 266–267
  CBT therapy for, 276–277, 278t–280t,
    281, 282t
  cognitions/beliefs in adjustment to,
    267–269
  disability and, 281
  telephone-delivered interventions (TDIs),
    283
  types of, 265
Ciarrochi, J., 185, 201
"Clinician's illusion," 321

Cognitions. See also Hot cognitions
  automatic vs. semantic, 208
  available vs. accessible, 209
  cold, 12, 13, 100–101
  cold vs. hot, 203–206
  conscious vs. unconscious, 206–208
Cognitive attention syndrome (CAS), 231,
    238–239, 241–242
Cognitive behavioral therapies (CBTs), 8,
    10, 222. See also Automatic thoughts;
    Barlow, David; Diathesis-stress
    model of anxiety; Hayes, Steven;
    Hutchins, Edwin; Linehan, Marsha;
    Meichenbaum, Donald;
    Mindfulness-based cognitive
    therapy; Rational-emotive behavior
    therapy
  acceptance-based, 224–225
  for chronic pain, 276–277, 278t–280t,
    281, 282t
  imagery and, 128–129
  irrational belief defined by, 63
  nosological syndrome focus of, 77
  pain theory of, 266–267
  prevention programs in support of,
    187–189
  rational and irrational beliefs in,
    201–209
  REBT vs., 75–76
  self-monitoring, 130, 137t–140t
  theory-driven questioning and, 127–128
Cognitive limitations and biases, 293,
    294–300
  availability heuristic, 295–297, 301, 308,
    311
  confirmation bias, 297–300, 311
  hindsight biases, 297–300, 305, 308, 312
  representativeness heuristic, 295–297,
    308, 312
Cognitive penetrability, 5
Cognitive processes/processing
  activation/maintenance of, 237–238
  cognitive penetrability and, 201
  conscious/unconscious, 5
  disambiguation from thought contents,
    116, 118
  irrational belief categories, 14, 18–19, 99,
    119, 253
  metacognition and, 234
  mindfulness and, 240
  pain catastrophizing and, 268
Cognitive Risk Profile for Pain, 275
Cognitive vulnerability, 196–197
Cognitive-behavioral therapies (CBTs)
Cohen, Jacob, 157, 320–321
Cohen, Patricia, 320–321
Cold cognitions. See also Schemas
  defined, 12, 100

Cold cognitions (*Continued*)
    effect on emotions, 13, 100–101
    hot vs., 13, 101, 203–206
Common Beliefs Survey-III (CBS-III),
    120–121, 185
Computational Level Theory, 12
Computer-assisted psychological
    instruments, 134
Computer-based adaptive testing, 134
Conceptual cognitions, 234, 236
Confirmation bias, 297–300, 311
Conscious vs. unconscious cognition (CBT),
    206–208
Constructivism, 4
Control of emotions scale (CBS-III), 121
Coping strategies
    chronic pain and, 267–268, 275
    juvenile offenders study, 184
    to overcome irrational thought patterns,
    59
Coping Strategies Questionnaire,
    Catastrophizing scale, 272
Cosmides, L., 71
Courtois, C. A., 128
Craighead, W. E., 198
Cramer, Duncan, 99–109, 177, 182, 183
"Credentialed Persons, Credentialed
    Knowledge" article (Meehl), 301
Critical incident stress debriefing (CISD),
    326
Critical rationalism (Popper), 4
Culture
    context of rational, irrational beliefs,
    56–58
    cultural power and rationality, 29–30
    defined, 50

Daily Record of Automatic Thoughts
    Concerning Pain, 277
Dalgleish, T., 85
Danziger, K., 24–25
Darwin, Charles, 66–67
Das, Lama Surya, 233
David, A., 104, 177
David, Daniel, 3–19, 49–60, 54–55, 99–109,
    173–190, 195–212, 253–262, 339–347
Davies, M. F., 106
Dawes, R. M., 293, 294, 305
De Beer, Z. C., 89
Deacon, Terrence, 65–66
Deception, beginnings with perception,
    64–65
Decision-making
    disciplinary vs. emancipatory rationality,
    43
    Ellis's failures regarding, 43–44
    guided discovery/Socratic questioning
    and, 126

Irrational Belief Inventory and, 122
    in master level Scrabble, 291–293,
    305–307
Deep cognitions. *See* Schemas
Deffenbacher, J. L., 158–159
Demandingness (DEM), 13,
    53, 57
    ABS 2/GABS and, 118–119
    and anxiety, 79, 158
    behavioral consequences of, 78–83
    depression and, 156–157
    desires and, 78–79
    irrational beliefs and, 123–124, 136, 149,
    153, 178
    perfectionism and, 158, 166
    self-downing and, 87, 92–93,
    166, 179, 253, 339–340
    Survey of Personal Beliefs and, 120
Dendato, K. M., 160
Depression, 6t, 7, 9t, 77. *See also* Beck
    Depression Inventory
    assessment process and, 124
    awfulizing and, 83
    demandingness and, 156–157
    Ellis on, 153
    Evaluative Belief Scale and, 123
    irrational beliefs and, 8, 122, 150, 153–157
    mindfulness cognitive therapy for, 18
    pain and, 269
    positive/negative correlations, 88
    REBT and, 149
    Survey of Personal Beliefs and, 120
Desires
    Buddha on, 7, 190
    components, 6–7
    demandingness and, 78–79
    leading to healthy results, 6t
    males vs. females, 164
    Plato on, 34–35, 36, 75
    rational beliefs and, 149, 175
    rationality's normative status and, 29
    REBT and, 8, 18, 173
Destructive disagreement belief, 183
Developmental disabilities, 180
Dewey, J., 32
Dialectical behavior therapy (DBT),
    223
Diaries, electronic, 130
Diathesis-stress model of
    anxiety (REBT), 150–151, 166, 196,
    198–199, 200
Diener, D., 160
DiGiuseppe, Raymond, 49–60, 82, 86,
    106, 118–119, 123, 126–127, 177,
    195–212, 342
Disabilities. *See also* Pain catastrophizing;
    Psychometric measures of pain
    beliefs

developmental, 180
maladaptive beliefs/thoughts and, 266
medical, 180
pain-related, 266–267, 269, 283
physical, 265, 281
Disability and Assertiveness Role-Play Test, 129
Disciplinary rationality (discrat), 34–35
    ABC(DE) model and, 39–40
    in rational psychotherapy, 37–40
    REBT and, 38–39
Discomfort anxiety, 84
Discrat. See disciplinary rationality
Discursive formations (Danziger), 24–25
    of technical rationality, 27
Disputation of irrational beliefs (IRBs), 4, 7, 9, 17, 28, 39–40, 116, 138t, 140t, 150, 161, 184, 195
Disputing (D) methods, 9, 18
Dowd, Thomas, 149–168, 173–190
Dryden, W., 24–25, 32, 54–55, 77, 106, 126–127, 149, 175–176
Durlak, J. A., 188
Dysfunctional beliefs, 8, 11, 185. See also Common Beliefs Survey-III
Dysfunctional emotions (feelings)
    assessment process and, 124
    assessment process identification, 124
    awfulizing and, 83
    causes of, 128–129
    client acknowledgment of, 130
    demandingness and, 79
    DiGiuseppe/Ellis on, 177
    functional vs., 101, 102, 104–105, 106, 177, 205
    intensity of, 177
    irrational beliefs and, 90, 105, 107, 109, 165, 340
    maladaptive cognitions and, 117
    negative/positive, 108–109
    self-downing and, 89
    unconditional self-acceptance and, 88
    Wessler on, 104

Eckhardt, C. I., 103
Egan, G., 27
Ego anxiety, 84
Ehde, Dawn M., 265–284
Einstein, Albert, 31, 38
Electronic diaries (ED) assessment, 134
Ellis, Albert, 3–19, 5–6, 23, 29, 32, 37–38, 39, 44–45, 52, 54–55, 78–79, 82, 90–91, 106, 149–150, 153, 173–190, 175–176, 177, 199, 209, 222
Emancipatory rationality (emanrat), 35–37, 37–40
EMDR (eye movement desensitization and reprocessing), 27

Emerson, Ralph Waldo, 17
Emmelkamp, P. M. G., 121–122
Emotion-cognition relation, 104
Emotion-eliciting strategies, 8, 17
Endes, R., 103
Enlightenment, search for, 7
Environment of evolutionary adaptiveness (EEA), 53
Epictetus, 5, 8, 34, 35, 37, 38, 46
Erwin, E., 43
Etiopathogenetic mechanisms in (psycho) pathology, IRBs as, 196–200
    correlational/cross-sectional studies B–C connection, 197–198
    during stressful events (A-B-C connection), 198–199
    self-referent speech/self-statement studies, 199–200
Evaluation scale (CBS-III), 121
Evaluative Beliefs Scale (EBS), 118, 122–123
Evaluative schemas, 14, 123, 166
Evans, C. E., 41
Evolutionary framework of rational, irrational beliefs
    as adaptations, 52–53
    as by-products, 53
    as exaptations, 54
    as noise, 53
    as spandrels, 54–55
Evolutionary psychology, 14, 50, 57, 58, 71, 340, 344
Exaptations, rational/irrational beliefs as, 54
Exner, T., 87
Experiential learning, 304–307
Expressive-experiential therapies, 326

Facing the Fire: Experiencing and Expressing Anger Appropriately (Lee), 324
Factual rationality, 63, 66–67, 69–70, 71
Farmer, R., 233
Fatsis, Stefan, 291
Feelings, theories of
    appraisal theory, 104
    binary model of distress, 102, 103–104, 106
    functional vs. dysfunctional, 101, 102
    unitary model of distress, 101, 103
Feminism/feminist writers, 29–30
Five Great Myths of Popular Psychology. See Myths of popular psychology
Follette, V. M., 11
Fong, J., 177
Försterling, F., 106
Foucault, Michel, 38
Four Noble Truths, 5
Fragility myth, 318–321

Freeman, Arthur, 149–168, 195–212
Freud, Sigmund, 8
Frey, R. B., 121
Fromm, E., 8
Functional feelings
Functional feelings (emotions). *See also*
    Dysfunctional emotions;
    Emotion-eliciting strategies
  CBT and, 124
  dysfunctional feelings vs., 101, 102,
    104–105, 106, 176, 177
  irrational beliefs and, 104, 117, 153
  rational beliefs and, 107, 109, 117, 178, 341

Gambrill-Ritchey Assertion Inventory, 161
Gangestad, S. W., 52
Gautama Buddha, 5, 7
Geller, Uri, 327
General Attitude and Belief Scale (GABS),
    118, 119–120
"Genetic" noise, 53
Gestalt therapy, 38, 326
Ghinea, C., 104
Global evaluation/self or other-downing
    (SD), 13, 78, 79, 81t, 92–93. *See also*
    Self-Downing, Perfectionism, and
    Importance of the Past scales; Self-
    downing scale
  ABS 2/GABS and, 119
  behavioral consequences of, 87–89
  CBS-III and, 120–121
  demandingness and, 87
  EBS and, 122–123
  as evaluative schema, 166
  identification by young clients, 131
  irrational beliefs and, 167, 178–179, 253, 339
  relational/marital problems and, 89
God, 35, 66–67, 203
Goldberg, G. M., 84
Goldfried, M., 198
Goldstein, Joseph, 220, 240
Gould, S. J., 52
Groves, P., 233
Guided discovery, 125–127, 223
Guided imagery, 128–129

Handbook of Pain Assessment (Turk and
    Melzack), 276
Harrington, N., 81
Harris, S., 106
Hart, K. E., 199
Hassles Scale, 181
Hayes, S. C., 226
Hayes, Steven, 11
Health/health outcomes
  irrational beliefs and, 254–256
  REBT and, 256–257, 257–259
  well-being promotion, by RBs, 201

Healthy People 2010, 187
Herbert, J. D., 224, 230
Heuristics (mental shortcuts). *See*
    Availability heuristic;
    Representativeness heuristic
Hewison, J., 31
Himle, D., 158
Hindsight bias, 297–300, 305, 308, 312
Hittner, J. B., 199
Hope, D. A., 129
Hopkins, Gerard Manley, 322
Horney, K., 8
Hot cognitions
  cold vs., 13, 101, 203–206
  defined, 12, 100
  Ellis on, 38
  irrational beliefs and, 14, 18
  rational beliefs and, 18–19
  theory-driven questioning and, 127
Humanistic-existential approaches, 221
Hutchins, Edwin, 67

Ideographic Role-Play, 129
Illusory correlation, 296–297
Imagery, 128–129, 151, 152
Implementational Level Theory, 14
Importance of the past scale (CBS-III), 121
Inductive questioning, 125–127
Inferential chaining, 127
Information processing, 64, 109, 196
  biased social, 161
  competitive Scrabble example, 291–293,
    305–307
  and metacognition, 236–237
  mindfulness-based therapies and, 220
  process-oriented theories and, 237
  types of, 207
Inglehart, R., 69–70
Inner child therapy, 316
Insight in apes study (Kohler), 31
Instrumental rationality, 25–26
Interpersonal therapy, 27
Ireland, J., 184
Irrational beliefs (IRBs). *See also*
    Awfulizing; Catastrophizing/
    awfulizing; Child and Adolescent
    Scale of Irrationality;
    Demandingness; Global evaluation/
    self or other-downing; Low
    frustration tolerance; Rational and
    irrational beliefs; Rational beliefs
    (RBs)
  and anxiety, 8, 157–160
  and assertiveness deficits, 160–163
  behavioral consequences of, 75–93
  bereavement and, 183
  categories of, 78
  of children, 51, 60, 82–83

cognitive process categories of, 253
cognitive vulnerability factors, 151
college student self-report measures, 181
creation of RBs vs., 8
defined, 3–4, 5–7
demanding, 179
and depression, 153–157
depression and, 8, 122, 150, 153–157
disputation of, 4, 7, 9, 17, 28, 39–40, 116, 138t, 140t, 150, 161, 184, 195
dysfunctional feelings and, 105, 107, 109, 340
as etiopathogenetic (causal) mechanisms, 197–201
evolution by design, 53
and general emotional disturbance, 151–153
global evaluation/self or other-downing and, 167, 178–179, 253, 339
health outcomes and, 254–256
judgment errors leading to, 291–309
mindfulness and, 219–243
procrastination and, 90
psychological instruments assessment of, 115
psychometric criticism of measures of, 155
psychophysiological reactions to, 107
religion and, 67–68
schemas, 166–167
self-challenging methods, strategies, 9–10
social science model, 50–52
and Type A coronary-prone behavior pattern, 151, 163–165
what is known/not known (summary), 339–340
Irrational Beliefs Inventory (IBI), 121–122
Irrational Beliefs Test (IBT), 117, 122, 153
Irrationality, 33
adaptive value of, 52
biological basis of, 52, 54–55, 60
chance and, 53
Ellis on, 41
marital adjustment and, 91
measures of, 86, 117, 122, 153, 178, 179, 181
predispositions towards, 59
procrastination and, 81–82

Jakubowski, P., 160, 162
James, William, 328
Janet, Pierre, 8
Jaycox, L. H., 188
Jenkins Activity Survey (JAS), 164
Jensen, Mark P., 265–284
Jones, J., 85
Jones, Jason, 75–93
Journal of Rational-Emotive & Cognitive-Behavior Therapy, 342

Judgment errors and irrational beliefs, 291–309
cognitive limitations and biases, 293, 294–300
availability heuristic, 295–297, 301, 308, 311
confirmation bias, 297–300, 311
hindsight biases, 297–300, 305, 308, 312
representativeness heuristic, 295–297, 308, 312
competitive Scrabble example, 291–293, 305–307
experiential learning, 304–307
illusory correlation, 296–297
personal influence, disproportionate influence of, 301–304
post hoc ergo propter hoc fallacy, 300
premature closure, 299
Justifications, logic of, and rationality, 28

Kabat-Zinn, J., 238
Kagan, Jerome, 322
Kallay, E., 104
Kassinove, H., 103, 186
Keefe, F. J., 269
Kelly, W. E., 160
Kohler, W., 31
Koopmans, P. C., 121–122
Kornfield, Jack, 223, 227
Krueger, J. I., 330
Kuehlwein, K. T., 202

Laidlaw, James, 68
Lakatos, I., 44
Lange, A., 160, 162
Lao Tsu, 7
Lazarus, R. S., 104, 177–178
Leaf, R., 87, 178
Lee, John, 324
Leslie, Y. M., 181
Letting go, 227–228
Lilienfeld, Scott O., 313–331
Limb loss, 265
Linehan, Marsha, 11
Lipsky, M. J., 151, 152
Locke-Wallace Marital Adjustment Test, 182
Locus of control scale (CBS-III), 121
Lorcher, P. S., 159
Low frustration tolerance (LFT), 76, 78, 79
ABS 2/GABS and, 118
behavioral consequences of, 84–87
Cognitive Process and, 119
irrational beliefs and, 339–340
Lynn, Steven Jay, 3–19, 232, 242, 313–331, 339–347

Macavei, Bianca, 104, 115–140
Mahoney, M.J., 206–207, 344
Maladaptive behaviors, 81, 90–91
Malouff, J. M., 199
Marlatt, G. A., 233
Marriage
    poor adjustment, self-reports, 85–86
    predictors in, 82
    rationality and, 80t, 81t, 89, 91, 181–182,
        199
    REBT efficacy study, 151
Master, S., 180
Matthews, G., 231, 237
McBride, C. M., 283
McClelland, T., 199
McDermut, J. F., 154–155
McMahon, James, 116–140
McNaughton, M. E., 255
Medical disabilities, 180
Meehl, P. E., 300, 301, 303, 318
Meichenbaum, Donald, 10
Mellinger, David I., 219–243
Mennin, D., 223
Metacognition
    control strategies, 237–239
    and information processing,
        236–237
    and mindfulness, 233, 234–236
Miller, George, 316
Miller, N. J., 160
Miller, S., 180
Mind of humans. See also Myths of popular
        psychology
    architecture of, 15–17, 50–51,
        56, 58
    as blank slate, 58
    deception and perception, 64–65
    and disciplinary rationality, 34–35
    misconceptions of, 314–315, 317
    modularity thesis portrayal of, 71
    symbolic belief systems, 65–66
Mindfulness-based cognitive therapy
        (MBCT), 232
Mindfulness-based stress reduction
        (MBSR), 232, 238
Mindfulness/mindfulness techniques, 11,
        219–243. See also Buddha/
        Buddhism
    acceptance-based approaches,
        commonalities with, 225–232
    attention, 230–232
    awareness, 230
    cognitive fusion/defusion, 226–227
    decentering, 228
    experiential avoidance, 225–226
    externalizing, 228–229
    focus on the present, 229
    letting go, 227–228

clinical applications, 232
historical background, 219–220
instructions, 220–221
limitations of, 239–242
and metacognition, 234–236
outcomes of, 219
and response set theory, 233–234
Mitchell, Tim, 29–30, 38
Möller, A. T., 89
Montgomery, Guy H., 108, 253–262
Moorey, S., 126
Morris, R. J., 84
Multiple personality disorder (MPD)
        schema, 296–297
Multiple sclerosis (MS), 265
Muran, J. C., 152
Myths of popular psychology, 317–331
    catharsis, 324–326
    critical importance of early experience,
        321–324
    fragility, 318–321
    self-esteem, 329–331
    unrealized potential, 327–329

National Association for Self-Esteem,
        329–330
Need for approval scale (CBS-III), 121
Neoplatonism, 35
Neuroimaging, 134–135
New Age entrepreneurialism, 327
Newton-Smith, W. H., 25
Nirvana, 7
No mind concept (Zen Buddhism),
        242
Noise ("genetic"), rational/irrational beliefs
        as, 53
Nondisputing methods, 11. See also Follette,
        V. M.; Hayes, Steven; Linehan,
        Marsha
Norris, P., 69–70
Norton, P. J., 129

Observations of patients during sessions,
        130
Obsessive-compulsive disorder, 122, 158,
        160, 232
O'Donohue, W., 43–44
Open-ended questioning, 125–127
Opioid analgesics, 265–266
Organisms, phenotypic characteristics, 50
Other downing. See Global evaluation/self
        or other-downing (SD)
Other-directed shoulds, 120
Overt operant behavior, 78

Padesky, C. A., 125–126, 223
Pain. See Chronic pain; Pain
        catastrophizing

Pain catastrophizing. *See also* Psychometric measures of pain beliefs
assessment/maladaptive beliefs, 270–276
described, 268–269
mediating role of, 269
research treatment support for, 269–270
Pain Catastrophizing Scale (PCS), 275
Pain Relief Screening Instrument, 275
Papageorgiou, C., 254
Paradoxical questioning, 125–127
Paras, K. C., 199
Paris, Joel, 321, 322–323
Past-life regression, 316
Penn Prevention Program, 188
Perceptual processing, 64–65
Perfectionism scale (CBS-III), 120
Perls, F., 8
Personal influence, 301–304
Person-centered therapy, 38
Phenotypic characteristics of organisms, 50
Physical disabilities. *See* Disabilities
Physical health and RBS/IRBS, 253–262
Plato, 34–35, 36, 75
Political power and rationality, 29–30
"Pop" (popular) psychology
industry background, 315–316
myths of
catharsis, 324–326
critical importance of early experience, 321–324
fragility, 318–321
self-esteem, 329–331
unrealized potential, 327–329
Popper, Karl, 28, 31, 44
Popular psychology. *See* "Pop" (popular) psychology
Positive and Negative Affect Schedule-Trait Version, 154
Positive psychology movement, 109, 204, 212, 330
Post hoc ergo propter hoc fallacy, 300
Postmodernism, 4
Posttraumatic stress disorder (PTSD), 226, 305, 319–320, 321, 326
Power, M., 85
Practical rationality, 66–67
Premature closure, 299
Prevention programs (primary) and rational beliefs, 186–189
Problem-solving (reflective) and rationality, 30–34
Procrastination, 81–82, 86, 90, 122, 124
Prud'homme, L., 154
Psychometric measures of pain beliefs, 271–276
Cognitive Risk Profile for Pain, 275

Coping Strategies Questionnaire, 272–273
Pain Catastrophizing Scale, 275
Pain Relief Screening Instrument, 275
Survey of Pain Attitudes Scale, 271–272, 273t–274t
Psychophysiological reactions to irrational beliefs, 107

Quine-Duhames thesis, 4

Rand, Ayn, 69
Rapgay, L., 231
Rational and irrational beliefs. *See also* Irrational beliefs (IRBs); Rational beliefs (RBs)
in architecture of human mind, 15–17
in cognitive-behavioral therapies, 201–209
automatic vs. semantic cognitions, 208
available vs. accessible cognitions, 209
cold vs. hot cognitions, 203–206
conscious vs. unconscious cognition, 206–208
cultural context and evolution, 56–58
defined, psychological vs. philosophical, 3–4
in the evolutionary framework, 52–55
feelings and, 105t
historical construct development, 3–11
in marital/close relationships, 181–182
multilevel analysis, 12–14
nature of, 11–18
physical health and, 253–262
psychological arousal studies, 178, 180
psychological reactions and, 106–107
in psychotherapy, 209–211
relationship between, 15, 16t
techniques/procedures for identifying, 125–132
about undesirable events, 101
Rational Behavior Inventory (RBI), 122, 154
Rational beliefs (RBs). *See also* Irrational beliefs (IRBs); Rational and irrational beliefs; Rationality
adjustment to stressors/general well-being, 179–186
creation of IRBs vs., 8
defined, 3–4, 5–7
desires and, 149, 175
Dryden on, 175
empirical literature on, 179
as health/well-being promoting mechanisms, 201
preferential, 179
and primary prevention programs, 186–189

Rational beliefs (RBs) *(Continued)*
  protective factors, 151
  as protective factors, 197
  social science model, 50–52
  state anger management with, 186
  what is known/not known (summary),
    341
Rational psychological health, 174–179
Rational psychotherapy, 23–46
"Rational Psychotherapy" article (Ellis),
    5–6, 23, 32, 37–38
Rational role reversal, 151–152
Rational stories (children's technique), 132
Rational-emotive behavior therapy (REBT).
    See also ABC(DE) model; Diathesis-
    stress model of anxiety; Irrational
    beliefs; Rational and irrational
    beliefs; Rational beliefs
  acceptance as focus, 222
  anxiety and, 149, 160
  behavioral intervention techniques in,
    91–92
  beliefs about activating events and, 254
  biological factors, 174–175
  as causal/prophylactic treatment, 10
  central tenet/goal of, 76, 115, 149, 150,
    152, 174, 176–177, 313
  couple dissatisfaction vs. couple
    disturbance, 82
  on demands, 79, 81
  depression and, 149
  desires and, 8, 18, 173
  diathesis-stress model of anxiety, 150–151,
    166, 196, 198–199, 200
  disciplinary rationality and, 38–39
  disputation of negative thoughts, 11, 18, 91
  dysfunctional feelings in, 103
  on emotional problems/self-defeating
    behaviors, 75
  high school student peer rating
    prediction study, 185
  hypotheses of, 6–7
  irrational beliefs defined by, 63
  on low frustration tolerance, 85
  methodology, 11, 17
  nondisputing methods, integration
    with, 11
  political dialectic and, 30
  promotion of self-acceptance, 89
  rational philosophies (3) taught by, 10
  rational psychotherapy as heart of, 23–46
  reliance on ABC(DE) model, 75, 76
  research agenda (new) for, 341–346
  on second basic biological tendency, 55
  self-help applications, 17
  theory-driven questioning and, 127–128
  undesirable events and, 101
  vs. REBT, 75–76

Rational-emotive behavioral consultation
    (REBC), 174
Rational-emotive education (REE)
    programs, 174, 184
Rational-emotive imagery, 151, 152
Rationality. *See also* Disciplinary rationality;
    Emancipatory rationality;
    Irrationality
  aspects/uses of, 33
  criticism of, 41–45
  cultural/political power and, 29–30
  disciplinary rationality, 34–35
  Dryden/Still on use of, 24–25
  emancipatory rationality, 35–37, 37–40
  factual and practical, 66–67
  instrumental and scientific, 25–26
  and the logic of justification, 28
  marriage and, 80*t*, 81*t*, 89, 91, 181–182,
    199
  meanings of, 41–42, 63
  as normative, 29
  as reflective problem-solving, 30–34
  Russell's view of, 42
  technical, and psychotherapy, 26–28
  as uniquely human, 30
Reason and Emotion in Psychotherapy
    (Ellis), 6
Rebirthing, 316
REBT. See rational-emotive behavior
    therapy (REBT)
Records (daily) of dysfunctional thoughts/
    diaries, 130
Reflective problem-solving, 30–34
Regression analyses, multiple/
    simultaneous, 152, 159, 185
Religions and stealth religions, 67–69
Representativeness heuristic, 295–297,
    308, 312
Response set theory, 233–234
*Riches and Renunciation: Religion,
    Economy, and Society among the
    Jains* (Laidlaw), 68
Rimer, B, K, 283
Robin, M. W., 87
Rogers, Carl, 8, 27, 230
Role playing, 17, 129–130, 161
Rosen, H., 202
Rosenbaum, M., 156
Rumination, active worry and, 240–242
Ruscio, John, 291–309
Russell, Bertrand, 42

Safran, J., 161, 162
Sagan, Carl, 328
Sanderman, R., 121–122
Satel, S. L., 318–319
Schema-based CBT, 242
Schema-focused therapy, 202

Schemas, 3, 12, 100, 202
  cognitive and behavioral, 233
  defined, 14
  evaluative schemas, 14, 123, 166
  irrational belief schemas, 166–167
  Mahoney on, 206–207
  MPD schema, 296
  theory, 241
Schnur, Julie B., 106, 253–262
Schön, D. A., 26
Schou, K. C., 31
Schreiber, F. R., 296
Schutte, N. S., 199
Scientific rationality, 25–26
Scrabble competition, 291–293, 305–307
Segal, Z. V., 238
Self-acceptance. See Unconditional self-
  acceptance (USA)
Self-control problems, 86
Self-defeating behaviors, 55, 79, 81, 84
Self-directed shoulds, 120
Self-downing (SD). See Global evaluation/
  self or other-downing (SD)
Self-Downing, Perfectionism, and
  Importance of the Past scales, 121
Self-downing scale (CBS-III), 120
Self-esteem myth, 329–331
Self-help personalities, 316
Self-oriented perfectionism, 81
Self-referent speech/self-statement studies,
  199–200
Sentence completion task (children's
  technique), 132
Shapiro, Francine, 27
Sherback, J., 84
Shortened General Attitude and Belief Scale
  (SGABS), 119–120
Shoulds, 10, 38, 43
  absolutistic, 6, 11, 13, 29
  biased rationality and, 30
  Ellis on, 38
  identification of, 150
  other-directed/self-directed, 120, 153
  REBT and, 30
Silverglade, L., 255
Silverman, S., 82, 86, 178
Similarity-based arguments/judgments,
  295, 308
Situational Self-Statement and Affective
  State Inventory, 121
The Six Pillars of Self-Esteem (Brandon), 329
Skilled helpers (Egan), 27
Smith, C. A., 104
Smith, T. W., 152, 163, 165, 177–178, 186
Sobocinski, D., 198
Social Skill Behavioral Assessment System,
  129
Socratic Questioning, 125–127, 223

Solomon, A., 155–156, 157
Solution-focused therapy, 221
Sommers, C. H., 318–319
SOPA. See Survey of Pain Attitudes Scale
Specific Demands on Self Scale (SDS), 157, 165
Spielberger, C. D., 85
Spinal cord injury, 265
Spörrle, M., 106
S-REF-based model, 237
Standards social science model (SSSM) of
  rational/irrational beliefs, 50–52
"Starting Over" psychotherapy tv show,
  324–325
State-Trait Anxiety Inventory (STAI), 102, 160
Stealth religions, 67–69
Still, Arthur W., 23–46, 24–25
Stoics/stoicism, 8, 35–37, 40
Strokes, 265, 327
Sullivan, M.J.L., 269
Surface cognitions. See Automatic thoughts
Survey of Pain Attitudes Scale (SOPA),
  271–272, 273t–274t
Survey of Personal Beliefs (SPB), 120, 181
Suzuki Roshi, 220
Sybil (Schreiber), 296
Symbolic belief systems, 65–66
The Symbolic Species (Deacon), 65
Szentagotai, Aurora, 75–93, 123

Tafrate, R., 186
Tan, B.-L., 181
Taoism, 7
Teasdale, J. D., 237
Technical rationality, 26–28, 33, 45
Techniques/procedures for identifying
  RBs/IRBs, 125–132
Theory-driven questioning, 127–128
Thorndike, Robert, 8, 31
Thorpe, G. L., 121
Thought Bubble with Rating Scale, 131f
Thought records (children's technique), 131
Thyer, B. A., 158
Tiba, A., 179
Tibetan Buddhism, 11, 18
Timmerman, I., 121–122
Todd, C. J., 26
Tolerance. See Low frustration tolerance
Toneatto, T., 234
Tooby, J., 71
Trower, P., 85
Turner, J. A., 270
Turner, S. H., 199
Type A coronary-prone behavior pattern,
  151, 163–165

Unconditional life-acceptance (ULA), 10
Unconditional other-acceptance (UOA), 10,
  78, 222

Unconditional self-acceptance
    (USA), 10, 87, 88, 89, 121, 122, 221,
    230
Unconscious information processing, 5,
    108, 200, 206–207, 231–232, 344
Unitary model of distress (qualitative
    theory), 103
Unity of Science movement, 28
Unrealized potential myth, 327–329

Valences (shared), 49
Vass, J. S., 43–44
Virtual reality assessment, 133
Vohs, K. D., 330

Wachtel, Paul, 323
Wallerstein, Judith, 320
Wampold, B. E., 210
Watson, John, B., 8, 84
Watts, Alan, 220

Wells, A. M., 188, 231, 237
Wessler, R. L., 44–45, 103
Wilson, David Sloan, 63–71
Woods, P. J., 162–163, 164, 165
Word Freak (Fatsis), 291
Worry Domains Questionnaire (WDQ), 159
Worry/worrying
    active worry and rumination, 240–242
    GAD-type, 231, 237
    Irrational Belief Inventory and, 122
    irrational beliefs and, 159–160
    overcoming, 159–160, 239–240
    postponement technique, 159–160
    about worry, 237

Young, J. E., 126

Zen Buddhism, 11, 242
Ziegler, D. J., 181, 186
Zisook, S., 106

LANCHESTER LIBRARY, Coventry University
Gosford Street, Coventry CV1 5DD Telephone 024 7688 7555

This book is due to be returned not later than the date and
time stamped above. Fines are charged on overdue books